Introduction to

TEXTILES

Introduction to

TEXTILES

EVELYN E. STOUT

Professor of Design and Environmental Analysis
New York State College of Human Ecology at Cornell University

THIRD EDITION

JOHN WILEY & SONS, INC.

NEW YORK · LONDON · SYDNEY · TORONTO

To Catherine J. Personius

PREFACE

To students and others who may use this book:

Extensive revisions have been incorporated in this third edition, many in order to keep information as current as possible, many to go further in some specific direction, often at the suggestion of users of the earlier editions, and others to incorporate additional pertinent topics or new developments of importance. This has necessitated deletion of most of the material on minor fibers that was formerly included. Chapters 2 and 15 are new and Chapters 13 and 16 have been so completely changed as to be almost entirely new.

In general, I have tried to keep my readers abreast of the rapidly changing technological developments in the field and their meaning to consumers, and to take into account the broader scientific background of most students of today as compared to those of a few years ago. I have considered end-uses of fibers and fabrics in both data and discussions and in textile furnishings, industrial, and medical, as well as apparel uses. Several new photographs have been added and photomicrographs have replaced most of the fiber sketches. Definitions are latest ASTM versions.

Some of the major changes specific to the chapters follow. In Chapter 1, the discussion has been made more truly an introduction to the broad field of textiles with projections for 1980. Chapter 2 is new; it incorporates some of the world and United States fiber production and consumption data that formerly appeared in Chapter 1 and has been expanded to include data on apparel, textile furnishings, industrial, and other end-uses of the various fibers and fiber groups. A section is included on world trade which considers duties, tariffs, trade agreements, and quotas, and their effects on the countries involved. Chapter 3 includes a simplified yet fairly detailed explanation of a new composite theory of the molecular structure of fibers that is gaining wide acceptance among world textile scientists. The position of glass and metallic fibers has been moved to the thermoplastic column in the table on fiber classification and trade names have

been deleted in order to emphasize generic classes. The trade names, however, are included at the head of the appropriate sections in Chapters 6, 7, and 8 as well as in the appendix. Chapter 4 discusses the history of cotton and includes much new material with more emphasis on the years since the Great Depression. It includes a survey of the United States government cotton subsidy program from its inception to the present and its effect on production, trade, quality, and related factors. Production and processing incorporate the newest trends and standards. Jute has been reclassed and discussed as a major fiber. In Chapter 5, the study of wool includes the government price-support program, modern methods of handling and grading, the new U.S. Standard Grades for Wool, and further consideration of the helical molecular structure of the fibers. In Chapter 7, new subsections are included on Nomex and Qiana nylons, and on Cantrece nylon as an example of a bicomponent fiber; the concept is pursued in some detail. A new section is included on polyamide/polyester biconstituent fibers and their structure. A new section on high-temperature organic fibers includes Teflon and PBI,BBB, and Pen-2,6 fibers which may be very important in the near future. In Chapter 8, the discussion on Beta glass has been expanded and a new section has been added that includes high-temperature, electrically-protective, and other new inorganic fibers. Chapter 9 includes a new texturizing process and information as to the extent to which the different texturizing processes are utilized. Nearly all sections in Chapter 10 have been expanded with inclusion of spun-bonded nonwovens, details of the needle-punch web process, and a new section on laminated fabrics. In Chapter 11, discussions of functional finishes have been expanded, particularly on flame retardance and resistance to include the new provisions of the Flammable Fabrics Act as amended in December 1968, and soil- and stain-repellency and soil release. Chapter 13 confirms that durable-press has superseded wash-wear and minimum-care fabrics and apparel in importance. Processes, fibers, and resins used, precuring and postcuring, and problems associated with permanent press as well as selection and care are discussed. Chapter 15 is a new chapter on stretch fabrics and apparel of the two general types—elastomeric and non-elastomeric stretch—with properties, end-uses, and other points of interest for both classes of fabrics. Chapter 16 discusses the new USASI L22-1968 textile performance standards in relation to history, specific end-uses, methods of evaluating performance, and recommendations for labels. The objectives and work of several textile-associated organizations and agencies are discussed as, for example, the American National Standards Institute, the American Association of Textile Chemists and Colorists, the American Society for Testing and Materials, and the National Bureau of Standards.

Many of the statements made in the original preface still hold for this revision. This book is planned for you as a consumer and scientist, to enable you to know what fibers are or may be on the market, their characteristics, how to choose wisely, what to expect of a fabric, and how to care for it. If you are interested in a career in the textile or clothing areas, this information will be no less important to you, for it is basic to an understanding of the textile field—whether for consumer use, teaching, research, merchandising, or any of the number of other applications—and to an understanding of allied fields as well. You with special interests in textiles will be expected to go much further in your chosen direction than can be covered in a volume such as this. Not all the details are spelled out; you are often expected to use your own intelligence, particularly in making the applications.

It is recognized that, by the time a book is published in a field which is changing as rapidly as the textile field, some statements made as facts may be superseded by new and better knowledge. This circumstance does not, however, excuse an author from giving as complete and factual a presentation of contemporary material as is possible at the date of writing. This book should be used with these statements in mind. With the best of intentions to present an unbiased picture, my own point of view has undoubtedly sometimes crept in and may lead to wrong inferences. The alert reader will be aware of these possibilities, will note questionable statements, and will explore further to arrive at the truth for himself. It is to be hoped that you will be stimulated to read from many sources, to question statements, to search for new facts wherever available, and to draw your own unbiased conclusions. References at the ends of chapters are for your convenience in starting out on roads of exploration. These, however, are all older than the present book, so for the newest data you must go to current publications, periodicals, and research reports.

Since it is not possible to cover in detail in one volume all phases of a subject as extensive as textiles, I have made concessions to space and time in this way: all through the book I have devoted considerable time to material which I consider likely to be new or unfamiliar, and for which little reliable reference information is available. Then, by contrast, I have spent a minimum of space on material which has been generally available for a great many years and for which there is a considerable amount of good, detailed, published information. Some of the references are guides to the latter.

I wish to acknowledge my indebtedness to the great number of authors whose work has been drawn upon; to commerical companies and government agencies which so kindly supplied information and sometimes also illustrations; to research groups and individuals whose data have been used

in arriving at certain conclusions and recommendations; to all those persons who encouraged me and who have helped in any other way in the preparation of this book.

Evelyn E. Stout

Ithaca, New York
October 1969

ACKNOWLEDGMENTS

I acknowledge my indebtedness to the persons, publishers, periodicals, organizations, or agencies who have given me permission to quote from their publications. A more complete citation is made with the quotation in the text.

American Association of Textile Chemists and Colorists.

American Dyestuff Reporter.

American Society for Testing and Materials.

Carrol-Porczynski, C. A., *Asbestos,* copyright 1956, The Textile Institute (England).

Chemical and Engineering News.

Chemstrand Corporation.

Daily News Record.

E. I. duPont de Nemours, and Company, Inc.

Hadfield, J. W., *Linen Flax Fibre Production in New Zealand,* copyright 1953, Whitcomb and Tombs, Ltd., Publishers (New Zealand).

Hamby, D. S. (Ed.), *The American Cotton Handbook,* Volume I (3rd edition), copyright 1965, Interscience Publishers, a division of John Wiley and Sons, Inc.

Leggett, W. F., *The Story of Linen,* copyright 1945, Chemical Publishing Co., Inc.

Mauersberger, H. R., *The American Handbook of Synthetic Textiles,* copyright 1952, Interscience Publishers, Inc.

Mauersberger, H. R. (Ed.), *Matthews' Textile Fibers,* fifth edition, 1947 and sixth edition, 1954, John Wiley and Sons, Inc.

Mauersberger, H. R. and Schwarz, E. W. K., *Rayon and Staple Fiber Handbook,* third edition, copyright 1939 by H. R. Mauersberger and E. W. K. Schwarz.

Merrill, G. R. Macormac, A. R., and Mauersberger, H. R., *American Cotton Handbook,* second edition, copyright 1949, Textile Book Publishers, Inc.

Modern Textiles Magazine.

National Advisory Commission on Food and Fiber, July 1967. U.S. Government Printing Office.

Owens-Corning Fiberglas Corporation.

Textile Chemist and Colorist.

Textile Organon.

Textile Research Journal.

Union Carbide and Carbon Corporation.

U.S.D.A. *Technical Bulletin No. 1210* (1959), Agricultural Marketing Service, U.S. Department of Agriculture.

United States of America Standards Institute.

Von Bergen, W., (Ed.), *Wool Handbook*, Volume I, third edition, copyright 1963, Interscience Publishers, a division of John Wiley and Sons, Inc.

Von Bergen, W., and Mauersberger, H. R., *American Wool Handbook*, second edition, copyright 1948, Textile Book Publishers, Inc.

Walton, Perry, *The Story of Textiles*, copyright 1937 by Perry Walton.

Weibel, Adele C., *Two Thousand Years of Textiles*, copyright 1952, published by Pantheon Books for the Detroit Institute of Arts.

CONTENTS

LIST OF TABLES

INTRODUCTION

Textile study, to the person starting it for the first time, is almost like engaging in the study of a foreign language, or trying to put together a complicated jigsaw puzzle when you have no idea of what the colors represent, or how the completed picture is supposed to look. But as terms become familiar and complete or extend knowledge which you already have, the pieces of the puzzle fall into place, fit in with things you already know through your experiences with clothes and fabrics, textile furnishings, and other uses of textiles, and the whole wide field becomes open to your view —from earliest historical times to the present, and with many hints of what the future may hold. Until tentative explorations are made, the novice has no idea of the fascinating trails and vistas that lie ahead to be followed and explored.

The subject of textiles is one of the most interesting available to man's study. It is both one of the oldest and one of the newest, old because the use of textiles predates recorded history, and new because textiles are rapidly and constantly changing with the introduction of new fibers, new developments for familiar fibers, and new processing and finishing for both. Production of fibers, yarns, and fabrics, with their allied industries, is one of the leading fields in numbers of persons gainfully employed in the United States, and it is rapidly gaining in importance in Canada, Mexico,

and many other countries. In the United States there has been some tendency in recent decades for the textile industry to shift in location from North to South, and from East to West. In Canada, a number of textile producing industries have sprung up in the southern part of the provinces of Ontario and Quebec.

Spinning fibers into yarns, the art of weaving, and the making of beautiful and delicate fabrics having lovely colors and design had already been perfected by the time of the earliest known records. Prehistoric fabric remnants have been found in widely separated sections of the world on different continents, confirming the widely accepted belief that weaving had been perfected by several groups or civilizations independently, who could not possibly have communicated with each other. Probably grasses, reeds, fur pelts, and felted wool from animals were used long before the development of fabric making. Walton, in *The Story of Textiles* (pp. 13, 14), wrote

. . . Older far than recorded history is the tale of fabrics.

To find its beginning, we must go beyond the dawn of history into the darkness of prehistoric times; for, when man first began to scratch his deeds on the rocks of his dwelling-place, fabrics, more or less perfect, were being fashioned, ornamented, and dyed.

Even the archaeologist cannot fully enlighten us. No matter how deeply he may delve into the most remote past to which he can sink the plummet of his research, evidences of spinning and weaving are found among the vestiges of the rude home of prehistoric man . . .

Flax fabrics dating back to a period thousands of years ago have been unearthed in England. The ruins of the Lake Dwellers of the Stone Age in Switzerland have produced them. Textiles of much beauty that belong thousands of years before Christ have been discovered among the earliest ruins of Peru, Mexico, and Egypt, and in the cave dwellings of New Mexico and Arizona.

*Matthews' Textile Fibers** (1947, p. 1) states

Although it is certain that primitive man fabricated coarse cloth from various fibers over 20,000 years ago, undisputed evidence is scanty. Textiles are relatively perishable. But in the dry, equable climate of Egypt and some parts of Asia textiles have been preserved in tombs and graves dating from about 2700 B.C.

Evidence has also been found that textile fabrics were in existence in the New World at least as early as 632 B.C.

Many of the tools and processes developed in these early days have been

---

* Unless otherwise indicated, all references to *Matthews' Textile Fibers* are to the 1954 edition.

used until the time of our modern, highly industrialized society and are still used today in the more remote areas of the world. Many ancient beautiful fabrics, designs, and colors have not been surpassed to this day.

Although he appreciates this interesting past, modern man does not spend all his time looking back! More changes have occurred in the textile field in the last three-quarters of a century—largely in the last 30 years— than in all previous history, with change continuing at a rapid pace. Seventy-five years is but a moment in historical terms. Probably few people in the developed and developing nations of today are unaware of the rapid pace and far-reaching extent of changes that affect the lives of all. Have you ever tried to visualize the possible world of the year 2000 A.D., which most of you will be around to see and perhaps to influence, and what your role will be in that world?

Many things have happened recently or are happening today that are likely to result in changes in our way of life. Some of these are easily identifiable; others require more searching study. Many, if not most, changes bring problems as well as benefits to many people; the problems often seem to be ignored and, if honestly faced, might seem to outweigh the benefits. The time lag between technological change and the consequent needed social change is too well recognized to merit discussion.

A few of the many things leading toward change follow: the population explosion with all the problems it poses on food supply, land use, employment, etc.; the emergence of many new independent or semi-independent nations in the world; ever faster travel with the probability soon of supersonic travel—each advance bringing the rest of the world within quicker reach; satellite-reflected television which brings both world events of great significance and innocuous nothings into homes in many countries almost simultaneously; man's success in landing on the moon and returning safely; future plans for landing on and exploring the surface of other planets; the European Common Market and other such trade associations; and the widespread unrest for a wide variety of reasons throughout a major part of the world. No doubt you can add to this list.

Many of these factors will have a direct bearing on the textile picture, and many, in turn, may be affected by the textile situation of a country, a region, or the world. As examples, as population increases, even with improvements in food production and more widespread birth control, it is likely that much of the most fertile land now used for fiber production may be required for producing food. Space exploration has required new materials that can resist the terrific heat of deceleration and reentry into the earth's atmosphere; these fibers must withstand extremely high and extremely low temperatures and yet, at the same time, be light enough in weight and flexible enough to be practicable in space garments. Research

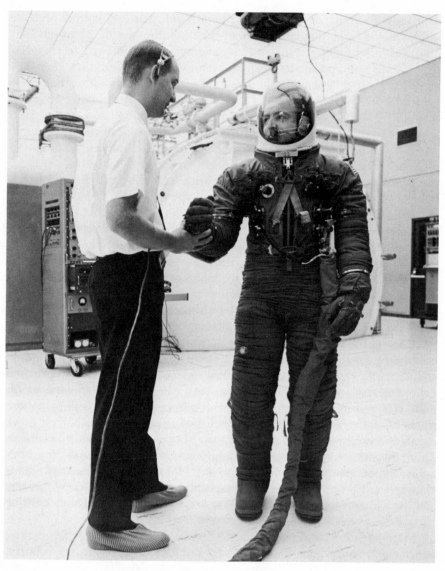

FIGURE 1-1. High mobility suit for space exploration. (Courtesy Hamilton Standard.)

for and development of such fibers and fabrics goes on intensively in a number of laboratories. Figures 1-1 and 1-2 are examples of a new (late 1968) high-mobility space exploration suit. The Apollo fire that took the lives of three astronauts has forced attention on the safety features of such assemblies and also has focused attention on the fire hazards, though they may be self-initiated, among the general population and certain segments of it. We cannot take time here to explore these developments but they are interesting and even exciting paths to follow in looking into the world's future. A knowledge of them is essential to understanding world events.

Not very long ago only the United States, the United Kingdom, certain of the West European countries, and Japan produced fabrics of any other kind than the natural fibers, or had a widespread industrialized system of production. But this too has changed. Man-made fiber industries are not only expanding in the highly industrialized countries but are also growing up in many countries around the world along with expanding natural-fiber industries. New mills, wherever found, tend to be very modern and are often highly mechanized and even automated. Old mills in many countries, including our own, are rapidly being replaced with modern mills. Competition for the world's markets is very intense and is likely to increase as time goes by. Many companies in developed countries are establishing branches in other developed countries in order to compete on the same level as the industries already established there. The number of man-made fiber producing plants in the world has grown from approximately 300 in 1955 to over 980 in 1969. They are found on every continent or its adjacent islands.

The fact that new and small countries can often begin their move to industrialize by establishing a textile industry poses many problems, both social and economic, for countries with well-established industries. Companies from the industrialized nations, or the governments of these nations, frequently build plants for the nonindustrialized countries and often supply the personnel essential to their operation until native personnel are educated, trained, and ready to take over their functions. These plants then compete with the industries that helped to establish them, with many resulting problems for the companies and the countries involved. Our newspapers, news magazines, trade journals, radio, and other media of communication frequently carry reports of efforts to reach agreements that will be fair to all concerned. Many of the meetings are held in Geneva, Switzerland. No doubt you have read or heard some of these reports on the efforts to reach agreement on quotas, tariffs, and trade, and to insure a fair share of the trade at desirable price levels for the developing countries. We shall take a brief look at these phenomena in Chapter 2.

FIGURE 1-2. Flexibility of the high mobility space suit is demonstrated. (Courtesy Hamilton Standard.)

Table 1 shows the average per capita consumption of textile fibers in the world and in the United States for 1957 and 1964, and for the United States for 1968. The figures include total fiber consumption for apparel, home furnishing, and industrial uses. Per capita figures vary widely in the different geographical areas of the world for many reasons, and from country to country within a geographical area according to the stage of development of the country. The developed countries (1964) had an average per capita consumption of 22.5 pounds as compared to 4.5 pounds for underdeveloped countries, with cotton usually the dominant fiber in the latter group. That the United States is both a developed and a wealthy country is apparent from these data. The European Common Market countries, the United Kingdom, and Japan are the highest per capita

TABLE 1. Per Capita Consumption of Textile Fibers for the World[a] and for the United States[b]

Year	Area	Total Pound	Cotton		Wool		Man-made	
			Pound	Per-cent	Pound	Per-cent	Pound	Per-cent
1957	World	10.9	7.5	68.6	1.1	10.1	2.0	18.3
1957	United States	35.1	22.6	64.4	2.6	7.4	9.9	28.2
1964	World	11.7	7.2	61.5	1.0	8.6	3.5	29.9
1964	United States	38.3	22.5	58.7	2.9	7.6	12.9	33.9
1968	World (figures are not available)							
1968	United States	50.9	22.0	43.2	2.3	4.5	26.6	52.3

[a] World figures for 1957 are from *Textile Organon* for July 1959; the figures for 1964 are from *Cotton and Other Fiber Problems and Policies in the United States,* Technical Paper, Vol. 2 (1967), by the National Advisory Commission on Food and Fiber.
[b] The United States figures for 1957, 1964, and 1968 are from *Textile Organon* for March 1969.

users of fibers among other developed countries, but most rapid change is being made by some of the developing countries. Trends on uses of different classes of fibers can be readily noted; all countries seem to be headed in the same general direction although the United States seems to be moving more rapidly.

In making projections for a period of years ahead, culminating in 1980, the President's Advisory Commission on Food and Fiber included projections for fibers. The projected 1980 per capita consumption of textile fibers for various countries has been assembled in Table 2. These proposals are based on projections for population and income for 1980.

There is no reason to assume that even were population ratios and incomes the same, all these countries or areas would use the same amount of fibers. There are too many reasons for differences for such divergent areas to be alike in their use of fiber.

Changes in the per capita use of fibers and in the amounts of different fibers used depend on many factors. Among these are the technology and economic wealth of a country, the education and culture of the people, local availability of raw materials, conditions of regional and world trade, fashion—particularly the phases of fashion that tend to make an item obsolete before it is worn out—and changes in living habits, and perhaps in standard of living, of the people. Particularly in our own country, other

TABLE 2. Projected Per Capita Consumption of Textile Fibers for 1980 [a]

Country or Area	Total Fiber Pound	Natural		Man-made	
		Cotton Pound	Wool Pound	Cellulosic Pound	Noncellulosic Pound
United States	54.0	22.1	2.7	7.6	21.6
Canada	35.0	13.0	3.2	6.6	12.2
Japan	35.0	12.3	2.5	6.3	14.0
Western Europe	34.0	12.6	3.4	7.1	10.9
Eastern Europe	30.0	11.1	2.4	9.9	6.6
USSR	29.0	16.0	2.3	6.1	4.6
Oceania [b]	25.0	12.0	4.5	3.2	5.2
River Plate	17.0	11.0	1.7	1.7	2.6
South Africa	13.0	6.5	1.2	3.4	2.0
Brazil	12.0	8.9	0.5	1.1	1.6
Western Asia	12.0	6.6	1.6	2.4	1.4
Mexico	10.0	6.5	0.5	1.7	1.3
Other South American	8.0	5.4	0.6	1.0	0.9
Central American, Caribbean	7.5	5.3	0.2	1.4	0.6
India	6.0	5.1	0.1	0.5	0.3
Other Asian	5.5	4.2	0.1	0.7	0.6
Mainland China	5.3	4.0	0.1	0.7	0.5
Other African	4.5	3.3	0.2	0.6	0.4

[a] From *Cotton and Other Fiber Problems and Policies in the United States.* Technical Papers Vol. 2 (p. 63), National Advisory Commission on Food and Fiber. Washington, D.C., July 1967.
[b] Australia, New Zealand, and neighboring islands.

factors have probably had an influence on the decrease per capita in amounts of certain fibers used.

1. There is a trend toward lighter-weight apparel, lighter not only in construction but also because many of our new fibers are lighter in weight (specific gravity) than the old. We also use fewer yards of fabric per garment and wear fewer garments than was the case less than a generation ago.

2. With modern laundering facilities in or near most homes, and an abundance of new washable fabrics, we probably tend to own fewer gar-

ments of a particular type than once was the case, particularly in undergarments and sleepwear.

3. With increasing industrialization, mechanization, and automation with their requirements for skilled rather than unskilled labor, decrease in the number of farmers and farm workers, and the growth of the service industries, the need for traditional "work clothes" decreases and need for more tailored, sporty, business type clothes, or uniforms increases.

4. With the shortening of the work week, higher incomes, and the trend toward outdoor living and recreation, many varieties of sport and

FIGURE 1-3. University coed, 1969 model.

other casual clothing has gained wide appeal. Witness the great number of persons of all ages who travel, ski, snowmobile, skate, boat, swim, bicycle, hike, hunt, to mention a few, and who own the special type of clothing for these activities.

5. Age changes of a population with the accompanying dependence on or independence from cultural patterns have a noticeable effect on apparel, furnishings, and many uses listed as "industrial."

6. Note the change in home furnishings; carpets are now used in many kitchens and bathrooms as well as living rooms, and outdoors as well as indoors, for sports stadiums as well as churches.

7. Space exploration and its possibilities have opened a whole new area of consideration. Try to imagine the difference in requirements in fibers, fabrics, finish, design, yardage, construction techniques, serviceability properties, handling cost, and marketing for the 1969 mini-costume of Figure 1-3 as compared to the high mobility space exploration suit of Figures 1-1 and 1-2.

8. With higher incomes, people may be more fashion-oriented. They tend to replace garments before they are worn out; this is also often true for furnishings for their homes, for their automobiles, and for their boats or other such items.

With this limited introduction we are now ready to launch into our exploration of the textile field.

FOR FURTHER READING

Current news reports and periodicals.
Mauersberger, H. R. (ed.): *Matthews' Textile Fibers.*
Scientific American.
Textile Organon.
Walton, P.: *The Story of Textiles.*
Weibel, A. C.: *Two Thousand Years of Textiles.*

FIBER UTILIZATION AND TRADE

The number of fibers available to the people of the world have varied through history with the geographical area, the state of culture of the people and their degree of affluence or poverty, technological developments, possibilities for trade with other peoples, and the degree and type of organization of their governing structure, which may stimulate or limit innovation. The developed countries of today have available to them a broad range of fibers of many types, both natural and man-made. In preparation for a detailed study of the various fiber groups, we need to have an overall view of the fibers available to people of the world, and to the United States in particular, and how this picture has changed over the years, what the trends are that indicate what the future will be, and to what extent there are attempts to regulate the ebb and flow of this vast array of fibers.

This chapter contains a concentration of data to which you will want to refer many times as you study various phases of textiles. Included are data on world and United States production and United States consumption by major fiber classes, and various apparel, home, and industrial end-uses for the major fiber groups in the United States for 1967, the latest date for which such figures are available as this goes to press.

We shall look first at the changing pattern of fibers produced in the

world, beginning with 1890 and carried through 1968. The availability of some of the new fibers and changes in the amounts of the major fibers produced in the world in these 78 years are reflected in Table 3. The method of reporting varies from country to country and the reliability of the data varies somewhat also, but data gathered as accurately as possible from so many sources give a good representation of the world's textile resources. This table reminds us of what relative newcomers the man-made fibers are and how quickly they have won a place for themselves.

You may notice as you analyze the information in the different tables that figures reported in one table may be slightly different from those reported for what is supposedly the same data in another table. This discrepancy is due to how, when, by whom, and for what purpose the data were collected and reported. Some data include waste fibers while others do not, some include all fibers produced in a classification while others exclude certain ones—glass is often excluded from data on man-made fibers. It seems advisable to compare in a single table those data gathered and reported together even though they may differ in some way from similar data appearing in other tables. There is no one coordinating body that assembles, verifies, and collates all this vast quantity of data for the world, or even for our own country.

The data in Table 4 are as close an approximation of Table 3 data as could be compiled for the United States production of textile fibers from the various sources listed as a footnote to the table. Although it is fairly easy to obtain production figures for commodities covered by government control and subsidy and for fibers for which there are many producers, it is more difficult to obtain figures when there is only one or a few producers. Sometimes, the totals are too small to be included in an overall table, and sometimes, especially for a new and highly competitive market, published figures might be too revealing to competitors, and perhaps to creditors.

By studying Tables 3 and 4 you can see how the United States production (in percentage figures) of some fibers has dropped and that of others has increased more than production of the same fibers for the world as a whole. To be meaningful, of course, the figures for the same years must be compared.

Table 5 shows United States consumption of different classes of fibers, as reported over a period of years. Very often it happens that more fiber is produced than is manufactured into yarn, fabric, or other products in the mills; this has particularly been true of cotton, and sometimes even of wool, in the United States. You will notice that percentages for a fiber have sometimes gone down from year to year although the actual number of pounds has gone up. As you study the total fiber picture you will see how

TABLE 3. World Production of Textile Fibers (Millions of Pounds and Percent)[a]

Year	Natural Fibers						Man-made Fibers				Total
	Raw Cotton		Raw Wool		Raw Silk		Cellulosic[b]		Noncellulosic[c]		
	Pound	Percent	Pound	Percent	Pound	Percent	Pound	Percent	Pound	Percent	
1890	5,965	78.6	1,600	21.1	26	0.3	—	—	—	—	7,591
1900	6,972	80.9	1,610	18.7	38	0.4	2	—	—	—	8,622
1910	9,261	83.5	1,770	16.0	51	0.5	12	0.1	—	—	11,094
1920	10,205	84.6	1,780	14.8	46	0.4	32	0.3	—	—	12,063
1930	12,942	82.2	2,210	14.0	130	0.8	458	2.9	—	—	15,740
1940	15,368	75.0	2,500	12.3	130	0.6	2,485	12.2	11	0.1	20,494
1950	14,654	70.6	2,330	11.3	42	0.2	3,553	17.2	153	0.7	20,732
1960	22,295	67.9	3,225	9.8	68	0.2	5,732	17.4	1,548	4.7	32,868
1965	25,432	62.6	3,284	8.0	73	0.2	7,381	18.0	4,516	11.1	40,636
1968	25,102	56.1	3,488	7.8	75	0.2	7,776	17.4	8,290	18.5	44,731

[a] Textile Organon, January 1962 and June 1969.
[b] Includes rayons, acetates, and triacetates.
[c] Does not include glass fiber.

TABLE 4. United States Production of Textile Fibers (Millions of Pounds and Percent)[a]

| | Natural Fibers | | | | Man-made Fibers | | | | | | | |
| Year | Cotton | | Wool | | Cellulosic | | Noncellulosic | | Glass | | Total |
	Pound	Percent	Pound	Percent	Pound	Percent	Pound	Percent	Pound	Percent	
1935	5,319.0	88.5	428	7.1	262.1	4.4	—	—	—	—	6,009.1
1940	6,283.0	87.4	426	5.9	471.2	6.2	3.2	—	1.4	—	7,184.8
1945	4,507.5	78.2	412	7.2	792.1	13.7	35.6	0.7	14.5	0.2	5,761.7
1950	5,007.0	74.6	248	4.5	1,259.4	18.8	122.4	1.8	23.5	0.3	6,713.3
1955	7,360.5	78.4	312	3.3	1,260.7	13.4	379.3	4.0	75.8	0.8	9,388.3
1960	7,136.0	76.4	323	3.5	1,028.5	11.0	677.2	7.2	177.0	1.9	9,341.7
1965	7,622.5	66.6	241	2.1	1,527.0	13.2	1,774.8	15.5	282.6	2.5	11,447.9
1968	3,600.0	40.1	200.0	2.2	1,594.3	17.8	3,187.5	35.5	399.6	4.4	8,981.4

[a] Sources used in compilation of these data:

(1) "Statistics on Cotton and Related Data 1925–1962," *Statistical Bulletin* 329, USDA. Economic Research Service, Economic and Statistical Analysis Division.

(2) "Cotton World Statistics," *Quarterly Bulletin* of the International Cotton Advisory Committee.

(3) "Base Book of Textile Statistics," *Textile Organon*, January 1958.

(4) "Base Book of Textile Statistics," *Textile Organon*, January 1962.

(5) *Textile Organon*, December 1954, November 1963, February 1964, October 1969 and December 1969.

TABLE 5. United States Consumption of Textile Fibers (Millions of Pounds and Percent)[a,b]

| | Natural Fibers | | | | | | Man-made Fibers | | | | |
| | Cotton | | Wool | | Silk | | Cellulosic | | Noncellulosic[c] | | |
Year	Pound	Percent	Pound	Percent	Pound	Percent	Pound	Percent	Pound	Percent	Total
1920	2,822.8	88.6	314.2	9.9	38.8	1.2	8.7	0.3	—	—	3,184.5
1930	2,616.6	85.0	263.2	8.5	80.6	2.6	119.3	3.9	—	—	3,079.7
1940	3,959.1	80.6	407.9	8.3	47.6	1.0	482.1	9.8	4.3	0.1	4,913.3
1945	4,515.8	75.2	645.1	10.7	1.0	—	769.9	12.8	49.8	0.8	6,007.0
1950	4,682.7	68.4	634.8	9.3	10.5	0.1	1,350.0	19.7	140.5	2.1	6,846.4
1955	4,382.4	65.3	413.8	6.2	11.0	0.2	1,419.2	21.1	432.2	6.4	6,709.7
1960	4,202.2	64.8	404.2	6.2	6.9	0.1	1,055.5	16.3	761.7	11.7	6,491.9
1965	4,477.5	52.7	387.0	4.6	5.8	0.1	1,550.4	18.3	1,955.9	23.0	8,494.4
1968	4,424.3	45.1	466.4	4.8	4.0	—	1,712.9	17.5	3,204.8	32.7	9,812.4

[a] Textile Organon, for March 1968 and March 1969.
[b] Figures include imports but not waste fibers so percentages sometimes total less than 100.
[c] Includes glass fibers.

15

this happens. The changes in percentages are the figures often referred to by producers who complain that they are losing their share of the market. Just what anyone's "share" of the market should be is not clear, for it is sure to change as the world fiber population, and developmental picture changes. It is interesting to see how the percentages vary for the different fibers when comparing figures for the world and those from both tables for the United States, even though the data are not directly comparable since some are production figures and the others consumption.

At present, the man-made fiber part of the United States textile industry is in good financial condition; although fibers ordinarily do not earn a high profit per unit volume, the enormity of the volume itself tends toward a reasonable profit. Not all fibers or fiber producers share equally in profit or loss, of course. The actual financial status of the natural fibers is more difficult to know because of government control on production and marketing, subsidies, protection through tariffs and quotas, and other such factors. In recent years, many old plants have been rebuilt and modernized, and many new plants have been and are being built. The rising "real" wages (in terms of purchasing power), the increased industrialization with accompanying mass production, and the rising standards of living in many other parts of the world are narrowing the gap between the United States and other trade areas more rapidly than once thought possible. This tends to make trade easier but also greatly increases its volume and competitiveness.

Textile fibers are used not only in apparel, but also in furnishings and industry as well. The percentage of the fibers that go into some of these various uses have not changed greatly in the United States over the past three decades, although the poundage has risen, as can be seen in Table 6, while others have changed considerably.

Although some of the apparel producers attribute a drop in the use of fiber in apparel to the miniskirt style of recent years and it undoubtedly has had a very noticeable effect, data from which this table was compiled do not show this clearly. There was an increase in use of fibers for women's apparel in 1967 as compared to 1966 although not as great an increase as for several years before. Men's apparel, however, showed an actual drop from 1966 in the amount of fiber going into apparel. You might like to think about these facts and the other trends apparent from the tables to see if you can account for some going up and others down. The use of fibers in industrial products has tended down over the years for several reasons, perhaps most important is the increased use of plastics. Why do you think the use of fibers in home furnishings has gone up? Rising income has played a large part, of course, but other factors have had an influence too.

TABLE 6. United States End-Use Consumption of Textile Fibers (Millions of Pounds and Percent)[a]

End-Use	1937		1949		1958		1967	
	Pound	Percent	Pound	Percent	Pound	Percent	Pound	Percent
Apparel	1,693	41.6	2,291	39.3	2,568	40.9	3,623	40.1
Home furnishing	927	22.8	1,157	19.9	1,458	23.2	2,580	28.6
Other consumer uses[b]	402	9.9	629	10.8	689	11.0	998	11.0
Industrial	947	23.3	1,391	23.9	1,216	19.4	1,597	17.7
Export	98	2.4	357	6.1	344	5.5	237	2.6

[a] From *Textile Organon*, January 1960 and January 1969.
[b] Other consumer uses include apparel linings, retail piece goods, narrow fabrics, handwork yarns, shoes and slippers, handbags, toys, and medical, surgical, and sanitary goods.

TABLE 7. Women's, Misses', Children's, and Infants' Apparel Consumption of Textile Fibers in the United States in 1967 (Millions of Pounds and Percent)[a]

Apparel Item	Total Pounds	Rayon and Acetate		Other Man-mades		Cotton		Wool	
		Pound	Percent	Pound	Percent	Pound	Percent	Pound	Percent
Suits[b]	30.8	11.3	36.7	7.5	24.4	4.2	13.6	7.8	25.3
Skirts	98.0	8.0	8.2	43.0	43.9	20.5	20.9	26.5	27.0
Slacks	120.7	21.0	17.4	40.5	33.6	46.0	38.1	13.2	10.9
Dresses, woven and knitted	435.0	212.5	48.9	78.5	18.0	114.0	26.2	30.0	6.9
Coats and jackets[c]	136.0	12.0	8.8	22.0	16.2	27.0	19.9	75.0	55.1
Rainwear	25.0	5.0	20.0	12.6	50.4	7.4	29.6	—	—
Playsuits, sunsuits, shorts[c]	129.0	14.5	11.2	31.3	24.3	80.7	62.6	2.5	1.9
Sweaters	95.9	0.5	0.5	65.1	67.9	3.9	4.1	26.4	27.5
Swimwear	18.1	2.9	16.0	8.9	49.2	6.3	34.8	—	—
Loungewear	75.0	21.0	28.0	20.0	26.7	33.0	44.0	1.0	1.3
Uniforms, washable, all types	18.3	0.8	4.4	13.0	71.0	4.5	24.6	—	—
Work clothing	62.1	1.0	1.6	15.3	24.6	45.8	73.8	—	—
Blouses and shirts	132.5	30.6	23.1	40.9	30.9	60.0	45.3	1.0	0.8
Foundation garments, all types[d]	44.5	11.7	26.3	22.0	49.4	10.8	24.3	—	—
Underwear, woven[e]	28.7	5.5	19.2	14.1	49.1	9.1	31.7	—	—
Underwear, knit[e]	121.7	47.8	39.3	46.2	38.0	27.7	22.8	—	—
Nightwear, woven	54.0	4.0	7.4	11.9	22.0	37.6	69.6	0.5	0.9
Nightwear, knitted	48.6	9.0	18.5	11.2	23.0	25.9	53.3	2.5	5.1

Hosiery, full length	48.1	0.1	0.2	47.4	98.5	0.6	1.2	—	—
Anklets and socks	33.2	0.1	0.3	13.6	41.0	18.0	54.2	1.5	4.5
Gloves	3.3	—	—	2.2	66.7	1.1	33.3	—	—
Apparel lace	13.7	2.9	21.2	8.6	62.8	2.2	16.1	—	—
Totals	1,772.2	422.2	23.8	575.8	32.5	586.3	33.1	187.9	10.6

[a] Compiled from *Textile Organon* for January 1969.
[b] Women's tailored uniforms are listed with men's (Table 8).
[c] Several types of children's garments included.
[d] Includes brassieres.

Tables 7 to 11 furnish detailed information on how much and what kind of fiber was used in 1967 for various end-uses in apparel, textile furnishings, and for industry. For example, in Table 7 you can note at a glance that more fiber is still going into dresses than any other item and that more dresses are made of rayon or acetate (or both) than any other fiber. One wonders how long it will be before change will force the inclusion of more classes of fibers. Also, perhaps there is more fiber going into lace than might be expected. Are you surprised to see that so large a share of lace is man-made fiber—probably nylon? You can also get an idea of the knitted as compared to the woven fabric in several items (in some of the other tables, too) and which classes of fibers are used for each method of construction. As you examine the totals at the bottom of the table, you will notice that a little more cotton was used than man-mades in either the rayon and acetate or other man-made classification, but when you add the man-mades together their total is considerably higher than for cotton. Are you surprised at wool's place in these end-uses?

For the other tables, we shall consider only an interesting facet or two, but you will want to study them in considerable detail and probably refer back to them as you study specific fibers.

In Table 8 you will notice that more fiber is used for utility clothing in men's apparel than for any other use. Also, you will see that a high percentage is cotton. Would you have expected this? When you consider that utility clothing includes most of what is known as "work" or "everyday" clothing, what a great variety of such apparel there is, and think of the various people in your own community who wear such clothing, you can probably visualize what such figures mean.

As you study Table 9 you can see how important the carpet and rug industry was in 1967 and how little of the market was going to wool which was the leading carpet fiber a generation ago. You will note that in sheets and bedding, cotton was still the overwhelming favorite. Consumer acceptance of polyester-cotton blends raises the question of how long this will be true. The great amount of rayon and acetate being used in drapery, upholstery, and slipcovers probably would be a surprise to many people—particularly to those people who have the idea that anything in this line that isn't cotton or wool is nylon.

Table 10 is included because such things as yard goods, lining fabrics, and such items are given separately from apparel or furnishings. This is due in part to the way data are reported and by whom, and also to the fact that until they are made up into end-use items it may be difficult to predict in what category many fabrics will appear. What is the most unexpected use of a fiber to you in this table?

You can believe that we are a people on wheels when you study Table

TABLE 8. Men's and Boys' Apparel Consumption of Textile Fibers in the United States in 1967 (Millions of Pounds and Percent)ᵃ

Apparel Item	Total Pounds	Rayon and Acetate		Other Man-mades		Cotton		Wool	
		Pound	Percent	Pound	Percent	Pound	Percent	Pound	Percent
Suits, medium and light weight	58.5	8.6	14.7	13.8	23.6	3.6	6.2	32.5	55.6
Uniforms, tailored civilianᵇ	43.5	1.5	3.4	16.3	37.5	0.8	1.8	24.9	57.2
Coats, separate, tailored	26.0	2.0	7.7	8.3	31.9	4.1	15.8	11.6	44.6
Slacks, shorts (outdoor)	240.1	39.4	16.4	100.0	41.6	79.7	33.2	21.0	8.7
Overcoats, topcoats, and rainwear	31.3	2.6	8.3	8.3	26.5	11.0	35.1	9.4	30.0
Jackets, athletic uniforms	108.0	9.0	8.3	33.1	30.6	49.3	45.6	16.6	15.4
Sweaters	59.9	0.7	1.2	19.9	33.2	2.3	3.8	37.0	61.8
Swimwear	12.5	3.1	24.8	2.9	23.2	6.4	51.2	0.1	0.8
Robes and neckties	24.7	5.9	23.9	2.3	9.3	12.7	51.4	3.8	15.4
Utility clothingᶜ	489.0	8.2	1.7	65.4	13.4	413.4	84.5	2.0	0.4
Shirts, business and dress	114.0	0.4	0.4	50.4	44.2	63.2	55.4	—	—
Shirts, sport, woven	134.0	25.0	18.7	35.0	26.1	71.0	53.0	3.0	2.2
Shirts, sport, knitted	139.9	2.9	2.1	27.5	19.7	109.0	77.9	0.5	0.4
Underwear, woven	37.5	3.5	9.3	5.9	15.7	28.1	74.9	—	—
Underwear, knitted	183.5	5.7	3.1	9.7	5.3	166.6	90.8	1.5	0.8
Nightwear, woven and knitted	46.2	0.2	0.4	3.9	8.4	42.1	91.1	—	—
Socks, all types	102.1	1.3	1.3	43.6	42.7	54.2	53.1	3.0	2.9
Totals	1,850.7	120.0	6.5	446.3	24.1	1,117.5	60.4	166.9	9.0

ᵃ Compiled from *Textile Organon* for January 1969.
ᵇ Includes women's tailored uniforms.
ᶜ Includes work and uniform shirts.

21

TABLE 9. Home Furnishings' Consumption of Textile Fibers in the United States in 1967 (Millions of Pounds and Percent)[a]

Home Furnishings Item	Total Pounds	Rayon and Acetate		Other Man-mades		Cotton		Wool	
		Pound	Percent	Pound	Percent	Pound	Percent	Pound	Percent
Bedspreads and quilts	149.0	35.6	23.9	6.0	4.0	107.4	72.1	—	—
Blankets and blanketing	132.6	63.7	48.0	26.7	20.1	27.8	21.0	14.4	10.9
Sheets and other bedding	571.2	24.8	4.3	12.2	2.1	534.2	93.5	—	—
Towels and toweling	225.4	1.8	0.8	—	—	223.6	99.2	—	—
Woven and lace napery	32.1	5.1	15.9	2.2	6.9	24.8	77.3	—	—
Carpets and rugs	900.1	113.1	12.6	614.6	68.3	88.5	9.8	83.9	9.3
Curtains	62.7	12.0	19.1	27.1	43.2	23.6	37.6	—	—
Drapery, upholstery, slipcovers	482.8	213.1	44.1	85.5	17.7	183.2	37.9	1.0	0.2
Miscellaneous[b]	24.3	2.1	8.6	6.9	28.4	15.3	63.0	—	—
Totals	2,580.2	471.3	18.3	781.2	30.3	1,228.4	47.6	99.3	3.8

[a] Compiled from *Textile Organon* for January 1969.
[b] Includes oil cloth, shower curtains, window shades, stamped art goods for embroidery, radio and TV grille cloth, and insect screening.

TABLE 10. Other Consumer Products' Consumption of Textile Fibers in the United States in 1967 (Millions of Pounds and Percent)[a]

Consumer Item	Total Pounds	Rayon and Acetate		Other Man-mades		Cotton		Wool	
		Pound	Percent	Pound	Percent	Pound	Percent	Pound	Percent
Apparel linings	267.7	96.0	35.9	45.7	17.1	122.8	45.9	3.2	1.2
Retail yard goods	183.5	44.0	24.0	26.0	14.2	99.0	53.9	14.5	7.9
Narrow fabrics[b]	136.8	24.1	17.6	31.9	23.3	80.8	59.1	—	—
Handwork yarns	32.4	3.6	11.1	5.0	15.4	8.8	27.2	15.0	46.3
Shoes, slippers (and linings)	74.8	3.7	4.9	2.0	2.7	69.1	92.4	—	—
Luggage, handbags, etc.	31.7	13.7	43.2	5.2	16.4	12.8	40.4	—	—
Toys	19.5	12.9	66.1	2.0	10.3	4.6	23.6	—	—
Medical, surgical, and sanitary	110.9	47.2	42.6	—	—	63.7	57.4	—	—
Miscellaneous[c]	140.9	92.0	65.3	46.0	32.6	2.5	1.8	0.4	0.3
Totals	998.2	337.2	33.8	163.8	16.4	464.1	46.5	33.1	3.3

[a] Compiled from *Textile Organon* for January 1969.
[b] Includes woven labels, braids, tapes, seat belts, belting, shoe laces, etc.
[c] Includes sports equipment, hand umbrellas, yarn to cover spandex or rubber, tricot fabrics for laminating, stuffing and filling materials, (except medical, surgical, and sanitary).

TABLE 11. Industrial End-Use Consumption of Textile Fibers in the United States in 1967 (Millions of Pounds and Percent)[a]

Industrial Item	Total Pounds	Rayon and Acetate		Other Man-mades		Cotton		Wool	
		Pound	Percent	Pound	Percent	Pound	Percent	Pound	Percent
Transportation upholstery[b]	67.3	9.0	13.4	6.3	9.4	52.0	77.2	—	—
Auto seat covers	8.4	0.4	4.8	2.0	23.8	6.0	71.4	—	—
Tires	451.0	122.8	27.2	323.2	71.7	5.0	1.1	—	—
Hose[c]	29.4	15.4	52.4	4.4	15.0	9.6	32.7	—	—
Belting	67.2	9.6	14.3	12.8	19.0	44.8	66.7	—	—
Laundry supplies[d]	14.8	—	—	7.0	47.3	7.8	52.7	—	—
Electrical applications	36.2	0.7	1.9	20.1	55.5	15.4	42.5	—	—
Felts[e]	25.9	4.7	18.1	5.6	21.6	6.7	25.9	8.9	34.4
Filtration (except cigarettes)	22.7	9.2	40.5	5.7	25.1	7.8	34.4	—	—
Sewing thread and medical sutures	105.2	3.4	3.2	15.7	14.9	86.1	81.8	—	—
Rope, cordage, fish lines, etc.	133.0	9.5	7.1	57.0	42.9	66.5	50.0	—	—
Bags and bagging[f]	128.0	—	—	12.3	9.6	115.7	90.4	—	—
Tarps, tents, chutes, etc.[g]	122.6	1.2	1.0	23.1	18.8	98.3	80.2	—	—
Paper and tape reinforcing	42.4	10.0	23.6	26.4	62.3	6.0	14.1	—	—
Plastic reinforcing	205.7	—	—	180.2	87.6	25.5	12.4	—	—
Miscellaneous[h]	136.5	31.8	23.3	11.3	8.3	93.2	68.3	0.2	0.1
Totals	1,596.3	227.7	14.3	713.1	44.7	646.4	40.5	9.1	0.6

[a] Compiled from *Textile Organon* for January 1969.
[b] Rugs are included in home furnishings.
[c] Includes fire, chemical, fuel, braided vacuum cleaner, etc.
[d] Wash nets, press and flatwork ironer pads, covers, marking tags, etc.
[e] Papermaker, roofing, mattress, cushioning, and wicking felts.
[f] Man-made yarn is used in nylon mailbags, olefin sandbags, etc.
[g] Parachutes, decelerator chutes, tow targets, awnings, beach, garden and tractor umbrellas, air-supported structures, tarps.
[h] Things such as book bindings, flags, bunting, linings for baby carriages, meat stockinette, wiping and tracing cloths, wall cover-

11. And isn't a surprising amount of fiber going into thread? We have to remember, however, that this is thread for all industrial users, textile furnishings manufacturers, apparel manufacturers including shoes, all sorts of plastic and leather goods, and other categories. A big share of the man-made fiber used to reinforce plastics is glass, though not so identified.

TRADE BETWEEN COUNTRIES

International trade, in general, is not permitted to flow freely from one country to another. There are many reasons, including some that are entirely political, others that are chiefly economic, some that are related to security, some that are designed to protect groups, commodities, or specific industries, some that are health-related, some that are designed to control quality of things bought and sold, or to maintain a balance between exports and imports. These categories, of course, often overlap.

We shall here be concerned briefly with trade between nations and not with regulations within countries although such regulations affect trade. For example, we shall include the effect of United States government subsidies for cotton and wool with the study of those fibers, through price support loans and incentive payments; such controls have an important effect on international trade.

Trade between countries is carried on by agreements of various kinds, some among groups of countries, others between pairs of countries, although most trade (in the free world) is carried on by business and industry of one country with those interested in its products or services in another in accordance with the agreements made between the governments. Several groups of nations have organized themselves as trade associations, for example, the European Economic Community (Common Market), the European Free Trade Association (those countries outside the Common Market), and a similar organization among the communist countries of East Europe and Russia.

Seventy-six nations have voluntarily formed an organization, GATT, which meets permanently in Geneva, Switzerland to work continually at regulation of trade between member nations. Even countries that do not belong send observers and are influenced by the agreements worked out by this organization. This body, which became effective in 1948, is officially the General Agreements on Tariffs and Trade. You have no doubt heard the "Kennedy Round" mentioned frequently in recent years as this deliberative body has tried to reduce trade restrictions between countries to promote freer trade. GATT represents primarily the industrialized nations. Another organization, the Organization for Economic Cooperation and

Development (OECD) is under sponsorship of the United Nations and represents primarily the developing countries. The aims of OECD, in many instances opposed to those of GATT, are to obtain special concessions for its member countries so that they may carry on effective trade with other nations—they are at a great disadvantage in dealing with industrialized nations—so there must be give and take on both sides. Such development must be encouraged and yet not destroy an industrialized country's own people engaged in such industry. There is presently quite a lot of sentiment in the industrialized as well as the developing countries for the industrialized countries to give up those industries that might well be carried on in developing countries and help the people who would thus lose their industry to convert to some other business.

Under GATT, a series of five-year agreements, known as LTA (Long Time Agreements) were worked out several years ago, and a great number have been extended, some with modifications, for several more years— many to run through 1971. According to *Textile Organon* for October 1964, 24 governments of North America, West Europe, and the Far East initially signed such agreements on cotton textiles, which were described as follows:

Under the terms of the agreement, an importing country threatened by, or subjected to, market disruption on any item or category of cotton textiles may proceed to freeze the imports of such items as follows: a. In the first year, the level of important restraint must not be below the level of actual imports during the first 12 months of the preceding 15 months; b. If necessary to continue restraint into a second year, the level of import restraint must be increased automatically by 5%, except under unusual conditions; c. In the third and subsequent years, the level of import restraint shall not be lower than 105% of the level for the previous 12-month period.

International restrictions or agreements include a variety of different measures such as duties, tariffs, and quotas.

Duties are taxes imposed on imports, exports, certain classes of raw, manufactured, or semimanufactured goods for purposes of revenue, primarily. For example, the English tax on tea that precipitated the American Revolution. Duties may operate to protect certain groups. For example, the duties on wool act to protect the United States wool growers as well as to furnish revenue to the government.

Tariffs also are taxes placed by a government on imports, though occasionally a tariff may be placed on an export. The purpose of a tariff ordinarily is protection of the industry at home, and is fixed at a high enough rate to discourage or even to exclude competitive products from abroad. For example, the United States has tariffs based on weight and

additional duties based on value (ad valorem) of fine quality wool and wool products imported from Australia and New Zealand, while carpet wool, which is not produced in the United States (with a minor exception) enters duty free, or at most, with a low duty. There are many arguments pro and con concerning tariffs; they are usually tied up with politics and powerful lobbies representing special interests until it is difficult to know wherein true justice lies. Tariffs are applied differentially by and to different countries, that is, some may have "favored-nation status" and have preferential treatment. Or a group of countries may agree among themselves to gradually remove all tariffs between them as is being done within the European Common Market.

A *quota* is an agreement made between an importing and an exporting country that only specified quantities of specifically listed goods will be shipped to the importing country within a given year, or each year for a given period of years. If the quota is exceeded, the excess is counted as part of the following year's quota. If a country fails to fill its quota, the deficiency is usually not added to the quota which may then be shipped the next year. Quotas are bilateral agreements between countries but operating within the general structure of GATT. The United States has quota agreements on cotton textiles or garments with Japan, Hong Kong, Portugal, China (Taiwan), the United Arab Republic, Spain, Jamaica, the Philippines, Israel, India, Greece, Turkey, and Ryukyu Islands. There are also restraints on imports of cotton products from Argentina, Brazil, Colombia, Mexico, Trinidad, Poland, and Pakistan. In all, about 90 percent of United States cotton imports in 1964 were admitted under restrictions of one type or another. Although figures are not available on present restrictions they seem to be at least as high. The largest present United States suppliers (through August 1968) in order were: Japan, Hong Kong, Taiwan China, Portugal, and Mexico.

Theoretically, quotas are worked out between the affected countries with the intent of considering the welfare of both—how they are judged seems to depend on which side of the fence one sits. After World War II, the United States encouraged Japan to rebuild by, among other things, shipping raw United States cotton and helping to establish a cotton processing and apparel industry. Japan quickly became a leader with highly modernized and mechanized mills; the fabric was made into garments which were then shipped back to the United States and sold at a price lower than that for similar goods produced within the country. It became necessary to establish quotas on manufactured cotton goods in order to sustain industry at home—much of which was much less modern and mechanized than that of Japan. This happened with other countries too, and the strict quotas imposed caused Japan to diversify into many

products of many types. In the last few years, Japan has failed to meet the quotas alloted to her by the United States; part of this is due to the swing of consumers away from all cotton toward polyester-cotton blended fabrics for many end-uses which Japan is already preparing for.

According to *Textile Organon* for December 1957, the wool quota system is somewhat different from the cotton system. To quote:

It should be noted that the Geneva Reservation proviso is not an absolute quantitative quota on imports, but one designed to keep imports on a low enough level to protect domestic woolen and worsted manufacturers from overburdensome imports.

In the 1967 Kennedy Round agreements which run through 1971, the United States agreed to reduce duty up to 50 percent on certain grades of raw wool and textile imports for those countries to which it extends most-favored nation treatment.

Some facts on importing and exporting countries may be of interest to you: The United States has been the leading exporter of cotton since the early 1800's but is rapidly losing that position because of the government programs and the resulting large quantity of cotton too poor in quality to meet mill demands (see pp. 49–50); other leading cotton exporters are the USSR, the UAR, Mexico, Turkey, and Brazil. The leading raw cotton importer is Japan; the cotton is manufactured into fabric there and may be finished or sold to Hong Kong or other countries for finishing, then sold back to the United States, Western Europe, or other countries. Other leading exporters of cotton goods are France, West Germany, Italy, the United Kingdom, and Hong Kong.

Biggest exporters of wool are Australia, New Zealand, South Africa, Argentina, and Uruguay. Biggest importers are Japan, the United Kingdom, the United States, France, and Italy. Biggest importers of rayon and acetate, in order are: the United States, West Germany, Belgium and Luxembourg, France, and the United Kingdom; for noncellulosic man-made fibers, the order is the same as rayon and acetate except that the United States and West Germany switch positions. Leading exporters of rayon and acetate are Japan, West Germany, Italy, the United Kingdom, and France and of noncellulosic man-made, West Germany, Japan, the United Kingdom, Italy, and France. You will note that sometimes a country both imports and exports fibers that belong to the same generic class. Some of the reasons should be apparent from the discussion in this chapter. Each country does not necessarily produce the whole range of possible fibers or fabrics within a type or the various products within a class and buys what it lacks from others.

The United States imports rayon and/or acetate chiefly from West Ger-

many, France, Austria, Italy, and Sweden and noncellulosics from West Germany, Japan, France, Italy, and Canada.

FOR FURTHER READING

Textile Organon
Daily newspapers
News magazines

FIBERS, THEIR CLASSIFICATION AND IDENTIFICATION

What is a fiber? How big is it? How strong? Are all fibers textile fibers? If not, why not? These and many other questions may occur to you as you begin your study of textiles.

Fibers are the very smallest visible units from which our fabrics are made, by one process or another. Take a piece of yarn, or a single yarn from a thread or fabric, and untwist it until it comes apart. Or pull a single strand from an opened cotton boll, or from a bunch of wool. The small, fine, individual hairlike strands are fibers. They are relatively small in diameter and long in proportion to their width, or diameter. Some fibers are short, others are very long, some are kinky, others are straight and smooth, some are scaly, and some are twisted. They may be weak, strong, transparent, opaque, colored, colorless, even or uneven in diameter, or they may vary in a great many other respects.

Although nature abounds in fibrous materials, and man has learned to synthesize many others, a relatively small number can be used for textile fabrics. What reasons can you give for this? To be used for textile purposes, it must be possible to make these materials into fabrics by one method or another. Some of the determining factors are length, strength, pliability,

diameter, abrasion resistance, and nature of the surface area. You will need to look for these characteristics as we study the different fibers.

In addition, to be suitable for clothing, fibers must be pleasant to the touch both in texture and temperature, absorbent to some extent so that they can be dyed, and comfortable to wear; cleanable by some method; of a weight and diameter suitable for garment fabrics that will meet the needs of the wearer in terms of temperature regulation, bulkiness, and freedom of movement; elastic; resilient; durable enough to warrant necessary expenditure of effort, time, and money on the part of producers and consumers; available in commercial quantities so that entrepreneurs can afford to establish an industry and laborers can afford to work in it; and at a fairly stable price which consumers can afford, with the exception of fibers used for luxury items.

If, in addition to the essential properties just listed, fibers are also beautiful, crease resistant, lustrous or dull as the desire may be, do not "pill," and do not accumulate charges of static electricity, so much the better.

Do you know the meaning of all these terms? It is essential that you do for a thorough understanding of this field. How would each affect making fibers into yarns or fabrics? You will find a textile dictionary extremely valuable in helping you to study textiles.

Not all the desirable properties are available in any one fiber, but some are essential if a fiber is to become a success for textile uses. Great length in relation to the diameter has been said to be the one property common to all the textile fibers. One property, or a combination of properties, must counterbalance the lack of others. As you study the properties of a fiber, you will see what compromise has been arrived at in determining its use. Modern production methods have overcome some of the difficulties in making fibers into fabrics and now make some fibers usable which were formerly unusable. No fiber is perfect. All are lacking in a few or many of these characteristics.

The different fibers are not all equally satisfactory for all uses, and researchers are fairly well agreed that never will there be found or produced a perfect fiber equally satisfactory for all textile uses. You will need to learn to discriminate between fibers on the basis of both fiber and fabric properties and the uses you wish to make of a fabric.

FIBER POLYMERIZATION AND STRUCTURE (not that important)

All fibers, whether natural or man-made, are carbon compounds of a type designated chemically as *polymers*. What is a polymer? The term is

derived from Greek words meaning "many parts." A polymer is a substance produced by combining two or more molecular units (monomers) into multiples (polymers) of the original molecular unit, the final product being very different in properties from the basic unit. Polymers usually consist of a high number of repeats of the basic molecular unit. The process by which monomers combine to form polymers is known as *polymerization*. In man-made polymers, high temperature, pressure, or both are usually necessary to induce polymerization.

Polymers may be classified according to the chemical nature of the units combining to form them or according to the method by which the units combine. We shall usually be more concerned with the nature of the combining units and the resulting properties but will take a quick look at both.

We shall look first at how monomers combine to form polymers. *Addition* is one method; in addition, the basic units link to each other end-to-end with no loss of any part of the original monomers. *Condensation* is another method of polymerization in which the ends of the monomers cannot link to each other until the end carbon of each monomer gives up a unit of a chemical element, usually hydrogen, oxygen, or nitrogen—freeing bonds that can then be shared by the combining monomers. The freed elements usually combine to form water or ammonia that is driven off as a gas during the polymerization process.

By either addition or condensation, polymerization continues until long, flexible, molecular chains—the basic units of textile fibers—are formed. Dr. Carothers, who first polymerized nylon, thought these chains must be at least 700 to 1300 angstroms (7 to 10 millionths of a centimeter) long. Each tiny, hairlike fiber is made up of thousands of such chains. We shall explore the theories of the structure of fibers in a few moments.

Perhaps polymerization can be better understood by means of a series of simple illustrations. Let us suppose that we have a simple compound A and another simple compound B. If, by one method or another, we can make a series of A's combine thus

A-A-A-A-A-A-A-A-A-A-A-A-A-A-A-A-A-A-A-A-A-A-A-A-A-A-A-A-

we have an example of simple, or *homopolymerization*, in which A units are combined into a long chain of A's. Or, we will make a series of B's combine, thus

B-B-B-B-B-B-B-B-B-B-B-B-B-B-B-B-B-B-B-B-B-B-B-B-B-B-B-B-

This is also a homopolymer. But if we can make units of A combine alternately with units of B into a molecular chain, thus

A-B-A-B-A-B-A-B-A-B-A-B-A-B-A-B-A-B-A-B-A-B-A-B-A-B-

we have a *copolymer*. The dotted lines indicate the repeating molecular unit of this polymer.

If we introduce a new substance C which we cannot make polymerize by itself, and can cause it to combine in a chain with either A or B (or with both), we will have a *heteropolymer*, possibly like one of these

A-A-A-A-C-A-A-A-A-C-A-A-A-A-C-A-A-A-A

B-B-C-B-B-C-B-B-C-B-B-C-B-B.

Perhaps the picture of different types of polymers can be made clearer by comparison to a railroad train. No doubt most of you have had the experience of waiting at a crossing for a long freight train to pass, or have been in a location where you could see trains go by, and maybe you have noted the different types of cars and have counted the cars on some of the trains. Can you imagine each car of the train as representing a molecular unit and of the whole string of cars as representing a polymer? The coupling between cars could represent the chemical bonds linking together the molecular units. Any train you have seen is very short in relation to the length of a fiber polymer. The train may have had a hundred or more cars, but polymers may be made up of hundreds to thousands of repeating units.

A train, excluding engine and caboose, representing a homopolymer would have all its cars identical no matter what type cars they were. One train might have all box cars, another all refrigerator cars, another all flat cars for carrying big pieces of equipment, another all tank cars, and still another all coal cars.

If you can then imagine hooking two different kinds of cars together, alternating them all down the line, your train would represent a copolymer. You might have one train made up of alternating box cars and refrigerator cars, another of coal cars alternating with refrigerator cars, another of piggyback cars alternating with tank cars, and so on.

A heteropolymer cannot be shown accurately by comparison with a train although a train of piggy-back cars loaded with trucks might seem to represent the idea. The trucks cannot be hooked into the line of cars but can be fastened to the top of the flat cars and carried along. A heteropolymer, however, would require the trucks to be hooked into the line of railroad cars though they could not be hooked to each other.

All fibers are polymers of one of these types. The natural fibers, insofar as is known, are simple polymers (cotton, linen) or copolymers (wool, silk). Among the man-made fibers may be found all three types of polymers.

Now that we have recognized the basic structure of a fiber, the polymerized molecular chain, how do the great numbers of chains that together

form a fiber do so? The present study of fibers by means of X-ray diffraction techniques and electron microscopy, in addition to the more familiar optical, infrared, and other physical measurement techniques is leading to new knowledge about the inner structure of fibers.

Many textile scientists, sometimes working alone, sometimes collaborating, and considering what others have reported, have proposed new theories or modifications of old theories about fiber structure. Since the various theories fall short in some way of accounting for fiber properties or behavior, a composite theory is now favored which, in part at least, incorporates the theories of a number of scientists from several countries. We shall consider the composite theory in a very simplified way in order to have a little better understanding of the fibers. A thorough understanding would require considerable knowledge of polymer chemistry which, it is hoped, some of you will be interested in pursuing as you continue your education.

To begin, we need to be familiar with the older concept of the structure of a fiber that was discussed briefly in earlier editions of this and in many other books. The fibers are believed to be made up of crystalline and amorphous areas varying in proportion in different fibers. In crystalline areas, the molecular chains were believed to lie parallel to each other and fairly close together; in amorphous areas, they were believed to be more or less helter-skelter. Crystalline areas were believed to account for strength, rigidity, brittleness, and such properties. Amorphous areas were believed to account for pliability, absorbency, and similar properties. This diagram illustrates the crystalline-amorphous concept.

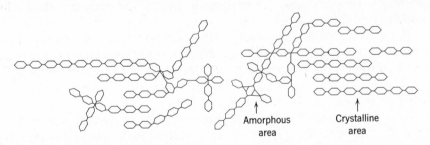

Amorphous area

Crystalline area

The new theories still consider that crystalline and amorphous areas exist and that their effect is about the same as in the older theory, but their meaning is somewhat different. Such areas are now attributed to smaller units than fibers—to microfibrils.

It has been learned that most of the fibers are composed of very complex and minute microfibrils, which are believed to be made up of the molecular chains. The microfibrils join in forming larger macrofibrils, and the macrofibrils, in turn, form the fibers. By means of the electron microscope micro-

fibrils have actually been seen in some types of fibers. It has been suggested that any fibril of approximately one micron in thickness be recognized as a macrofibril.

There is evidence that single crystals may form molecular chains that fold back and forth in a regular, layered pattern, often with chain ends free, something like this sketch.

Microfibrils are believed to be made up of imperfect folding-chain crystals, with some chain ends (fringes) and some chains (known as "tie" molecules) carrying across the space between crystals—the amorphous area— and with some chains forming parts of two (perhaps more) crystals. As natural fibers grow and as man-made fibers go through the drawing process, the tensions cause the crystals to deform, with some layers of the chains sliding past each other and forming still more tie molecules, thus helping to give the fibril its stable structure and characteristics. Of all the chains, 30 percent or more are believed to act as tie molecules. The amorphous areas are areas of crystal defects, tie molecules, chain ends, and impurities. Some scientists think that the folded chains assume a helical or coiled shape when relaxed. A fibril cross section presumably has several crystalline and amorphous areas within it. It has been suggested that the folded chains in fibrils may line up something as represented in this sketch.

←— microfibril —→

Although we shall not be much concerned with such chemical structure in this book, it is hoped that an explanation will help you understand the complex nature of the textile fibers we shall be studying and will stimulate those of you who have a scientific interest to explore further.

TEXTILE FIBER CLASSIFICATION

In the classification of the textile fibers of the United States shown in Table 12, the usual major classifications of the group into natural and man-made fibers has been followed, as has the usual classification of natural fibers into animal, vegetable, and mineral. The man-made fibers have been classified as thermoplastic and nonthermoplastic, with an additional group of unclassified fibers placed in the nonthermoplastic column for conven-

TABLE 12. Classification of United States Textile Fibers[a]

Natural Fibers	Man-made Fibers	
	Nonthermoplastic	Thermoplastic
Cellulosic (vegetable)	Alginate	Cellulosic
cotton	none at present	acetate or triacetate
linen	Cellulosic	acetate
jute	rayon	triacetate
minor fibers	cuprammonium	Mineral
abacá	high wet modulus	ceramic
banana	saponified	glass
cattail, cisalpha	viscose	metallic
coir	Protein	aluminum
fique	azlon	chrome
hemp	casein	copper
hennequen	zein	gold
kapok		nickel
kenaf		silver
mesta		steel
milkweed		tungsten
piña		Noncellulosic
ramie, rhea, grass		
linen		acrylic
redwood		anidex
roselle		modacrylic
sisal		nylon
Spanish moss	Unclassified	high temperature
sunn	PBI	nylon 6
urena	polycarbonate	nylon 66
Mineral	polystyrene	nytril
asbestos	potassium titanate	olefin
Protein (animal)	quartz silica	polyethylene
silk		polypropylene
wool		polyamide/polyester
minor fibers		polyester
alpaca		rubber
angorra (rabbit)		latex (natural)
		neoprene
camel		(synthetic)
cashmere		lastrile
		saran

[a] Italicized names are the generic terms specified in the Textile Fiber Products Identification Act or covered by it. Trademarked fiber and/or yarn names under the various generic classes are listed at the beginning of the discussion of each class and in the appendix.

TABLE 12. Classification of United States Textile Fibers[a] (*Continued*)

| Natural Fibers | Man-made Fibers | |
	Nonthermoplastic	Thermoplastic
cow hair		*spandex*
feathers		*vinal*
fur fibers (mink,		*vinyon*
etc.)		
guanaco		*tetrafluoroethylene*
horsehair		
llama		
mohair (goat)		
qiviut (musk ox)		
rabbit		
vicuna		

ience and not because of their properties. With the exception of the unclassified group, those fibers are thus grouped together that have some characteristics in common, of which some similarities in performance properties may be expected, and for which similar care will be required in most cases. Within these major divisions, fibers have been grouped by the generic names of the natural fibers and man-made fibers as defined in the Textile Fiber Products Identification Act; these are italicized. Fibers in the various groupings are listed alphabetically for convenience in locating them. The trade-named fibers within the various generic classes are not listed in this table but are listed at the beginning of the discussions of the various generic classes of fibers and also in the appendix.

Because of changes in fiber end-use over recent years, the glass and metallic fibers are here listed as thermoplastic fibers although they were listed as nonthermoplastic in earlier editions of this book. At the temperatures to which they ordinarily are exposed in apparel, homes, and buildings, these fibers may be considered to be nonthermoplastic. But in the very high temperatures associated with space exploration, in various types of uses where danger of very high temperature fire exists, and in a growing list of industrial applications, these fibers melt or burn as do the fibers better known as thermoplastics.

The order of the table, however, will not be followed in our detailed study of the various fibers. There we shall begin with the more familiar in a group and progress to the unfamiliar. New fibers, as developed, can be added to this list in their proper places. When this has been done, you will automatically know something of what may be expected of them and how to care for them.

Some fibers we shall study in considerable detail as typical of their class; others will not be studied at all. A large number of these fibers are available on world markets; some of them have a limited availability in various areas of the world; some are in the experimental stage and may never be placed on the market; a few were made at one time but have been discontinued temporarily or permanently for varying reasons; others, for which there are as yet no names, and which are still highly secret in the companies where they are being developed, may be on the market by the time this book is printed. A practice that has sometimes added to the confusion of trying to learn the identity of fibers is the naming of yarns dyed by a special process, or yarns produced in different ways, with trademarks that sound very much like fiber names. Often the advertising and labels on these products lead the consumer, who is used to hearing of new fibers, to believe that these, too, are fibers. Until the passage of the Textile Fiber Products Identification Act, labels were often only fiber trade names and carried no generic names at all. Now, however, this is illegal, although stores may still be found that violate the law and have accepted unlabeled merchandise or have removed the labels before the merchandise is displayed for sale.

In the past, trademarks have often not carried a fiber name at all. Now, however, such labeling is prevented by the provisions of the Textile Fiber Products Identification Act. Since this law covers all the fibers used in wearing apparel and furnishings, with specified exceptions, it is important for consumers to know and understand certain of its provisions. Therefore a brief description of the most essential provisions, from the consumer viewpoint, follows, although other laws of more limited scope will be discussed with the fibers to which they pertain.

THE TEXTILE FIBER PRODUCTS IDENTIFICATION ACT

The Congress of the United States, on September 2, 1958, passed the Textile Fiber Products Identification Act; it was signed by President Eisenhower and became effective March 3, 1960. During the interim, the Federal Trade Commission held hearings and established a set of rules and regulations for its interpretation and enforcement. The law covers all textile fibers except those covered by the Wool Products Labeling Act of 1939.

The three provisions of most importance and interest to consumers are

1. (Sec. 4*b*1) A stamp, tag, label, or other means of identification must be affixed showing in plainly legible English or figures

. . . the constituent fiber or combination of fibers in the textile fiber product, designating with equal prominence each natural or manufactured fiber

in the textile fiber product by its generic name in the order of predominance by the weight thereof if the weight of such fiber is 5 percentum or more of the total fiber weight of the product, but nothing in this section shall be construed as prohibiting the use of a nondeceptive trademark in conjunction with a designated generic name. . . .

With one exception, fibers present in amounts of less than five percent may not be designated by generic name, and fibers used for ornamentation only need not be designated by generic name if the label states that ornamentation is excepted. The reason for this ruling is that it takes more than five percent (usually considerably more) of a fiber to influence fabric properties effectively. The exception is spandex; it has been demonstrated that only two or three percent of spandex fibers in blends will influence the "give," that is, the stretch potential of a fabric. Presumably, this exception will also cover other highly elastic fibers such as rubber and lastrile and proposed new classes of fibers with high elasticity.

2. (Sec. 4c) A textile fiber product shall be considered to be falsely or deceptively advertised

. . . if any disclosure or implication of fiber content is made in any written advertisement which is used to aid, promote, or assist directly or indirectly in the sale or offering for sale of such textile fiber product, unless the same information as that required to be shown on the stamp, tag, label or other identification . . . is contained in the heading, body, or other part of such written advertisement, except that the percentages of the fiber present in the textile fiber product need not be stated.

In simple terms, an advertisement does not have to say anything about fiber content but if it does, the same rules apply as to labels except that percentages do not have to be stated.

3. The required stamps, tags, labels, or other means of identification *must be* affixed to and remain on the product itself, or on the package intended for sale to the ultimate consumer, until the consumer himself removes it. If products packaged together and labeled with a single label (usually on the package) are separated for sale either as retailer practice or at the request of a consumer, each item from such packages must be stamped, tagged, labeled, or otherwise identified with the original information. Presumably, the consumer who asks to have a package broken may ask for the item with the original label, ask that the item he purchases be labeled, or take it without a label, trusting to his own memory to retain the pertinent information.

Fabrics cut from bolts, rolls, or other large-quantity holders do not have to have stamps, tags, labels, or other identification affixed to the removed portions *if* the information is on the bolts or rolls at the time of sale. There

seems to be a loophole here, as you may already have discovered, in that stores often reroll or rebolt materials on different types of holders than those on which the fabric was shipped, especially for display tables, and frequently do not transfer the information to the new bolt—nor is it made available on a placard on the table for consumers to see.

Some uses for the fibers are specifically exempted from coverage, that is, fibers for upholstery stuffing; outer coverings of furniture, mattresses, and box springs; linings, interlinings, and padding incorporated for structural purposes and not for warmth; stiffenings, trimmings, facings, and interfacings; backing and padding of floor coverings; sewing and handicraft threads; bandages, surgical dressings, and other products covered by the labeling requirements of the Federal Food, Drug, and Cosmetic Act of 1938; waste materials not intended for textile products; and fibers used in footwear, headwear, handbags, luggage, brushes, lampshades, toys, catamenial goods, adhesive tapes and sheets, chemically impregnated cleaning cloths, and diapers.

Other provisions of the act cover definitions, country of origin on imports, keeping of records, misuse of fur names, guarantees, and prosecution. Labels carry codes by which manufacturers may be identified.

The Federal Trade Commission established a set of rules and regulations for enforcing the law, and interpretations of the meanings of the various portions of the law have been made over the years since its passage. New additions and modifications will necessitate additional interpretations. Among the most important rules are those establishing generic names and definitions for manufactured fibers (Rule 7), and the procedure for establishing generic names for manufactured fibers not covered by Rule 7.

The generic names established for immediate use by Rule 7 are acrylic, modacrylic, polyester, rayon, acetate or triacetate, saran, azlon, nytril, nylon, rubber, spandex, vinal, olefin, vinyon, metallic, and glass (see Table 12). In late 1969 Rule 7 was amended to include a new generic name, *anidex*.

Rule 8 provides for the establishment of other generic names for fibers for which the FTC definitions for interpretation and enforcement of the 1958 law are not accurate. New fibers that are now in the early stages of development, in actual pilot plant production, or that may be synthesized in the future are thus assured of new generic names if such establishment is warranted by their chemical composition.

This law can be of great value to the consumer as he becomes familiar with its terms and requirements and carefully reads the tags, labels, and stamps. Although at first it may seem confusing to you, how can you see this law operating to the advantage of the individual consumer? How can he benefit most by its provisions?

It may become imperative, if a consumer is to know what he is purchasing, to become acquainted with all the generic names, although it is likely that an increasing number of producers of fabrics or garments will use both trademark and generic names on the labels, for example "Orlon Acrylic Fiber." A manufacturer with a desirable product will want the consumer to be able to identify it.

The labeling required by this law should prove to be a boon to consumers who take the trouble to observe the types of phenomena about which we are talking (classification as to thermoplasticity, etc.), in knowing what to expect of the fabrics and how to care for them, what to look for in rebuying satisfactory merchandise, and what to avoid as unsatisfactory for certain uses. With this type of labeling, a consumer's experience accumulated over the years should be valuable to him in choosing fabrics and fibers according to whatever uses he intends to make of them.

Although a great many persons believe that this law does not go far enough in its labeling requirements, it is a big step in the right direction. But much of its value must be the responsibility of the consumer himself.

As we study the list of fibers and their grouping, a few definitions are in order.

Natural fiber refers to all fibers that occur in fiber form in nature. All may not be readily apparent as we study their sources, but the fibers are there. Our problem is to locate them and to ascertain what is necessary to make them available for use.

Man-made fibers are textile fibers that do not occur in fiber form in nature but must have something done to them by man to get them into fiber form; or they are fibers that have been broken down from their original fiber form and reassembled into a different sort of structure. The latter are often designated as "regenerated" fibers. The rayons are examples. The Textile Fiber Products Identification Act uses the term *manufactured fiber* for man-made fibers and defines them as "any fiber derived by a process of manufacture from any substance which, at any point in the manufacturing process, is not a fiber" (Sec. 2*d*).

Thermoplastic fibers are those that soften with heat and thus become pliable, or, if the heat is sufficiently high, will in most cases melt, or may burn, or both, sometimes at extremely high temperatures.

Nonthermoplastic fibers are those that do not soften or melt with heat but will in most cases scorch or burn if the temperature is sufficiently high. The natural fibers could be placed in this grouping too, with the exception of asbestos, which neither scorches nor burns.

Staple fibers are short-length fibers which must be spun together to form a yarn. These may vary in length from ½ inch for the shortest usable cotton to 18 to 30 inches for the long linen fibers. Man-made fibers cut to these

lengths are also known as "staple" length fibers. Yarns and fabrics made from staple length fibers are known as staple yarns or fabrics.

Filament fibers are those of a continuous long length, from 400 to 1300 yards or more for silk to the relatively unlimited length of some of the man-made fibers. Yarns or fabrics made from such fibers are known as filament yarns or fabrics.

Tow refers to the short fibers remove in processing flax and also to the multiple-filament strands of man-made fibers (rayon specifically) that are cut or broken into short lengths for spinning into *spun* yarns.

FOR FURTHER READING

Federal Trade Commission: Rules and Regulations under the Textile Fiber Products Identification Act

Joseph, M. L., *Introductory Textile Science*

Kaswell, E. R., *Wellington Sears Handbook of Industrial Fabrics*

Labarthe, J., *Textiles: Origins to Usage*

THE NATURAL CELLULOSIC (VEGETABLE) FIBERS

The natural cellulosic fibers, usually called "vegetable fibers," of which cotton, linen (flax) and jute are the three most important from the textile viewpoint, in common with other plants are largely cellulosic in structure. Vegetable fibers are obtained from various areas of the parent plants—some are seed hairs, some are stem fibers (bast), and others are leaf fibers. Cotton and kapok are examples of seed fibers; flax, hemp, and jute of bast fibers; and piña and sisal of leaf fibers. Raw cotton is approximately 90 percent cellulose, and when waxes and other extraneous materials are removed in preparation for textile uses, it may be as high as 99 percent cellulose. Flax and the other vegetable fibers have much lower percentages of usable cellulose, although their original cellulose content is approximately the same as for cotton. The cellulose in plants may be combined with lignin, pectin, and other substances.

After many many years of experimentation and research, chemists agreed upon the chemical structure of cellulose as being a condensation polymer of glucose (the same glucose with which you may be familiar as a simple sugar) in which water (HOH) was split off at the point of union of the units which form the longer chains. This theoretical structure has been

sustained by further years of intensive research, except that whereas formerly a cellulose molecular chain was believed to be a union of 1500 to 2000 of the glucose units, recent research has led to the belief that the molecular chain is much longer, involving perhaps 10,000 glucose units per chain in the case of cotton. A chain of such a great number of units would give a length-breadth ratio of about 7000 to 1, a fineness which gives some idea why it is so difficult to study the inner structure of a cotton fiber, even with the electron microscope, when it is remembered that each tiny fiber is composed of many fibrils which are in turn composed of many such chains of units.

Cellulose is a carbohydrate made up of carbon (44.4%), hydrogen (6.2%), and oxygen (49.4%). The repeating unit of the cellulose chain, within the dotted lines of the diagram, may be pictured structurally as follows:

$$
\begin{array}{cccc}
CH_2OH & CH_2OH & CH_2OH & CH_2OH \\
\end{array}
$$

Notice that cellulose is a homopolymer that has been polymerized by condensation, with a molecule of water (HOH) split off where two units join. This is the chemical structure of all the natural cellulosic fibers and of the man-made nonthermoplastic cellulosic fibers—the rayons.

The cellulosic fibers have a number of properties in common that are of significance in their use and care as fabrics. Fabrics of these fibers tend to be absorbent and comfortable to wear, to lack elasticity and resiliency so that they may wrinkle easily unless specially finished, to be almost as strong (or even stronger) wet as dry, and to be free (unless specially finished) from accumulations of static electricity. They may be dry-cleaned but ordinarily are restored to freshness by laundering. They are not subject to attack by moths but may be subject to bacterial and fungal attack, that is by mildew and mold.

When a flame is touched to them the cellulosic fibers burn readily and rapidly with a yellow flame and the odor of burning cotton rags, paper, or straw. When completely burned they leave little, or no, powdery gray ash. They are sensitive to and easily damaged by acid solutions but may have some properties improved by certain alkaline solutions.

We shall note these and other properties as we turn now to a detailed study of the more important fibers of this group.

COTTON

History

Cotton, together with linen and wool, was in use long ages before historical records began. Students of archaeology and history do not agree whether the use of cotton began first in the Old World or the New, or whether inhabitants of both may have learned to use cotton at about the same time. India, however, is usually credited with being the originator of the first cotton fabrics as well as many of the finest.

It is generally assumed that early civilizations learned to use wool before they learned to use cotton. Evidence for this exists, among other things, in early descriptions of cotton as "vegetable wool." Many legends grew up around the origin of the early fibers. Crawford, in *The Heritage of Cotton* (p. 5), attributes one such legend to "the delightfully unveracious" Sir John de Mandeville thus:

Cotton was supposed to be the wool of certain mysterious Scythian sheep. These lambs grew on shrubs, each cradled in its downy pod. Except for the fact that the stalk was attached to the soil, they were like the little downy creatures who gamboled in the English fields. Fortunately this stem was flexible and permitted them to bend down and graze on the adjacent herbage. When, however, all grass within this narrow orbit had been eaten, the lambs naturally and wisely proceeded to expire. Both wool and flesh were then available.

The Bible mentions that King Solomon, who lived from 1015 B.C. to 975 B.C., used cotton hangings for the temple built during his reign. Herodotus, one of the earliest of the Greek historians, wrote (445 B.C.) "There are trees which grow wild there (India), the fruit of which is a wool exceeding in beauty and goodness that of sheep. The Indians make their clothes of this tree-wool." Theophrastus, a little later, left a complete account of the cultivation of cotton in India.

When Columbus first stepped ashore in the New World he had discovered, he was greeted by natives dressed in cotton garments. He found cotton cloth being beautifully woven, with colored yarns and delicate feathers interwoven to obtain decorative designs.

In the United States, from the introduction of slavery and the growth of the plantation system until relatively recently, cotton growing was concentrated in the southern and southeastern states. Following the abolition of slavery, large farms and plantations were subdivided into small plots of

one to a few acres, which were farmed by tenant farmers whose livelihood depended almost entirely on the cotton raised on these plots. In addition, there were many small, owner-cultivated farms. All cotton work was largely hand labor, or mule and human labor combined (see Figure 4-1). The human labor is still typical of cotton production in the less developed areas of the world.

During the depression years following the stock market crash of 1929, and through the years of World War II, a great change took place. Tenant farmers and other small farmers, hit doubly by depression markets and unfavorable growing seasons, gave up and left the farms. With rising factory and shipyard employment in cities, especially in the North and West, with the spread of armed conflict, a shortage of labor and the consequent high wages attracted an ever-growing number from the cotton farms to the industrial cities. At the same time, increasing mechanization of cotton production, as well as mechanization of other farm equipment, led to consolidation of small farms into larger ones, and reversion of small tenant plots to the larger plantation farms which could be cultivated with tractors and other mechanized equipment by a relatively few people, thus forcing small farmers to sell out and tenants to leave the cotton farms. With the successful invention of cotton production machinery, the need for many laborers at seasonal times was largely eliminated, although much human labor is still used to get the cotton picked in some areas. The depression years story of the disrupted life of many of the forced-out, emigrating cotton families is told vividly in John Steinbeck's novel *The Grapes of Wrath*.

Because of the effects of the Great Depression in the early 1930's and the resulting federal programs that have profoundly influenced life in the United States and that are now taking a new direction, we need to go back to trace the history of these programs.

The Great Depression hit the United States very hard and spread over most other developed countries as well, bringing trade to a virtual standstill and thrusting a large proportion of the people into deep poverty. The federal government of the United States attempted to rescue farm families who were, as a group, hardest hit of all. Regulations of the farm economy were instituted which, with changes over the years, persist to this day. These regulations, together with our rapidly changing technology with the accompanying drastic changes in rural and urban life have been influential in changing the face of America and have had world repercussions. We probably are at the very beginning of great changes in direction that farm production and rural life as it has been known over the centuries will take, and we need to have a closer look at what has happened to cotton production since World War I (1914–1918) and the portents for the future. Many of the things that have happened in relation to cotton are typical

FIGURE 4-1. Hand picking of cotton—a back-tiring job. (Courtesy National Cotton Council.)

of other farm crops that are primarily food and feed crops. Because there is as yet no substitute for food, but fibers may be supplied in other ways, cotton-producing areas are the sections most likely to be permanently changed; also, a high proportion of the less economic and small farms seem destined to disappear. This, of course, is a disturbing prospect to those whose livelihood presently depends on cotton production and whose

families have never known any other manner of living than as cotton producers or processors.

Since Colonial times, and especially with the Industrial Revolution which began with the cotton industry in the United States, cotton has been the most prevalent and traditional cash crop, with about 60 percent of the total crop being produced for export as a raw material to other countries until the mid-30's. Until the last few years, the United States has been the largest producer of cotton in the world; this, of course, resulted in United States' policies being the dominant factor in world cotton trade throughout most of this time period.

Prices of many commodities and consumer products fluctuated wildly after World War I but had begun to stabilize when the stock market crashed in 1929 with the resulting world money chaos followed by the Great Depression of the early 1930's. Price for cotton dropped from a high of 35 cents per pound during World War I to five cents per pound in the early 1930's. At the same time prices of all other farm products dropped —for instance, eggs brought (to the farmer) ten cents a dozen and corn was so cheap that farmers in the Midwest burned it for fuel since they had no money to buy relatively expensive coal. Prices of many things people needed to buy were also cheap, but with no money people could not buy them. Many people in the cities lost their jobs and those who had held very good jobs were sometimes reduced to selling apples on street corners. Soup kitchens were established in the cities to try to give the starving poor one hot meal a day to enable them to survive. The generation who lived through those years—now middle-aged and older—can give you many fascinating stories of some of their experiences as individuals, in their families, and in their communities, and the efforts made to pull out of the miserable conditions. There were, of course, many bright spots in the situations as well as dark ones, since many humans are very resourceful in adversity and are capable of many creative ideas and solutions to problems.

The measures taken by the federal government to begin to alleviate the situation during Franklin Roosevelt's early years as president are well documented. The majority of United States' citizens still lived in rural areas at that time; farmers were those most deeply caught, and their recovery was basic to the recovery of the rest of the economy.

Some of the measures taken first by the government were price supports based on price-cost relationships of the years 1909–1914 as a "normal" base, often called "parity." Some direct payments were authorized to farmers who would sign up in acreage control programs in which a part of their crop was plowed under. All participants in the program were able to borrow on the cotton (and other basic crops) they produced from the

Commodity Credit Corporation without waiting to sell them in the markets of the country or the world. These loans, called "nonrecourse loans" worked this way. A farmer could borrow from the CCC up to a given percentage (this varied over different years from 65 to 105 percent) of the anticipated value his crop would bring on the market. If he was then able to market his crop at a higher price than that of the loan he could repay the loan, reclaim the cotton, and sell it where he desired. But if the price were lower than the loan, after June 30th of the crop year, the cotton was considered sold at the loan price to the CCC. This, in effect, put a floor under the prices farmers received and was an indirect method of income payment. This was the way in which huge surpluses in various farm products began and continued building up because the loan price was often higher than the particular commodity would bring on the open market. Often no effort was made to sell in the marketplace. Within a few years cotton exports had dropped to 40 percent of the crop. With many products, the tendency was to produce varieties that would give the maximum yield per acre, regardless of quality, and much was too poor in quality to be used for human food or textile fiber.

It was soon apparent that acreage controls were necessary if surpluses were ever to be controlled and such controls became a part of the cotton program after excessive cotton production in 1937 for which there was no market anywhere. Although acreage controls were imposed and have continued, quality controls still have not been imposed. Additional regulations took the form of soil conservation and diversion payments which were attempts to divert land use to soil-building and conservation uses. The latest legislation consists of direct payments to maintain farm income. This is meeting with objection from many of those receiving large payments because direct payments are so much more visible to taxpayers than those for support or land diversion. These direct payments are still supplemented with price supports on crops and CCC loans, but acreage diversion payments have been discontinued as of 1969. The government regulatory program has led to ever-decreasing exports and to subsidies to manufacturers and exporters in recent years (though now discontinued) as well as to producers. The total payments per farm vary from a very small amount to many small farmers, especially those in the Southeast, to hundreds of thousands of dollars, and in some cases to more than a million dollars each per year to some large farmers who have large-scale, efficient operations and probably should never have been given any government aid. The program, since its inception, has been politically involved with the difficulties this means in effective control or change. There are many ramifications of the problem. There seems little doubt that many unproductive farms and farm areas have been influenced to take up or to continue cotton produc-

tion when their use should have been diverted to something else. A big part of the surplus cotton held by the CCC in recent years has been from one area of the country which produces a poor quality cotton and probably should not be producing it at all. Other problems associated with the program are inequity of payments to different farmers from one area to another and even within the same area, variations in supports for the same grade in different areas, more than one person in the same family being paid for acreage diversion on the same farm, etc. Some of the references, particularly the report of the President's Advisory Commission on Food and Fiber under the title *Cotton and Other Fiber Problems and Policies in the United States* will give you much interesting data and insight into differing viewpoints on the same problems, as well as the arguments used to justify some of the practices. As potential taxpayers you will be interested in how programs sometimes develop and grow out of reasonable control.

The latest federal program, which is a change in direction, seems to hold out some hope for solving the cotton problem. It is the Food and Agriculture Act of 1965 which went into effect for four years beginning with the 1966–1967 season. The huge cotton surplus held in the United States has almost disappeared already (1969) in this program, even though much of it was an inferior quality. The provisions of this act are, according to R. Whitaker in the report to the President's Advisory Commission on Food and Fiber (p. 135):

(1) Participation in the program was made voluntary with a minimum reduction of 12.5 percent from effective farm allotments on all but small farms. (2) Farm allotments continued to be based on the 16-million-acre minimum national allotment. Effective acreage allotments consist of the farm allotment plus or minus adjustments for "release, reapportionment, sale or lease." (3) Price support payments are provided on the farm's domestic allotment (65 percent of the effective farm allotment). (4) Diversion payments are provided for acreage diverted out of cotton and put to conserving uses. The farmer has a choice of reducing 12.5 percent, 25 percent, or 35 percent below his effective farm allotment. Diversion of acreage is a prerequisite for receiving program benefits. (5) For farmers who wish to grow for export only a limited acreage allocation will be available, but no program benefits will be received by such producers. (6) CCC loan rates are reduced to 21 cents for "Middling 1" cotton in 1966–67 and 90 percent of the world price for the three succeeding seasons. (7) Cotton producers have an opportunity to divert their cotton acreage from production for a long-term period under the Cropland Adjustment program. (8) The law also authorized the Secretary of Agriculture to offer participating growers an additional choice as to the use of acreage diverted for payment.

Farmers signed up for this program and diverted land to other things than cotton. With all the payments involved, the cotton farmers got approximately 35 percent of their gross income from cotton in the form of government payment in 1966–1967; the figure is estimated at 65 percent for 1968–1969. Few took up the option to produce for the export market without price supports. Mr. Whitaker called attention to the fact that the government did not mention disadvantages that went with advantages of the program. It is expected that this act will result in United States cotton competing at world prices in world markets with production and consumption plus exports being brought into balance. That this new direction may succeed in stimulating production of desired qualities of cotton was implied in a USDA release in early 1968 which confirmed a shortage of $1\frac{1}{16}$ inch and longer fiber cotton and that only 60 to 65 percent of the 1968–1969 crop was expected to be this length. The reason given was producer response to price levels of $1\frac{1}{16}$ inch or longer fiber on world markets.

This discussion has not taken into account other government programs that help (or that subsidize farmers) such as irrigation projects, research programs, grading, and testing, nor has it considered the effect of federally regulated programs and markets on related industries such as gins, mills, spot markets, stock exchanges, and others. Many of the related industries have been thousands of small operations scattered over the cotton-producing areas of the country. Many of these, too, are changing to conform to a changing technology, but others are disappearing from the scene. How many cotton mills and related industries may disappear, how many might switch to other fibers, and how much consolidation might occur, or how much attrition to age of plant and outmoded methods cannot be foreseen at this time.

Other cotton-producing areas are not happy about developments that again give the United States a more competitive position in world cotton markets. There are many differing opinions among different groups of people with varying interests in what is ahead and what should be done. Many Congressmen now believe that developing countries must be given priority in world cotton markets, while others think only of preserving an ever bigger share of the market for United States cotton. Thus, the long-range direction and how far the United States will go is not now apparent. Governments in some other countries have also subsidized cotton through free fertilizer, irrigation projects, price supports, or other action. But most of them are facing the need to switch land to food crops to feed their growing populations. It would seem that cotton will never again have the importance among world, and particularly United States, fibers that it has had in the past. Some breakthrough in cotton as dramatic as

the development of nylon in the man-made fibers could, of course, change the whole picture. In his discussion, Mr. Whitaker questioned the wisdom of doing anything to increase production of cotton in the developed countries and as a consequence driving developing countries out of the markets. He said, "Finally, it is assumed that the number of U.S. people dependent upon cotton for a living will decrease further and that it will become increasingly difficult to justify large federal subsidies to fewer and fewer cotton growers."

Cotton is one of the fibers that has been most protected by quotas and other trade agreements and by import duties on some types of cotton. Rigid quotas are now in force for raw cotton although there is no duty on any type except extra long staple, and duty on that has been reduced in a late round of agreements.

Production and Source

Cotton grows well in some parts of all the continents of the world except Antarctica. The pattern of world cotton production has changed considerably over the past decade both in the number of countries producing cotton and the volume produced. Note world figures in Table 3, Chapter 2. Some of the developed countries are producing less cotton and many developing countries are producing more. In many instances, the increased production in the developing countries will no more than keep up with population increases and rising standards of living but in others cotton is becoming, or will become, an important item in international trade. Most of these countries still do not produce enough to make much of a showing in world production figures for cotton.

In the 1910–1911 season, according to figures from the New York Cotton Exchange, world commercial production of cotton totaled about 9½ billion pounds. Of this total, 61.4 percent was produced in the United States, 16.1 percent in India, 7.6 percent in Egypt, 5.2 percent in Russia, 4.0 percent in China, and 1.4 percent in Brazil.

According to the July 1968 *Quarterly Bulletin* of the International Cotton Advisory Committee, figures for world cotton production for 1966–1967 (August 1 through July 31) indicated that a total of about 23.3 billion pounds was produced. Ten countries produced 85.0 percent of this total as follows: the United States 20.3 percent, the USSR * 19.1 percent, Mainland China 13.4 percent, India 9.4 percent, Mexico 4.6 percent, Pakistan and the UAR 4.3 percent each, Brazil 4.2 percent, Turkey 3.6 percent, and Sudan 1.8 percent.

Preliminary figures for 1967–1968 indicate that world cotton production

---

* Includes Latvia, Estonia, and Lithuania.

had dropped to about 22.6 billion pounds and that the USSR, apparently for the first time ever, produced more cotton than the United States. The 1966–1967 total for cotton produced in the United States was down almost 34 percent from that reported for 1965–1966. Preliminary figures for 1967–1968 indicated a further drop of almost 25 percent. Such drastic changes inevitably have far-reaching effects on all segments of the cotton industry as well as the producers. USDA cotton crop predictions for 1968–1969, however, show an increase to a little more than the 1966–1967 levels. This increase was expected to be too little to satisfy domestic and export needs.

Total world mill consumption of cotton for 1966–1967 was almost 25 billion pounds. The ten highest consuming countries and the percentage of the world total consumed was: the United States 18.1 percent, the USSR 14.2 percent, Mainland China 13.4 percent, India 11.6 percent, Japan 6.2 percent, Pakistan 2.7 percent, France 2.4 percent, Brazil and West Germany 2.3 percent each, and Italy 2.1 percent. This leaves 24.7 percent of the world's cotton for all the rest of the countries. The countries themselves did not always actually use all the cotton their mills consumed; a number manufactured cotton goods for sale to other countries as fabric, apparel, or other items. And, of course, needs vary greatly among countries with differences in climate and with the other variables discussed in Chapters 1 and 2. Cotton consumption for the various countries, and for the world also, does not necessarily correspond to production for numerous reasons. If world consumption of a specific fiber is greater than world production the difference must be made up from surplus stocks held by some countries, much of which may be of inferior quality. The United States has long been the chief source of surplus cotton; other countries have neither the storage facilities nor the economy to permit much stockpiling. Before all surplus is exhausted, the problem of fiber supply must be faced. Solutions may vary from country to country, and in time, over the world. Can you think what some of the alternatives may be in such a situation? Perhaps the decision would be to use more poor quality fiber even though this would lead to other problems, including dissatisfaction of consumers. Or perhaps a decision would be made to substitute other available fibers, or to do with less, or even to do without. A poor country might have to do with less fiber than it needs as richer countries outbid it for the scarce supply, or because it simply could not pay the high price even if everyone shared cooperatively. Limitations may be made as to how the scarce fiber (or all fibers) may be used, thus perhaps affecting the mills, the apparel and furnishings industries, and fashion. During World War II, the United States government placed restrictions on the use of fabrics for apparel that limited the total amount of yardage that could be used in garments of the various types. Use of cuffs on sleeves and trousers,

and other unnecessary appurtenances were forbidden. The effect on fashion was very quickly apparent—design lines became simple and uncluttered, skirts were narrow and short (though not as short as the miniskirts of the late 1960's). Suits with wide-legged trousers and double-breasted jackets, along with other styles requiring other than a minimum of fabric disappeared from the marketplace. One of the fairly early effects of removal of the restrictions was the "new look" in which skirts became full and were dropped to mid-calf or lower, trouser legs became wider, and cuffs, big collars, and other ornamentation reappeared.

In 1910, the states leading in production of cotton in the United States, in the order of amount produced from most to least were Texas, Georgia, Mississippi, Alabama, South Carolina, Oklahoma, Arkansas, North Carolina, Tennessee, Louisiana, Missouri, Florida, Virginia, and California.

In 1966 fourteen states were reported as producing cotton in amounts varying from about 3.18 million to 93 thousand bales (of 478 pounds each) of upland cotton with a few other states producing a total of 18 thousand bales among them. The latter group were not listed separately. The amount of long-fiber (American-Egyptian) was too small to affect overall figures though, if available, might possibly change the position of one or two of those states producing it. The order of cotton production for states, from highest to lowest in 1966, was: Texas, Mississippi, California, Arkansas, Arizona, Alabama, Louisiana, Tennessee, Georgia, South Carolina, Oklahoma, New Mexico, Missouri, and North Carolina. The first six of these states have been in the top six positions since 1957 and in the same order except that California and Mississippi interchanged positions for a year or two during this time. This relatively unchanging pattern is probably largely a reflection of government acreage allotments and subsidy programs. The same eight states were also in the next group of eight places in both these report years but their positions varied; this is sometimes a reflection of changing to other crops, to greater industrialization, or to other sources of income.

With successful power machinery available it became profitable to produce cotton on irrigated land. Consequently, the high plains of the Southwest (Texas, western Oklahoma, and parts of New Mexico and Arizona) and the flat valleys of Arizona, New Mexico, and California have replaced part of the traditional cotton area in importance in cotton production. The shift from the Southeast to the Southwest is very considerable and is well known; another shift within the "Old South" has been little noted though it may be as important. This shift is from the small family farms, many of 15 acres or less, in the hilly country and over all sorts of topography, to the large farms of thousands of acres in the flatlands of the Mississippi Delta where mechanical equipment, chemicals, and other

modern innovations can be used both satisfactorily and profitably. The change in cotton production has forced some of the southeastern states to turn to other crops and to industry. Several states have been notably successful in attracting much industry of varied types and are thus on a more diverse and less rural base than just cotton farming.

These factors together have led to the concentration of four-fifths of United States cotton production on only about 25 percent of the cotton farms. This trend toward disappearance of the family farm is continuing in cotton production as well as in nearly all other types of farming. As other countries develop and industrialize this probably will happen to them too.

The name *cotton* is derived from the Arabic word *qutn* (or Katan). Cotton plants are found growing in almost all subtropical areas of the world, although relatively few varieties have attained commercial importance.

Cotton is the seed hair of the shrub that bears the botanical name *Gossypium*, a member of the Mallow family. According to the *American Cotton Handbook, Volume I* (3rd edition) there are four species of Gossypium varying in fiber characteristics and commercial importance; each species had a different domestication if not origin.

Gossypium hirsutum, believed to have been domesticated in Mexico, Central America, and the West Indies, embraces the more than six hundred varieties known primarily as "Upland" cotton of which only a few United States varieties predominate. These are the variously numbered and described Lankart, Deltapine, and Stoneville cottons. The Upland cottons comprise approximately 87 percent of the world's cotton and 99 percent of the cotton produced in the United States. These are medium staple cottons varying in average fiber length from ⅞ to 1¼ inches. These are the cottons produced on the small farms of the Southeast and on the large mechanized farms of the Mississippi Delta, natural rainfall areas, in which good quality cotton with length of 1 to 1¹⁄₁₆ inch is common. Shorter varieties (⅞ to about an inch) of Upland cottons are produced in the deep-well-irrigated areas of the high plains of the Southwest. Much of the latter cotton is not of an evenness or quality acceptable to fabric mills.

Gossypium barbadense, originally the cotton of the Inca Indians of Peru and later transplanted to and known as the Sea Island cottons of the Caribbean Islands and the coastal areas of the United States, was progenitor of the modern Egyptian, American-Egyptian, Peruvian, and most of the Pima cottons. Pima S-2 (officially Acala 4-42), which is the only cotton permitted by state law to be grown in the San Joaquin Valley of California, is a barbadense that includes in its germ plasm several barbadense varieties.

It has medium length staple but is stronger than the hirsutum cottons. The barbadense cottons account for about 8 percent of the world's total and one percent of United States cotton production. The barbadense are the long-fiber cottons (average length 1¼ to 2½ inches) in great demand because of fineness, length, and strength for threads and high quality fabrics.

Gossypium arboreum, believed native to India, and *Gossypium herbaceum*, whose origin has not been established but seems to be in Arab lands, together account for about 5 percent of world production but are almost entirely used in the countries where produced, now India and Pakistan. These cottons are characterized by coarse, short fiber lengths (½ inch to somewhat less than an inch) and low yields. They are known as short staple cotton.

Cottons are subject to a number of diseases at various stages of development and to insect pests of which the boll weevil and its effects on the Sea Island cottons is best known. With selective breeding, chemical sprays, treatments of various kinds, and the use of fertilizers, pests and diseases are now under better control, and yields per acre have increased greatly from a generation ago. Average yield for Upland cotton for 1968–1969 has been estimated at 515 pounds per acre. Costs have also risen, so the question of balance between added costs and added receipts must be carefully weighed when various treatments are considered. Long-fiber cottons yield fewer pounds per acre but bring higher prices than other cottons.

Cotton is classified according to fiber length, fineness, luster, and geographical location where it is produced. According to R. Whitaker (*Cotton and Other Fiber Problems and Policies in the United States*) a number of changes in quality of United States cotton—some good, some not—can be noted since the early 1930's. These are: staple longer but more variable in length, reduction in amount of trash even with mechanical harvesting, less desirable color, increase in strength, and improvement in fineness.

Cotton is an annual plant in temperate climates, but is sometimes a treelike perennial in tropical climates. In general, the shrub grows from 4 to 6 feet tall over a growing period of 6 to 7 months. It thrives best in sandy soil, in a warm or hot, humid climate, or in irrigated areas of suitably warm temperature. The yield, quality, and value of the fiber largely depend on a suitable growing season and on fair, calm weather during the picking season. Rain and dirt on the opened bolls is likely to cause damage and discoloration, and strong winds may blow some of the fiber from the bolls. Figure 4-2 shows the stages of cotton boll development.

From 80 to 110 days after planting, the plant produces beautiful, creamy white blossoms which change to pink or red, fall off after a day or

FIGURE 4-2. Stages of cotton boll development: A, square or flower bud; B, new bloom; C, two-day-old bloom; D, full-grown unopened boll. (Courtesy National Cotton Council.)

two, and are replaced by the small, green, three-, four-, or five-celled triangular pods called *bolls*. During the next 55 to 80 days the bolls mature, that is, the seeds and fibers develop within the boll, which increases in size to about that of a walnut. The seed hair, which begins to grow on

the day the blossom appears, reaches a maximum length of about 2½ inches in long-fiber varieties and is known as *lint*. About ten days after these fibers begin to grow, a second, shorter, darker growth appears that adheres tightly to the seed, especially in Upland cottons. This second growth is called *linters* or *fuzz*; it may have considerable color. Gray, yellow, green, and brownish fuzz are quite common. The uses for the two types of fibers vary considerably. All these growth processes go on simultaneously, that is, flowers appear throughout the period of growth, and development of individual bolls proceeds accordingly, so that a plant may have flowers and ripe bolls at the same time amid other bolls at various stages of maturity. The mature boll bursts open from the fiber pressure, exposing the fluffy mass of white cotton fibers, each section or "lock" of which contains seven to nine seeds imbedded in the fibers, and with fibers in the different adjacent cells intertwined to a considerable degree. According to Mary L. Rollins (*American Cotton Handbook, Volume I*, p. 50):

FIGURE 4-3. Fully ripened cotton boll. (Courtesy National Cotton Council.)

It has been estimated that a single cotton seed has no less than 10,000 to 20,000 lint fibers so that a 5-lock boll could well have half a million fibers within it, not counting the fuzz fibers. No two of these fibers are exactly alike in length, shape, or wall thickness.

The fiber with its seeds is known as *seed cotton*. About one-third of the weight of seed cotton is fiber, and the other two-thirds is the weight of the seeds, which also have commercial value. Figure 4–3 shows a fully ripened cotton boll.

To insure that the quality be at its best, the cotton should be picked very soon after the boll opens. When picked by hand, the picker can discriminate and pick only what is ripe and has not been badly discolored or otherwise damaged. A mechanical picker, however, cannot discriminate, so its vacuum mechanism picks up anything that will come loose, including leaves and trash, some immature cotton, damaged and discolored cotton as well as good cotton, thus lowering the grade, and hence the price, of the cotton. Spraying from airplanes to defoliate the cotton plants just before picking time has helped to eliminate some of this difficulty. Newer machines are more able to discriminate between ripe and unripe, and cotton and trash.

Processing

Before processing can start, the cotton must first be picked from the plants. Picking has been a hand labor operation the world over and has only recently become a mechanical operation in the United States to any extent. Hand picking is still common in areas of small farms, on terrain unsuited to mechanical harvesting, and sometimes for early-ripening cotton in fields to be mechanically picked later. The worker picks into a long sack which is dragged behind him; picking is hard work and requires skill to remove the cotton from the sharp, dried bolls. There are two general types of mechanical pickers, spindle pickers (Figure 4-4), which remove the cotton from the open bolls by catching the plant between revolving spindles, and strippers (Figure 4-5), which take boll, leaf, and branch too. Stripper cotton requires cleaning and sometimes drying before ginning. Mechanical pickers are used much more extensively than strippers, though the latter are favored in the Southwest where plant growth is low to the ground and yield is rather light. About 8 percent of United States cotton was mechanically picked in 1950 as compared to 70–80 percent today. Hand picking is cheaper on small farms, in hilly areas, and where most of the cotton has not matured sufficiently to be picked at the same time.

Processing, too, has been modernized and mechanized so that many processes are much more complicated than in the past. In some types of

FIGURE 4-4. Machine picking of cotton: spindle type picker. (Courtesy National Cotton Council.)

machinery two or three steps have now been combined into a continuous operation. Continuous processing throughout all the steps still is not practiced and may never be practicable. More cleaning is necessary with mechanical picking than hand picking but, in general, though the machines are more sophisticated, the processes have the same purposes as in years past. Excellent illustrations of various types of modern machinery may be seen in the two volumes of the *American Cotton Handbook* (3rd edition). These books also give considerable descriptive detail on processing. There are also a number of good illustrations in some of the other books listed at the end of this chapter.

The steps between picking and weaving or other means of constructing fabric include: ginning, baling, classification (commonly known as grading), marketing, opening and picking, carding, combing, drawing and roving, spinning, and winding and twisting. One or more steps may be omitted, depending on the type of fabric and the end-use for which it is

intended. Beginning with opening and picking, these processes may be required for any staple length fiber, regardless of source. These processes are discussed in Chapter 9 on yarns. We shall discuss those listed before opening and picking here. Please refer to Chapter 9 for the other processes.

GINNING

Ginning is the process by which the lint is removed from the cotton seeds. Roller gins are used for long-fiber cottons and saw gins for inter-

FIGURE 4-5. A cotton stripper; it really strips the plants clean. (Courtesy International Harvester Company.)

mediate and short-fiber cottons. Roller ginning is both slower and more expensive than saw ginning. Eli Whitney, with whose name you have long been familiar, is famed for the invention of the cotton gin, an invention of great importance in the development of the cotton industry. A special ginning process, carried on at seed-crushing mills, removes the linters.

Many modern gins have a drier and cleaner unit that operates ahead of the ginning process itself. Gins may have additional feeders, cleaners, stick and green leaf removers, hull removers, and lint driers set up in such a way that all can be used or some bypassed according to the condition of a specific lot of cotton.

BALING

Baling is carried on at the gin after the lint is removed from the seeds. The lint is compressed into low density, rectangular bales weighing approximately 500 pounds each which are quite large, measuring about 54 × 27 × 45 to 48 inches. Bales are wrapped in burlap and banded with steel bands to keep the bale in shape and to enable handling. At some gins a sample of the cotton in each bale is automatically compressed in a special tube and is then attached to the bale to make unnecessary the usual sampling practices of cutting or coring into bales for grading. Cutting or coring is sometimes done several times by different people, damaging the bale, wasting fiber, making handling more difficult, and adversely affecting bale appearance.

Classification

A method of classifying cotton so that interested people everywhere may buy by standard descriptions and not have to examine actual samples has grown up in the United States which is now used almost universally for Upland cotton. The need for such a procedure is apparent in these statements made by W. H. Fortenberry in the *American Cotton Handbook, Volume I* (p. 110) when he says:

> From 14 to 16 million bales of cotton are produced in the United States annually on about a half million farms, and much variation is found in the quality of this production. These quality variations result from differences in varieties planted, soils, rainfall, irrigation practices, fertilizer, temperature, cultural practices, insect damage, length of growing season, exposure of open cotton before harvest, and methods used in harvesting and ginning. The *grade factors* of *color, leaf,* and *ginning preparation* are affected to a great extent by the weather and length of exposure in the field after the bolls open, by plant characteristics, and by harvesting and ginning practices.

Cotton manufacturers require certain qualities in the cotton to be used for

any particular product. The manufacturer wishes to purchase cotton which will be consistent in these qualities over a relatively long period of time, in order that he may maintain the uniformity of the product being manufactured from a quality standpoint under optimum spinning conditions. Therefore, it is highly important for the manufacturer to be able to specify what quality factors are desired so that cotton merchants may locate and deliver the specified raw cotton.

The three elements of classification are: *grade, staple,* and *character;* each has a varying number of subdivisions. The federal government, through the Department of Agriculture, has established official standards for a number of factors in relation to classification and maintains supplies of standard cottons that can be obtained for use in classifying.

GRADE

The *grade* of cotton is based on three factors, all related to appearance: *color, leaf,* and *preparation.* Color of raw cotton varies in hue, intensity, and value with differences in varieties planted, various factors in the growing season, age, and what happens to it in processing and in storage—to name a few things. Grade standards for color are listed as White, Light Spotted, Spotted, Tinged, and Yellow Stained as variations of white. There are additional categories outside the white to yellow range to take into consideration the effect of leaf and other hues. These are: Plus, Light Gray, and Gray. In general, the more nearly white the sample, the higher the grade insofar as color is concerned.

Leaf refers to bits of leaf, stem, hulls, seeds, grass, oil, sand, and other foreign materials that have persisted through or been picked up during processing. The less the leaf, the higher the grade insofar as this factor is concerned because it affects the degree of readiness for spinning.

Preparation refers to the degree of smoothness or roughness due to anything that causes uneven appearance or texture, such as neps (small tangled knots of fibers), naps (matted clumps of fibers), damaged fibers, or other types of nonuniformity.

Grade designation is determined by considering the rating on all three factors. In order to facilitate grading, the U.S. Department of Agriculture since 1909 has established standard grades for Upland cotton, known as *Universal Standards for the Grade of American Upland Cotton,* which are used the world over for grading American cotton. Since 1914 the standards have been published, revised, and expanded as necessary. Forty grades were defined in 1962, the most recent revision. Each year, boxes containing 12 samples of cotton representing 15 of these grades are prepared for reference from cottons of different varieties, grown in different regions, differing in color, and containing different amounts of leaf and qualities of prepara-

tion. There are official descriptions for the other 25 grades but no sets of samples for them.

The person who decides on the grade for a bale of cotton (each is graded separately) must try to arrive at an average of the three factors. For some types of variation a lower grade is given and for others a higher. When a lower grade is given than it seems a sample might have been assigned, the reason for the lower grade must be stated on the grade notation so that buyers may know the reason for the reduction. Irregular and special cottons are graded also but are handled separately; these include fire-damaged or other-damaged cottons, water-packed, reginned, mixed packs, and other nonusual types.

The United States has also established nine standard grades for American-Egyptian cotton which, because of its very different properties, cannot be graded by Upland cotton standards. The U.S. Department of Agriculture has prepared reference boxes of cottons that meet these standards too. A tenth grade is anything that, for any reason, falls below the nine defined grades.

STAPLE

Staple refers to measured length of cotton fibers and the degree of uniformity of length within a sample. The USDA has set official standards for length of Upland cotton, based on a linear inch and covering a range (by fractions of inches) from 13/16 to 1½ inches, and has prepared reference samples of cotton of the various defined lengths. Fibers within a sample vary greatly in length but the bulk of them must be fairly close to the stated staple length. Arriving at a figure for staple length has usually been a hand process that required much skill acquired over years of practice. There are now instruments available for this process that are coming into considerable usage. Uniformity in length is important in making high quality goods and in processing on high speed machines.

CHARACTER

Character refers to fineness, luster, strength, body, spirality, frictional behavior, and any other property not covered by grade or staple which will affect yarns or fabrics made from the cottons.

Market, support, and loan prices are based on a classification known as 1-inch Middling. Thus any bale or lot of cotton classified above this standard would be considered a better quality and would command a higher price than the Middling standard cotton, and lower qualities would sell at a lower price than the Middling standard. Distance from Greenville, South Carolina, that is, cost of shipping to that point, is a factor in price that is actually set in 16 different regions of the United States.

With increasing use of instruments for classifying the quality of cottons it has become necessary to have certain standard qualities of cotton available for calibrating the instruments of different laboratories both within and outside the United States. To meet this need, through cooperation among a number of interested organizations, ten "International Calibration Cotton Standards" were established in 1957. The program is carried on through the USDA where samples for use in calibration are prepared and distributed. Many laboratories in many countries now use some or all of these standards for calibrating their instruments. The USDA has also made available standard cotton samples for other test methods not yet included in the international series.

MARKETING

Marketing includes all transactions from the time the cotton leaves the producer until it is accepted at the mill. Some cotton is sold directly from producer to mill, but most of it goes through a more devious series of selling operations. Most cotton is actually handled, often in lots of 100 bales of the same grade and description, in the large cotton markets of the world, at last report the largest being New York, Liverpool, New Orleans, Memphis, and Houston.

Many of the series of marketing steps are carried on in the *spot* markets or in the *cotton exchanges*. The spot markets are the small markets throughout the cotton-producing areas and the cotton mill areas of the country where the cotton farmers sell their cotton to small merchants, to representatives of large merchants, or to cooperatives. Actual exchange of bales of cotton may take place at the spot market, or delivery may be made at any specified time and place. The Cotton Exchange, an organization somewhat like the Stock Exchange, deals only in "futures" marketing, with no actual cotton bales and sometimes no samples of cotton present, but with futures sales made on the basis of description and grade. This is possible primarily because of standardization of description and grading. Futures selling permits sales of contracts against a supply for future delivery, a practice that enables mills to buy their cotton at a somewhat more stable price throughout the year than by spot sales. Cotton exchanges of the United States were formerly located in New York, New Orleans, and Chicago; with the closing of the New Orleans Exchange in July 1964, only the New York Exchange remains in operation. The government-controlled policies and prices of today's United States market for cotton has almost eliminated the need for the exchanges.

All the processes, so briefly described in this section, may be explored in much greater detail in some of the references given at the end of this chapter.

Fiber Properties

Properties of fibers may be categorized (arbitrarily) as microscopic, chemical, physical, and biologic. Each of the various kinds of properties is affected by all the others so that it is not really possible to study one group of properties entirely separate from the influence of all the rest. For example, mildew is a biologic organism which attacks cotton and grows on it, destroying the cotton fibers and changing the physical, chemical, and microscopic properties. It is customary to look at the fiber characteristics in relation to one or more of the categories listed, and because this method offers a convenient way to study the individual fibers, we shall use it.

Microscopic properties are size, shape, distinctive markings, and general appearance of the individual fibers as viewed under magnification. Compound, polarizing, and electron microscopes, used with different light sources, are all valuable tools for studying details of fiber structure. We shall be concerned primarily with structure that is visible by means of a compound microscope.

Chemical properties are reactions of fibers to contact with acids, alkalies, bleaches, dyes, stains, and other such chemical substances, including water. Since all substances are chemical, it would be impossible to make a complete chemical reaction analysis.

Physical properties are often more apparent than other properties. These include color, length, diameter, weight, specific gravity, nature of the surface, spinnability, elasticity, resilience, flammability, and many other such characteristics for which there are usually methods of measurement.

Biologic properties are the ways in which fibers react to insects, molds, bacteria, and fungi—their attractiveness or unattractiveness to such organisms.

MICROSOPIC APPEARANCE OF COTTON

When viewed with an ordinary compound microscope cotton fibers are seen to have a twisted ribbonlike appearance—that is, the fiber looks as if it is a flat ribbon that has been held at each end and one end rotated until a series of 180-degree turns are spaced all along its length. The twists, known technically as convolutions, are due to changes that occur in the fiber as it matures. As it grows, each fiber, which is generally considered to be a single, long cell, develops both a primary and a secondary wall and a central canal, or lumen. The lumen carries liquid to the living cell. When the ripened boll opens, the liquid dries rapidly, causing the lumen to collapse. As it dries, the fiber assumes the characteristic twisted or spiral form, caused in part by the collapse of the lumen. The cell walls appear as thickened edges of the ribbonlike strand. Longitudinal sections of fiber

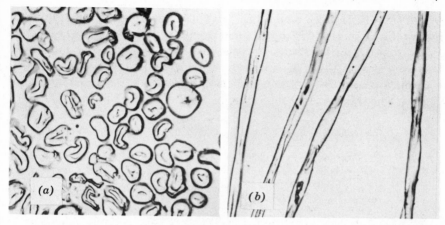

FIGURE 4-6. Photomicrographs of cotton: (*a*) cross sections; (*b*) longitudinal. (Courtesy E. I. duPont de Nemours & Co. Inc.)

readily show the characteristic twists and thickened walls by which cotton may be easily and reliably identified, for no other fiber has these characteristics. The number of twists per inch length vary from 150 to 300 for different varieties and types of raw cotton. Long-fiber cottons have more twists per unit length than other cottons, and mercerized cottons of all types often show fewer twists than the similar unmercerized fiber. Figure 4-6 is a photomicrograph of a cross section and a longitudinal view of cotton fibers.

Cross sections of cotton fibers show the wall and flattened lumen; the fibers are usually more or less bean-shaped but may vary considerably in outline. Mercerized cotton fibers may be almost round. A group of cotton cross sections looks much like a handful of uncooked, rolled oats cereal which has been spilled on a flat surface.

Immature cotton fibers often do not show the usual cotton characteristics, either longitudinally or in cross section. Sometimes neither twist nor lumen is visible in these fibers. Immature fibers may have thin walls, and the cross sections may be U-shaped.

The cotton fibers which seem rather like smooth, fine hairs to the unaided eye, and are shown to have convolutions all along their lengths when seen with the microscope, show still more complex detail when viewed under the high magnification of an electron microscope (Figure 4-7). Some of the detailed fibril structure of fibers discussed in Chapter 3, p. 34 is visible in cotton fibers. Although Figure 4-7*a* is a schematic diagram of the layers of a cotton fiber, the area designated as "secondary lamellae" shows the reversals in direction which actually occur in the fibrils of a

cotton fiber. It has been established that the convolutions of a mature fiber follow this reversal pattern of the secondary wall underneath exactly. When some of the convolutions of the fiber are removed in the mercerization process it is thought there may be some straightening of the fibril reversals underneath. Cotton is the only known fiber to have this pattern of fibril reversals and convolutions. The cross section of Figure 4-7b is an

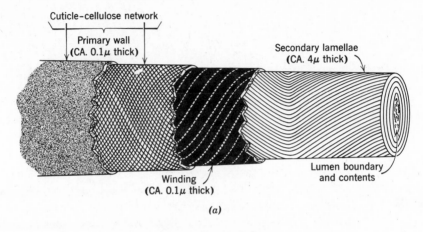

Cuticle–cellulose network

Primary wall
(CA. 0.1μ thick)

Secondary lamellae
(CA. 4μ thick)

Winding
(CA. 0.1μ thick)

Lumen boundary
and contents

(a)

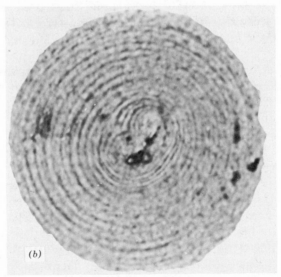

(b)

FIGURE 4-7. A cotton fiber: (a) schematic diagram showing the component layers of the fiber cell wall; (b) photomicrograph of cross section swollen in cuprammonium hydroxide to show growth layers. (USDA photographs by Southern Regional Research Laboratory.)

actual electron photomicrograph showing the day-by-day growth rings of an individual cotton fiber. The cotton fiber has been swollen by means of a cuprammonium hydroxide solution to make the rings visible.

CHEMICAL PROPERTIES

The chemical composition of typical cotton is 94.0 percent cellulose, 1.3 percent protein, 0.9 percent pectic substances, 1.2 percent ash, 0.6 percent wax (in the primary wall), and 1.9 percent other things, including sugars. The cellulose content of raw cotton varies from 88 to 96 percent, depending on the variety of cotton, soil, and growing conditions. Cotton that has been scoured and bleached to remove as much of the other materials as possible is about 99 percent cellulose.

Cotton fibers, in common with other cellulosic materials, are quite absorbent. This accounts in part for their comfortableness, especially in hot climates. In the process of absorbing, the fibers tend to swell considerably in cross-sectional area, although their length is apparently little affected. This fact is utilized in some of the finishing processes applied to cotton and to other cellulosic fibers.

Cotton is decomposed by strong acids, hot or cold, and is deteriorated by weak, hot acids. Acids are used, however, in obtaining certain finishes, described in *Matthews' Textile Fibers* (p. 231) as follows:

> Strong sulfuric acid is used as the basis of several special cotton finishes. A momentary treatment is sometimes used to increase the transparency of cotton, and various strengths of acid have been suggested. It is always a matter of treatment for seconds and at low temperatures. Methods employing strong sulfuric acid have been operated especially under patents owned by the Heberlein interests (Swiss), sometimes combined with treatment with strong caustic soda. Details of the processes actually used have not been made public. The finishes vary greatly and have been characterized by such terms as "transparent," "linen-like," and "wool-like." A specific example is the permanent organdie finish which upon washing and ironing recovers its stiffness without starch.

It is difficult to control acid treatment sufficiently to avoid degradation of the cotton fibers.

Weak alkalies have little or no effect on cotton, but strong alkalies are used to obtain special effects and for improvement of some fiber and fabric properties. Mercerization is a widely used process for obtaining luster. Can you recognize a mercerized finish?

In 1844, when filtering caustic soda solution (sodium hydroxide) through cotton cloth, John Mercer (of England) noted that the cloth swelled then shrank. About 1890 it was discovered that if cloth wet with

sodium hydroxide were dried under tension, the cloth did not shrink but became stronger and developed a high luster. The latter process is the one known today as *mercerization,* and it is widely used for many cotton fabrics and for thread. Treatment without tension, to allow swelling and shrinkage, has long been used to obtain the special effects of some plissé and seersucker fabrics; this is called "slack" mercerization today and is the basis for producing one type of stretch cotton fabrics and has been recommended for three-dimensional effect cotton lace. Slack mercerization is discussed further in Chapter 15.

Mercerization is accomplished by treatment with an 18 to 23 percent concentration of caustic soda for ½ to 2 minutes, at room temperature or a little higher, with the cloth held under tension to prevent shrinkage. Then the cloth is washed, neutralized to remove any remaining alkali, and washed and dried under sufficient tension to maintain the desired yardage. The increase in luster is due to the increased reflection by the fibers, which have become more cylindrical and have lost some of their twist during the treatment.

Mercerized cotton not only has increased luster over unmercerized cotton but also is stronger, has increased affinity for dyes so that less dye is needed (or darker or brighter shades may be obtained with the same amount), dyes more evenly, has greater affinity for resins and other finishing compounds, and may be somewhat more sheer in appearance. It is sometimes said to soil less easily than unmercerized cotton.

Overbleaching in finishing or in laundering causes degradation of cotton. Bleaching is discussed in Chapter 11.

PHYSICAL PROPERTIES

Cotton fibers are most often creamy white in color, although the color varies with variety, chemistry of the soil in which grown, climatic conditions, and the weather from the time the boll opens until the cotton is picked. Rain on the opened bolls, dust and dirt blown in, and other stains from insects, wet foliage, and such things may cause spottiness of color and make the fiber darken to bluish or grayish tones. Egyptian cotton has a reddish-brown cast and is darker in color than Sea Island and Upland cottons. Cotton grown in the Cajun area of Louisiana has a lovely deep reddish-tan color. Experiments in which different chemicals were added to the soil resulted in green, orange, pink, gray, and other color lint in cotton, but colored lint has not been practical to produce in quantity. You can perhaps think of several reasons for this.

Usable cotton fibers of the different varieties vary in length from 0.5 to 2.5 inches and in diameter from 6 to 26 microns, with specific gravity of

1.50 to 1.55 and breaking tenacity of 2.0 to 5.0 grams per denier,* roughly defined as an indicator of toughness. The higher tenacity is characteristic of the long-fiber varieties. Cotton is thus one of the shorter fibers, intermediate in width, and its specific gravity is higher than that of most other fibers. Because of its short length, the twists and "cling" are very important in making cotton fibers into yarns. Cotton has medium strength compared to other fibers, but when wet its strength increases, sometimes as much as 30 percent. The increase in strength when wet is very important in durable work clothing and other clothing for use in tropical or very humid climates, where moisture and perspiration are likely to be factors that must be considered. Cottons that have special resin finishes usually lose the property of being stronger when wet and may even be weaker wet than dry. Special finishes are considered in Chapters 11 and 13.

Cotton has medium abrasion resistance and high flex resistance. Cotton's low resilience and low elasticity mean that cotton fabrics will wrinkle and that the wrinkles will not "hang out" but will require pressing for their removal. Elongation of cotton—stretch continued to the breaking point—varies from 3 to 10 percent with 7 percent considered average, which is low compared to that of many other fibers. Cotton may be stored for long periods of time with no apparent loss of strength, although it may yellow somewhat. Prolonged exposure to ultraviolet rays and sunlight causes great loss of strength and may also cause white cotton to become yellow.

Cotton will scorch if ironed with too hot an iron, causing damage and loss of strength. But the ironing temperature of cotton is relatively high before damage occurs. Note the "cotton" setting on an iron. Cotton is readily refreshed by washing and ironing and, in the resin-finished or modified cottons, may require no ironing. One of cotton's values is its resistance to degradation in a high number of severe launderings. It is often considered to be the least expensive fiber in terms of upkeep. Because cotton, without damaging the fiber, can be sterilized in boiling water or in a steam autoclave, it is usually considered to be the most antiseptic of all fibers. It is widely used in hospitals for operating room materials and uniforms, partially for this reason as well as for the fact that untreated cotton presents no problems with dangerous accumulations of static electricity. Why is this so important?

Immature cotton fibers tend to be weaker and less opaque than mature

---

*Denier, in this usage, refers to unit of linear density. Data on breaking tenacity have been gathered from several sources and in a few instances conditions of testing were not specifically stated; for all such data in the following pages, except linen, the conditions were stated or implied to be 21°C temperature and 65 percent relative humidity.

fibers, to form tangled fiber bunches (called "neps") in spinning, to dye unevenly, and to have poor affinity for mercerization and other chemical treatments.

BIOLOGIC PROPERTIES

Mildew, bacteria, and yeasts will grow on cotton under conditions of high humidity and temperature. Starched or soiled cottons are more likely to be attacked than clean, unstarched cottons. Such attack causes discoloration and weakening or destruction of the fabric, and may be accompanied (always with mildew) by characteristic disagreeable odors. Can you recognize such attack? The organisms may be on the cotton in the field but lie dormant until conditions for growth become right in the mills or in the home, or they may make their initial contact in the mill or in the home. Mills lose thousands of dollars each year because of mildew.

Silverfish and termites will also attack cotton, and instances have been reported of crickets eating starched cottons.

Cotton fabrics may be chemically treated to protect them from attack by microorganisms, but the treatment may change the fabric appearance or texture so much that its uses are limited. These treatments are important for outdoor fabrics such as tents, awnings, lawn furniture, and camp furnishings where appearance is, perhaps, not as important as at home or for clothing.

Uses and By-products

The range of uses for cotton covers thousands of items in many areas. It has been said that there is practically no textile need anywhere for which cotton has not served, is not serving, or could not serve. It can vary from sheerest, softest or crispest, and loveliest batiste, organdy, lace, and other fabrics for babies' most delicate garments or for evening wear of unsurpassed beauty to heavy, coarse, strong fabrics for the toughest of work garments, shoes, sails, belts, and canvas. Did you know that the glamorous wardrobe of the "Maid of Cotton" is all cotton? And that cotton in the Arctic keeps out the wind and maintains warmth? And that in the tropics it protects the wearer from insects and from excessive radiation exposure from the sun as well as keeping him cool? It is used for all members of the family and for all types of home furnishing materials. Cotton is used for dress, for sports, for sleep, to keep the wearer warm or cool or dry or even moist, in some instances. It is truly a versatile fiber. Its uses have been extended still further by some of the new finishes now being applied.

Although we are more familiar with the uses of cotton in apparel and textile furnishings, there is a considerable amount used for other consumer and for industrial uses, as can be noted by study of Tables 7, 8, 9, 10, and

11 in Chapter 2. You may find it worthwhile to read the comments concerning the individual tables in Chapter 2, and you will find it useful to refer to these tables as we consider further the uses of cotton.

From Tables 7 and 8 it is apparent that almost twice as much cotton is used for the male part of the population for apparel as for the female, even though infants are included with the latter. This probably reflects not only their differing occupations but also the way in which the different segments of the apparel industry (or is it their patrons?) have or have not accepted the man-made fibers. Although the conservative, traditional nature of men's and boys' apparel seems to be changing now, there is a question as to how far it will go. If you examine advertisements, you will probably notice that though styles change, they still tend to be carried out in the traditional fibers.

It would be interesting to speculate as to why such a high percentage of fabrics sold over the retail counter (Table 10) is cotton. What do you guess? In recent years, some textile furnishings items (Table 9) for which cotton has long been considered the most suitable fiber, sheets and pillowcases for example, are now being made of other fibers such as polyester/cotton or rayon/cotton blends. It is perhaps surprising to see that towels are not all made entirely of cotton. On the other hand, the thermal blanket has restored a share of the blanket market to cotton which had been taken over by other fibers. Some of these trends are too new to be seen clearly from the tables.

The high percentage of cotton used for transportation upholstery (Table 11) is surprising. Such fabrics are usually blends of fibers with cotton being the very important basic fiber in the blend, in part because of price, and in part because of its desirable properties. Study of specific items in the various tables will probably suggest to you many ideas, including why some of the industries cluster together and why they are in specific geographical areas.

The by-products of the cotton industry are largely from the seed, although the linters may also be considered by-products. The linters are used chemically in the making of writing paper, rayons, acetates, plastics, explosives, sausage casings, and such products, and nonchemically as filler in mattresses, mattress pads, upholstered furniture, and automobile cushions.

The seeds themselves are a valuable crop with many uses. After the linters are removed, the seeds are crushed under great pressure to obtain a high yield of oil. Uses for the oil include cooking and salad oils, hydrogenated fats, and oleomargarines. Are you familiar with any of these products? If not, you may be interested in looking for them the next time you visit a supermarket. With the high incidence of heart disease and

arteriosclerosis among adult Americans today and the medical evidence associating these diseases with high cholesterol levels in the blood, the unsaturated fats such as cottonseed oil are being given wide use in diets and in many food products. Examination of the description on the containers for such products may reveal them to you. Other uses for the oil are soaps and synthetic detergents, paints, explosives, varnish, cosmetics, oilcloth, linoleum, phonograph records, and many other products. The cake which remains after the oil is removed is ground and used for a rich feed for cattle, particularly for dairy herds. Waste from the seeds is used as fertilizer. The value of the seeds is sometimes almost as great as the value of the fiber itself.

With the introduction of the nylons, polyesters, triacetate, and acrylics and their wide acceptance by consumers, cotton's position in the markets of the developed countries, especially in the United States, has been seriously threatened for the first time, despite the higher prices per pound of the man-made fibers. To meet this threat a great many research programs have been initiated and many types of studies have been or are being made of ways to improve the properties of cotton or to modify the chemical structure of cellulose so that cottons will have many of the properties of the man-made fibers and be competitive with or, as cotton producers fondly dream, supersede them. But such programs are small and poorly financed as compared to the research programs carried on by the man-made fiber producers.

There are several reasons for this: in contrast to the man-made fibers that are produced by a relatively few large companies, cotton is still produced by thousands of producers who have not tended to cooperate in research or promotion except as the USDA programs have provided these services. Nor do they cooperate with man-made fiber producers who are using great quantities of cotton in mixed-fiber fabrics for durable press, wash-wear, and such developments. Cotton men tend to attribute their ever-decreasing percentage of the fiber market to promotion of man-made fibers by their producers, and tend to shut their eyes to the special properties of man-made fibers and fabrics that make them desirable to consumers. A payment of one dollar per bale of cotton from all producers willing to make this contribution is now going into a fund for research and promotion for cotton, but the larger part of this fund has thus far been designated for promotion. Although cotton has an advantage price-wise except in comparison with the rayons, cotton and man-made fibers do not displace each other pound for pound. Most of the man-made fibers have a lower specific gravity (thus are lighter in weight per given area) and higher strength and elongation for a fiber of the same size; therefore, they have a "cover" advantage in that the same weight of fiber produces more

yardage of similar fabrics. Perhaps a part of the problem results from the fact that cotton has for such a long time been such a widely accepted and widely used fiber that no one considered what might be possible in improving its properties in ways that consumers might demand if they knew what was possible. We tend to cry out for things we have never had only when it seems that attaining them has become a possibility.

What of the future of cotton? No one can foresee with certainty what the future holds but it seems safe to assume that cotton will always have an important place among the fibers of the world although it has now lost its supremacy as the most-used fiber. Cotton, however, must increasingly give way to food and feed crops, especially on highly productive land, if world populations continue to grow as predicted.

Cottons, as all of you are aware, have undergone many improvements in recent years and the cottons of the future are certain to have properties not yet achieved. Functional finishes of a number of types are applicable to cotton, perhaps even more than to other fibers. Some examples of these are wash-wear, durable press, soil release, flame retardance, water repellence, and shrinkage control. In addition to finishes, efforts are being made to modify the fibers themselves by chemical changes such as efforts to alter the homopolymer structure by grafting other compounds into the chains, or substituting other elements for those in certain positions in some of the basic cellulose units. Whether the resulting fiber is still cotton is open to question. It is interesting to speculate as to what might lie ahead.

LINEN

History

Linen, obtained from the flax plant, is known to be one of the most ancient of textile fibers in point of use. W. F. Leggett, after very intensive research into the history of linen, has written in *The Story of Linen* (p. x, Introduction):

It is truly impossible to learn which of the many natural fibers were first used for textile purposes, or even to be sure how that particular fiber came to be used, but of the four chief textile fibers, wool, cotton, silk and flax, the last is unquestionably the most ancient. Some anthropologists even declare that it is possible that linen had its origin not long after the advent of man.

It is known that linen cloth was produced in Egypt long enough ago to be a well-developed art by 3400 B.C. This fact is attested to by the linen cloth in a number of varieties and textures found in the tombs of the dynasties which ended about that time. Although handmade, some of the

cloth was very fine and sheer—some of it was even called "woven air"—
having more than 500 threads per inch, a weaving feat which is not
duplicated even by modern machines. A robe of this fabric, it is said,
could be drawn through a small finger ring. On the other hand, coarse
linen cloth comparable to the canvas of today was also produced. The rank
of the wearer is believed to have been designated by the type of linen
burial cloth, the nobles and priests being wrapped in as many as a thousand
yards of fine, smooth linen, and slaves being wrapped in a few yards of
coarse canvaslike linen. All, however, were wrapped in linen for burial,
for this fiber alone was believed to be "pure" and thus had religious
significance.

From ancient Egypt, with the rise of sea travel and trade, the use of
linen spread all around the Mediterranean, thence on to other inland
territories, and with the Roman conquest of England, to that country;
at least fairly sophisticated manufacture of linen began in England at
that time. Linen is frequently mentioned in the Bible as clothing and as
partitioning and furnishing the temple of the Exodus in various ways.

In time, France, Belgium, and Holland became famous for the quality
of the linen they produced. Ireland became the most important producer
of beautiful linen fabric, a position that it still commands today. The
Irish climate is ideal for the spinning and weaving of linen, for dampness
keeps the fiber tough rather than brittle.

In our own country, colonists early turned to the production of flax to
supply their own clothing, household, and other fabric needs not satisfactorily met by the more easily obtained wool. It was essential to their
survival that each family be almost self-sufficient. In addition, with the
increasing restrictions on manufacturing and trade that England imposed
on the colonies, it became a patriotic duty for colonists to produce their
own fabrics. Linsey-woolsey, a sturdy fabric made with linen warp and
wool filling, attained considerable prominence among colonial and pioneer-
ing groups. Linsey-woolsey was popular for outer wear for both civilian
and military uses—even up to the time of the American Civil War. *The
Story of Linen* (pp. 86, 87) says

All the American colonies were energetic in promoting the cultivation of
flax and its manufacture into linen cloth, and in a short time almost every
colonist devoted at least a small field to the raising of flax. . . .

The raising of flax and the preparation of its textile fibers was done by
men on the farm, usually in their spare time, while, as in Europe, spinning,
weaving and such limited dyeing as was at that time attempted, was the duty
of the women folks. . . .

The production of linen cloth in the United States was superseded by
cotton with the invention of the cotton gin in 1793; this resulted in cotton

cloth being both cheap and plentiful. The growth of the factory system also tended to discourage home production of fabrics. Although subsequent attempts have been made to establish a linen fabric industry in this country, they have proved largely unsuccessful to date because of the great amount of hand labor involved and its cost.

Production and Processes

It is difficult to interpret figures on fibers because there seems to be no uniform method of reporting for different fibers, or by different reporting groups. This situation seems to be especially true for linen. In some instances actual production figures are given, but in other instances only those fibers appearing in international trade, as exports and imports from the various countries, are reported. Flax figures are usually given on the basis of fibers exported.

According to figures from the FAO *Yearbook of Statistics* for 1952, in the years 1934–1938 the USSR produced 73.1 percent of the world's flax—much more than all other countries combined. Some of the other countries and their shares were Lithuania 3.6 percent, Poland 3.0 percent, Belgium 2.8 percent, Latvia and France 2.6 percent each, Germany 1.6 percent, and on down to the Irish Republic 0.1 percent. The United States produced too small an amount of flax fiber to be counted. Some of the flax-producing countries used a large share of their flax fiber at home, and some exported fiber to other countries—at times to be manufactured into fabric in those countries and exported to still other countries, as Ireland does, for example.

During World War II flax production decreased in many countries that were invaded or that were unable to obtain labor for such crops. Japan, Egypt, and Argentina increased their flax fiber production in order to supply the needs of their own and their allies' navies and merchant shipping, and for other marine uses (primarily) during the war. During this period New Zealand also developed a fairly extensive flax industry to help meet the needs of the British armed and supply services.

J. W. Hadfield, in *Linen Flax Fibre Production in New Zealand* (p. 3, Introduction), mentioned reasons for the instability of the flax fiber supply:

Flax values are very unstable. They are affected by government policies in view of the strategic importance of flax in time of war, the development of synthetic fibres, and the utilization of cheaper competitive vegetable fibres such as Italian hemp and jute.

A 1968 issue of *Textile Organon* carried a table with recent data on some of the natural fibers from which the data in Table 13 have been

taken. Flax (linen) had regained its pre-World War II position within a few years after the close of that conflict and now seems to be increasing in production a little. Of the total, in 1966 the United States imported a little more than 15 million pounds of the linen, or approximately 3.3 per-

TABLE 13. Estimated [a,b] Total World Production of Flax, Hemp, and Jute (Millions of Pounds)

Fiber	Year				
	1951–1956 [c]	1956–1961 [c]	1962–1963	1964–1965	1966–1967
Flax (linen)	1012	1402	1523	1404	1590
Hemp [d]	2278	2585	2641	2831	2675
Jute and allied fibers	4700	5663	6711	7069	8012

[a] Data from *Textile Organon* for May 1968 had been obtained from *Industrial Fibres* (17 edition), Commonwealth Secretariat.
[b] Figures based on data available from non-Communist countries and estimates of Communist countries.
[c] Average of years listed.
[d] Excluding soft hemp in China.

cent, including raw fiber, semifinished, and finished linen. New developments in production and treatment, and a growing trend toward combining linen with other fibers may lead to a greater revival of the linen industry. The supply of linen tends to reflect demand reasonably well.

The United States produces considerable flax, but almost entirely for seed because of the value of the oil. A small amount of native linen has, in the years since World War II, been supplied to fabric designers for the interior decoration of homes and other buildings. Linen, for apparel and textile furnishings purposes, is the most important of the bast fibers.

Linen's botanical name is *Linum usitatissimum*, a name indicative of its many early uses. The term *flax* is derived from Anglo-Saxon and old High German words and is usually applied to the plant in English-speaking countries, whereas the fiber is called *linen*. In a great many other countries, "linen" designates both plant and fiber. Flax may be produced for its fiber or for its seed; it is rarely produced to yield both from the same plants. In this country, however, fiber from seed flax is sometimes used in paper making and has been used to a limited extent for upholstery filler.

Flax is a slender, straight-stemmed plant with narrow, medium-green, lancelike leaves, which grows to a height of 2 to 4 feet. The longest-

stemmed varieties are planted for fiber. The plant separates near the top into a few branches which, in turn, bear the ½-inch-wide blossoms and the seed bolls. Figure 4-8 is a photograph of a flax field. The blossoms of different varieties may be colored pink, purple, white, or azure blue; the latter two are the varieties of commercial importance. Blue-flower flax is considered to have better spinning qualities than varieties with white blossoms. The flowers are open only in the morning. From a distance, a field of open blue flax blossoms often appears to be a lake.

Flax grows in a temperate climate under a wide variety of climatic conditions but does best with cool, even temperature and considerable rainfall. It requires a growing season of 85 to 100 days. The height of the plants, hence the fiber length, and the quality of the fiber vary greatly with soil and climatic conditions.

Flax does not require a rich soil. The seedbed must be carefully prepared, but, once planted, no special care is required except to keep the weeds down while the plants are young. Because flax is subject to some rather severe plant diseases, it is usually rotated from field to field rather than grown in the same fields year after year.

Flax fibers occur in bundles just inside the relatively stiff cuticle (outer) wall and surrounding the woody central part of the stem. See Figure 4-9. The fibers are bound together within the bundles by a cellular tissue, sometimes called the phloem, and by gums and waxes. These sub-

FIGURE 4-8.   A flax field. (Courtesy Crops Research Division, USDA.)

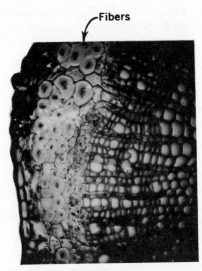

Fibers

FIGURE 4-9. Cross section of a portion of a flax stem showing the linen fibers just inside the stiff cuticle. (Courtesy Crops Research Division, USDA.)

stances are largely removed during processing, allowing the individual flax fibers to be separated.

Methods of cultivation vary from country to country, depending in some instances on the extent of the labor force available and its price. Formerly flax cultivation was almost entirely a series of hand operations, but now, as in other agricultural endeavors, it is becoming more mechanized. The trend is toward greater mechanization everywhere, including Ireland, which has long depended almost entirely on hand labor to grow and prepare linen fiber.

The stage at which flax is harvested depends on the end product desired. Flax is harvested for seed when stems and seed bolls are quite dry and are yellowish brown in color, and for fiber when the bolls are set and the stem is yellow, but still rather moist and supple. If harvested when the stalk is too green, the yield is low and the fiber may be weak.

Regardless of the methods chosen, linen production uses a few processes distinctive to bast fibers, and to linen in particular. Among these processes are pulling, retting, and scutching. Once the purified fiber has been obtained, the processes for making it into yarn and cloth are similar to those for many other fibers.

PULLING

Pulling is the removal of the whole plants, including the root systems, from the soil. Unbroken stems give maximum fiber length and also prevent

staining of the fibers within the stem during the drying and retting processes. Although flax stems are tough, to avoid breaking them in the pulling operation they must be grasped near the ground, whether they are pulled by hand or by machine. Very successful pulling machines have been invented and are in fairly general use in many flax-producing countries. The size of the fields and amount of the rainfall often determine whether machines can be used. After being pulled, the root ends of the plants are placed evenly (butted) and the plants are tied in bundles to dry, perhaps to be stored for a time. Bundles facilitate removal of the seed (rippling) before retting is begun.

RETTING

Retting is a process by which the brittle outer cuticle layer of the stem is broken down and at least partially destroyed by fermentation through bacterial action and by moisture, allowing the fiber groups within the straw to be removed. There are several methods of retting, all of them slimy, odorous, and unpleasant, making this a very disagreeable process of flax production. Although removing the cuticle by applying chemicals has been tried successfully, this process, sometimes called "chemical retting," is not much used and is said to result in fiber of harsher and poorer quality than do the various other methods of retting, that is, dew, running water, stagnant pool or bog, and tank.

Dew retting is most successfully carried on in areas that have heavy dews at night and warm temperatures during the day. The flax is spread out in rows on the grass and is turned regularly so that all stems and areas are equally exposed to moisture and sunshine, which dissolve the cellular tissue of the stem cuticle and the gummy substances holding the fibers together. Dew retting is ordinarily slower than other processes, taking at least two or three weeks. Since it is slower, it may also be less likely to result in over-retting and damage to the fiber. The fibers sometimes darken because of the long exposure period and may be of inferior quality, although some of the finest-quality linen obtainable is dew-retted.

Running- and stagnant-water retting are carried on in similar fashion except that stagnant-water retting is likely to be considerably faster because the products of bacterial action are not carried off and thus have a cumulative effect. The flax bundles are placed in crates that are weighted down with stones or other weights to keep the entire length of the stems submerged after bacterial action commences and gases form. In running-water retting, it is often necessary to construct a fence or barrier to prevent crates from being carried downstream. Flax being retted by either method must be watched closely, for getting it out of the water (thus stopping fermentation) at just the right moment is critical to the quality of the

resulting fiber and fabric. Water from pool retting has largely had the oxygen removed, and, until aerated, is unfit for human or animal use, or aquatic life. A number of countries now prohibit the retting of flax in streams and rivers.

Tank retting is the method used in Oregon and New Zealand, and it is tending to replace other methods of water retting in other countries. Tank retting is water retting carried on in specially built tanks (usually concrete) in which a constant lukewarm water temperature is maintained at all times. Color from stems and dirt is usually leached out and drained off in the first few hours, resulting in a lighter-colored, non-stained fiber. Some of the water is drained off each day and fresh water added so that fermentation can be more carefully controlled. The disagreeable aspects of retting may be cut down somewhat by this method.

Water for retting must be clean and free from minerals, especially iron, that might discolor or otherwise damage the fiber, and preferably should be soft water. Tank retting may take only a few days, but running-water retting may take as long as dew retting, depending on the temperature of the water and the swiftness of the current.

Whatever the method of water retting, according to *Matthews' Textile Fibers* (p. 291), this is what happens:

The water penetrates to the inner part of the stalk via small flaws in the cuticle or bark, causing the inner cells to swell and burst cuticle. This in turn increases moisture absorption and permits greater penetration of bacteria, which act on pectins in the substances surrounding the fiber bundles, changing them into soluble sugars.

Thorough drying is necessary after retting to prevent further fermentation. Mechanical driers are now being tried more or less successfully and, when improved, will undoubtedly be influential in determining the future of linen production. Flax is sometimes stored for a long period of time to cure before further processing after retting.

DECORTICATION

Although decortication, a process of scraping the cuticle and woody center from the fibers in green stems, has been tried as a substitute for retting, this process is used only experimentally at present because the resulting fiber is inferior to retted fiber.

SCUTCHING

Scutching is the process of removing the dried, retted fiber from the woody remainder of the plant stem. The first step is a *breaking* operation in which the butted, parallel stems are passed through a series of fluted

metal rollers; the rollers break up the woody portion of the straw into fine pieces, called "shives," which can then be beaten out (scutching), leaving the long linen fibers largely undamaged. Scutching also helps to separate the individual fibers in the bundles by breaking down the gums and other cementing substances. Machines sometimes combine breaking and scutching steps into one continuous operation. The resulting long fibers are called "line" flax. The fibers that are broken in the scutching process are recovered, rescutched, and used as various qualities of "tow." When flax production was familiar to nearly everyone, the term *towhead* was often applied to children who had hair similar in color and texture to tow flax. If you examine some scutched flax, you can easily see how the term *towhead* came to be so used. About one-tenth of the weight of the original flax stem is fiber.

There are no standard grades or descriptions for linen fiber as there are for cotton, although in the limited production in Oregon, flax fiber has been designated by five grades according to fiber length and color, general condition, and luster. A good quality spinning fiber is fine, soft, and strong and has a somewhat cold and oily feel and a glossy sheen.

Properties

When viewed through a microscope, linen can be distinguished from other commonly used textile fibers by its distinctive appearance. Longitudinally, the fibers have somewhat the jointed appearance of bamboo or various types of cane, because of transverse lines or nodes, a characteristic of most of the bast fibers (see Figure 4-10). As seen in cross section, the

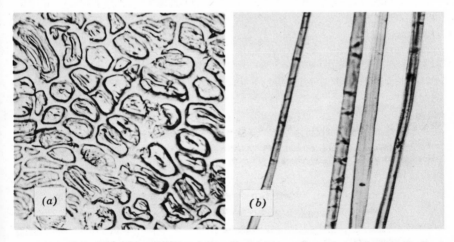

FIGURE 4-10. Photomicrographs of flax fiber: (*a*) cross sections; (*b*) longitudinal. (Courtesy E. I. duPont de Nemours & Co. Inc.)

fibers are round to polygonal, usually five-sided with rather rounded corners, with the small central lumen visible, and with considerable variation of fiber diameter apparent. The "joints" are individual cells within the fiber. Immature fibers are oval in shape with much larger lumen.

Raw flax fibers are composed of about 71.5 percent cellulose, 10.7 percent water, 9.4 percent gums, pectins, etc., 6.0 percent aqueous extract, 2.4 percent fat and wax, and 1.3 percent ash. When boiled off and bleached, linen is almost all pure cellulose.

Very few specific data are available concerning chemical reactions of linen, but since it is a cellulosic fiber, about the same reaction can be expected to alkalies and to acids as cotton exhibits. Since linen has a natural luster, it is not often mercerized.

Linen may be satisfactorily bleached, treated with chemical resins for crease resistance and other properties for which resins are commonly used, and dyed in fast colors. Linen fiber may be damaged by boiling water and by overbleaching; its waxes are thus removed, leaving it harsh, brittle, and subject to several types of damage.

Linen, diameter for diameter, is the strongest of the vegetable fibers and is sometimes claimed to be the strongest of all natural fibers, whatever their origin. Strength, as in all fibers, depends on quality of the fiber, cross-sectional area (diameter, more or less), conditions under which processed, and many other factors. Linen is stronger wet than dry.

Linen varies from a creamy white to grayish brown, the depth of color depending largely on the time and condition of retting. It may be bleached to white or near white, or to any stage between the original color and white, and is found on the market at the various stages of bleaching. Linen fibers vary from 12 to 30 inches in length and 5 to 28 microns in diameter, with great variation among fibers. It has an average specific gravity of 1.50 and breaking tenacity of 2.9 to 3.1 grams per denier. Linen has low elongation and resilience and therefore crushes and wrinkles readily unless treated for crease resistance. Ironing when quite damp is necessary to restore untreated linen to its wrinkle-free freshness. Linen possesses a natural crispness when ironed damp, thus does not require starching, and has a natural luster. It becomes softer and more lustrous with use and laundering, so that a fine, long-used piece of linen may have almost the feel and appearance of silk. Heirloom linens handed down from generation to generation may display these qualities.

Good-quality linen is very durable and will wear a long time. It is readily refreshed by washing and ironing, and can be ironed at a somewhat higher temperature than cotton, but it will scorch if the iron is too hot. When it is ironed, linen has an odor somewhat like straw. Ironing develops a luster, so if a dull finish is desired, linen garments should be

ironed on the wrong side. Table damask is ironed on the right side to develop the luster and enhance the pattern.

Untreated linen feels cool to the touch and is one of our most absorbent fibers owing partially to its "wicking" ability. It absorbs very rapidly and also is quick drying, so it is one of the most comfortable fabrics for warm climates. Resin finishes for crease resistance, while improving that quality, cut down on absorption and evaporation and thus decrease the cooling effect of linen. However, the improvement in wrinkle resistance is usually of more importance to the consumer than the difference in coolness.

Linen has sometimes been considered an expensive fabric, but today it is competitive in price with many other fabrics, particularly imported ones. Its durability should be taken into account when considering its cost.

Linen yarns can be flattened and made more lustrous and soft during manufacture by a beating process called *beetling*, in which the fabric is pounded with hundreds of tiny hammers. This process does not harm the fibers but destroys part of the cementing substances between fibers.

Linen may be attacked by mildew but is less likely to be so attacked than starched cotton. Resin finishes tend to cut down on the likelihood of microorganism attack on both linen and cotton.

Uses and By-products

Apparel uses for linen include men's slacks, suits, robes, neckties, and jackets; women's suits, skirts, coats, jackets, sportswear, blouses, and shirts; and accessories for both men and women, such as handkerchiefs, shoes, handbags, luggage, and hats. Textile furnishings include the luxury items of linen sheets and pillowcases as well as drapery and upholstery fabrics, table damask, lace, and other napery, and nonpile rugs. Industrial uses include linen piece goods and lace, as well as the more prosaic sewing thread for leather goods, twines, belts, and fire hose. Linen has long been the principal fiber for fire hose because of its great strength, low elasticity, and quick absorption of water, so that it becomes wet through and can be handled comfortably (temperature-wise) and is not likely to catch fire as long as water is going through it. Marine and armed services uses (largely ropes) have been important in past years, but now other natural and man-made fibers are tending to replace linen for these purposes.

By-products of linen are largely from the seed. The most important by-product is linseed oil, which is a valuable oxidizing (thus drying) ingredient in many outdoor paints, is used in making linoleum, and is often used in making explosives, thus creating shortages of some of these products in war time. Flaxseed is an ingredient in some medicines and drugs and in many wave-set solutions used by women of this country.

Linen was one of the first fibers to be successfully resin treated for

wrinkle resistance, and most linen fabrics for apparel use are now so finished. Dry cleaning may preserve the finish, and with it dimensional stability, longer than laundering. Linen/triacetate rough-textured knitted fabrics have been quite fashionable in women's summer dresses and suits over the past several years, and polyester/linen combinations have had a place in woven fabrics for such purposes. The combination of fibers takes advantage of the absorbency, comfort, and crispness of linen and the crease resistance, pliability, and resiliency of the other fibers. Efforts to promote such blended fabrics in men's wear have met with little success thus far. To many persons, particularly those of the older generation of today, pure linen (also pure silk) garments or textile furnishings are still the epitome of beauty and luxury. The future of linen is dependent on price, available labor, available land, and developments in properties to keep it competitive with other fibers. Linen is covered by the Textile Fiber Products Identification Act although, as a natural fiber, it is not defined in the law.

JUTE

Jute is the most important of a class of fibers known as bast fibers throughout the world. Data for world production of jute and linen are given in Table 13. *Matthews' Textile Fibers* (p. 258) says of this group of fibers:

The large group of plants included in the bast fiber group represents, in relation to the number that are cultivated and processed on a commercial scale, a very rich potential supply of textile fiber. As methods of cultivation and processing are improved, many of these plants will undoubtedly be utilized to a greater extent.

We shall consider general properties that apply to all the bast fibers here, though all except jute appear under the minor fiber classification. The bast fiber plants are tall, slender plants growing to a height of 5 to 16 feet, with stalks ½ to ¾ inch in diameter. Height varies for the different plants and with the geographical area, soil, climate, and conditions of growing season. The plants have relatively few leaves, which are borne near or at the top. The fiber grows inside the cuticle of the stem as does linen in the flax plant. The individual fibers are short, but because cementing substance within the fiber bundles is not removed, the fibers overlap and may be removed and used as long continuous strands, limited only by the lengths of the stems.

The fibers are removed from the stems by retting, decortication, or

a combination of methods. Sometimes, after cutting, plants are left on the ground until the leaves wither and fall off or can be easily shaken from the stalk. Several of these fibers may have their luster and flexibility increased by hand rubbing while drying, but this is done only for some end-uses.

Jute is the name given to the bast fiber from the plant *Corchorus* of the Tiliaceae family, but it is also known by several other names, including pat, or pata, and saluyot. Fibers from other plants, especially some leaf fibers, are sometimes erroneously called jute. In *Matthews' Textile Fibers* (pp. 260–262), B. Montgomery has given something of the assumed history of jute:

> Use of fiber from plants of the genus *Corchorus* for fabrics and cordage is of great antiquity. The jute plant generally thought to be C. *olitorius* is mentioned for its food uses in the Bible, Job 30:4, as well as in ancient Egyptian and other early literature of the Mediterranean area. This may indicate that the genus originated in the Mediterranean area and was brought to the Indo-Pakistan subcontinent in prehistoric times. Its use as a textile fiber by the people of the Mediterranean area is somewhat obscure, though it may well have been used for the "sackcloth" of ancient times. It is possible that the plant, which in the Mediterranean area is only 4 to 5 ft tall, did not yield sufficient fiber to make it of unusual interest for this purpose but that, when it began to grow in the warm, moist climate of Asia, the greater height of the stalks resulted in its utilization as a fiber plant. Ancient literature from Asia makes frequent mention of the fiber for textile use.

Jute ranks next to cotton in the amount of fiber produced in the world and in commercial value. It has been said to be the world's most plentiful, cheapest, and weakest fiber. But the picture has changed considerably during and since World War II, and several other fibers are now being produced in competition with jute.

Although jute is grown in limited quantities in many countries, by far the largest amounts are grown in Pakistan, India, and Brazil, with only the two former exporting fiber or fabrics. Before partition into India and Pakistan, India produced and manufactured nearly all the world's supply of jute. After partition, Pakistan held much of the production area and India the mills for processing. The friction between the two countries led to low production, high cost, and fluctuating supplies. Pakistan needed much of its land to grow food and, in addition, World War II had disrupted transportation. Consequently, other governments encouraged their citizens to grow jute or other fiber plants in order to supply cordage and bagging for their own national needs. Jute production is largely dependent on a plentiful supply of cheap hand labor; thus there are a limited number of areas where it can be grown.

The United States imports raw, semi-manufactured, and finished jute fabrics, the former for twine and cordage and the latter two as bagging and burlap—almost the only fabric made from jute.

Microscopically, jute resembles flax, but it usually lacks the cross markings characteristic of bast fibers. Raw jute is 62 to 64 percent cellulose, with a high lignin content which accounts for the woody nature of the fiber. The lignin, gums, waxes, and other materials that cement the fibers together within bundles are not usually removed in jute—hence the fiber is never so fine and soft as linen but is harsh and stiff.

Jute is harvested by hand-cutting the stalks a few inches above the ground. The fiber is removed by retting and stripping from the remainder of the deteriorated stalk tissue by one of four hand methods; then it is washed repeatedly to remove bits of bark, gum, etc., and dried away from sunlight, which would cause darkening and weakening of the fiber.

The color and quality of the fiber depend considerably on the degree of maturation of the plant when harvested; if harvested when the plant is in flower the fiber is finer and lighter in color, but the yield is lower than for more mature jute. Jute is graded by a variety of rather poorly defined standards at various stages in marketing; no set of standards has been generally accepted on a wide basis.

Jute is a weak, harsh, brittle fiber, with low elongation and little elasticity. The color varies from creamy white to dark brown; the best quality is lightest in color. Jute fiber has considerable luster. Jute darkens and weakens with age and exposure to light and is thus not a durable fiber. It is easily attacked at high humidity and temperature by the organisms that cause rot and mildew, and it cannot be completely bleached without considerable damage to the fiber. It may be dyed, but usually colors must be chosen dark enough to mask the natural fiber color. Jute is weaker when wet than dry and is not particularly strong at any time. Without special finishing, it cannot be either laundered or dry cleaned satisfactorily; however, with some of the new chemical finishes it can now be treated so that it may be washed or cleaned, and it may now be flame proofed and made water repellent.

Because it is cheap, jute has long been the primary fiber used for bagging and wrapping fabrics, especially for world food supplies for animal and man. Much fiber is used for rope, twine, cord, other forms of cordage, and backing for carpets and rugs.

Burlap, the fabric made from jute, has many uses: as undercovering for upholstered furniture, as backing for linoleum, for bulletin boards, and sometimes for curtains and slip covers in vacation lodges and cabins. From time to time jute makes fashion news, as a few years ago when it

was made into circular skirts and matching shoes with bright felt trim. Specially finished jute has limited possibilities for apparel use.

THE MINOR NATURAL CELLULOSIC FIBERS

Bast Fibers	Leaf Fibers	Seed or Fruit Fibers
hemp	abacá	cattail
kenaf	fique	coir
mesta	hennequen	kapok
ramie	piña	milkweed
sunn	sisal	
urena		

In addition to the three major natural cellulosic fibers—cotton, linen, and jute—there are a great number of vegetable fibers of lesser importance to the textile field, and potentially many more that at present are not being utilized. Most of these fibers are bast, leaf, and seed or fruit fibers. A great many minor fibers are used to a considerable extent in small areas of the world but are little known outside those regions. With ever-growing ease of travel, we shall have more opportunity to become acquainted with peoples in the far reaches of the world and with their fibers, many of which are being brought back to this country by our mobile countrymen.

General properties for the minor cellulosic fibers that are designated as "bast" are given at the beginning of the discussion on jute. If you are interested in detailed information about the individual fibers of this group and their usage please refer to the earlier editions of this book or to other sources listed in them.

Bast or stem fibers have considerable present or potential commercial importance. These are often called "soft" fibers in contrast to leaf fibers which are called "hard" although there may be little or no actual difference. Few leaf fibers are of commercial importance although some are widely used in their native habitat.

The leaf fibers, as do most of the bast fibers, grow in bundles with ends of individual cells overlapping to produce a continuous strand, and individual fibers within the bundles are held together by gums, pectins, and other materials. The fibers, although found in various places in the leaf, are usually important in supporting and giving structure to the leaf. Most of the leaf fibers are from closely related plants.

Seed hair fibers other than cotton and coir are, at present, not used in fabric making; they are of importance in apparel and furnishing fields,

however, because their buoyant qualities make them especially valuable for water-safety articles such as life belts and jackets, for stuffing materials where buoyancy and insulation are desired, and for articles such as pillows, toys, and comforters, used by persons allergic to feathers or wool. Foam rubber and some of the man-made fibers have in many instances replaced seed fibers for stuffing.

In addition to the classes of minor fibers already listed should be added Spanish moss and redwood fiber because they are fibers of some commercial importance in our own country.

FOR FURTHER READING

Crawford, M. D. C.: *The Heritage of Cotton.*

Hadfield, J. W.: *Linen Flax Fibre Production in New Zealand.*

Hamby, D. S. (ed.): *The American Cotton Handbook,* Volumes I and II.

Hollen, N. R. and Saddler, J.: *Textiles.*

Joseph, M. L.: *Introductory Textile Science.*

Kaswell, E. R.: *Wellington Sears Handbook of Industrial Textiles.*

Labarthe, J.: *Textiles: Origins to Usage.*

Leggett, W. F.: *The Story of Linen.*

Linton, G. E.: *Natural and Manmade Textile Fibers.*

Mauersberger, H. R. (ed.): *Matthews' Textile Fibers.*

National Advisory Commission on Food and Fiber: *Cotton and Other Fiber Problems and Policies in the United States.* Technical Papers, Vol. 2, July 1967. U.S. Government Printing Office.

Stout, E. E.: *Introduction to Textiles* (1960 and 1965).

Walton, P.: *The Story of Textiles.*

THE NATURAL PROTEIN
(ANIMAL) FIBERS

The natural protein fibers, obtained from the animal kingdom, are fewer in number than the vegetable fibers used for textiles. The two most important are wool and silk. There are, in addition, a number of minor fibers, often called specialty wool or hair fibers.

The protein fibers, both natural and man-made, in common with other protein substances are extremely complicated molecules composed of varying kinds and numbers of amino acids which have polymerized to form long polypeptide chains of high molecular weight. The amino acids themselves vary greatly in complexity with varying kinds of side chains which may be acidic, basic, aromatic, aliphatic, heterocyclic, hydroxylic, or sulfuric. The proteins are commonly described as being made up of "amino acid residues" because as they proceed to polymerize by condensation each acid loses a molecule of water (HOH). Relatively little is known about the structure of proteins since only recently have the first ones (*insulin* was first) been synthesized—the way in which chemists arrive at an analysis of their complicated structure.

The general chemical structural formula for all amino acids, no matter how complicated, is

$$R\text{-}CH\text{-}COOH$$
$$|$$
$$NH_2$$

and the general chemical structural formula commonly used to represent a protein is

which can be added to almost indefinitely. This segment represents three amino acid residues, as signified by the dotted lines. The R's represent the side chains.

The chemical structures of the wool and specialty fibers are similar to each other, but silk is very different; therefore no one formula can be given for this group of fibers as a whole, as was possible for the cellulosic fibers. All fibers in the group, however, contain carbon, hydrogen, oxygen, and nitrogen, and the wool and specialty fibers also contain sulfur.

As a group, the protein fibers are elastic and resilient, thus free from problems of wrinkling and creasing, and they are absorbent. Silk differs greatly from the other fibers in the group in most of its other properties.

The protein fibers burn at varying rates, with an odor of burning hair or feathers that is mostly due to the nitrogen content, and leave a brittle black residue which can be crushed readily between the fingers. Protein fibers are damaged by alkaline solutions; a hot weak solution of sodium hydroxide (NaOH) will destroy them.

We shall first examine wool, next the minor or specialty wool and hair fibers because they are much like wool, and finally silk, which bears a resemblance to the man-made fibers in some respects and will prepare us for their study.

WOOL

Wool may well have been the first fiber that man learned to make into fabric, either by matting and felting, or by spinning a yarn and weaving. Walton, in *The Story of Textiles* (pp. 15, 16, 32), in reference to the ruins of the Swiss lake dwellers discovered in 1853–1854, said

Some of the lowest villages were many feet down, and belonged to the earliest Stone Age. In them were found crude but serviceable fabrics of bast, flax,

and wool, and signs that the growth and manufacture of cloth of flax and wool at so early a date was an important industry. . . .

At the dawn of history, wool, flax, cotton, and silk were being woven in the East with the greatest skill, and which was the first material used in weaving is not known. It is probable, however, that the possession of flocks and herds led to the spinning and weaving of wool before either cotton, flax or silk was so used; and the fact that here and there ancient records speak of fabrics of cotton and silk as if they were rare luxuries would indicate that linen and woolen fabrics were too common to receive much attention, and that those of the other materials were relatively novel. . . .

The spinning and weaving of wool has been practiced, as we have seen, from a most remote antiquity, and in the Far Western America as well as in remote Eastern Japan and China. Remnants of wool as well as linen are found in the barrows of the Britons and also in other tombs.

Wool is the hair or furlike covering of the sheep. Originally sheep had two coats, a coarse, protective, wiry "guard" or "beard" coat, and a soft, warm, fleecy undercoat of very fine texture. With domestication and selective breeding, the outer coat disappeared and most types of modern sheep have only the fleece coat, which has now attained considerable length.

The sheep is believed, of all animals, to have been the most adaptable to varying local conditions throughout the world and throughout its history, and to have been the most influenced by environment. The many variations in shape, fleece, and other characteristics attest to this fact as well as the fact that sheep cannot be traced back to any original breeds.

The *American Wool Handbook* (1948, p. 63) says

In the beginning sheep were covered only with hair, and wool was merely a soft slight down next to the skin. The Scotch blackface sheep is one of the present breeds most closely related to this primitive type.

In the earliest pastoral industry one finds that Abraham, the patriarch of the Old Testament, thrived and prospered because of the value of his great flocks and herds. According to Crawford, the oldest evidence of wool comes from Asia Minor, from Tell Asmar, the great hill or mound. Under a succession of ruined cities were found seals indicating an elaborate system of personal ownership of wool and flocks of sheep. There is evidence that trade existed in this venerable fiber. The date set for this mound is 4200 B.C., or 6000 years ago. The pastoral industry was apparently one of the first agricultural pursuits to be established. From central Asia, the cradle of civilization, the sheep gradually were introduced into new localities until today they are found over the entire globe. Sheep, probably of the fine wool type, had been introduced into Spain by the Phoenicians hundreds of years before the Christian Era. There is little doubt that a number of different types of finer "wool" sheep from Asia, Africa, Greece, and Rome were brought into Spain and the various blood

lines fused to form the famous Spanish merino sheep, the ancestor of the finest wool-bearing sheep of today.

Although other animal hair or fur fibers are used in the making of fabrics, the term *wool* is generally understood to refer only to the fiber obtained from sheep.

Breeds of sheep are classified, on the basis of the fineness and length of their wool, into five types. Figure 5-1 is a photograph of these different types. These are long, medium, fine, carpet wool, and crossbreeds, the dual-purpose sheep. Breed influences wool characteristics such as length, fineness, strength, color, luster, waviness, elasticity, resiliency, shrinkage potential, and felting properties. Breed also influences the quality and character of the meat. Some breeds are valued chiefly for their wool and their mutton is of minor importance, but other breeds have been developed for the best possible compatible quality of wool and mutton. There are hundreds of breeds of sheep falling into the five types, each a little different from the others in some respect.

Indians of the Americas had no sheep until they were introduced by

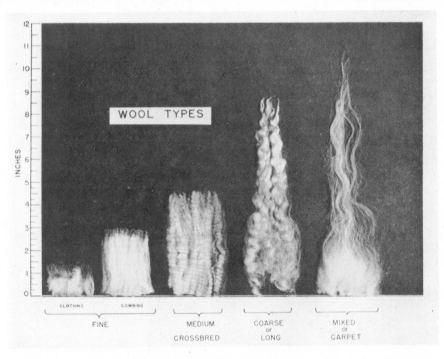

FIGURE 5-1. Variation in fiber length between different types of wool. (Courtesy E. M. Pohle and W. Von Bergen, Interscience Publishers.)

the Spanish into Central and South America and into our own Southwest, and from England into colonial North America along the eastern seacoast. The Indians of South America, however, made use of the fleece from llamas, alpacas, and vicunas, all of which were native to their regions.

In colonial America, although some fabrics were imported from England, families were dependent on themselves, or small groups shared work, for their fabric supply. Nearly every farm had a few sheep which were regularly shorn. The wool was washed, carded, spun, woven, and fashioned into garments or needed household articles by the women and girls of the family. Weaving was sometimes done by men, however, because of the heaviness of the wooden looms. In fact, all over the world wool fabric production was a household handcraft until modern times.

About 1640–1650 groups of artisans set up fulling, dyeing, and finishing establishments for wool cloth which was brought to them from the looms in the homes, and from this start factories were established where spinning and weaving were also carried on. All early wool fabrics were woolens. The more exacting processes for making worsted fabrics, notably combing, were not adequately enough mastered until the last quarter of the nineteenth century for worsteds to become a considerable part of the wool fabric industry.

Source and Production

Tables 3, 4, and 5, in Chapter 2, give us a brief glimpse of wool in the world fiber picture. From these tables you can see that world production of wool has doubled since 1890 but that both production and consumption in the United States are dropping. The increase in wool consumption (Table 5) as shown for 1945 and 1950 was undoubtedly due to World War II, with 1945 reflecting military requirements and 1950 probably civilian replacement of wardrobes depleted by scarcity during the war years. Reasons for changes in production and consumption of fibers were mentioned in the latter part of Chapter 1, and some of the changes in wool will be discussed in more detail here.

Apparel-type wools are produced in largest amounts in Australia, New Zealand, the Union of South Africa, and the United States and constitute about 81 percent of total wool production. Carpet wools account for the other 19 percent. Argentina is the leading producer of carpet wool, with smaller amounts produced in New Zealand, Uruguay, India, and Turkey. Every state in the United States produces some wool, with Texas producing almost a fourth of the total. All wool produced in the United States is the apparel type because, under the conditions in which wool is produced here, sheep with a suitably coarse wool for carpets cannot be raised, as a general rule. A few fat-tailed carpet-wool type Karakul sheep are raised in the

United States for the production of lambskin for fur, though most of this type sheep are raised in the Soviet Union and a few European countries. Some of the Navajo sheep produce a carpet type wool used for hand weaving of rugs by the Navajo Indians. C. E. Terrill, in the *Wool Handbook, Volume I* (p. 113), says:

> Sheep-raising is an important occupation of the Navajo Indians but the handweaving of wool appears to be decreasing. A weaving-wool type of sheep has been developed at the Fort Wingate Laboratory and a little coarse Navajo wool is still produced and handwoven into rugs.

In studying Tables 4 and 5 you may have noted that we consume more wool in the United States than we produce. The balance is made up by imports. United States imports of wool have risen sharply over the past 25 years—from about 15½ million pounds in 1945 to almost 122 million pounds in 1967, which is the latest figures available. This despite the high prices because of tariffs and duties. The imports include both apparel and carpet type wools.

According to F. Lowenstein *et al.*, in *Cotton and Other Fiber Problems and Policies in the United States* (pp. 38–40):

> Wool prices in the United States reflect world supply and demand conditions. Thus, domestic prices have generally fluctuated directly with foreign prices. However, on a duty-paid basis, prices of imported wool at Boston normally are 10 to 20 percent higher than similar grades of domestic wools, reflecting the better preparation of foreign wools.
>
> U.S. farm prices also reflect changes in foreign prices for wool. Domestic producers sell their wool at market prices, but they are eligible also for a payment rate to equal the difference between the national average price of all shorn wool sold and a higher incentive price level. Government payments to growers are intended as an incentive to increase production.

Competition with other fibers, particularly the polyesters and acrylics, affect the price of wool. And as with cotton, the lower specific gravity of the man-made fibers has a cover advantage that tends to make price differentials even greater. Lowenstein, in the reference cited above, continues (p. 40):

> . . . In addition, producers of synthetic fibers have been aggressive in research, in technical and marketing service, and in product development and promotion of end products. However, wool is able to compete with manmade fibers because it is often superior in quality factors that include warmth, comfort, fabric "hand," and appearance of the garment or end product.

The United States government, through the Department of Agriculture, has maintained a system of price supports since the early years of World

War II to encourage wool production at levels believed to be necessary for national security and general economic welfare. This level is 300 million pounds per year of shorn wool, greasy basis.

The first supports were government purchases to maintain military supplies and CCC loans to producers, based on world market prices for wool. These loans have usually been set at 103 to 109 percent of world prices for sheep's wool and somewhat less than 100 percent for mohair.

Price support loans alone were not successful in stimulating production of wool to the desired levels so the program was expanded by the National Wool Act of 1954 to add incentive payments to the loan programs. Incentive payments are financed from duties and tariffs on wool and wool fabric imports but cannot exceed 70 percent of the total received from these sources. The incentive payments were fixed at 62 cents per pound through 1965 and were raised to 65 cents per pound in 1966. According to E. M. Pohle, in the *Wool Handbook, Volume I* (p. 652):

After the marketing year is over and the average price received for shorn wool by all producers is known, the rate of the incentive payment for the marketing year is announced. The rate of payment will be the percentage required to bring the national average price received by all producers up to the announced incentive price. Use of the percentage rate recognizes quality production and encourages producers to improve the quality and marketing of their wool to get the best possible price in the open market.

In addition to loans and incentive payments, wool producers are paid for unshorn lambs that they have marketed, to make up for their wool. This payment is based on the weight of the lambs to approximate the weight of wool on each at the time of marketing. This price has varied from about 35 cents to 65 cents per 100 pounds weight of the lambs over the years it has been in effect.

Despite all these efforts, the number of sheep in the United States and the overall production of wool continue to decrease. The estimated total of shorn wool for 1968 was a little less than 176 million pounds, greasy basis, down 6.5 percent from 1967.

A program of promotion and advertising for wool and lamb was also authorized in the National Wool Act of 1954; it is carried on by the American Sheep Growers Council, Inc. This program is financed by a deduction approved by sheep growers, and will run through 1969. The deduction amounted to 1 cent per pound on shorn wool and 5 cents per hundredweight on unshorn lambs through 1965 and was increased to 1½ and 7½ cents respectively, effective in 1966.

Why has wool production declined in the United States, and what of its future? Wool production has in recent years become more a small-scale

"farm" activity than a large-scale "range" activity typical of the days when range land was plentiful at little or no cost, and there were few restrictions on its use. The maximum number of range sheep in the United States is believed to have been reached in 1884. With increased population spreading out into all areas of the country, growth of cities and suburbs, more land utilized for cultivation through irrigation, new varieties of adaptable plants, and new agricultural practices, the amount of land available for the range production of sheep has been greatly restricted. Much, if not most, of such range land is now part of the nationally owned system of parks or forest preserves in the mountainous areas of our country, particularly of the West, for which strict and effective regulations for grazing have been established in order to maintain these lands undamaged, or to repair the ravages of earlier thoughtless or careless policies that allowed overgrazing and overcutting. Although there has been a great deal of grumbling about the current regulatory policies and much lobbying in Congress by persons who would benefit financially from unrestricted use of public lands, such policies are necessary and may have to be made more stringent in years to come. It is probable, however, that much of the present area of grazing land will be continued as such, for its use for other purposes is very limited.

The difficulty of maintaining a supply of reliable sheepherders is a real problem to sheep ranchers. The sheepherder lives a lonely existence far from the comforts that most of us consider necessary; and his life, cut off from human contact for weeks or months at a time, with his only companion his valuable dog, appeals to very few people. It is not a life conducive to family living. Such work also requires a skill with sheep that is possessed by very few men. With trailer houses, radios, and other modern inventions, the sheepherder is not so isolated as he once was, but much of the range country remains in regions inaccessible to motorized vehicles and remote from areas where electricity and such conveniences are available. Sheepherders still face many of the dangers of old—wild animals, sudden storms, and the remoteness of help. Wages, although much higher than a few years ago, still do not compare with those offered by many other types of employment. However, the high labor costs of sheepherders and shearers do tend to make the expense of wool production very great for the producer.

The fact that people in the United States demand lamb or young mutton for meat rather than older mutton has also had an influence on wool production and marketing, especially in certain types of fibers. Development of refrigeration has probably had an effect too.

In the Eastern half (approximately) of the United States, sheep are raised in small flocks of 25 to 50 ewes on farms devoted primarily to other

products. Wool from such areas is called "domestic." In the Western half of the country, where range lands are available, sheep are raised in flocks of thousands on unfenced ranges, with little or no shelter available. Wool from such flocks is called "territory" wool. Texas and California flocks are kept in fenced pastures and shelter of some sort is provided, although the pastures are often of the large range size; range breeds of sheep are preferred for these huge fenced pastures. Texas wool produced from these flocks is of good quality, but California wool is likely to vary more and to be of poorer quality. Both of these wools, however, must be classed separately from the clip from other states because of the short length of the fibers; the sheep are sheared twice a year in both Texas and California.

The methods of handling sheep determine to a considerable extent what type of sheep is produced. It would seem logical that with fenced pastures and shelter the finest-fibered sheep might be raised in the farm flock areas. This, however, is not the case. Farm flocks are largely medium-wool crossbreed varieties, valued for meat as well as for wool. On the other hand, in order to handle sheep successfully on the open range, they must be breeds with a herding instinct, who will stay together. This instinct is seemingly present only in certain of the fine-wooled breeds, of which some of the merino breeds are the most famous. Some of the farm flock sheep, notably those in Ohio, are noted for their fine wool, equal to or better in quality than that of range sheep. The finest diameter wool produced in the United States (80's), as fine as any produced in the world, comes from the fenced pastures of Texas. There are great differences in wool quality within the same breed of sheep because of differences in climate, soil, pasturage, supplementary feed, and health of the animal. There are also differences in quality in the various parts of a sheep's fleece, the most exposed areas being poorest in quality.

Marketing and Grading

The leading wool markets of the world are in Sydney, Boston, Buenos Aires, and London, in that order. The amount of wool handled in Boston far exceeds that handled by other United States markets in Philadelphia and Chicago. New York City handles the bulk of the carpet wool in the United States. As was the practice for cotton, wool is sold in local spot markets and in futures markets through the wool exchanges. Much wool is sorted and graded locally by cooperative organizations of producers, who may also do their own marketing. Wool may be sold directly by the producer to a market representative at the spot markets, through cooperative producing and/or marketing associations of producers, or at public auction.

Auctions are relatively unimportant in this country, but the auction method of selling is spreading. The most famous world wool auction is in London. Futures markets deal with tops exclusively, or with unprocessed wool.

The *American Wool Handbook* (1948, p. 378) defines *tops* as "The wool top is wool that has been scoured, carded and combed; in other words semi-manufactured. It is in the form of a ball of about 8 or 9 pounds. These balls are packed in bales of about 250 pounds each."

Wool is classified or graded twice—once called "grading" to determine diameter, length, and condition for classifying individual fleeces and lots for initial marketing operations. The second classification—called "sorting"—is a further finer classification for specific end-uses. Two systems of grading have developed, one is the system used in the United States which is largely warehouse grading, and the other the system used in Australia which is also fairly typical of wool grading in South America, South Africa, New Zealand, and some Asian and European countries also. Grading and sorting operations are often combined in countries other than the United States.

E. M. Pohle, in the *Wool Handbook, Volume I* (pp. 556–558), describes warehouse grading in the United States as follows:

. . . When a lot of wool reaches the warehouse, the bags are hand trucked one at a time to the grading table and opened up. The grading table used by the grader is a large wooden table which rests on wooden saw horses, allowing it to be moved and taken down easily. Surrounding the table on two sides are large baskets on rollers. Most grading today is done under fluorescent lights, many of which are movable to locations convenient to the grading table setup near large tiers of wool bags or near scales. These lights provide a constant source of illumination, all important in the grading operations. This also makes it possible to have the same type of lighting any day of the year. However, there is still some grading done where the table is placed either under a skylight or in front of north windows, if possible. The grader stands on the free side of the table; his needs are a pencil and a notebook to check the lot and bag number.

To be a good grader it is essential to have good eyesight and an average memory; the grader's memory is the result of practice and experience and enables him to make a quick decision about the grade of wool as represented in the fleece. To have an official standard set on hand is an excellent aid for any grader. The grader is assisted by two helpers, one to truck the bags to the table and the other to pass the fleeces one by one up to the table after the bag has been opened on the floor. The grader opens up the tightly tied fleece a trifle, pulling out small samples about the size of a lead pencil, from several places over the fleece. He tests it for strength by trying to pull it apart with his fingers and, using his thumb as a ruler, he estimates the length of the staple. His eyes will note at a glance the fineness. He then turns the fleece over to the other side and repeats the procedure. If both sides are equal in grade and

length he throws the fleece into a designated basket containing other fleeces of similar grade and length. After the baskets are filled, they are removed and emptied onto a pile of fleeces of the same grade, where they remain until the entire lot has been graded. If they have been sold, the graded wools are immediately rebagged and shipped. Fleeces of the same grade, but of various lots, may be piled together, and such graded piles before being bagged may contain as many as 5000 fleeces or approximately 40,000 pounds. This constitutes about one railroad car load or transport truck, and is the quantity wool buyers usually prefer when purchasing in the country . . .

Wool that for any reason is offgrade—removed from carcasses of sheep that have died from disease or exposure, black and gray wools, damaged wools, and those with large amounts of foreign materials—are not graded but are sold by examination of the individual fleeces.

The second grading is the breaking up or *sorting* of the various qualities of wool from each individual fleece, and is based on the finest possible count to which each quality can be spun in the mills; there are thirteen grades for sorting. The person who does the first grading, called a "wool classer," must have some familiarity with grades in sorting as well as with the initial fleece grades. The second grader, called a "wool sorter," must be familiar with both the mill processes and grades required for each type of fabric, and with the wool classes for fleece as well. Sorters in the United States work in the mills and often are familar only with the type of sorting used at a specific mill.

In addition to fineness, length is also an important factor in the utilization of wool fiber, particularly if combing is one of the processes to be used. Although there are no standard grades for wool fiber length, designations are made on the basis of common usage which has developed over the years in the markets. The terms used are *strictly combing* for fibers over 2½ inches long, *French combing* for fibers 1½ to 2½ inches in length, and *clothing* for fibers under 1½ inches. The coarser wools are the longer ones; length varies approximately ¼ inch per grade for comparable periods of time between shearings. "Fine staple" wool refers to combing length wool in one of the three fine diameters.

Internationally accepted terms for grades are adapted from the English numerical system. The U.S. Department of Agriculture established a series of twelve standard grades for wool which were enacted into law in June 1926. This early system, called "blood," and originally having something to do with breeding, has now been replaced by the numerical system. The latest revision of the U.S. Standard Grades for Wool became effective January 1, 1966. It defines 16 grades that are based on average fiber diameter and variations of fiber diameter. The United States standard grades are as follows.

	Average Fiber Diameter (microns)	Standard Deviation (microns)
Finer than grade 80's	17.69 or less	3.59 or less
Grade 80's	17.70–19.14	4.09 or less
Grade 70's	19.15–20.59	4.59 or less
Grade 64's	20.60–22.04	5.19 or less
Grade 62's	22.05–23.49	5.89 or less
Grade 60's	23.50–24.94	6.49 or less
Grade 58's	24.95–26.39	7.09 or less
Grade 56's	26.40–26.84	7.59 or less
Grade 54's	27.85–29.29	8.19 or less
Grade 50's	29.30–30.99	8.69 or less
Grade 48's	31.00–32.69	9.09 or less
Grade 46's	32.70–34.39	9.59 or less
Grade 44's	34.40–36.19	10.09 or less
Grade 40's	36.20–38.09	10.69 or less
Grade 36's	38.10–40.20	11.19 or less
Coarser than grade 36's	40.21 or more	—

Boxed standards for both grading and sorting are supplied by the USDA, as are the cotton standards. The USDA has also developed methods for sampling and for determining length and diameter.

The Australian method of grading is described in the same reference as the American method (p. 559–61) as follows:

The bulk of the Australian wool is graded or classed and assigned a type number at the shearing shed. The shearing is performed in the same manner as shearing in the United States, except that the wool from the belly is cut free from the rest of the fleece and handled separately. Special care is taken to protect the fleece from contact with foreign substances. The shearing room is presided over by head classer, whose job it is to separate the fleece into the various classes or grades and to keep the wool of the same money value together as much as possible.

*   *   *

On being brought from the shearing floor the fleece is thrown, skin side down, on the wool classing table, so as to open widely. . . .

Skirting is the next step; it consists of removing from the body of the fleece any objectionable sorts. Two skirters usually work together at one table, one skirter operating on each side of the fleece. The inferior portions or objectionable sorts are heavy shrinking parts such as tags, leg pieces, neck pieces, bellies, locks, and stained portions. The various skirtings are separated by skirts as follows: A small portion of the wool skirted from the forequarters of the fleece is normally finer and of lighter shrinkage than the inferior "plucking" of the britch end. They are known as "first pieces" and "second

pieces." First and second pieces are looked over, together with the bellies and sweepings from the shearing floor, at the piece picker's table. The tags, stained parts, and locks are sorted into individual bins . . .

The next step is the actual grading by the wool classer who grades the wool fleece as 70s, or 60s super-combing, or whatever grade and quality it may be. The fleece is then placed in its respective grade bin. The fleeces from ewes, wethers, rams, and lambs are kept separate.

Australian fleeces are rolled, packed about 40 to a bale, and compressed by hydraulic presses into a compact bale weighing about 300 pounds. These, of course, pack well into shipping space, which is important since much Australian wool is exported.

In addition to knowing what the various grades and lengths mean in terms of utilization, the wool buyer has the additional responsibility of judging correctly, usually within 1 percent, the "shrinkage" of the different groups of wool he is examining, even within the same lot. Shrinkage refers to the amount of foreign matter, not fiber—foreign matter such as grease, suint, dust, sand, burs, tar, and paint—present on the wool which will be removed in scouring or other cleaning processes. Shrinkage runs from as low as 25 to as high as 85 percent of the weight of the raw wool, and varies not only with breed but also with sex, the part of the animal from which the wool was obtained, and the area of the country in which the animal was raised; it varies from state to state within an area, and in different regions within the same state. Buyers must examine the actual wool lot to arrive at these judgments; they cannot as yet buy from a sample description, as is possible for cotton.

Wool sheared from living sheep is called shorn or *fleece* wool. Wool removed from the pelts of slaughtered animals or those otherwise deceased is designated as *pulled* wool because the fiber is loosened by one of several chemical treatments on the skin on the side away from the fiber, and the fiber may then be pulled, root and all, from the skin. The ratio of pulled wool to fleece wool in the United States is usually about 15 percent pulled to 85 percent fleece. Fleece wool is more desirable than pulled wool for several reasons; one important reason is that the root end of pulled wool interferes with even dyeing and may affect other processing. Fleece wool is also said to be livelier.

Wool Legislation and Fabric Classification

Although wool may be classified in a number of ways, those of primary importance to the consumer are the three classes designated by the Wool Products Labeling Act and the two fabric classes based on yarn processing.

The Wool Products Labeling Act of 1939, effective since July 15, 1941, was designed to protect the consumer from misbranding of wool and wool

products, including some of or all of the specialty fibers. It requires labeling of manufactured apparel and wool fabrics intended for apparel use that are made up of 5 percent or more of wool, exclusive of ornamentation. Carpet wools, not covered in this law, are covered by the Textile Fiber Products Identification Act. The 1939 law specifies three types of wool, which must be labeled in order of amount and with percentages of fiber content stated.

1. *Wool, new wool,* or *virgin wool* is wool fiber that has been through manufacturing processes only once.

2. *Reprocessed wool* is wool fiber reclaimed from woven or felted wool products that have not been utilized in any way by the ultimate consumer. This class includes fibers reclaimed from cutters' scraps and from woven and knitted garments and fabrics that for some reason have failed to sell.

3. *Reused wool* is wool fiber reclaimed from knitted, woven, felted, or spun wool products that have been used in any way by the ultimate consumer. Much of this fiber is reclaimed from old garments collected by the ragman or junkman. The wool is often reclaimed by garnetting and carbonizing processes, which may do considerable harm to the wool fiber.

Although the law makes no requirements concerning the quality of wool fiber that must be used for each of these classes, and good quality wools may be used in both reprocessed and reused wool, there are likely to be fewer damaged fibers in fabrics made of new wool that has been through the manufacturing processes only once. Were it not for the practice of reclaiming and reusing wool from previously manufactured fabrics, however, the price of many wool articles would be considerably greater than now. For 1964 a little less than 13 percent of the wool used in the mills in the United States was reprocessed wool and a little less than 2 percent was reused wool. These figures are typical of the past several years. Of the total reprocessed and reused wool utilized in this country, almost a third goes into carpet yarns.

The two fabric classes based on processing with which we are concerned are *woolens* and *worsteds*. A very good explanation of the differences between worsteds and woolens has been given in *Economics of American Industry* (p. 373), which says

The worsted division uses a larger proportion of virgin wool than the woolen branch. Wools used in worsted are long fibers combed from virgin wool, i.e., wools that have not been previously used or processed. In the combing process, in which the short fibers, or noils, are eliminated, the long fibers are made to be parallel to each other so that they may be tightly spun. The fabrics, as a result, are closely woven and have a smooth appearance, and the pattern of the weave is easily discernible.

Woolens, on the other hand, are made from short-fiber wools, or from noils and also from reworked wools, such as chips and rags. Unlike the straightened fibers used in worsted, the woolen fibers are more or less crossed and intermixed and are less tightly spun, and the fabrics for the most part are loosely woven and rather rough surfaced.*

Because of the differences in fiber length, often of quality, and of processing, worsteds are more expensive. They are highly desirable for so-called "man-tailored" suits and other garments. They tend to become shinier with wear than do the duller-surfaced, rougher-textured, or napped woolens.

The Fur Products Labeling Act (1951) will be mentioned here only because furs are animal fibers that are still attached to the animal's skin; fur fibers obtained from cutting scraps and unusable pelts are often blended and spun with wool or other fibers for woven and knitted apparel and furnishing fabrics.

The Fur Labeling Act requires that all furs be labeled with the name of the true animal of origin; if portions of the pelt other than the back are used, the portions must be specified; and if the fur is dyed, this must also be stated. The Textile Fiber Products Identification Act covers the combination of fur with other fibers as for other fibers with each other.

Processes

Among processes used in converting raw fiber to fabric, only shearing, sorting, and carbonizing are unique to wool. Carbonizing and other processes are described briefly in the chapters on yarns and on finishing.

SHEARING

This is the process of clipping the fleece from a living animal. In most parts of the world shearing is done once a year in late spring or early summer, depending on climatic conditions of the area. Sheep are usually shorn twice a year in Texas and California. Sheep shearing is hard work and is one of the highest-paying jobs in range areas. Large shears, operated by hand or motor, are used. Skill is required in order to remove as much wool as possible and still leave enough to protect the animal from sun, storm, and chill and to avoid injuring the animal's tender skin. The belly wool is taken off first and separately; then the rest is removed in such a manner that the fleece is unbroken with all the parts in their natural positions on each side of the central wool along the backbone ridge. The natural position facilitates grading. Then the whole fleece is rolled in a commonly accepted method, tied (preferably with nonfibrous string), and packed in bags for marketing.

* By permission from *Economics of American Industry,* by Alderfer and Michl: third edition. Copyright 1957, McGraw-Hill Publishing Company.

PULLING

This process is covered briefly on page 103.

SORTING

Sorting is the separation of the previously graded fleeces (seven grades) into the spinning qualities, based on the second standard set of grades (thirteen) at the mill. The best wool comes from the shoulders and sides of the sheep, the next best from the lower back, loins, and upper front legs, and the poorest from back legs, neck, and head. Some bits are thrown away after shearing, before the fleece is rolled.

Mills buy and sort according to the type of product or quality of fabric they wish to produce; mill sorts vary from two or three to the full thirteen. The *American Wool Handbook* (1948, p. 389) says

. . . A mill manufacturing high quality goods will always make us many sorts as possible to get the full benefit of each fleece, whereas mills running lower grades of goods may make only two main sorts by throwing out the edges of the fleeces only. In other words, the higher the quality of the goods to be manufactured the more carefully the sorting is done . . .

Wool may be *bench* sorted, as in most countries, or *trap* sorted; about 75 percent of United States wool is trap sorted. Bench sorting is done by one man working at a table, with the whole fleece spread out before him and receptacles around him for all the different grades that are to be made. In this way the maximum number of grades and most even quality within a grade can be achieved; the process takes long years of practical experience or several years apprenticeship as a sorter. The greater the number of grades, and the finer the qualities, the slower the sorter. Trap sorting is a cruder and faster method and is thus less expensive. Teams of four men work together on an endless-chain basis, in which two men cut the twines and open the fleeces, one does the sorting, and the fourth checks to catch any obviously overlooked mistake in sorting. In this method only badly stained or damaged wool is removed. Australian wool has such unusable parts of the wool removed after shearing, before the fleece is rolled for marketing. Dried tar, paint, and other branding or treating materials are usually clipped from the fleece by hand to save the maximum amount of wool.

The difference in sorting methods accounts for much of the difference in quality between imported and domestically produced wool. Much of the American wool could be made into fabrics of as high quality as any in the world if the more discriminating sorting practices were followed. Intense competition between mills is said to be the reason that sorting is not done by bench methods. It will be interesting to see whether increased mechani-

zation and larger markets in Europe will bring about a change in wool sorting methods used there; the coming of refrigeration to more remote parts of the world, in New Zealand, for example, tended to lead to production of crossbreed sheep (for both mutton and wool) rather than the breeds for wool alone.

Structure of Wool

Wool is composed of five elements varying somewhat in the different amino acids, in approximately the following percentages: carbon, 50 percent, oxygen, 22 to 25 percent, nitrogen, 16 to 17 percent, hydrogen, 7 percent, and sulfur, 3 to 4 percent. Wool (including hair and fur) is the only fiber that contains sulfur. Eighteen amino acids have been identified in wool analyses with the presence of a nineteenth questioned. These are glycine, alanine, valine, leucine, isoleucine, phenylalanine, proline, serine, threonine, tyrosine, aspartic, glutamic, arginine, lysine, histidine, tryptophan, cystine (sulfur-containing), and methionine (sulfur-containing). Hydroxylysine is the questioned acid. Those acids present in greatest amounts are glutamic, serine, arginine, cystine, and proline.

Although the structural formulas for amino acids and for proteins (peptide linkages) given at the beginning of this chapter are common to all protein fibers, beyond that the chemical structure differs for each fiber so that no chemical structure common to all can be assumed. Wool, hair, and fur fibers are classed as "keratin" proteins, that is, they contain high amounts of cystine (sulfur-containing) while silk fibroin contains no cystine, thus no sulfur. A most interesting chemical structure for wool has evolved from the work of many scientists, beginning with Speakman in England in the 1930's, taking a new direction with the work of Pauling and Corey in the early 1950's, and proceeding through the work of a number of other scientists today. We shall examine the theoretical structure which, while not accepted by everyone, has won fairly wide acceptance among textile chemists.

Wool is one of the fibers that has been shown to be composed of the complex fibril structure discussed in relation to cellulose, though the crystalline structure for wool is quite different from that of cellulose because of its greater complexity and the side chains which do not permit the same type of layering or close packing. Wool molecules are therefore now generally believed to be coiled in a spiral α-helix arrangement with probably three amino acids per complete turn, as proposed by Pauling and Corey. These complex molecular chains permit disulfide bonding, hydrogen bonding between side chains of different acids, and perhaps salt linkages between acidic and basic elements of side chains.

Because it is impossible to show such a complex structure as wool dia-

grammatically and clearly it may be possible to gain some understanding from some simplified diagrams. The structure proposed by Speakman in 1936 is still much used to indicate how the various bonds may be formed. This formula, which follows, is considered to be only schematic and not structural since it cannot show some of the configurations necessary in the coiled chains as now accepted.

$$
\begin{array}{ccc}
& \diagdown CO & \diagup CO \\
-CH & & CH- \\
& \diagdown NH & NH \\
& CO & CO \\
& CH-CH_2-S-S-CH_2-CH \\
& NH. & \text{Cystine linkage} & NH \\
& CO & CO \\
-CH & & CH- \\
& NH & NH
\end{array}
$$

$$
\begin{array}{ccc}
CO & & CO \\
-CH & & CH- \\
NH & & NH \\
CO & & CO \\
CH-CH_2-CH_2-COO^- \quad {}^+NH_3-CH_2-CH_2-CH_2-CH_2-CH \\
NH & \begin{array}{c}\text{Glutamic}\\\text{acid}\end{array} & \text{Lysine} & NH \\
CO & & CO \\
-CH & & CH- \\
NH & & NH \\
CO & & CO \\
CH-CH_2-COO^- \quad {}^+NH_3-C-NH-CH_2-CH_2-CH_2-CH \\
NH & \begin{array}{c}\text{Aspartic}\\\text{acid}\end{array} & \underset{NH}{\overset{\parallel}{C}} & \text{Arginine} & NH \\
& & \text{Salt linkages}
\end{array}
$$

For a better idea of what the α-helical molecular structure is like, imagine taking a very long molecular chain of the type diagrammed as a peptide chain at the beginning of this chapter, fastening it at the top of a tube,

then coiling it around and around the tube, beginning at the top end and slanting the coils enough to avoid overlap as you work down. You would have a structure something like the following diagram for which we are indebted to L. F. Fieser and M. Fieser who used such a model to represent the conformation of protein molecules in their book *Advanced Organic Chemistry*. They called attention to the fact that this structure corresponds to distances derived from X-ray diffraction studies and would permit bonding of C-O groups, which always point down in the diagram, and N-H groups, which always point up.

Of course, molecular chains are not coiled around tubes, so if you could imagine removing the tube carefully so that the helical structure remained essentially in place, you could then imagine some turning and twisting of the side chains toward the hollow center of the coil, bringing others to the outside surface, and perhaps bringing appropriate elements close enough together for additional bonding. Pauling and Corey also proposed that the central straight α-helix (as shown) may have as many as six other chains twisting around it and with other nearby α-helices. (A real can of worms!) So we begin to understand how very complex these fibers are and to gain some insight into why they behave as they do.

Statements made by L. Rebenfeld in an article titled "Chemical Mechanism of Wool Setting," published in the *American Dyestuff Reporter* for June 21, 1965 (pp. 38–40) sums up the complex structure of wool and some of the ways in which it functions. He says

Wool is characterized by one of the most complex organo-chemical structures and by a unique and complicated intermolecular organization. Indeed, it is the organo-chemical structure of the keratin protein which is largely responsible for the complexity of the intermolecular organization. A variety of

side functional groups from the amino acids which form the protein chain interact into a system of intra- and inter-molecular bonds resulting in the formation of relatively stable cohesive aggregates. The keratin protein chain, in its native configuration, is wound upon itself into an α-helix which is stabilized primarily by hydrogen bonds and disulfide cross-links. The α-helices are further aggregated into protofibrils, microfibrils and ultimately into cortical cells. These various elements of wool fiber structure are held together by a network of intermolecular forces which may be classed as (1) disulfide cross-links, (2) salt bridges, (3) hydrogen bonds, (4) hydrophobic bonds, and (5) Van der Waals forces.

One of the unique properties of textile fibers, particularly of wool, is the ability to undergo severe dimensional changes when subjected to various combinations of chemical, mechanical and thermal stresses. While each fiber type requires its own specific conditions, the essential sequence in causing such dimensional changes to take place is the severance of intermolecular forces, the relative motion of polymer chains after intermolecular forces have been ruptured, and the subsequent reformation of intermolecular forces which will hold the polymer chains in their new position. The wool fiber presents the best example of such dimensional changes occurring once intermolecular bonds have been broken or at least partially disrupted. . . .

Although the scales and cortex of wool contain the same amino acids, they are not present in the same amounts in each; the scales apparently contain greater amounts of cystine (sulfur-containing acid) than the cortex. In some ways the sulfur linkages are the weakest parts in the structure of wool in that they are the parts most readily attacked by oxidizing and reducing agents, alkalies, and even by light, and are the avenues by which forces leading to the eventual destruction of the fiber make their initial attack.

Properties

Wool has easily identifiable characteristics, when viewed through a microscope, particularly in longitudinal views. In cross section it is similar to other round fibers (see Figure 5-2).

In cross section wool is made up of two, and sometimes three, distinct parts: (1) the outer, horny, transparent, flattened scales (cuticle or epidermis); (2) a cylindrical cortical layer (cortex), which makes up the soft, plastic bulk or body of the fiber; and (3) in the medium and coarser grades, a medulla, or central air-filled canal. These different layers are often made visible by microscopic magnification.

The scales vary in size and in the shape of the projecting ends according to the different types of wool and hair fibers, with the free ends projecting outward and upward toward the tip of the fiber. In the finest wools the scales each encircle the fiber and fit one into another like stacked cups or bowls. In the coarser wools the scales overlap like shingles on a roof, and

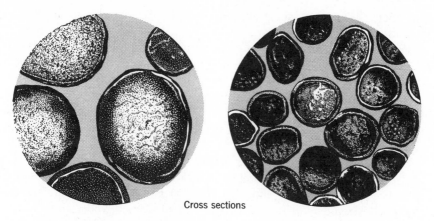

Cross sections

FIGURE 5-2.   Sketch of wool cross sections.

there may be several in an encircling row, depending on the diameter of the fiber. The scale structure makes wool easily identifiable in longitudinal view by means of the microscope alone. Figure 5-3 shows different kinds of scale structure.

The scale structure forms a protective "hide" for the more delicate part of the fiber and gives it form and a certain degree of rigidity. The cortical layer is responsible for the strength and elasticity of the fiber. The medulla increases the insulative property of the fiber by incorporating a built-in air space—the medulla apparently is not needed for fiber growth.

Wool is sometimes said to be the only fiber that possesses all the desirable characteristics of a textile fiber. It is considered one of our most dur-

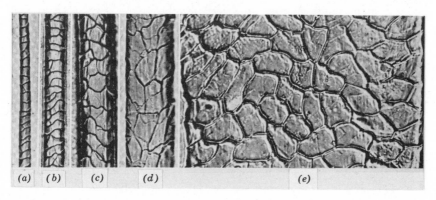

FIGURE 5-3.   Photomicrographs of various types of wool scale structure. (Courtesy E. M. Pohle and W. Von Bergen, Interscience Publishers.)

able fibers, in spite of some weaknesses, because of its combination of properties.

Wool, like human hair, is an outgrowth of the skin. It grows from hair follicles which also have sebaceous (sweat) and oil glands attached; these glands serve the same functions as those for human hair. But where human hairs grow individually, five to ten wool fibers grow in a group, which accounts for the denseness of a fleece. The number of fibers per square inch varies from 8000 to 60,000 in different breeds, with variation on an individual animal.

Fineness of diameter, or fiber width, varies in wool from 0.00039 to 0.00276 inch, or in microns from 10 to more than 70, with fibers from the same fleece varying greatly, especially in carpet wools which contain fibers from one extreme of diameter to the other. Carpet wools also contain kemp fibers that may be up to 200 microns in diameter. The finest wools are most nearly equal in diameter, but they too vary. The fineness of the wool largely determines its use. Except for the trained eyes of experts in the wool industry, human eyes can distinguish differences only between fine and coarse wool fibers. The inability to make finer distinctions is probably partially due to the effects of the crimp and luster of wool.

Lengths of wool fibers vary from 1½ to 15 inches, with the finer types being shorter. Intervals between shearings affect length, and fiber lengths from the same area of the same sheep vary greatly. A standardized method has been devised for arriving at a general average for fiber length of a given quality from a fleece. Diameter and length must be considered together in determining uses for wool fibers. True length is difficult to determine accurately because of the crimp of the fiber.

Fine wools are 1½ to 4 inches long and are noted for softness, fineness, strength, elasticity, and superior spinning and felting qualities. They are used for high-quality flannels and knit goods, broadcloths, meltons, and other face-finished fabrics, for example, uniform and billiard cloths.

Long wools are from 6 to 9 inches in length, coarse, strong, lustrous, and with rather poor felting qualities; they are used for the coarser tweeds, serge, overcoating fabrics, blankets, felts, braids, buntings, and lustrous worsted fabrics.

Medium wools fall between fine and long wools in length and other characteristics and are used for knitted goods of all kinds and for fine tweeds, serges, overcoatings, flannels, and blankets. Crossbreed wools fall into the medium wool class as far as usage is concerned.

Carpet wools, as the name implies, are largely used in the manufacture of carpets and rugs, for other coarse fabrics, felt boots, horse blankets, coarse upholstery fabrics, etc. They contain a mixture of coarse outer hair and finer down from the only types of modern-day sheep that produce

these two coats. Carpet wool properties vary greatly, depending on the qualities and proportions of these two types of fiber and on the proportion of kemp fibers among them. Carpet wools are graded as coarse, medium, and good.

Most clean wool is off-white in color, although gray, brown, and black-wooled sheep are not uncommon in the various breeds, and types of gray-wooled and black-wooled sheep are bred in Russia for their pelts, to be used as certain types of fur. Whiteness of the wool varies from pure white in Australian wool to light and dark ivory in other white wools. Wyoming wool is the whitest produced in the United States. Color is due to pigment in the cortical and medullary areas of the wool; the scales are not pigmented. Colored fleeces must be handled separately from white, and the variations in whiteness mean that wool must often be bleached before it is dyed.

Luster is due to the nature and transparency of the scale structure of wool; it varies among animals and breeds, with the area of a fleece, and with climatic conditions. It is more apparent in aggregates of fibers than in individual fibers, and varies from soft luster for fine, crimpy wools to high luster for some carpet wools and for mohair, a specialty fiber. Luster is more apparent in worsted than in woolen fabrics, and is utilized in design detail and in emphasizing vividness of color in certain types of materials. Shine which develops with use, especially of worsted fabrics, is probably associated with the degree of initial luster of the fiber as well as the type of yarn and fabric, and with the methods used in caring for the fabric—especially pressing.

Wool has a breaking tenacity of 1.0 to 1.7 grams per denier, rather low compared to that of most other fibers, although low strength tends to be compensated for by a high degree of elasticity and elongation. Strength, as with most other properties, varies widely for wool but is fairly constant within grade qualities. There is a direct relation between fiber diameter and strength, with the finest diameter wools being weakest and the coarsest wools strongest. Wool is weaker wet than dry, losing from 10 to 25 percent of its strength when wet but regaining it when dry. What are the implications in this for wear and care of wool fabrics?

Elongation of wool is from 20 to 50 percent, and both elongation and elasticity are usually higher when the wool is wet. It has been shown that wool fibers may be stretched as much as 30 percent for short periods of time without permanent damage. When the strain (stretching force) is released, the fibers recover much of this stretch immediately and within 24 hours have returned fully to their original length. This elasticity is believed to be due to the natural crimp of the fiber and to the helical structure of the molecules, and is important in accounting for the very satisfactory performance of wool fabrics in use. Durability is very de-

pendent on this factor, when the relative weakness of wool is considered. Wool's resistance to wrinkling and creasing, and the fact that wrinkles and creases hang out if a garment is hung where it has room to recover, is largely due to the great degree of elasticity of the fiber. A steam room speeds up such recovery, so that a wrinkled wool garment hung near a steaming tub or shower will be effectively "pressed" in a short while and with no damage such as might occur in pressing with an iron. People who travel often use this method of keeping their clothes pressed. Care must be taken, of course, not to put the garment where the water will splash on it. The steamed garment should be removed to a dry room and allowed to dry before being worn.

Closely associated with elasticity of wool is its resiliency, or ability to recover from compression. Wool is the most resilient of fibers, a factor that makes it eminently suitable for carpets and rugs. Resiliency also contributes to the draping qualities and crease resistance of wool fabrics, and to the fact that it holds its shape well. Resiliency varies with the quality of the wool—damaged wools lose this quality, as well as their elasticity. Associated with resiliency may be a certain amount of rigidity, especially in coarse carpet wools, which helps to prevent their twisting when compressed.

Wool has a natural crimp, often described as "kinky," which varies considerably in numbers and in sizes of the waves, the appearance changing from flat waves to ringlets in different fleeces. Although the number of waves per inch is often considered to bear a direct relation to fineness, and there is a slight tendency toward this relation, crimp is by no means a reliable indication of fineness. The crimp contributes greatly to the elasticity and resiliency of wool and to its crease resistance. Together with the scale surface, the crimp makes possible the spinning of fine and few fibers into yarns and also permits the utilization of very short fibers (noils) that accumulate from processing, as well as those fibers reclaimed from previously manufactured wool products.

Most wool resists abrasion very well. This factor, accounting in part for the durability of wool, is dependent on crimp, elasticity, and resilience of the fibers.

The specific gravity of wool is 1.30, which is about the same as that of silk (1.35) and between those of cotton (1.55) and nylon (1.14). Ability to absorb moisture from the humidity of the air is called *hygroscopicity,* and the amount of such moisture picked up when an oven-dried sample is placed in a room with air at a controlled relative humidity is called *moisture regain.* Wool is the most hygroscopic of fibers; it will pick up 13 to 18 percent moisture from air at the controlled relative humidity (its moisture regain), and as high as 30 percent from air with high relative humidity (90% or more). It does this without feeling damp or uncom-

fortable to the touch. This characteristic presents a problem in buying or selling of either fiber or fabric because a change in climatic conditions can make a considerable change in the weight of the lot of wool. It is now a common practice in many countries to buy and sell on the basis of a certain regain, and temperature- and relative humidity-controlled rooms have been established in various cities for checking on these data.

Because wool reaches moisture equilibrium with saturated air slowly and gives up its moisture slowly, it is a good insulator against sudden chilling; thus it is one of the most comfortable fibers to wear in a cold, damp climate or for a swimsuit.

There has long been considerable controversy over what accounts for the warmth of fabrics. A few years ago many researchers were agreed that warmth depends on the thickness of a fabric and its ability to maintain that thickness (its resilience) rather than on the type of fiber. If this were true, fabrics of equal thickness would be equally warm, regardless of fiber, as long as the thickness remained constant. Wool fabrics, because of fiber crimp, resilience, and elasticity, may retain their original thickness. There is some reason to suspect that for some of the new fibers, however, warmth does not depend solely on the thickness of the fabric.

In fabrics that are worn there are factors other than thickness involved in warmth—factors such as perspiration and its evaporation, the extent to which the mass of fibers entrap and hold air, and the surface roughness or smoothness of fibers and fabrics which determines the extent of actual contact between fabric and human skin.* Softness of fibers and fabrics is probably a factor in warmth because of its effect on drape and conformity to body contours. Much work remains to be done to determine the true factors that constitute warmth of fabrics.

Although wool is a poor conductor of electricity, friction caused by rubbing against the scales will easily generate a static charge. Such static electricity is discharged when the fabric, or person wearing or handling it, comes into contact with a good conductor. This phenomenon is especially noted indoors in winter when relative humidity falls to a low level. Then layers of clothing cling together when the wearer moves and a shock is experienced when the accumulated static electricity is discharged on contact with a conductor, all of which is very annoying to many persons.

* In temperate and warmer climates, comfort necessitates some circulation of air between the skin and the garments covering it in order to permit evaporation of perspiration; there is some evidence that this may not be true in extremely cold climates. In many climatic regions, if moisture is not evaporated from the skin and from the clothing next to the skin, chilling may occur. Studies have shown that the area of contact between fabric and skin is very important in chilling; the greater the area of contact, the greater the degree of chilling. Wool, because of its crimp and resilience, should make little contact with the skin and thus be accompanied by little chilling.

Humidifiers are often installed in mills to keep the moisture content of the air high enough to prevent difficulty in handling on various processing equipment.

Felting, a purely physical phenomenon, is the matting together of fibers in such a way that they cannot be separated again. True felting ability is possessed by only a few animal fibers, of which wool is the most important. Ability to felt is an important characteristic of wool; just how and why it occurs is not definitely known. *Matthews' Textile Fibers* (p. 590) says

. . . To make felting possible a fiber must possess a surface scale structure, ease of deformation, and the power of recovery from deformation. Under the influence of pressure, heat, and moisture the wool fiber tends to migrate in the direction of its root end, owing to its scale structure.

Felting is important in shaping wool fabric to the contours of the human body, without bulk, especially in tailored garments, in making felt fabrics for many uses, in shaping felt hats, and in other ways. It can be a disadvantage, too, if soft sweaters or other wool garments are handled carelessly in washing or pressing.

Wool scorches rather easily and becomes shiny with pressing; it should always be pressed at low temperature on the wrong side, with a pressing cloth or wet paper next to the fabric if a dry iron is used. Scorching damages wool permanently, discoloring it and making it harsh.

Wool is sensitive to degradation by sunlight. Actual photochemical decomposition occurs during weathering, even while on the back of the animal. This leads to brittleness, loss of strength, and yellowing. White wools yellow with age, even if protected from light, although protection slows the process down considerably.

Prolonged dry heat (at temperatures of 212°F or over) damages wool so that it becomes weak and harsh, but prolonged cold has no chemical effect on the fiber. Steam, used over short periods of time, has no damaging effect and permits setting of creases and pleats which are fairly permanent (unless the setting temperature is exceeded) and felting out of excess fullness. Steam under pressure destroys wool rather rapidly; therefore wool cannot be sterilized by boiling or autoclave methods, but it can be sterilized by means of formaldehyde. Formaldehyde also acts as somewhat of a buffer to prevent alkali damage.

Wool is reactive with all types of acids, although not to the same degree for each type. Acid dyes and other acid compounds may be used to obtain color and special effects or to change certain properties, such as the ability to felt.

Alkaline solutions of all types degrade wool very readily. A 5 percent

solution of boiling sodium hydroxide (NaOH) dissolves wool very quickly; this fact is made use of in the laboratory in removing wool from mixture and blended fabrics, and also as an identification test for wool. Even the soaps and soda ash used in scouring (removing grease, suint, and dirt) will damage the fiber unless concentration, temperature, and time are all kept low and are very carefully controlled. Damage is often not revealed through loss of strength because felting and shrinking of the fibers may lead to greater strength. Harshness and low resilience are indications of damage, but they may be difficult to detect until considerable damage has occurred. Ammonium carbonate, borax, and sodium phosphate have less effect on wool than other alkalies and are safe if used carefully. These facts about the effect of soap and other cleaning products, temperature, and time have important implications for the care of wool garments, for example, sweaters that are washed at home. What procedures would you recommend for washing such garments?

Both oxidizing and reducing agents attack the sulfur bonds and must be used judiciously. This fact causes much concern at the mills, for bleaching is carried on by one or the other of these agents. Hydrogen peroxide, an oxidizing agent, gives the best permanent white and is used most often for bleaching wool. Reducing agents produce an initial whiteness which is not permanent.

Although wool does not usually absorb metallic salts readily, magnesium chloride (most often), magnesium sulfate, or zinc chloride gives increased weight to the fabric; the method used is similar to the one for weighting silk. Sometimes calcium or barium thiocyanate solutions are used in conjunction with steam to produce crepe effects in fabrics.

Wool is one of the fibers least likely to be attacked by mildew and bacteria. But from the earliest days in the life of a lamb, wool harbors microorganisms, some of which may be pathogenic, occasionally causing disease in animal or man. Anthrax is a disease sometimes acquired by man from contaminated fleece. Mildew, mold, and other such organisms may be held in the fleece over years of storage, to appear when growing conditions are favorable, unless the wool is treated to prevent this happening. Soaps, wool creams, vegetable oils, and other materials used in conditioning wool for processing may render it more susceptible to attack.

Wool is attacked by both clothing moths and carpet beetles who actually use the fiber for food. The damage is done by larvae. Today there are a number of effective compounds to prevent such attack, many of which can be used in the home; others, which must be applied in the mill or factory, give immunization for periods of time ranging from a year to the life of the article. Mothproofing is discussed further in Chapter 11.

Uses and By-Products

There are probably few ways of utilizing textiles for which wool has not been used sometime, somewhere. Many of today's uses are different from those of former years, but many remain the same. Tables 7, 8, 9, 10, and 11 in Chapter 2 all contain detailed information on the end-uses of wool in the United States. As we examine these tables, we see that most of the wool goes into apparel, with somewhat more being used for women's, children's and infants' apparel than for men's and boys'. Do you find this surprising? Also we note that the wool for apparel is going primarily into coats of various types, jackets, suits, sweaters, skirts, slacks, and dresses— probably about what we would expect from our own experience and observations. It would be interesting to see the geographic distribution for these various items.

You will see from Table 9 that there is still quite a lot of wool going into carpets and rugs although the amount is small in comparison with the man-made fibers. The amount of wool being sold as yard goods (Table 10) may seem low, especially in comparison with the amount of yarn sold —no doubt most of this for hand knitting. Felt is the only industrial use of wool that has any meaning (Table 11). As you study these tables, you will note many interesting details that perhaps give some hint of the future for wool.

Wool has very valuable by-products, largely recovered from the *yolk* removed from the fleece in scouring. Yolk is made up of the wool grease, suint (perspiration products), as well as materials acquired during the time it is attached to the mobile sheep. The amount of yolk, as well as the proportion of the different constituents, varies greatly among breeds, individuals, and different areas. The wool fat forms a protective coating on the surface of the wool fiber, preventing damage and also preventing matting and felting and water absorbency, which, considering the hygroscopicity and high absorption rate of wool, would make a sheep almost helpless in wet weather because of the weight of its wool.

The grease of wool is really an unusual type of wax rather than a grease. In purified form it is called *lanolin*. No doubt you are familar with some of its pharmaceutical and cosmetic uses. Lanolin is a unique product in its ability to penetrate human skin, carrying with it pharmaceutical or other desired products. It is also used a great deal in engineering fields and in the leather goods trades. Potash compounds are recovered from the suint.

New Developments

One of the most important developments attempted in the last quarter century has been the production of nonfelting, washable, and shrink-

proof wool. The processes are not yet perfected, but some are successful enough for a great many million dollars' worth of fabrics and garments to be processed each year.

Shrinkage in wool fabrics or garments is of two kinds, relaxation and felting shrinkage. Relaxation shrinkage is common to all fabrics; it occurs when yarns stretched in one or both directions in weaving or knitting relax from this tension when put in water. This can be controlled by relaxing the fabric during finishing. Relaxation shrinkage occurs the first time the fabric or garment is placed in water; it also occurs (more slowly) with steaming and steam pressing.

Felting shrinkage occurs in washing because there are present the conditions previously discussed that cause fibers to travel toward their root ends and to mat together. Felting shrinkage may occur at any time the correct conditions (heat, pressure, moisture, alkalinity) are present and may occur in more than one washing. Its control depends on altering or destroying the scale edges, or destroying the elasticity of the cortex; the former is the more desirable, for the elasticity of wool is one of its greatest assets. Nonfelting wool is attained most often at present by chlorination treatment with either an acid chlorine solution (called "wet chlorination") or gaseous chlorine. It is difficult to control these processes, especially the wet process, and to affect only the surface because wool has a great affinity for chlorine.

Another process for controlling felting shrinkage is treatment with melamine-formaldehyde resin. After application, heat curing causes this resin to polymerize both in the cortex and on the scale surface so that elasticity and friction are both reduced, and conditions for felting are thus removed. This process, too, is not entirely successful.

The various processes are successful enough, however, that the U.S. Quartermaster Corps, which is responsible for much of the research reported in controlling shrinkage of wool, requires wool for socks, undergarments, and shirts for the armed services to be so treated; it accepts either process which meets specifications for dimensional stability. During and since World War II, millions of dollars per year have been saved just on wool socks alone. Before nonfelting wool was required, socks worn in the services shrank so much because of the methods by which the men cared for them that they had to be discarded after a few washings, sometimes after the first one.

These treatments, however, are not desirable for all wool garments and fabrics. The properties they destroy are sometimes those most valued in attaining or maintaining desirable effects in other garments, especially in tailoring. A nonfelting sock yarn (wool) may be most undesirable for a sweater; nonfelting wool yarns sometimes stretch in washing.

One of the newer procedures for controlling felting shrinkage of wool and adding to its washability is a process developed at the USDA Western Regional Research Laboratory in Albany, California. The name "Wurlan" has been given to the process. The Wurlan process, commonly described as interfacial polymerization (IFP), changes the surface of the wool fibers by inducing polymerization of a polyamide on the surface of the wool fiber, thus forming a "skin." Any one of a number of polyamides might be used; hexamethylene sebacamide has given the best results in experimental work.

The process consists of immersing the wool in an aqueous solution of the diamine, removing excess solution, then immersing briefly in a diacid chloride solution, again removing the excess, rinsing, and drying. A polyamide resin forms almost instantly at the fiber surface. The treatment is said to have only a minor, and not a degrading, effect on the physical and chemical properties of the wool. The wool can be treated in fiber, yarn, or fabric state, but the latter two seem to result in the most desirable product. The process seems to be suited also to polymerization by means of polyesters, polyureas, and polycarbonates on wool fiber surfaces.

Interfacial polymerization does not result in completely shrinkproof wool. Interest now has gone further along this line to development of durable press wool fabrics. Australia, too, has much interest in such developments and is concentrating considerable research effort in achieving washable, drip-dry, no-iron wool fabrics.

Experimental attempts to replace sulfur linkages with metallic salt linkages, thus leading to a more stable wool, have been more or less successful and may lead to modified wools with still more advantages and fewer disadvantages than today's wool.

There is a trend today to mix and blend wool with some of the man-made fibers in order to obtain special properties or different effects than can be achieved with any one fiber alone. Washable easy-care fabrics are an example. These topics are discussed in Chapters 13 and 14.

THE MINOR NATURAL PROTEIN FIBERS

alpaca	feathers	mohair
angora (goat)	fur fibers	qiviut
camel	guanaco	rabbit (not Angora)
cashmere	horse hair	vicuna
cow hair	llama	

The minor natural protein fibers are often known as specialty fibers since they, too, form the fur or hair coating of animals. They can be

expected to have the same general structure as wool and to behave similarly. The name "specialty fibers" is recognized for such fibers in the Wool Products Labeling Act. These fibers are used to a much lesser degree than wool, and some have very limited usage because of the nature of the fiber, its scarcity, cost, etc. They include camel, guanaco, llama, alpaca, vicuna, cashmere, mohair, angora, rabbit, qiviut, cow, and horse wool or hair fibers, and may even include feathers. A number are used as fur as well as fiber.

Except for cashmere, in which scales are visible, and mohair, in which they are faintly visible, these fibers have indistinct scales, although scales on all may be seen with equipment that is discriminating enough. They have the same burning and chemical properties as wool, and they resemble wool in cross section. All are subject to attack by moths. Human hair is the strongest of all the hair or fur fibers, followed by mohair, long-fiber wools, horsehair, camel's hair, alpaca, medium-fiber wools, and fine-fiber wools.

Most of these fibers are used in apparel fabrics, and a few are used in textile furnishing fabrics. They may be used alone or with wool to produce softness, luster, design, or other special effects. The quality of the resulting fabric depends not only on the quality of the special fibers, but also on the quality of the wool or other fibers with which they are blended.

A more detailed study of these fibers may be found in earlier editions of this book and in the *Wool Handbook, Vol. I*. The latter also contains photographs of some of the animals.

SILK

Throughout the many centuries of its use, dating back at least to 2640 B.C., silk has been considered one of the most elegant and luxurious of fibers. It is still so considered by many people of the world, despite all the advances in fiber technology which have given us a great array of competitive man-made fibers. Silk, in the Western world at least, has had a long, erratic history.

The discovery of the method for raising silkworms, of removing the silk filaments from the cocoons, and of using the silk in weaving for garments is credited to Si-ling-chi, a little empress of long-ago China, from whose name the fiber has derived its name.

Walton, in *The Story of Textiles* (pp. 45, 46–48), has made these interesting statements concerning the history of silk:

Like wool, cotton, and flax, the date of the origin of silk is uncertain. Very early it was in use in the East, and well into modern times it continued

to be the fabric used exclusively by the nobility, or royalty. In fact, the earliest historic reference has a royal setting, and comes from the East. According to Chinese history, silk was used in China thousands of years before Christ. . . .

The art subsequently spread to India, where it was introduced by a Chinese princess, who carried the silkworm eggs and seeds of the mulberry-tree concealed in the lining of her head-dress; and by India the silk was made known to Europe. For many centuries, however, the Chinese had a monopoly of the industry, and Tartar caravans carried loads of silk, which they sold to Persian and Arabian traders.

The knowledge of silk was brought to Europe by Alexander the Great (356–323 B.C.) when he returned from India, and Aristotle gave full particulars of the silkworm, describing it as a horned worm which he called Bombyx. . . .

The knowledge of silk brought by Alexander seems, however, to have been lost, for the Romans later obtained silk from the Greeks and thought that it was a fleece that grew upon trees. This became the early belief of the western world. Nearchus evidently confused silk with cotton; Virgil supposed silk was carded from leaves; Dionysius thought it was combed from flowers; while Pliny (23–79 A.D.) describes the Bombyx, but makes it a native of Assyria.

It is impossible to say when silk came into use among the higher classes of Rome, but there is authority for believing that it was first worn in Rome during the supremacy of Julius Caesar (61–44 B.C.), and from then on became the dress garment of the Roman nobility. Its price was very high, selling for its weight in gold. Nevertheless, silk had such a vogue among the wealthy classes that the Emperor Tiberius prohibited men from wearing it on the ground that it was effeminate, and Roman satirists denounced the wearing of the transparent silk of Cos by either sex because of the indecency. Emperor Heliogabulus, in 222 A.D., shocked his subjects by appearing in a garment of thin silk, while Emperor Aurelian in 273 A.D. refused the plea of his wife for a single garment of purple silk on the ground of extravagance, saying that a pound of silk sold for its weight in gold, and that wearing it would be an example of extravagance.

Ammianus Marcellinus, 380 A.D., stated that silk had come within the reach of the common people. A decree of the Emperor Justinian (518–565 A.D.), that silk should be sold for eight pieces of gold per pound, or about $15, together with a war with Persia whose traders were the carriers of silk, cut off all importation and ruined the silk merchants.

The situation was relieved by two Persian monks, who had become familiar with the silk industry while on a religious embassy to the Chinese, and who informed Justinian that they could secure from China the means of establishing the industry. Accordingly, at Justinian's command they returned to China, observed carefully the whole process of the industry, and 536 A.D. brought back to Constantinople the seeds of the mulberry-tree and the eggs of the silkworm concealed in hollow staves, and thus was the silk industry

established in Europe. Byzantine silk soon came much in demand for ecclesiastical purposes.

From these beginnings the use of silk spread throughout Europe, and by the Middle Ages it was so much in vogue that a thousand knights, and presumably their ladies, appeared dressed in silk for the wedding of the daughter of Henry III of England in 1251 (or thereabout). Queen Elizabeth I and her court are credited with being the first to wear silk stockings, and the queen, at least, had some that were especially knitted for her. The silk trade was well established in France by 1600.

Attempts to establish a silk industry in a number of colonies in colonial America were encouraged in many ways, both by England and by the local governments. The American effort was aided, if not made possible, by immigrations of skilled silk workmen from France and England because of religious persecution or the competitive situation at home. Attempts were also made later to establish a silk industry in the Midwest, in the Far West, and, even as late as during World War II, in the Southwest. The silk industry in America, however, with the exception of a few famous mills in Connecticut and a considerable industry centered around Paterson, New Jersey, was largely a series of beginnings and failures, with one small group taking up an attempt as another small group failed, often with the same equipment and in the same mill. Poor and outmoded mill equipment, widely fluctuating silk prices, and high labor costs contributed to the failure of the industry; competition from the man-made fibers was the final blow to the already ailing mills. Those silk mills still remaining work with man-made fibers too, and silk fabrics are the lesser part of their production. Silk for women's hosiery, which used a large part of all silk coming into the United States, was almost entirely replaced by nylon as soon as sufficient supplies of that fiber became available. Silk has made little return to this end-use.

Although silk is popular again today in certain fashion circles, the fabrics or garments are often those imported from France, Italy, Japan, and, in some instances, from Thailand. Some of the silk imported into the United States is still manufactured into fabric or items here.

Production and Source

Although silk is not produced in the United States and only a small part of the world's silk production is used here, we need to have some knowledge of its present position and to consider its future status. Because so little silk is produced today in relation to the other major fibers, few data are available here covering the industry as a whole. Japan, Thailand,

Italy, and France apparently remain the leading producers of silk but data on their relative positions are not readily available.

Silk is an expensive fiber, and prices of raw silk fluctuate rapidly and widely. This affects its use, especially among producers of fabrics for mass markets, even in blends where a fairly low percentage would likely be used. As was reported in *Daily News Record* for March 15, 1966, one mill man said

A 20 percent silk fabric represents five or six pounds of silk per one hundred yards. An upsurge of $2 a pound is not unusual, and that means 10 cents a yard. A high style fabric is another matter, but a silk content fabric cannot be mass produced and merchandised on this basis.

Silk has always been a very small percentage of the total amount of fiber produced in the world (see Table 3, Chapter 2) and used in the United States. In no year since 1890 has world production of silk totaled more than 1 percent of total fiber production, and it has not reached that level since 1943. A few months before the United States was forced to enter World War II, silk supplies were cut off entirely, and on July 16, 1941, the considerable supply of silk in the United States was "frozen" for military uses by the Office of Production Management; at that time and throughout most of that war, no fiber other than silk had ever been used as a parachute for human beings.

Consumption of silk in the United States is shown in Table 5 (Chapter 2) for five-year intervals beginning with 1920, and for 1968. All this silk was imported.

Silk, as a luxury fiber and the only fiber of its general type until the nylons and polyesters were developed although a few filament rayon and acetate fabrics more or less simulated silk in appearance, presents an interesting reflection of the economic condition of the country during the years shown. The figure for 1920 is quite low for the era and undoubtedly reflects the high prices and unstable economy following the end of World War I. The economy recovered quite well and stabilized in the 1920's, to be hit by the stock market crash in late 1929. Since this was not fully felt throughout the economy for another year or two, the 1930 figures for silk are still pretty high. The 1945 figure shows the effects of World War II, and those for 1950 and 1955, the beginning of the return of silk to the market, but also the new factor of competition with nylon. The later figures reflect the ever-increasing effect of the new nylons, polyesters, and other fibers on silk.

Silk is not the hair or fur covering of an animal, as are other natural protein fibers, but is the material extruded from glands in the body of the animal in spinning its cocoon or web. In several ways the processes used by

caterpillars and spiders are similar to those used by man in producing man-made fibers; in fact, man has attempted to imitate the animal kingdom. The man-made fibers are more like silk than are any of the other natural fibers, and in some ways silk itself resembles the man-made fibers more than it does the other natural fibers.

Commercial silk is produced by the cultivated silkworm, *Bombyx mori*, really a caterpillar, which feeds on mulberry leaves, or by one of its relatives, the most important being the *Antheraea pernyi*, which produces wild or tussah silk. The wild caterpillars feed on a specie of oak leaves. Spiders also produce a limited amount of very beautiful and delicate silk fiber. One or two species of spiders produce a fiber that is utilized in the optical industry for crosslines in sensitive instruments such as microscopes, telescopes, and surveying instruments.

The silk caterpillar goes through four distinct stages in its life cycle: egg, larva to caterpillar, pupa or chrysalis, and moth. Each stage of the cycle is very carefully and scientifically controlled in the major silk-producing countries. The life cycle takes 36 to 63 days, depending on conditions, and germination of the eggs can be controlled to permit year-round cultivation of caterpillars in all their life cycles. The silk caterpillars are subject to a number of diseases, all of which affect the quantity and quality of the silk produced; since most of the diseases can be controlled through X-ray detection of disease in the female moth and her eggs, the egg-producing part of the industry is extremely important. The silk fiber is produced at the end of the larva cycle. The larva emerges from the egg as a tiny "ant" about 3 millimeters long; during the following period of 20 to 30 days it eats mulberry (or oak) leaves voraciously, sheds its outgrown skin four times, and achieves a length 160 to 300 times its original length and a weight almost 10,000 times that of the ant. This period has prepared it for the rest of its life, for it has no mouth in subsequent stages. The silk filament is produced for the cocoon for the dormant stage when the caterpillar is becoming a stub-winged moth which will never be able to fly, as most moths and butterflies can.

The silk is formed in two glands, one on each side of the caterpillar's body, which come together in one exit tube in the head, called a *spinneret*, where a silk glue, sericin, from another pair of glands is also secreted. As the two tiny filaments of silk fibroin are extruded from the glands into the tube they begin to "set," are coated with the glue, and all together, when extruded from the spinneret into the air, harden into the continuous-filament raw silk fiber. Each raw silk fiber, then, consists of two fine filaments of silk, coated and glued together with sericin. The twin-fiber filament is silk; the sericin is usually removed in later processing and is not silk.

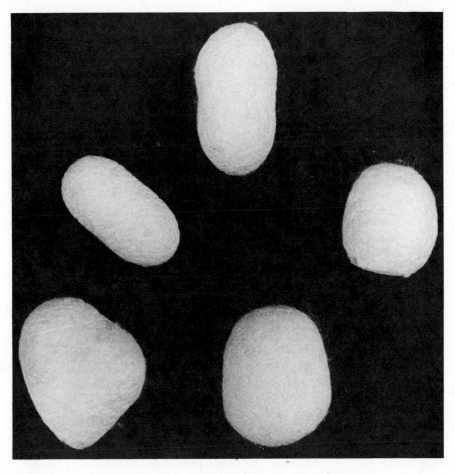

FIGURE 5-4. Silk cocoons. Cocoon at lower left is a double cocoon.

The caterpillar spins its cocoon from the sericin-coated silk filaments, beginning at the outside and working in, in a figure-eight motion of its head and upper body. During the 2 to 5 days it takes to complete the cocoon, the caterpillar spins a continuous filament 400 to 1300 yards long. The gum helps to hold the cocoon together. (See Figure 5-4).

If allowed to emerge from the chrysalis in the normal life cycle, the moth would damage an end of the cocoon, so only those moths desired for reproduction are permitted to cut through the cocoon with the aid of a secretion from their bodies. Others are killed by heat, or are stored under freezing conditions to keep the pupae dormant until the silk is to be unwound from the cocoons. Quite often two caterpillars working to-

gether produce a double cocoon, the silk from which is called "Dupion silk." It is difficult to unreel and varies much along its length, having thick and thin spots and knots. Dupion silk is used in making slub-textured fabric, at times very much in demand.

Processes

Since silk comes from the cocoon, with certain exceptions, as a continuous filament, there are relatively few processes involved in producing yarn or fabric. Only *reeling* and *throwing* will be discussed here.

REELING

This is the process of unwinding the silk filament from the cocoon. The fiber is of great delicacy, and in order to handle silk in subsequent processes, filaments from several cocoons (two to five) must be unwound at the same time and combined. The cocoons are usually placed in warm water to soften the sericin, and the outside of the cocoon is brushed to locate the end of the filament. Then the filaments are placed together and given just enough twist to hold them. The gum helps to hold the filaments together. Great skill is required to handle the filaments without tangling or breaking them. Since filaments become finer toward the center of the cocoon, as they are unwound it is essential to start new cocoons at intervals so that the resulting thread will be fairly even in diameter.

THROWING

Throwing is the operation of combining several reeled strands to make a yarn. The number of strands combined and the amount of twist they are given is determined by the use to be made of the yarn.

Short pieces of filament from punctured cocoons from which the moth has been allowed to escape, short pieces brushed off the outside of the cocoons in preparation for reeling, matted pieces from the inside of the cocoon, and pieces resulting from breaking in the various processing manipulations are spun, as any short fiber, in making dull-textured spun silk fabrics.

Structure

Raw silk is composed of two proteins: *fibroin*, which is the fiber itself, accounts for 75 to 85 percent of the total fiber weight, and *serecin*, the gum that cements the twin filaments together (and is usually removed in processing), which accounts for 15 to 25 percent of total fiber weight. Only the fibroin is of particular interest to those concerned with fibers.

Silk fibroin, according to the *Harris Handbook of Textile Fibers* (Table 3, p. 60), is composed of 15 amino acid residues, several in trace amounts.

It is composed in greatest amounts of glycine, alanine, serine, and tyrosine. Silk is made up of most of the same amino acid residues as wool but in very different proportions. Silk contains no tryptophan, hydroxylysine, cystine, or methionine, thus no sulfur. Silk is composed of considerably higher proportions of glycine, alanine, serine, and tyrosine than wool, and considerably lower proportions of glutamic and aspartic acids, arginine, and threonine. If you look at a table showing the chemical structure of these various amino acids (such as Table 9, p. 222 in the *Wool Handbook, Vol. I*) you will note that most of the acids present in greatest amounts in silk are relatively simple acids of low molecular weight with simple side chains. By contrast, the acids present in greatest amounts in wool are the acids of high molecular weight with complex side chains. These differences largely account for the differences in physical structure and behavior between silk and wool fibers.

With the relatively simple and uncluttered molecular chains of silk, the chains can fold more readily into a regular structure and can pack closer together than can wool with its more bulky structure and complex side chains. Silk is believed to form the pleated-sheet structure theorized by Pauling and Corey, in which the zig-zag folded individual chains form CO and NH bonds with adjacent chains. Such pleated sheet arrangements may be either parallel or antiparallel as shown in these diagrams.

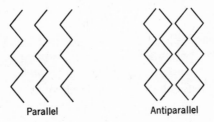

Parallel   Antiparallel

Silk probably assumes the antiparallel form. Such a structure could account to a great extent for the elasticity and resiliency of silk.

Silk, though a smooth, continuous filament fiber, is composed of fibrils just as the other protein fibers. These fibrils can be faintly seen as longitudinal striations in wild silk by means of a compound microscope, and can be made faintly visible in cultivated silk with certain acid treatments.

Properties of Silk

Longitudinally, degummed silk appears as a smooth, lustrous, translucent filament and may show slight variations in diameter along its length. Raw silk, with the gum still on, appears irregular and bumpy.

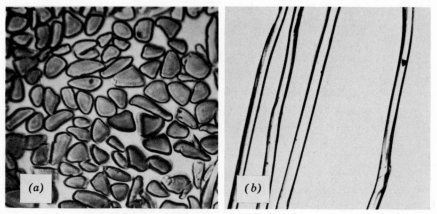

FIGURE 5-5. Photomicrographs of silk: (a) cross sections; (b) longitudinal. (Courtesy E. I. duPont de Nemours & Co. Inc.)

Striations may sometimes be seen along the length of wild silk. In cross section, silk is triangular in shape, with the corners somewhat rounded. Cultivated silk cross sections resemble equilateral triangles, and those of wild silk, isosceles (elongated) triangles. (See Figure 5-5).

Silk burns about like wool, with an odor (less strong than in wool) of burning hair or feathers, and leaves a black residue. Thin silks flame readily. Weighted silk holds its shape as it burns (the metallic weighting) and does not crumble; pure dye silk rolls up into tiny black beads that are easily crushed with the fingers.

Silk varies from 5 to 23 microns in diameter, with wild silk being coarser and sometimes exceeding these figures. Length of a filament, if taken unbroken from the cocoon, varies from 400 to 1300 yards. There is considerable variation among cocoons, depending on the type of caterpillar, its health, care, surrounding environment, and the amount, cleanness, and quality of its food, and other less obvious factors.

Silk is a lightweight fiber with a specific gravity of 1.25 to 1.33. It has hygroscopicity about equal to that of wool, which it also resembles in absorbency and electrical properties.

Cultivated silk fiber is white, although the raw fiber may appear to be yellow to gray because of the color of the sericin. Wild silk is a tan color, possibly best illustrated in natural-colored pongee, which is made of wild silk. Silk has a natural, rich, soft luster.

The breaking tenacity of silk is 2.2 to 4.6 grams per denier; it is slightly weaker when wet than when dry. Its elasticity and resilience are good, ranking between cotton and linen at one end of a scale and wool

at the other. Although the fiber itself is washable, fabrics and garments are often so constructed that dry cleaning is advisable.

Silk is warm and pleasant to the touch and is generally considered comfortable to wear.

Chemically, silk reacts much as does wool to different acid and alkaline substances, although it often reacts less quickly.

Silk is readily dyeable with a variety of dyes and has an affinity for metallic salts; the affinity for metallic salts has led to the process of *weighting,* and often to overweighting of silk.

WEIGHTING

Weighting is the process of treating silk with certain metallic salts to give weight and body to the product. It originally was supposed to have been used to replace the weight of sericin (up to 20 percent of raw-fiber weight) removed in degumming, which left the amount of expensive fiber very much reduced. For various reasons, silk was often overweighted, that is, given higher percentages of weighting than that which would just replace the gum removed. It was found that by repeating certain processes several times, the amount of weighting could be increased with each "pass" until it far exceeded the weight of the fiber. Metallic salts of lead, zinc, and tin have been used for this purpose, although lead was largely discontinued years ago because it is a health hazard. Some weighting apparently does not harm the fiber and does improve the "hand" and body of fabrics for certain uses. Overweighting, however, damages the fibers, causing the fabric to become tender and to split easily and rendering it more sensitive to light degradation.

Because overweighting of silk had become a widespread, highly competitive, and unscrupulous practice in many instances, the Federal Trade Commission, in its *Trade Practice Rules for the Silk Industry* (1938), ruled that any silk fabric, except black, that has more than 10 percent metallic weighting must be labeled *weighted silk.* Black silk may have up to 15 percent weighting without being so labeled because of the nature of the processes required for dyeing a good black on silk. Fabrics with less than these specified amounts of weighting may be labeled *pure dye silk,* a term that has nothing whatever to do with dyes or their purity.

With the public acceptance of cheaper man-made fibers, which do not require weighting to achieve desired properties, and the virtual disappearance of silk from the market in the 1940's, weighted silk has not returned to the market to any considerable extent.

Silk is affected adversely by sunlight (ultraviolet), being degraded considerably within a few months' time, and white silk tends to yellow with age. Weighted silk, in particular, is subject to perspiration degradation,

and dyed silks of all types are likely to be considerably discolored, if not damaged, by perspiration. Silk can withstand somewhat higher pressing and processing temperatures than wool.

Silk is not subject to moth attack and is less likely than cotton and linen to be attacked by mildew, rot, and mold.

Uses

A United States end-use survey (*Textile Organon,* January 1969) included a number of uses for silk, but the amount of silk was included with other fibers and cannot be ascertained. The uses, however, are interesting. Silk was listed for the following end-uses: for men's and boys' wear—light- and medium-weight suits, separate coats and slacks, robes, neckties, business, dress, and sport shirts, nightwear, and hose; for women's, misses', children's, and infants' wear—suits, skirts, slacks, dresses, jackets, coats, loungewear, blouses and shirts, knit and woven underwear and nightwear, hosiery, gloves, and apparel lace; for home furnishings—sheets and pillowcases, woven and lace napery, upholstery, and drapes; for other consumer products—apparel linings, retail piece goods, narrow fabrics, shoes and slippers, luggage, handbags, and sports equipment; and for industrial uses—electrical applications, cordage, and casket linings.

Some silk producers have been carrying on a campaign in the United States to recover markets for silk; some are quite optimistic about the prospects. The consensus among mill men in the United States, however, seems to be that silk has lost out forever to man-made fibers for most end-uses. The announcement of the new Qiana nylon has added to the uncertainties for silk. And in late 1968 came the announcement from Japan that production of silk had been on the rise for the year but that consumption had not risen, so a silk surplus was in prospect. No one was ready to predict what effect this would have in world silk markets.

FOR FURTHER READING

American Fabrics.

The Encyclopedia Americana.

The Encyclopedia Britannica.

Fieser, L. F. and Fieser, M.: *Advanced Organic Chemistry.*

Harris, M.: *Handbook of Textile Fibers.*

Hollen, N. R. and Saddler, J.: *Textiles.*

Linton, G. E.: *Natural and Man-made Textile Fibers.*

Mauersberger, H. R. (ed.): *Matthews' Textile Fibers* (1954).

National Advisory Commission on Food and Fiber: *Cotton and Other Fiber Problems and Policies in the United States.* Technical Papers Vol. 2.

Stout, E. E.: *Introduction to Textiles*. (1960 and 1965).
Von Bergen, W. (ed.): *Wool Handbook* Vol. I.
Walton. P.: *The Story of Textiles*.
Weibel, A. C.: *Two Thousand Years of Textiles*.
The World Book Encyclopedia.

THE NONTHERMOPLASTIC
MAN-MADE FIBERS

The whole man-made fiber industry is a fantastic development of the past three-quarters of a century, during the early part of which attempts to produce "artificial silk" commercially, resulting in a fiber now known as "rayon," was the modest beginning. From this early success, which was a real breakthrough in textile development, research into fiber structure and polymerization grew until the first truly man-synthesized fiber, nylon, was produced in 1938. The successful synthesis of fibers from materials having none of the characteristics of fibers, together with the making of new fibers from materials originally fibrous in nature, has led to the present group of seventeen generic classes of man-made fibers in the United States with the many trademarked names for fibers, yarns, and fabrics seen everywhere today. We certainly need the classifications of the Textile Fiber Products Identification Act and other provisions to guide us in selecting those that best meet our various needs. According to *Textile Organon* for June 1969 there were, when the data were assembled, 981 plants in the world for production of one or more kinds of man-made fiber. These were widely distributed among countries with 290 in Western Europe, 218 in Africa, Asia, Australia, and environs, 223 in North America,

103 in Eastern Europe, and 87 in South America. The number of plants in Communist countries were usually estimates. Of all these plants, 191 produce rayon, 52 acetate, 70 acrylics, 81 glass, 228 nylon, 157 olefin, 128 polyester, and 74 produce a variety of other fibers that were not designated.

All the man-made fibers have some processes in common. They have been produced from nonfibrous materials, or, if fibrous to begin with, have somewhere in processing lost their fibrous structure and must then, from a viscous state, be reformed into fibers. This is usually done by forcing the solutions through devices called *spinnerets*. All the fibers must then coagulate or harden within a reasonable time after leaving the spinnerets so that they will not stick together and may be wound on bobbins or cones, or be deposited in "pots" as cakes of yarn, and readied for conventional processing into fabrics.

The man-made fibers described in this book are divided into two major classifications, nonthermoplastic and thermoplastic. These classifications are based on properties that largely determine the use and care required by the fibers and the fabrics made from them.

The nonthermoplastic group of man-made fibers includes several subgroups, those of cellulosic origin, alginates, minerals, and protein-base fibers. The largest group at present are the fibers of cellulosic origin, all of which are identified as rayon in the Federal Trade Commission (FTC) rules for interpreting the Textile Fiber Products Identification Act.

The nonthermoplastic fibers, except for the mineral fibers, may be cared for much as cotton, linen, silk, or wool, whichever they most resemble, both in their visible characteristics and in their reactions. They are not softened by heat and therefore will not melt if ironed, although they will scorch if ironed at sufficiently high temperatures. As a group they are soft, absorbent, pliable, and comfortable to wear, do not pill, do not accumulate charges of static electricity, and are not subject to attack by moths. In longitudinal view under the microscope, nonthermoplastic fibers, like most other man-made fibers, look very much alike. All appear as smooth rods, black-speckled if delustered, but with no characteristics by which the individual fibers can be positively identified from longitudinal microscopic views alone, as can cotton and wool.

The mineral fibers, both natural and man-made, are different in many ways from all the other fibers and are discussed separately in Chapter 8.

THE RAYONS (CELLULOSIC FIBERS)

We shall begin our study of rayon by defining it according to FTC rules for interpretation of the Textile Fiber Products Identification Act, which says

rayon—a manufactured fiber composed of regenerated cellulose, as well as manufactured fibers composed of regenerated cellulose in which substituents have replaced not more than 15% of the hydrogen of the hydroxyl (OH) groups.

It is an interesting fact that much of rayon's early development is tied to the attempts to develop filaments for incandescent electric lamps, then newly developed by Thomas A. Edison and his co-workers. Not, however, that the search for filaments for lamps necessarily led to the invention of textile fibers!

Many accounts of the development of rayon explore in considerable detail the early suggestions and attempts for making artificial silk without benefit of silkworms. Some of the men and their dates are Dr. Robert Hooke and René F. Réaumur, who predicted such a possibility in 1664 and 1710, respectively; F. G. Keller (1840), inventor of a mechanical process for producing wood pulp, and Louis Schwabe (1840), who experimented with a crude type of spinneret for drawing various solutions through holes into thread form.

Since nitrocellulose rayon was the first rayon to be produced successfully and commercially, the early history of this kind is of importance here. The work of Keller and Schwabe was basic to the development of all types of rayon. In 1855, George Audemars (Switzerland) patented a process for transforming nitrocellulose solution into fine threads; and in 1877, Sir Joseph Swan, co-worker of Edison, turned his attention to textiles for lamp filaments. The result of his efforts, displayed in 1885 at the London Fair, was an "artificial silk" fabric made from fibers that he obtained by forcing collodion through fine holes into a coagulating and denitrating bath. If Swan had exploited this feat, he might have been called the "Father of Rayon," the title bestowed on Count Hilaire de Chardonnet, of France, who purposely set out to find a method for producing artificial silk for fabric use.

The _Rayon and Staple Fiber Handbook_ (pp. 2–3) has given this account of Chardonnet's work:

From a textile point of view, Count Hilaire de Chardonnet began his work in 1878 and obtained his first French patent on November 11th, 1884, culminating all the efforts of his predecessors Hooke, Réaumur, Audemars, Ozanam, Weston, Hughes, Powell, Evans, Wynne, Crooks, and Swinburne. His labors have won him by general acclaim the title of "Father of the Rayon Industry." . . .

He was a purposeful research worker, a pupil of Pasteur and trained at the Ecole Polytechnique of Paris. Chardonnet made a careful study of the silk worm, its habits and its method of producing silk. He based his procedure on this study and proceeded to exhibit the fruits of his labor in 1889. The great

Paris Exhibition attracted the attention of capitalists, who provided the funds for the first artificial silk factory at Bensançon, his birthplace, using the nitrocellulose process. Within two years, many technical problems were overcome in connection with large-scale production, denitration, and rendering the filaments non-inflammable. *This marks the birth of the commercial rayon industry.* Of course, the process was still in a new, crude state and many modifications and improvements had to be made. The Tubize Co. established the use of the process in Belgium and in 1920 in the United States.

The interesting part about Chardonnet's work is that he lived to see the commercial culmination of his labor before he died in 1924.

The other rayon processes, for cuprammonium, and viscose, followed soon after and are the two processes still used. Acetate, a cellulose derivative developed about this same time, is not considered a rayon in the United States but is still so regarded in a great many other countries. Except for its early history when it was considered a rayon, acetate will be discussed with other man-made thermoplastic fibers. The production of nitrocellulose rayon, Chardonnet's original process, required denitration steps to control explosiveness and flammability of the fiber, and was more expensive than the other processes; this rayon is no longer produced anywhere in the world, and in the United States (where it was known as Tubize) it was discontinued in 1934.

Several developments which over the years have been of considerable interest to the man-made fiber industry as a whole, and for the cellulosic fibers in particular, are mentioned here briefly, with their dates.

Charles F. Topham, in 1902, developed the "pot" system of spinning which, by rapid centrifugal force, permits the filaments (with a little twist) to be deposited into a hollow-centered "cake" form, in which shape the filaments are adaptable for further processing and dyeing without the necessity of rewinding.

In 1916, a German company produced the first staple rayon yarn, a process little noted at the time but destined to become important later on.

In 1919, the price of silk reached $20 per pound, whereas rayon, which hit a high of $6 per pound early that year, dropped to $2.50 by October— the high price of silk hastening the day for man-made fibers to dominate the silk market.

In 1924, the name *rayon* was coined and voluntarily adopted by the industry; efforts were then concentrated on developing the new fibers as fibers in their own right rather than as substitutes for silk. Among other things, protests of silk manufacturers over the term *artificial silk* were instrumental in causing the National Association of Manufacturers to appoint a committee to suggest a new name. *Rayon* was their recommendation.

In 1926, rayon consumption in the United States moved up to third place, following cotton and wool, and exceeded silk for the first time. In this same year the first rayon with a dull luster was made. This development permitted the eventual control of luster to any degree of brightness or dullness desired, replacing the extremely bright metallic luster of early rayon, then considered cheap looking. This advance was of special significance to hosiery and lingerie manufacturers.

In 1927, it was discovered that rayon was adaptable to making crepes of all degrees of pebble, and it quickly took the lead in the crepe fabric field; in 1927 the first rayon staple length fiber in the United States was produced, but few mills were interested.

In 1937, the first synthetic resin finish was offered for rayon; the first high-strength rayon was produced (DuPont's Cordura); three companies in collaboration succeeded in producing the first rayon tire cord; the first plant in the United States devoted exclusively to staple fiber production began operation; Japan took its place with the United States, as a leading rayon-producing country; and the FTC promulgated the first Rayon Trade Practice Rules, to be discussed later.

In 1946, viscose staple rayon undersold cotton in price per pound for the first time.

In 1951, the FTC promulgated the trade practice rules establishing regenerated cellulose fibers as rayon and removing cellulose acetate fibers from the rayon classification. Since this practice went into effect in 1952, it explains why books published before or about 1952 and persons accustomed to the old nomenclature call acetate "acetate rayon." A few garment manufacturers still indiscriminately put rayon labels in garments made of acetate as well as in those that really are rayon.

In 1954, in the United States, the production of staple fiber first exceeded that of filament fiber, and it has held this place ever since.

In 1958, Courtaulds (Alabama)* announced the new cross-linked cellulosic fibers Corval and Topel. These were the first of a growing number of cross-linked and high-wet-modulus fibers which may well be destined to revitalize the cellulosic fiber industry.

Improvements have been made constantly since the first successful rayon fiber was produced by Chardonnet, and they continue to appear in all processes all the time, so that today's fibers bear little resemblance to their originals. Many of the fiber-producing companies are research leaders today. We now have rayons varying in luster from dull to very bright, in a wide range of deniers from very fine to very coarse, in varying strengths from low to very high, and with varying degrees of bulk, to

* Now Courtaulds North America, Inc.

mention only a few possibilities. Today rayon ranks second only to cotton in the amount produced and consumed in the United States and, pound for pound, is often cheaper than cotton.

Economic Status

Although rayon first went into production in the United States in 1910, it today ranks second in amount produced among United States fibers, represents a huge investment in money and machinery, and gives employment to a large segment of our population. Whereas textile industries used to be concentrated largely along the Atlantic seaboard, now many are found in the Southeast as well as in other parts of the country. Many factors have entered into the decisions of manufacturers to move from the East and to locate textile and other industries in the South. From your knowledge of the history of our country, how many of these factors can you identify? How many of the following reasons do you think have influence on the decisions and to what extent? Available supply of laborers from largely rural areas, because of the shift to mechanized farm production, many of whom are already familiar with textile millwork; cheap electric power from government-built dam projects; community programs for development of resources which offer desirable building sites and sometimes the buildings themselves for industry to lease or purchase, and local tax exemption while the industry is being established; nondominant status of labor unions in many areas; the drawing power of one established industry for other related industries; and availability of library and special research services within a reasonable distance.

A study of the cellulosic-fiber columns of the man-made fibers of Table 3 (Chapter 2), which cover world production of rayon and acetate (and triacetate also in recent years), reveals how this growth has taken place on a worldwide basis. What factors account for this phenomenal growth, and why have the rayons been so widely accepted? Tables 4 and 5 (Chapter 2) show that United States production of this group of fibers was less than consumption—imports account for the difference.

Before proceeding further we should note the customary methods used for reporting statistics concerning the cellulosic man-made fibers. Until recently all man-made cellulosic fibers were reported as one, making it difficult, and sometimes impossible, to find data in which the amount of each separate type of fiber is reported. Even at this date, with the rayons holding a major place among the world's fibers, the different types of rayon are lumped together—and often even acetate is included—in much of the available data. The "Base Book of Textile Statistics," which is the January 1962 issue of *Textile Organon*, reports all rayons and acetates as a single fiber group in nearly all the data presented, but some other issues of the

publication report data separately since 1940 for rayon and acetate. Data on fibers still covered by patents are released reluctantly, if at all, except in strictest confidence.

Table 14 includes data on the forms in which United States rayon has been produced since 1940 as well as the amounts. The competition of other man-made fibers is reflected in the decline after the peak year of

TABLE 14. United States Production of Rayon (Millions of Pounds and Percent)[a]

| | Filament | | | | Staple and Tow | | |
| | High-Tenacity | | Regular | | | | |
Year	Pound	Percent	Pound	Percent	Pound	Percent	Total
1940	9.8	3.0	247.3	75.5	70.6	21.5	327.7
1945	202.2	35.0	246.6	42.7	129.1	22.3	577.9
1950	308.2	37.8	319.1	39.1	188.5	23.1	815.5
1955	432.7	44.5	202.3	20.8	337.8	34.7	972.8
1960	279.3	37.7	147.0	19.9	314.0	42.4	740.3
1965	264.6	22.8	169.2	15.6	648.0	59.9	1,081.8
1968	202.4	18.3	162.9	14.8	739.1	66.9	1,104.4

[a] Compiled from *Textile Organon*, February 1968 and 1969.

1955, especially in high-tenacity rayon. But note the figure for 1968 which reveals a surge to new high levels for the total rayon produced; the increase is due to a slight increase in regular tenacity filaments and a large increase in staple and tow. We shall look at this again. The high level for high-tenacity filament rayon in 1955 reflects the period when rayon had replaced cotton for tire cord and dominated that market. Since that time nylon has taken a large part of the tire cord market away from rayon and now nylon, in turn, is threatened by the polyesters. New radial type tires now being developed, however, may restore this market to rayon. The staple and tow forms of rayon have shown continual growth except for an occasional year of decline.

Another interesting development in the man-made fiber industry has been the shift in emphasis between filament and staple length yarns from time to time. This shift has sometimes been due to the great versatility of staple yarns and to the increasingly common practice of blending various types of fibers. Sometimes the shift has been due to the development and use of texturizing processes for filament yarns with the resulting greater versatility in end-use this has made possible. The first plant for staple

length rayon began operation in the United States in 1937; Table 14 indicates how important this development has been. World production figures for staple and tow acetate and rayon (always reported together) as compared to filament acetate and rayon increased from 51.9 percent in 1940 to 59.1 percent in 1968, although this has not been a consistent or steady trend. On the same basis, considering acetate and rayon together, in the United States staple and tow production was only 49.5 percent of total rayon and acetate production in 1968. Many of the texturizing processes were developed in our country and their use is obviously of greater importance to us.

In 1950 the world's ten leading countries producing man-made cellulosic rayon and acetate *filament* fibers were the United States (49.5%), United Kingdom (10.0%), Italy (5.8%), West Germany (5.7%), Japan (5.4%), France (5.2%), The Netherlands (2.5%), Canada (2.0%), Brazil (1.9%), and Spain (1.2%). The leading producers of rayon and acetate *staple* were the United States (18.8%), West Germany (15.3%), East Germany (10.6%), United Kingdom (10.6%), Japan (9.2%), Italy (7.2%), France (4.9%), Austria (4.2%), Czechoslovakia (2.9%), and Spain (2.0%).

A total of 2,262,000,000 pounds of filament rayon was produced in 1968, according to *Textile Organon* for June 1969, of which 78.9 percent was produced by these ten countries: the USSR (17.5%), the United States (16.1%), Japan (11.1%), Italy (6.9%), West Germany (6.4%), the United Kingdom (5.6%), India (4.7%), France (4.0%), the Netherlands (3.5%), and East Germany (3.1%).

World rayon staple and tow produced in 1968 totaled 4,580,000,000 pounds of which 81.4 percent was produced by these countries: East Europe—including Mainland China—(25.3%), Japan (16.7%), the United States (16.1%), West Germany (8.5%), the United Kingdom (7.7%), France (3.1%), India (3.0%), and Canada (1.0%).

End-uses are often still reported for rayon and acetate together, and often they are blended together or with other fibers for many of the listed purposes. Because they are reported together, we shall look at the end-uses as they appear in Tables 7, 8, 9, 10, and 11 in Chapter 2 before we study the fibers separately. The larger share in most end-uses is rayon but some uses refer primarily to acetate; however, we shall not be able to distinguish them.

Home furnishings make use of the largest percentage of rayon and acetate with drapery, upholstery, and slipcovers accounting for the most extensive end-use. Carpets and rugs are next, and the least is reported for towels and toweling. The next greatest total amount is for women's, misses, children's, and infants' apparel, with the greatest amount being

used for dresses; hosiery and socks of all kinds use the least amount, almost too little to be worth reporting. There isn't much rayon and acetate used in sweaters either.

The third greatest total amount goes into the category of consumer products with apparel linings being the greatest end-use. This would include not only linings for suits, coats, jackets, and such but also the large amount of acetate tricot which is bonded as a backing or lining to rather thin or otherwise stretchy woven and knitted fabrics which are so popular in women's and girls' apparel. Industrial uses account for a large amount of rayon and acetate too, largely in tires, which would be rayon.

The least amount of rayon and acetate in these tables is used for men's and boys' apparel with most of that used going into slacks, shorts, and shirts for sport or other outdoor wear. Most of these fabrics are probably blends. The smallest amount is reported for nightwear, though a number of uses do not include much of these fibers.

The rayon fibers have a number of properties in common with each other and with cotton and linen, in addition to properties listed at the beginning of this chapter. They burn readily with a yellow flame, and with the odor of burning paper or cotton, leaving a small amount of cobwebby residue (or none at all), which crumbles into fine, powdery, gray ash. The rayons may be successfully treated to retard fire. They are all sensitive to reaction with acids but are not generally damaged by alkalies. Most of them have low resilience and elasticity, and without special crease-resistant treatments, wrinkle considerably and need to be pressed frequently. Crease-resistant treatments, however, are very commonly applied to many of the fabrics made from these fibers.

Laws, Rules, and Standards Affecting Rayon and Acetate

The development of regulations and standards for rayon and acetate will serve to illustrate how such regulations rise and change, both in importance and scope.

As already mentioned, in 1924 the term *rayon* was first used to denote the cellulosic man-made fibers, and this term rather than *artificial silk* was recognized by the FTC in certain of its rulings in 1925. The first trade practice rules applying specifically to rayon were promulgated in 1937, with new rules and changes over the years, as follows:

RAYON TRADE PRACTICE RULES,
EFFECTIVE OCTOBER 27, 1937

This group of rules, declared by the FTC under its powers to prevent "misinformation, misrepresentation and deception, in the interest of fair competition and consumer protection," arose largely from the urging of

the silk industries, probably, in part, because of the great expansion underway in the rayon industries at that time.

These rules (1) defined rayon as "the generic term for manufactured textile fiber or yarn produced chemically from cellulose or with a cellulose base and for thread, strands or fabric made therefrom, regardless of whether such fiber or yarn be made under the viscose, acetate, cuprammonium, nitrocellulose or other processes"; (2) required that the term rayon be used in advertising, distributing, selling, branding, or labeling of items made of rayon, and that the word rayon be as conspicuous as the other descriptive words used with it; (3) required fabrics and garments of rayon in combination with other fibers to have listed all the constituents (in order of percentage) of each fiber present in amounts over 5 percent, all to be in the same size type.

THE RAYON TRADE PRACTICE RULES, EFFECTIVE FEBRUARY 11, 1952

These superseded the 1937 rules, most of which were incorporated in the new rules, except for the definition which now excluded acetate from the rayon definition. The new definitions were

Rayon: Man-made textile fibers and filaments composed of regenerated cellulose and yarn, thread, or textile fabric made of such fibers and filaments.
Acetate: Man-made textile fibers and filaments composed of cellulose acetate, and yarn, thread, or textile fabric made of such fibers and filaments.

THE TEXTILE FIBER PRODUCTS IDENTIFICATION ACT, EFFECTIVE MARCH 3, 1960

This act of Congress superseded the Trade Practice Rules of 1952 and incorporated them in the general regulations covering all the textile fibers. Provisions of this law were discussed briefly in Chapter 2 and will not be repeated. The definition for each classification of man-made fibers is included with the discussion of the fibers falling within it.

THE L-22 MINIMUM STANDARDS FOR RAYON AND ACETATE FABRICS

This group of standards for rayon and acetate fabrics was approved December 31, 1952, by the American Standards Association on the recommendation of its Committee L-22, appointed for this specific purpose and representing all segments of interests, from fiber producer, to retailer, garment manufacturer and cutter, and consumer. The 1952 standards were replaced with revisions in 1960 which covered end-use minimum performance requirements for fabrics of all types of fibers. These have now been superseded by 1968 revisions and are discussed in Chapter 16.

Processes

Since all the man-made cellulosic fibers, whether thermoplastic or not, depend on cellulose as their basic material, the processes for obtaining purified cellulose for fiber production is a first step in manufacture and will be considered before we examine the individual fiber processes. And because all man-made fibers (except metallics) depend on spinnerets for formation of the fiber, we shall consider them here.

Cellulose is found extensively in the walls and skeletons of all trees and plants. Trees, cotton, ramie, hemp, straw, bagasse from sugar cane, bamboo, and many other plant forms are potential sources of cellulose, in varying degrees of purity. Wood pulp and cotton linters have proved to be the best sources to date because of the quantities available, a certain degree of uniformity, and more or less stable price. Since the early 1950's an ever-increasing percentage of the cellulose used in fiber production in the United States has been obtained from wood pulp; in 1963 wood pulp accounted for 99½ percent of the cellulose used and continues to stay at about that percentage. Wood pulp has been considerably cheaper and the price more stable than for pulp made from linters. A tendency toward increased use of wood cellulose in recent years has been attributed largely to the great price fluctuations in cotton linters since 1951, whereas the price of wood pulp has remained fairly constant.

PREPARATION OF WOOD CELLULOSE

Logs for the United States textile fiber industry come from the Pacific Northwest, the South, and from Canada. Modern practice permits utilization of a number of kinds of trees. Logging practices vary in each area but must be carefully controlled in order to insure a continuous supply of logs within an acceptable quality range. To meet these requirements a whole wood pulp industry, with its allied research, has arisen to serve the textile industry. As fiber processes change in the plants, adjustments and controls are made in the pulp industries to insure adequate supplies of the desired quality of cellulose. Controlled tree-cutting practices, and the reseeding of cutover areas with improved nursery stock especially developed to meet more adequately the specific needs of the industry, are too well known to warrant discussion. Although to a considerable extent the processes for preparing wood pulp for the textile industry parallel steps for the paper industry, more careful controls are required all along the way for textile cellulose.

The *Rayon and Staple Fiber Handbook* (p. 72) says

The main object of the pulping process is to isolate the cellulose in the wood from the other constituents in such a way as to leave the cellulose as

pure as possible, and furthermore to avoid any radical physical change of the isolated cellulose fibers.

The first step is to select and cut sound, healthy trees of the right sizes for easy handling in subsequent processing. At the mill, the trees are debarked and stored until they have reached the right degree of seasoning. Knots and decayed or damaged areas are removed, then the trees are cut into very small chips and screened to eliminate oversize pieces and sawdust. Chipping is necessary to remove undesirable wood and to control within very close limits the processes that follow. Cooking, using the sulfite process similar to the papermaking process, is next. Huge cooking chambers are each loaded with 40 tons of dry woodchips and 50,000 gallons of bisulfite solution, which has just been freshly prepared at the cooking site in special towers; there sulfur is burned and combined with limestone and water to form a mixture of sulfurous acid and calcium oxide, thus making the bisulfite solution. All these processes require careful control to insure uniformity of the bisulfite solution, of pressure, cooking time, and temperature. As "digestion" proceeds, chemical checks are made hourly of the cooking mass, and when the desired state is reached, the mass is immediately blown into a vat and washed several times with pure, soft water to stop any further reaction. The pulp is then diluted with water and passed over screens which remove any coarse materials remaining. Since the pulp at this stage is pale yellow, it is next treated with hypochlorite to bleach out the color and to oxidize remaining lignin so that it can be flushed out with water. Sheets of cellulose are then formed, pressed, and dried. These sheets are almost pure cellulose and resemble thick white blotting paper. They are cut to the size specified by a particular user, counted, stacked, baled, and wrapped for shipment to the fiber-processing plants. Improved reforestation policies and better control at all stages of wood production are resulting in improved yield and quality of cellulose. New and better processes are also being developed for pulping.

PREPARATION OF COTTON LINTER CELLULOSE

The steps for preparing cellulose from cotton linters must be as carefully controlled throughout as those for preparing cellulose from wood. You will recall that the linters are the short fibers adhering to cotton seed after the original ginning. They are removed at the mills where the seed is to be utilized for its oil and other products. All linters may be removed in one process, called "mill run" or in two ginning processes. If two are used, the first ginning or "cut" removes only the longer fibers, together with

much of the trash and foreign matter adhering to the seed. This cut is used largely by the mattress and furniture industry, or for cheap qualities of cotton fabric. The second and shorter cut is less expensive and is cleaner; it becomes the cotton for chemical cotton, much of which is utilized in the man-made fiber industries. The initial quality of the linters depends on their quality and condition when the seed is received at the mill and, in their subsequent use, on the condition and cleanliness of the mill equipment.

Different lots of linters are blended to achieve a uniform quality of chemical cotton. The cleaned, blended linters are carried to the top of huge digesters where the fibers are mixed with dilute caustic soda solution (NaOH); then they are carried into the digesters for the cooking process. Temperature, pressure, time, and proportions depend on the product desired; all processes are carefully controlled throughout. Constant checks enable the linters to be removed from the digester at the right stage; then they are washed with soft water to stop the action of the alkaline solution. The cooked linters are finally bleached with chlorine, rewashed thoroughly, and dried.

For some fiber processors, the fluffy, white, purified fibers are baled or rolled and wrapped for shipment as chemical cotton. For other processors, the wet fibers are made into sheets like those from wood cellulose. All cellulose from linters is dried to a specified uniform moisture content. Cotton cellulose is usually designated by its viscosity, that is, the time required for its dispersion in a standard cuprammonium solution. Various end-uses require different degrees of viscosity for optimum handling by their different methods. Maximum allowable ash content is often specified by the users of chemical cotton.

The method for utilizing the purified wood or cotton cellulose in production of fibers varies with each process, and the differences in methods result in characteristic differences in the fibers.

SPINNERETS

Spinnerets, sometimes called "spinning jets," must be made with extreme precision and care, and polished until no possibility of the slightest roughness remains anywhere. The instruments for making the holes in the spinnerets are finer than human hair, and the holes must be of uniform size and exceedingly great smoothness. Spinnerets are made of platinum and platinum alloy for viscose rayon and other processes where fibers coagulate in chemical baths, but they may be made of steel or other metals for air- or water-coagulating processes. Concerning the cost of platinum

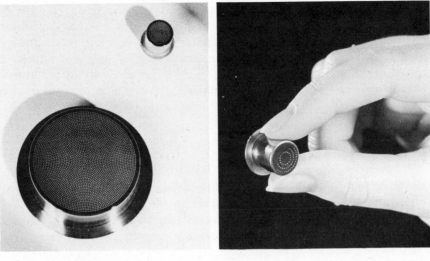

FIGURE 6-1. Three types of spinnerets used in the production of rayon. (Courtesy American Viscose Corporation.)

spinnerets, the American Viscose Corporation several years ago said, "The cost is dependent upon the size of the jet and the number of holes in it. For spinning a typical textile yarn, such as 150 denier/60 filament, the total cost of a 60 hole jet is about ten dollars. One jet with several thousand holes, including the cost of the platinum, could total $1000." No doubt the price is higher now.

The number of holes in a spinneret depends on the number of filaments desired for a yarn, or if staple or tow is being made, on the amount of fiber that can be handled satisfactorily at one time in further operations. Each spinning unit (or system) uses many spinnerets. Figure 6-1 is a photograph of three spinnerets of the types most commonly used.

Special spinnerets having various unusual shapes have been developed in recent years to be used primarily with melt-spun types of fibers such as the nylons and polyesters, though they may sometimes be used with other spinning systems too. Some of the new type spinnerets may be used in forming bicomponent fibers, or to produce triangular-, lobed-, star- or H-shaped fibers. Some of the new spinnerets are designed to produce hollow fibers of different shapes with smooth circular surfaces, or with projecting corners at triangular or Y-shaped turns. The purpose of these designs is to increase surface area for improved flexibility, dyeability, absorption, control of luster, transparency, or cover, to improve thermal

properties, or to permit two different types of materials to be spun together to form a bicomponent fiber.

When special-shaped spinnerets are used, the spinning process becomes a much more critical operation than with common types of spinnerets and drawing, too, requires a different type of precision control if the special shape is to be maintained.

Viscose

Avicolor [a] *	Englo [b]	Krispglo [b]	Strawn [d]
Avicron [a]	Enka [b]	Lowland [b]	Super L [a]
Aviloc [a]	Enkrome [b]	Narco [e]	Super Narco [e]
Avron [a]	Fair Haven [f]	Narcon [e]	Super Rayflex [a]
Briglo [b]	Fiber 24 [d]	Newbray [h]	Suprenka [b]
Coloray [c] *	Fibro [c]	New-Color [h]	Tusson [e]
Comiso [e]	Fibro DDC [c]	New-Dull [h]	Tyron [d]
Cuprussah [e]	Fortisan [g]	Purilon [a]	Tyweld [d]
Drapespun [d]	Hi-Narco [e]	Rayflex [a]	Villwyte [d]
Dream Slub [e]	IT [a]	Skybloom [b]	Xena [e]
Dul-Tone [d]	Jetspun [a] *	Skyloft [b]	
Dy-Lok [d] *	Kolorbon [a] *	Softglo [b]	

[a] Trade name granted to FMC Corporation, American Viscose Division.
[b] Trade name granted to American Enka Corporation.
[c] Trade name granted to Courtaulds North America, Inc.
[d] Trade name granted to Midland-Ross Corporation, IRC Fibers Division.
[e] Trade name granted to Beaunit Corporation, Beaunit Fibers Division.
[f] Trade name granted to Fair Haven Mills, Incorporated.
[g] Trade name granted to Celanese Corporation, Celanese Fibers Marketing Co.
[h] Trade name granted to Mohasco Industries, Inc., New Bedford Rayon Division.
*Solution dyed.

Viscose rayon is the most used of the rayons, primarily because it is the least expensive, being competitive with cotton. Patents have expired on the rayons, acetate, and nylon, so that their processes are no longer secret but are part of the public domain, accessible to everyone. Hence the widespread production, throughout the world, of these fibers. Because more information is available about the processes on which patents have expired, and because they will serve to illustrate for us some of the similarities and differences in production of the man-made fibers, we shall consider the processing of these fibers in more detail than others.

Viscose rayon was developed very soon after Chardonnet succeeded in his attempts to produce nitrocellulose rayon commercially. C. F. Cross and E. J. Bevan, chemists at Courtaulds, Ltd., of Great Britain, obtained

patents in 1892 for the chemical processes underlying the viscose process, but fibers were not successfully made until the necessity for "aging" the solution was discovered accidentally about 1900. Between these dates, however, the viscose solution was used in finishing linen fabrics and other materials, for paper sizing, and for a cellulose film similar to cellophane. Cellophane, first made in 1908, is viscose which has been extruded in a flat stream and rolled into a thin sheet rather than extruded through spinnerets.

The first viscose yarn was exhibited in Paris in 1900. Production began in Great Britain, France, Belgium, and Switzerland about the same time, around 1904, and Courtaulds, who owned the British patents, established a small plant in the United States under the name of the Viscose Company of America, which, as the American Viscose Corporation,* has since become the largest rayon-producing company in the world. Courtaulds sold their interests in this company during World War II but have since established a new company in the United States under their own name.

Today viscose rayon is produced by eight companies in the United States and by companies in thirty-seven other countries in the world, under a great many trade names which often indicate the producer but not necessarily the fiber. The resulting fiber is not all alike. Since viscose is man-made, it can be varied in many ways, depending on the end-product desired. This fact is also true of other man-made fibers.

Viscose rayon is largely cellulose, as is cotton, but in dissolving the original cotton or wood and regenerating the cellulose in a new fiber, the degree of polymerization has been reduced. This reduction accounts for many differences in the properties of rayon and cotton, especially the greater sensitivity of rayon to physical and chemical change.

PROCESSES

Viscose rayon can be made from purified cellulose, which is prepared by processing wood or cotton linters, or a mixture of the two. Wood constitutes almost the entire source of cellulose for viscose rayon in the United States. When received at the rayon plants the cellulose sheets are unpacked and stored for several weeks in rooms where the temperature and relative humidity are rigidly controlled, in order to insure that all sheets have the same moisture content, a very important factor in maintaining uniformity in the subsequent processing and, ultimately, uniformity of the resulting rayon. The diagrammatic sketch of viscose rayon processing, Figure 6-2, will help the reader in following the cellulose through a rayon plant, from sheet form to rayon fiber or yarn.

* Now a division of FMC Corporation.

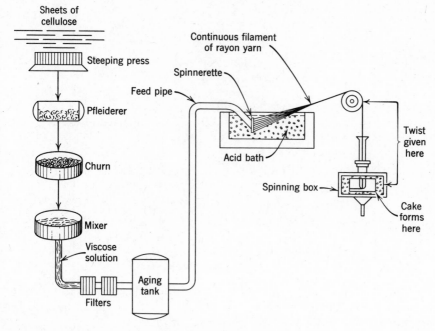

FIGURE 6-2. Flow chart of viscose rayon production. (Courtesy American Viscose Corporation.)

A pound of viscose fiber requires approximately these amounts of various raw materials: 1.067 lb wood cellulose (or somewhat less of chemical cotton because of its higher cellulosic content), 1.0 lb sodium hydroxide, 0.4 lb carbon disulfide, 1.5 lb sulfuric acid, 1.0 lb sodium sulfate, 0.2 to 0.5 lb glucose or corn sugar, and 800 to 1700 lb soft, chemically pure water.

Various descriptions of the viscose process name six to eight steps, depending on the detail given. We shall consider seven, in accordance with the diagram. Then, after the fiber is coagulated and wound or deposited in some manageable form, there are still other steps in preparing it for use.

The first step is a mercerizing process; in batches of 500 to 1000 pounds, the sheets of cellulose with uniform moisture content are placed on edge in compartments within big, rectangular vats called "steeping presses." The vats contain 18.5 percent sodium hydroxide solution at a temperature of 70°F. The cellulose sheets are left in the vats for an hour, and here conversion of the cellulose to sodium cellulose begins. The chemical reaction (with considerable disagreement about the position of the sodium) is as follows:

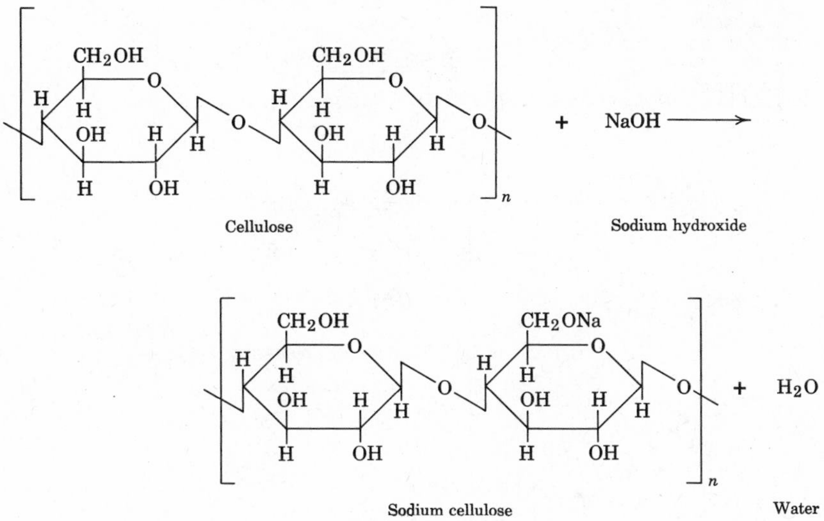

Cellulose   +   NaOH ⟶

Sodium cellulose   + H_2O

Water

The presses then operate to push together the partitions, thus squeezing out part of the sodium hydroxide solution so that the sheets have picked up only five to six times their original weight.

The next step is a shredding process. The moist sheets of sodium cellulose go into shredding machines that have heavy, notched-edge, spiral blades which gently tear the sheets apart, until the whole is a mass of small, fluffy, white "crumbs." The crumbs are then stored in cans for 40 to 80 hours and kept at a temperature of 85°F, while the sodium

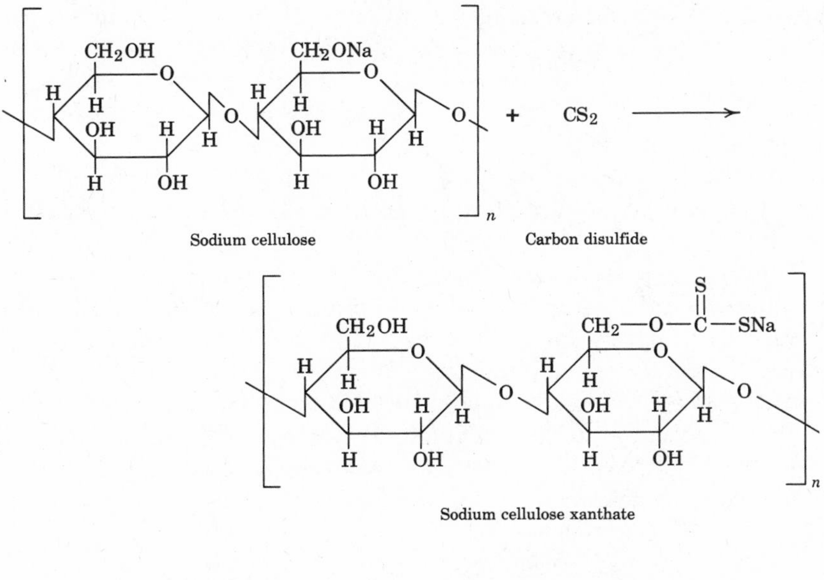

Sodium cellulose   + CS_2 ⟶

Carbon disulfide

Sodium cellulose xanthate

hydroxide continues to react with the cellulose; this is one of the two aging periods in the production of viscose rayon.

The third step (formulas for chemical reaction at bottom of page 150), determined by viscosity measurements of the sodium cellulose, is churning the crumbs with carbon disulfide in a huge rotating drum under exact temperature control. This process converts the sodium cellulose to cellulose xanthate. The *Rayon and Staple Fiber Handbook* (p. 91) describes the visible part of the process this way:

. . . As the carbon bisulphide is gradually absorbed, the batch shrinks in volume to about one-half its original size; and, as can be observed through the sight glass, the color of the cellulose changes from white to canary yellow and finally to orange, the color being an indication of the completion of reaction. Further, most of the loose and fluffy crumbs originally introduced are now rolled into balls ranging in size from marbles to baseballs.

The fourth step is preparation of the spinning liquid: cellulose xanthate (taken from several churns in order to insure uniformity of a large amount of viscose) is mixed with dilute sodium hydroxide until all the sodium cellulose xanthate material is dissolved, and a golden-brown liquid, the consistency of honey, is formed. This takes about 3 hours at 60°F. The typical reaction is

$$2\ \text{[Rayon (regenerated cellulose)]}_n\ +\ 2CS_2\ +\ Na_2SO_4$$

Rayon (regenerated cellulose)

Carbon disulfide

Sodium sulfate

$$2\ \text{[Sodium cellulose xanthate]}_n\ +\ H_2SO_4\ \text{(dilute)} \longrightarrow$$

Sodium cellulose xanthate

Sulfuric acid

If the rayon is to be dull or semidull, delustrant is added at this stage, and if it is to be solution-dyed, the color pigments or dyes are added between this time and the time of spinning. Titanium dioxide, finely divided white pigment, is the delustrant ordinarily used, although mineral oil is

sometimes used. You will note that the rayon formula is like that of the cellulose with which we started.

The solution is then passed through a series of filters in order to remove bits of wood cellulose and any other undissolved material which would interfere with pumping the viscous liquid through the spinnerets. Since further aging must occur before the solution is ready for spinning, a period of 12 to 24 hours elapses during the blending and filtering processes; the right stage of ripening is determined by frequent tests. When ripened to the correct degree of viscosity, the solution is stored in vacuum tanks for a few hours to remove air bubbles which would cause the filaments to break in spinning.

Spinning is the seventh step. Metered pumps force a measured amount of solution (depending on the denier desired) through the spinnerets, which are arranged in a row in a long trough, and horizontally into the coagulating bath. The bath contains sulfuric acid, sodium sulfate, glucose or corn sugar, and water. The acid neutralizes the sodium hydroxide and causes precipitation of the cellulose; the sodium sulfate adds strength and is believed to be responsible for the serrated cross-sectional shape; the glucose or corn sugar gives pliability and softness to the yarn. The coagulated fibers are led through a guide to a bobbin or to a spinning pot that rotates rapidly, inserting a little twist in the filament and, by centrifugal force, throwing the resulting yarn to the outside edges of the pot so that the cake of yarn is built from the outside in toward a hollow center.

The diameter of the fibers is determined largely by the degree to which they are stretched. Stretch is determined by the difference between the speed at which the fibers emerge from the spinnerets into the coagulating bath and the speed at which they are deposited in the rapidly spinning pot. The greater the difference in speed, the finer the denier of the fiber.

The size of the holes in the spinneret has some initial influence on fiber diameter. The degree of stretch affects the physical properties of the fiber and yarns too; the stretch orients the molecular chains in the fibers, making more of them parallel, thus increasing crystallinity and giving added strength and rigidity, and at the same time reducing pliability somewhat. Coagulating the fibers in a liquid bath is known as "wet-spinning."

Viscose filaments are most often spun into yarn cakes in spinning pots, but they may be wound as nontwisted filaments on bobbins for further processing, or they may go from the coagulating bath through continuous processing, with no break or further handling until all additional processes are complete. Pot spinning is most used, and is preferred over bobbin spinning, because filaments have been twisted to make yarns and, with the

small amount of twist given, are easier to handle and less subject to damage in further processing than are the nontwisted groups of filaments on the bobbin.

FILAMENT, STAPLE, AND TOW. The processes described have been for filament rayon, but those for staple and tow are the same through the coagulating bath; staple and tow are not centrifuged to form cakes, nor are they wound on bobbins.

Filaments emerging from the spinnerets may be cut to any length staple fibers, depending on whether they are to be spun on cotton, silk, or wool systems, and if they are to be blended with other fibers. For staple fiber and staple tow, the larger-type spinneret with 2000 to 3000 holes is used, and all the fiber coming from a spinneret is collected into a tow or rope. It may be cut into the staple length desired while wet, and go through other processes in short-fiber form, thus taking whatever shape and size the other processes may induce. Then the fibers are baled or boxed and handled just as any other short-length fibers.

Instead of being cut into short lengths, the tow may be put through the final processing as a continuous long rope and sold to the yarn spinner or fabric manufacturer in this form. He then cuts it, or sometimes breaks it, to any length desired for a particular type of yarn or fabric.

FINAL PROCESSES. After being coagulated in the acid bath as filaments, and collected in pots, on bobbins, or as tow, or cut into staple lengths, the fibers or yarns are washed to remove all traces of the processing chemicals. Sometimes they are bleached, although most rayon comes through processing in a nice white color. Fibers in all forms are dried on a trip through a tunnel dryer. Fibers and yarns are then ready for handling on regular equipment in the same way as other fibers of comparable lengths. Oil is often added to the fibers as a lubricant before packaging to soften and protect them in spinning and weaving. Bobbin filaments must be twisted into yarns and rewound into skeins before packaging.

Instead of individual steps for these processes, a continuous method has been developed and is in use in several plants. By this method the filaments, as they come from the coagulating bath, are run over a series of moving reels with very accurate controls, where continuous sprays of the various finishing solutions fall upon each filament along a fixed part of the route; by the time the last reel has been reached the filaments have had all the treatments and are dry and ready for twisting and winding in skeins or on cones. The reels are adjustable so that any degree of stretch may be applied to the fibers, which are still not completely set from their coagulating bath. This process cuts down on the amount of handling the

yarn must take, is faster, and is said to result in more uniform fibers and yarns than step-by-step handling. High-tenacity yarns are made by imparting a high degree of stretch in spinning, either in the bobbin or cake method, or on the reels of the continuous method.

Automation has been introduced in some of the newer rayon plants so that many steps formerly handled manually now proceed mechanically, with electrical controls directing the complete movement of materials through the plant.

PROPERTIES

Under the microscope, in longitudinal view, viscose rayon fibers appear much as smooth glass rods, although under high magnification striations may be visible parallel to the fiber length, owing to the indentations of the fiber surface.

In cross section, the fibers may be round, oval, or quite flat, but all show serrated edges. The typical serrated cross section is a positive means of identifying viscose. In the cross sections delustering materials show as black specks. Photomicrographs of longitudinal and cross-sectional views of viscose rayon may be seen in Figure 6-3.

Viscose rayon is made in different deniers, according to the end-use; these may be as low as 1 denier or as high as 25 per individual filament. The length may be controlled to any desired staple or filament length, and the luster to any degree.

Viscose rayon is made in different tenacities—regular, medium, and high—with other properties varying accordingly. Breaking tenacity varies from 1.5 to 2.6 grams per denier for regular viscose to 3.0 to 5.7 grams for high-tenacity fiber. Viscose is thus among the medium-strength fibers in regular-strength types, but it is among the stronger fibers in the high-tenacity types. Viscose loses from one-third to one-half its strength when wet but regains it when dry. Wet strength has been considerably improved in recent years, but this is one of the limiting factors in the use and care of this rayon. What are the implications for use and care of viscose?

Elongation, which varies from about 9 to 30 percent, is greater when viscose is wet, compensating in some measure for fiber weakness when wet; it exhibits a property termed "creep" or "delayed elasticity." When stretched within its elastic limits and released, rayon immediately recovers some of its stretch; this is elasticity. Then over a period of several hours, or even days, it will gradually creep back to its original length. A number of man-made fibers exhibit this property.

Elasticity and resiliency are both low, so that viscose wrinkles badly unless treated with special finishes. Wrinkling is not the problem it might seem for many manufacturers treat these rayons with resin finishes, even

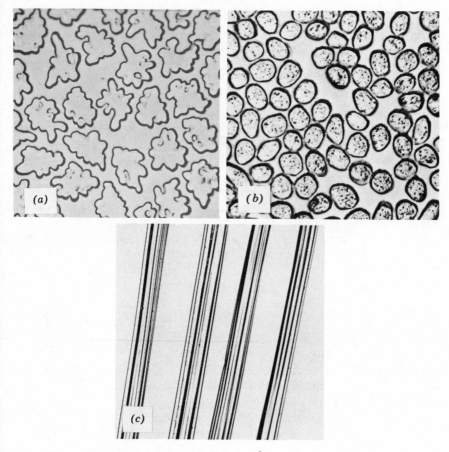

FIGURE 6-3. Photomicrographs of viscose rayon: (a) cross sections of regular viscose; (b) cross sections of high-wet-modulus rayon; and (c) longitudinal. (Courtesy E. I. duPont de Nemours & Co. Inc.)

though they may not be so labeled, if they are intended for outerwear type of clothing, such as dresses, blouses, shirts, and slacks. Rayon was the first fabric in the United States to be successfully and extensively treated for wrinkle resistance. Resin treatments on the rayons seem to be more successful than on most other fabrics. Affinity for resins seems to be a chemical reaction with viscose and is usually quite permanent.

The specific gravity of viscose is 1.52, about the same as that of cotton, which is medium among fibers. It is very absorbent and exhibits about 11 percent moisture regain. Its absorbency makes it easy to dye with the cotton colors. It dyes in darker colors than cotton does, and so rapidly

that it is sometimes necessary to add retardants to slow down the process in order to have a uniform color. Dyes must be chosen carefully for mixtures and blends containing viscose, or the rayon will exhaust the dye before the other fiber has had a chance to get wet. Viscose is comfortable to wear; it is soft, has excellent draping qualities, and is said to be the only man-made fiber that can be given sufficient twist for the construction of true crepes. Viscose does not accumulate static electricity. Resin finishes may alter some of these properties. Viscose loses strength during prolonged exposure to daylight, especially if the light is coupled with high humidity. It is more resistant to light than silk, but less resistant than acetate, Orlon, and Fortisan.

Rayons may be satisfactorily laundered by the same methods as cotton of similar color and structure, and require no special care in handling unless the fabric is a very weak one. They can be ironed at the same temperatures as cotton. Viscose does not melt when pressed with a hot iron, but it will scorch. Nor is boiling or sterilizing in an autoclave advisable. Seam finishes of a type that will not ravel are highly desirable in viscose garments which are to be laundered. Viscose swells in water, so the fit of a garment may be affected by the amount of moisture in this rayon when it is pressed. Viscose is more sensitive to acids than cotton and is quickly degraded by acid bleaching or other acid treatment.

Clean, dry viscose is rarely attacked by mildew and mold. If it is stored where temperature and humidity are high, or if it contains starch or is spotted with food, there is more chance of such growth. Discoloration and weakening of the fabric result.

Solution dyeing is a process for adding coloring matter to fibers. The pigment or dye is added during the final blending before the solution goes through the spinnerets; thus the fibers are colored throughout. Statements have been made that such methods give a much greater degree of color-fastness, and to all types of fading agents, than do conventional dyeing methods. The use of these processes is limited, however, in matters such as color range, the difficulty of predicting future color fashion, and the necessity for processing different colors separately. What other limitations can you see?

USES

The uses of the rayons (and acetates) have been discussed earlier in this chapter, so only a few things still need to be mentioned in relation to viscose. Special types of viscose have been developed for carpets and rugs; much of the carpeting in automobiles is viscose or a combination of viscose and acetate. The high-tenacity yarns, initially developed for tire cord and still important in that market, are being used in upholstery and drapery

fabrics, work clothing, and in other items for which high strength is essential. Viscose is an inexpensive and versatile fiber adaptable to all spinning systems and to various finishing resins. It is one of the fibers most often mixed and blended with other fibers, both the natural and the man-made.

Some out-of-the-ordinary textile yarns have been produced from viscose, although not all are in production now. *Bubblefil* was the name given to a type of yarn made by forcing viscose solution through a spinneret with only one fair-sized hole to which an air jet was attached. As the filament was extruded, small amounts of air were blown in at frequent intervals, causing discontinuous small air bubbles to form within the fiber skin, like small balloon-like beads; or with greater force, like a string of large, hollow beads. The resulting filaments were very lightweight and buoyant because of the entrapped air. They were used in life jackets and such types of equipment during World War II when kapok and milkweed fiber could not be obtained. Small amounts of other materials, such as casein or synthetic resin, have been incorporated in the viscose solution in attempts to give different properties, but none of these attempts has been successful enough to be continued.

A very interesting new use for cellulosic fibers—whether rayon, acetate, or triacetate was not specified, and perhaps it could be any of them—was described in *Chemical and Engineering News*, August 21, 1967 (p. 13) as follows:

Five years of development in two industrial laboratories have now culminated in the first trials of a new artificial kidney on a human volunteer. . . . The device is as efficient as conventional artificial kidneys, the large units that are wheeled to the bedside for use.

Artificial kidneys remove uremic wastes from the blood of persons whose own kidneys are diseased and cannot function. . . .

The developers of the new device call it a capillary kidney. It contains hollow, hair-size cellulose fibers, slightly larger than the capillary vessels of the human vascular system. The fibers—11,000 of them—are packed into a compact case which can be held in the hand.

Although actual cost of the new kidney can't be determined exactly until clinical trials are over and commercial production begins, it appears that the cost will be far below that of a conventional large hospital unit. . . .

Cuprammonium

Bembella [a]	Flaikona [a]	Ondelette [a]
Cupioni [a]	Multi-Cupioni [a]	Parfé [a]
Cupracolor [a]	Multi-Strata [a]	Strata [a]
Cuprel [a]	Nub-Lite [a]	Stratella [a]

[a] Trade name granted to Beaunit Corporation, Beaunit Fibers Division.

The cuprammonium process was the second one developed to make rayon. It too is a regenerated cellulose, possessing many characteristics in common with cotton and with viscose rayon, and can be pictured with the same structural formula.

The history of cuprammonium rayon began with the discovery that cellulose could be dissolved in Schweitzer's reagent, a common reagent in chemical laboratories. Before the possibility of making a fiber was suggested, during the attempts to find incandescent light filaments, the cuprammonium solution was found to be of value as a finish in waterproofing and rotproofing textile fabrics. A patent for such finishing under the trade name Wellesden was issued to Scoffern (of England) in 1859. In 1891, the first cuprammonium rayon was produced in Germany by M. Fremery and J. Urban, but the process was not successful until E. Thiele, in 1901, devised (and patented) the "stretch-spinning" process. The industry, after an early but small spurt, died down until the 1920's, when the stretch-spinning procedure was modified somewhat and made more usable.

The cuprammonium process, although the fiber has many desirable qualities, has never been established on a widespread basis, as has the viscose process. Only one company in the United States, the Beaunit Fibers, Division of Beaunit Mills, produces cuprammonium rayon. This type of rayon is produced in four other countries.

Production of cuprammonium rayon is always reported with viscose in available economic reports, but it stays constant at about 5 percent of total rayon production.

PROCESSES

The cuprammonium process has fewer steps and seems to be considerably simpler than that for viscose. Cotton linters have usually been the preferred source of cellulose, but in recent years wood cellulose has become increasingly important and is sometimes preferred because of its greater reactivity with the solvent.

The first step is to moisten the cellulose with dilute sodium hydroxide, then to mix the moist cellulose thoroughly with a semi-gelatinous form of copper hydroxide $Cu(OH)_2$. The right proportions of copper, ammonia, and cellulose are necessary if the cellulose is to dissolve eventually as a spinning solution. These proportions are, approximately, 4 percent copper and 29 percent ammonia to 9 or 10 percent cellulose.

The free liquid is pressed out and the mass washed with water, which does not affect the copper hydroxide that is left on the cellulose fibers; these are again pressed to remove about 60 percent of the water. The mass is then squeezed through a metal sieve and placed in a vacuum tank where

all air is removed to prevent oxidation during the next, the "ripening," stage.

The air-free mass is mixed with ammonium hydroxide and left to ripen for 24 hours. During this stage, Schweitzer's reagent, a dark blue solution, is formed by reaction between the ammonia from the hydroxide and the copper hydroxide deposited on the cellulose; the mixture dissolves the cellulose and forms a thick, viscous fluid that is the spinning solution. This solution may be kept indefinitely and spinning done at will, in contrast to viscose which must be spun within specified hours after the aging process is completed.

Spinning cuprammonium rayon is quite different from spinning viscose. Here we encounter the first stretch-spinning method devised, a process

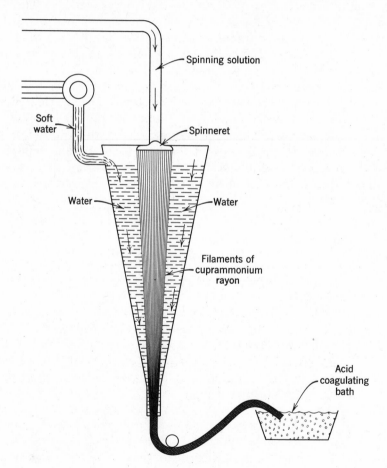

FIGURE 6-4. Diagram of the stretch-spinning system for cuprammonium rayon.

which with variations is used for spinning several other man-made fibers. The diagrammatic sketch of Figure 6-4 may help in understanding this spinning process.

The spinneret used is made of nickel and has larger holes than those used for viscose. In addition to the spinneret, the apparatus consists of a long glass funnel with a glass-nippled end, a source of constantly running, soft, warm water introduced at a top area of the funnel and running out at the bottom, a steel rod below the tip of the funnel, and a coagulating trough containing a weak acid solution.

As the spinning solution is forced by a metered pump through the spinneret, the filaments begin to coagulate in the water as they are drawn down through the nipple, under the bar which removes part of the water, and into the acid bath which completes the coagulation. The water circulating downward in the funnel exerts considerable pull on the filaments, which, together with the drawing operation, greatly reduces the diameter of the filaments. The stretching also orients the molecules of the cellulose, thus increasing the strength of the filaments.

From the coagulating bath the filaments are wound on bobbins or collected in spinning pots for final washing and drying, or they may be carried on through a recently developed continuous process for these final treatments. Cuprammonium rayon may be used with or without twist. Although the American Bemberg Company (now Beaunit Fibers) in 1952 announced plans for producing staple-form cuprammonium rayon on a commercial scale, all this rayon on the market is apparently still the filament type.

PROPERTIES

Except for microscopic appearance, the properties of cuprammonium rayon are almost the same as those of viscose, so only their differences need be mentioned.

When seen through the microscope in cross section, cuprammonium fibers appear as tiny, smooth, featureless circles (see Figure 6-5).

Breaking tenacity of cuprammonium rayon varies from 1.7 to 2.3 grams per denier. Cuprammonium rayon has always been made in fine diameters, and for many years it was the only fiber that could be made in diameters finer than silk. This fineness gives it great flexibility and has made it adaptable for many of the uses to which silk is especially suited; it also blends well with silk, has a soft hand, silky feel, and subdued luster. Its flexibility and softness probably account for its very good wrinkle resistance. Cuprammonium has good resistance to perspiration damage. White

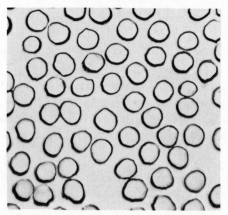

FIGURE 6-5. Photomicrograph of cuprammonium rayon cross sections. (Courtesy E. I. duPont de Nemours & Co. Inc.)

cuprammonium rayon does not yellow with age. Because of the traces of copper remaining, it is more resistant to mildew and mold than are other cellulosic fibers. Cupracolor is the trademarked name for the solution-dyed cuprammonium rayon. Cupioni is a popular trademarked filament yarn with built-in slubs.

A flame retardant filament yarn for use in drapery fabrics was announced in early 1968.

USES

Cuprammonium rayon is used largely for sheer dress and curtain fabrics, for tricot lingerie, and to some extent for hosiery.

Fortisan

Fortisan is not a new fiber, but owing to the circumstances since its introduction, it has been little known to most civilians; even now it is found in very few civilian applications, and these are largely industrial.

As early as 1935, British Celanese, Ltd., had begun work on a high-tenacity acetate fiber. In 1941 the Celanese Corporation of America began to produce the new fiber under the trade name Fortisan. The new fiber was one of the strongest and most stable known, and made some of the lightest-weight fabrics and other products because of the extreme fineness to which it could be drawn. As a result, Fortisan was "drafted" and most of its life has been devoted to military and scientific uses. If you have not

heard of Fortisan, in spite of its admirable qualities, the following paragraphs, written by M. Whitehead of the Celanese Corporation for *Matthews' Textile Fibers* (pp. 924–925), may explain why:

. . . It came to be used in place of silk for many different types of parachutes, ranging from light flare chutes to heavier cargo chutes, which could withstand severe conditions of loading and impact as well as climatic conditions. Of it were also made shroud lines, sewing thread, tapes, balloon valve cords, fine strong core threads for tinsel conductors in radio and radar headsets, heating elements for flying suits and gloves, fine strong tracer threads, heavy strong fabrics as a base for resin laminates in aircraft work, antiblackout suits, and tent liners. It was also used satisfactorily for man-carrying parachutes, because it has a higher[?] specific gravity, making its volume less for any given weight and making it packable in a smaller space than for any other fabric. . . .

With the outbreak of the Korean War, Fortisan returned 100 percent into the Defense Program for all uses of World War II and also such new items as large and small inflated radomes, and larger, lighter, and stronger airships with greater lifting capacity. Many millions of yards of light, strong fabric went into and are still being purchased for the linings of combat garments, arctic clothing, and the like, where the demonstrated dimensional stability and strength, and durability including that to severe mobile laundering, were needed. These fabrics at first were vat dyed but were later produced as dope-pigmented yarns of OD shade, giving even greater fastness than that supplied by vat dyes, and other properties required by the Armed Forces.

We are interested in Fortisan primarily because it is our only saponified rayon fiber.

PROCESSES

The processes for making Fortisan bear little resemblance to those for other rayons. In fact, the Fortisan production begins with the use of already spun acetate filament yarns, which are carried through saponification to remove the acid radical and convert the acetate to regenerated cellulose. Saponification is possible because, in the process of producing acetate (an ester of acetic acid), acids have been used which permit substitution of acetyl groups (CH_3CO) for OH groups; in the reversal the acids are thus available for hydrolysis with sodium hydroxide. Although Fortisan is often called an acetate rather than a rayon, it is a rayon because in saponification it has regained many of its original cellulosic properties and behaves as the rayons do. There are two steps in the Fortisan process.

The first step consists of stretching acetate yarn in the presence of compressed air and steam, so that the molecules in the molecular chains

become more perfectly oriented than in any other cellulosic fiber. The yarn is first guided through a chamber of compressed air (at a pressure of 32.5 pounds per square inch) on rollers set at a controlled speed, and then through a 6-foot-long steam chamber where the pressure is about the same as in the air chamber (33 pounds per square inch). At the end of the steam chamber the filaments are pulled through rollers that rotate ten times as fast as the first set, thus stretching the filaments to ten times their original length and reducing their diameter accordingly. The filaments are then wound on plastic bobbins with perforated sides, for saponification.

In the second step, the stretched yarns on their bobbins are placed in a pressure machine in a solution containing about 1 percent sodium hydroxide and 15 percent sodium acetate, and the solution is pumped through the filaments, to the inside of the bobbins and back, until saponification is complete. The yarn is then oiled, dried, and wound on skeins or bobbins for use. Saponification results in a loss of 38 percent of the original weight of the acetate; this in part accounts for the cost. Fibers may be used as filament or cut into staple lengths for spinning.

PROPERTIES

Under the microscope Fortisan cross sections resemble the original acetate, being three- to five-lobed in appearance.

The strength of Fortisan equals that of glass, high-strength polyamides and polyesters, and the new high-wet-modulus rayons—all of which are among the strongest of the textile fibers. Fortisan retains about 85 percent of its strength while wet. The diameter can be varied, for it is possible to draw Fortisan out to a small fraction of a denier, far finer than any other fiber can now be drawn. Elongation at break is about 6 percent, wet or dry, and elasticity is low—very important factors in some uses where, through all weather conditions, the same length is essential. Although initial elasticity is low, elastic recovery is good, and creep may continue for as long as two weeks in dry fabric, although it is rapid for wet fabric. The high degree of orientation could be expected to result in rigidity, which shows up in low elasticity and elongation, but this is said to be overcome, when desirable, by a special type of heat treatment at 200°C.

Fortisan is one of the most resistant of all fibers to light and weather degradation and is ideal for curtains and other products for which light exposure poses a problem.

Fortisan burns like the other cellulosic fibers and can be given the fire-retardant treatments that work on them. It can be washed and ironed like

cotton and linen, and withstands higher ironing temperatures. Fortisan fabrics are absorbent.

Fortisan exhibits the same chemical properties as the other cellulosic fibers. Like cotton, it can withstand steam and autoclave treatment and dyes with the same dyes in fast colors. It is not affected by dry-cleaning solvents.

"Opus" treatment for Fortisan acts in somewhat the same way as mercerization of cotton. The temperature is kept low for the treatment, which is done (apparently) without tension. The result is increased elongation and slight shortening of the yarn—changes that make Fortisan very desirable for sewing thread, the availability of which, unfortunately, seems to be practically nil.

Fortisan apparently is subject to attack by the same organisms as are other cellulosic fibers, when conditions are right.

USES

Military and scientific uses of Fortisan have been mentioned at the beginning of this discussion. Fortisan is being utilized in space suits and for other textile needs in space vehicles and explorations, and in other high-speed and high-impact experimentation. Civilian uses vary from fine, practically invisible cords for hearing aids to sheer glass curtains, sheer dress fabrics, foundation garments, lightweight coated rainwear, sewing thread, parachutes, sailcloth, surgical sutures, high-pressure surgical bandages, typewriter ribbons, dental floss, plastic-coated baby pants, and myriads of other items.

The few fabrics available of 100 percent Fortisan are expensive compared with fabrics of the other cellulosic fibers; they are priced more like silk and wool. Sheer curtain fabrics of 100 percent Fortisan look and feel about like cuprammonium fabric of the same type but cost two to four times as much. The much greater durability of Fortisan, however, needs to be taken into account in reckoning its cost. It is the custom of some curtain fabric manufacturers to use a weave with Fortisan in one direction and cotton, silk, or other light-sensitive fibers in the other. This deplorable practice allows the fabric no opportunity to benefit from Fortisan's superior qualities in strength and light resistance.

The future of this fiber will probably lie primarily in military, scientific, and industrial fields unless production can be increased and the cost considerably reduced. With so many other fibers in the apparel field, the producers of Fortisan may prefer not to tailor their fiber to meet such needs.

THE HIGH-WET-MODULUS AND CROSS-LINKED RAYONS

Avril [a]   Nupron [d]
Fiber HM [b]   Polynosic [b]
Fiber 700 [b]   Zantrel [b]
Lirelle [c]   Zantrel 700 [b]

[a] Trade name granted to FMC Corporation, American Viscose Division.
[b] Trade name granted to American Enka Corporation.
[c] Trade name granted to Courtaulds North America, Inc.
[d] Trade name granted to Midland-Ross Corporation, IRC Fibers Division.

There are at present only eight trade-named fibers in this group, with only seven in actual production. Some of the earlier ones and those on the market five years ago are no longer being produced. There may be quite a lot of these rayons produced without trademarks or other identification than "rayon."

The chief disadvantages of regular rayons have always been their high degree of swelling in water and low resistance to distortion and elongation when wet, which together resulted in dimensional instability. It has thus not been possible to predict or to control rayon shrinkage because swelling, in particular, depended on the amount of water imbibed; return to any given dimensions was dependent on the extent of the decrease in swelling with removal of water. Rayons, unless resin finished, have also been noticeably subject to wrinkling with poor wrinkle recovery, and their wet strength has been considerably lower than their dry strength. Scientists set out to find ways to overcome these disadvantageous properties. Cross-linked and high wet-modulus rayons were the result.

The first of this group of new rayons, Corval and Topel, trade-named fibers of Courtaulds North American, Inc., were announced as new cross-linked cellulose fibers in 1958. They were followed in 1960 by announcements of Avril and Zantrel, new high-wet-modulus fibers that are also cross-linked.

All these fibers, whether cross-linked only or high-wet-modulus, have properties in common that are considerably different from the older or "traditional" rayons. This group of fibers seems to combine the desirable properties of both cotton and the man-made fibers in a desirable fashion, and their price is competitive with cotton.

Producers of the new high-wet-modulus rayons attempted in 1960 to establish a new generic class for these fibers under the provisions of the Textile Fiber Products Identification Act. The FTC ruled that the new fibers still fell within the chemical definition of rayon and denied the re-

quest. Efforts to have the ruling overturned in the courts were not successful.

Although Corval is not now being produced, we shall look briefly at Corval as typical of the cross-linked rayons and more closely at Zantrel as an example of the high-wet-modulus rayons which seem destined to become the rayons of the future. Then, since both types are similar in properties, we shall explore the potentialities of their future together.

Corval

Cross-linking is the process of forming a three-dimensional polymer structure by adding an organic radical between CH_2OH side chains of the original cellobiose units. To state a complicated process simply, in developing Corval it was found that a combination of a form of formaldehyde and any of several catalysts or curing agents, in solution at pH anywhere under 9.5, could be used successfully to cause cross-linking of cellulose. The curing agents are Lewis acids (metallic salts) in the solid state, which are slightly soluble in water. The reaction is said to be a heat-activated, solid-state reaction which does not proceed in the presence of water. The reaction with the cellulose is believed to take place at the end of a drying process.

The success of the process was evident in the properties of Corval. Other than the following properties, Corval was comparable to the older rayons. Corval was reasonably stable in dimensions and did not exhibit progressive shrinkage. Its wet strength and resistance to distortion were much improved over those of the older rayons, yet its dyeability, texture, and wearing comfort were not impaired, Like cotton, it could be mercerized and slack-mercerized for stretch fabrics. Crimp was "set" because the fibers tended to retain the configuration in which they were cross-linked; this resulted in a mild degree of loft and bulk.

Zantrel

A high-modulus fiber is one that has relatively little initial distortion or elongation with a given applied force; high-wet-modulus fibers retain this resistance to distortion and elongation when wet.

The basic research work which resulted in the high-wet-modulus rayons was begun in Japan in 1938 by Schozo Tachikawa, the late president of the Tachikawa Research Institute. His work has been reported under the trade name Toramomen, the name given to the fiber in Japan. Tachikawa's purpose was to develop a man-made fiber with all the desirable properties of cotton. A high measure of success was announced to the English-speaking world in 1951. A European group, under option to produce the fiber when commercially feasible, helped to modify the research techniques

Tachikawa used in developing the fiber. Although the method of manufacture of Zantrel is protected by patents, the other high-wet-modulus rayons are undoubtedly made by similar processes. Zantrel is frequently described as a "polynosic" fiber although, after the FTC ruled that these fibers are rayons, the name Polynosic was granted as a trade name to the American Enka Corporation.

PROCESSES

The Zantrel processes are best described in the words of C. Eugene Coke, as they appeared in *American Dyestuff Reporter* for January 9, 1961 (pp. 35–40). He said

Involved in the manufacture of Zantrel is a radically new concept in cellulose chemistry. This concept is concerned with maintaining maximum cellulose chain length throughout the production of a very dilute cellulose zantrate solution. The concept also includes the formation of reconstituted cellulose in such a manner that the fiber has a stable and homogeneous microfibrillar structure. This structure is similar to that of the natural cellulosic fibers, such as cotton and flax, in which the cellulose molecules forming the structural elements or fibrils are closely and uniformly arranged with strong chemical bonds between them. This is in contrast with "old" rayon in which the fiber is built up from irregular bundles of cellulose molecules which are randomly arranged and which therefore have fewer and weaker chemical bonds. These differences in chain length and in structure are responsible for the differences in physical, chemical, and performance characteristics between Zantrel and the natural cellulosic fibers on one hand, and "old" rayon on the other hand. They account for the much lower resistance of "old" rayon toward swelling agents such as water and alkalis, which pentrate between its molecules readily and thereby further weaken the chemical bonds holding the structure together. This also accounts for the low wet strength and low initial wet modulus of "old" rayon.

To produce this new man-made cellulosic fiber, there is involved a new and unique manufacturing technique, including new chemical compositions, concentrations, and temperatures throughout the process. New chemical controls are involved and control limits are much narrower than ever employed in the manufacture of "old" rayon. A large portion of the equipment used to produce Zantrel has been especially designed and engineered for this fiber. Raw material for the manufacture of Zantrel is either cotton linters or wood pulp of the highest quality to meet rigid specifications for a high and uniform cellulose chain length (DP). The average DP * of cellulose molecules in the Zantrel fiber is not less than 520, as compared with 240–280 for "old" rayon.

PROPERTIES

The longitudinal microscopical appearance of the high-wet-modulus rayons is like that of other man-made fibers, including the traditional ray-

* DP is the abbreviation for degree of polymerization.

ons; the cross sections tend to be circular and look like a number of other fiber cross sections, including the thermoplastic fibers. The properties discussed for Zantrel are also applicable to Avril, Lirelle, and potential new fibers in this class.

Zantrel (and the other high-wet-modulus rayons) has retained all the good dry properties of the other rayons and has much improved wet properties. It is dimensionally stable to such an extent that it can be compressively preshrunk to less than 1 percent residual shrinkage; thus it can qualify for the Cluett, Peabody and Company "Sanforized" trademark. It has good wrinkle recovery but can be improved to easy-care standards by adding a small amount of resin; it retains its strength following such treatment. Zantrel has a crisp, lofty, pleasing hand and soft luster; it can be dyed in as wide a variety of colors and is as fast to light and washing as cotton. It is, in fact, more like cotton than like traditional rayon. Zantrel can be washed by machine and ironed like cotton. It is comfortable, absorbent, and does not accumulate static electricity.

Some of the properties of the new rayons are given in Table 15.

TABLE 15. Properties of the High-Wet-Modulus Rayons [a]

Properties	Avril	Zantrel	Lirelle
Specific gravity	1.50	1.51	1.53
Breaking tenacity (grams per denier)			
Standard [b]	5.1	3.4	5.0–5.5
Wet	3.5	2.7	4.0
Breaking elongation (percent)			
Standard [b]	18.0	10.0	6.5
Wet	21.0	12.0	7.0
Water absorbency (percent)	13.0	11.5	12.5

[a] Compiled from Textile World 1964 Man-Made Fiber Chart, July 1964.
[b] "Standard" refers to testing conditions of 70°F temperature and 65% relative humidity.

USES

Zantrel and Avril are appearing primarily in blends, both with natural and other man-made fibers. They are found in a wide range of woven fabrics which have traditionally been made of 100 percent cotton and in many types of knit goods. These fibers have been on the market since 1961 in ready-made dresses, blouses, and other items of apparel and are also found in blends with other fibers in drapery and upholstery fabrics, sheets and pillowcases, and table napery. The high-wet-modulus rayon sheets on

the market are of a quality and price comparable to cotton percale but softer in "hand." The high-wet-modulus rayons are commonplace in wardrobes for both sexes and all ages and for home furnishing fabrics of many types. Do you have anything that contains any of these fibers? You may be interested in looking on labels to see where you find them.

Future

The early success and consumer acceptance of the high-wet-modulus rayons is believed to be responsible in part for the recent resurgence of the rayon industry. Many rayon producers have converted their production systems so that they may produce these rayons. Present plant capacity is being expanded and new plants for rayon are still being built. These rayons have quietly replaced much of the older type rayon on the market. They are direct competitors to cotton in price. FMC Corporation has developed a new one of these rayons for belted and radial tires.

Present producers of Avril and Zantrel have established a policy, which if continued by these and adopted by other potential producers, will insure the quality of the fabrics produced from the new fibers. These fibers are being sold by letter or number and not by trade name. Only when the fabrics produced are shown to meet a specified standard, usually the L-22 standard for the specific end-use for which the fabric is intended, may the trade names Avril and Zantrel be used.

THE AZLONS (PROTEIN FIBERS)

Aralac (U.S.)   Sarelon (U.S.)
Ardil (U.K.)   Silkool (Japan)
Caslen (U.S.)   Vicara (U.S.)
Lanital (Italy)   Wipolan (Poland)
Merinova (Italy)

Azlon has been defined by the FTC, for enforcement of the Textile Fiber Products Identification Act, as "a manufactured fiber in which the fiber-forming substance is composed of any regenerated naturally occurring proteins." This group includes fibers made from the casein of skim milk, the zein of corn, and the proteins of soybeans and peanuts. Experimental work has been done with keratin of feathers; proteins of cotton, pumpkin, and tobacco seed, hemoglobin, and lactoglobulins; proteins from horse serum, fish, and egg albumin; and practically all other proteins that can be made soluble.

These fibers are defined as "regenerated" protein fibers, but this defini-

tion does not have the same meaning as it has for regenerated cellulosic fibers. Although the raw materials were formerly protein substances, they were not originally fibrous in nature as were the celluloses used for rayon. All the man-made protein fibers need to be cross-linked by artificial means, that is, cross-links are not present naturally as in wool. This has been a big problem in their production.

Azlons have a number of properties that are similar to the natural protein fibers; they bear more resemblance to wool than to silk. Azlons are composed of varying amino acids, but the structure is believed to be more like silk than wool. The protein molecules, though having many side chains, are believed to be in a different form than in wool, so that stable cross-links have not developed, although there are some salt linkages.

Azlons burn less readily than cellulosic fibers, but perhaps somewhat more readily than wool, with an odor of burning hair or feathers not quite as strong as the odor for burning wool or silk. There is a black residue, which is brittle and can be readily crushed between the fingers. Azlons are similar to wool or weaker in strength, and have considerably lower strength wet than dry; elongation is fairly high. All are absorbent and do not accumulate charges of static electricity. They are resilient, pleasant, and warm to the touch, have good insulative value, and do not felt. All have the same appearance under the microscope, both longitudinally and in their round cross-sections, with no distinguishing characteristics.

Vicara is the strongest of the man-made protein fibers to date, and has the highest wet strength in relation to dry. Comparisons reported with one type of wool show these dry and wet tenacity relations in grams per denier between the commercially prepared fibers: wool 50's dry tenacity 1.2, wet 75 percent of dry; zein fiber dry tenacity 1.2, wet 62 percent of dry; casein fiber dry tenacity 0.7, wet 43 percent of dry; and peanut fiber dry tenacity 0.8, wet 38 percent of dry.

Attempts to make protein fibers began a great many years ago, but none was successful enough for commercial production. In 1935, Antonio Ferretti of Italy developed a successful process for casein fiber made from skim milk which was produced under the trade name Lanital, by the Snia Viscosa Company in Italy. The second such fiber was Vicara, trade name for the zein protein fiber from corn, produced by the Virginia-Carolina Company of the United States. These, with soybean and peanut protein fibers, are considered to be the most promising for resuming, continuing, or increasing protein fiber production. Each fiber is chemically different, although there are similarities in the reactions of peanut, milk, and soybean fibers. The zein fibers differ from the others in several properties, although they are vegetable protein fibers, as are peanut and soybean protein fibers.

At various times one or another fiber has been produced in another

country, but Vicara (zein fiber) has been produced only in the United States, Ardil (peanut fiber) is being produced only in the United Kingdom, and Merinova (casein fiber) is produced only in Italy.

The future of the man-made protein fibers is very uncertain. Corn, peanuts, milk and soybeans are all important sources of food proteins. In the United States, emphasis on producing fibers from these sources was often due to the desire to discover new methods for utilizing surplus food-stuffs. This is no longer true. Large segments of the world's population are underfed, and the problem of protein fibers is tied to questions of philosophy, politics, nationalism, economics, sociology, transportation, trade, and many other factors, as well as the food habits and food preferences of the different areas of the world. The situation is complicated by a multiplicity of interrelating conditions. Can you think of examples of some of these problems? We all need to think of ways in which progress can be made toward solving them.

For all these reasons, and also because there are so many other sources of materials for fibers in the world, there seems to be considerable doubt how far experiments with these types of protein substances will be pursued. Regardless of their future, it has been demonstrated that it is possible to utilize some of the protein substances in making fibers. A brief discussion of certain of these fibers follows.

Vicara

In 1935, L. C. Swallen of the Corn Products Refining Company applied for a patent for a protein fiber made from zein of corn, but much work was done at the Northern Regional Research Laboratory of the USDA, at the Harris Research Laboratories, and at the Virginia-Carolina Chemical Corporation before the process was perfected enough to go into commercial production in 1948. It was manufactured in small quantities and found ready acceptance; facilities were being expanded, but production was halted, for unexplained reasons, in 1958. The projected sale of process and plant to another company was not made, and the plant has been dismantled. Although it is no longer being produced, the processing is typical for this class of fibers and therefore is of interest to us.

Vicara is made from zein, the protein found in the gluten of corn. It is extracted from the corn gluten meal by means of isopropyl alcohol during processing for corn starch, corn sugar, and other such products. Zein is dried and milled as a pale yellow powder. The zein from many batches of corn gluten in the mills is blended to give uniformity of fibers.

Vicara processes are quite similar to those for viscose rayon through the fiber-coagulating stage; then several curing steps are required to stretch

and orient the molecules within the fiber and to cross-link the molecules with each other.

The first step is to dissolve the zein in a dilute alkaline solution, which is believed to uncurl the protein molecules sufficiently for them to be acted on by processing chemicals and to be forced through the spinnerets. When thoroughly dissolved, the viscous liquid is stored in aging tanks, usually for 24 hours, where viscosity increases until the material has become a solid gel.

The gel is then filtered and forced through spinnerets into the coagulating bath, which contains an acid to precipitate the fiber, a small amount of formaldehyde to form enough cross-links to give stability for further processing, and perhaps salt. The spinnerets are the large, thousands-of-holes type for producing tow. The filaments go through the rest of the processing as tow collected from many spinnerets—as many as 270,000 filaments may be processed in a single tow. After leaving the coagulating bath, the filaments pass through a heated precuring chamber that "fixes" the cross-links. They then go through the same general stretching procedure as the rayons. It is necessary to treat the filaments again with more formaldehyde to form more cross-linkages, then again to cure in order to stabilize the structure, which now has many cross-links between molecular chains, as does wool. This structure is dimensionally stable and will not felt or shrink in subsequent washing or cleaning.

After curing, washing is necessary in order to remove the remaining traces of chemicals. Then the fiber is dried, crimped for some uses, cut into staple lengths of ½ to 6 inches, and baled in 300- or 500-pound bales. Vicara is a relatively expensive fiber to produce.

PROPERTIES

Vicara has a very luxurious hand, resembling the softness of the finest wools (Vicuna and cashmere). Its diameter can be made similar to these fibers. Vicara is pale yellow unless bleached; then it is slightly creamy, about like white wool. Its strength is comparable to fine wool, both dry and wet, and it has high elongation and elasticity, insuring excellent wrinkle resistance and rapid recovery from creasing. Its specific gravity is 1.2, making it a little lighter in weight than comparable wool. Moisture regain is 10 percent. It may be washed and ironed like cotton and rayon. Vicara is not damaged by boiling water. Deterioration by sunlight is very slow, but sunlight gradually bleaches undyed Vicara.

Vicara is much more resistant than wool to alkaline solutions; separation is sometimes made by dissolving out the wool in hot dilute alkaline solutions. The fibers, which are resistant to a wide variety of chemicals, can be

dyed with most of the dyes used for wool. Vicara is not attacked by moths or carpet beetles and is resistant to mildew, molds, and rot.

Because of its cost and limited quantities, Vicara, during its short history in this country, had limited usage. It was used for cashmere-like sweaters and in soft, lightweight, Vicara-wool blend fabrics for sport shirts, dresses, suiting materials (both for men and for women), robes, blouses, and knitted garments. It imparted a softness, drape, and luxurious feel that is often very desirable.

Casein Fibers

The first man-made protein fiber was Lanital, produced in Italy as the result of the work of Ferreti, mentioned earlier. Merinova is the casein fiber now produced in Italy, and Wipolan is produced in Poland. Aralac was the name given a similar fiber produced for a few years in the United States during World War II but it was not well accepted by the public. The plant was sold to the Virginia-Carolina Chemical Corporation in 1948 for production of Vicara. A small amount of another casein fiber, Caslen, was produced in the United States. Merinova is produced in sufficient quantities in Italy to warrant attention and is marketed in the United States. Have you seen anything made of it, or any of the advertisements?

In many countries, casein fiber, produced from milk, has been made in a purposeful effort to find a substitute for wool, partly because of the expense of wool, and partly to make the country in question more self-sufficient. This situation was particularly true for those nations planning the acts of aggression against others that developed into World War II. The motive in the United States has not been economic self-sufficiency but rather interest in experimentation.

The method for producing the casein fibers is essentially the same as that for Vicara and does not need to be repeated.

Many of the properties of the casein fibers are similar to those of wool. They lack the wet strength and stability of wool, however, and are said to be subject to moth and mildew attack. These fibers have been used as wool substitutes and mixed with wool or rayon for wool-like woven and knitted goods. When wet some casein fabrics have a disagreeable odor. They require careful handling when wet and in pressing, and they scorch at temperatures lower than for cotton. Casein fibers are white.

Casein fibers seem to have won limited acceptance in some other countries, but not for apparel and textile furnishing uses in the United States. The industrial casein fiber Caslen attained considerable acceptance in high-denier bristles, in curled fiber for paint roller covers, and in other such items. The curled fiber in the coarse deniers was said to be springier than wool.

Soybean Fiber

Countries producing large quantities of soybeans have exhibited interest in producing a soybean protein fiber. Early investigations were made by the Japanese, although patents were granted for processing soybean fiber in the United States as early as 1940. From 1939 to 1943 the Ford Motor Company carried on work with soybean fiber as a possible automobile upholstery fabric. The processes were taken over by the Drackett Products Company in 1943 and continued a few years longer, then discontinued. Work on the Japanese soybean fiber Silkool was also dropped at the end of World War II.

Soybean protein is removed from the meal by steeping the meal with a solution of sodium sulfite after the oil is extracted from the bean. Processing of the protein is then similar to that for Vicara.

Soybean fiber varies in color from white to tan, has a density of 1.3, which is the same as that for wool, and is similar to casein fiber in other properties and in its uses. The fiber has crimp as it comes through final processing.

Peanut Fiber

Peanut protein fiber, named Ardil in the United Kingdom where it was first developed, and Sarelon in the United States, was first made in experimental fibers in 1938 at the Ardeer factory in Scotland. World War II stopped the work, which was resumed when hostilities ceased. Experimental work on peanut protein fiber, as well as on cottonseed protein and other fibers, has been carried on at the USDA laboratory, commonly known as the Southern Regional Research Laboratory.

First the oil is removed, then the meal is dissolved, and then the protein is precipitated out and carried through processes approximately the same as for Vicara. To produce crimp for some uses, after other processing is complete, the fibers are wetted, stretched, and then released.

Peanut fiber is creamy white to light tan in color, and can be made in fine deniers or deniers coarse enough for carpet fiber, for which it was sometimes used in the United Kingdom. Other properties and uses are the same as for casein or soybean fiber.

THE ALGINATES

Alginate is not defined by the FTC since no alginate fiber is produced in the United States, and it is of slight importance elsewhere. The United Kingdom is the only country producing the fiber—calcium alginate—at the present time.

Calcium alginate fiber is derived from the alginic acid of the cell wall of several types of brown-colored seaweed; the acid is closely related, chemically, to cellulose and to pectic acid. The acid is a polymer composed of long chains of d-mannuronic acid. Brown seaweed contains 15 to 40 percent alginic acid. The acid groups are very reactive, especially with alkalies. Alginic acid is used in a number of food products and in finishing agents for paper and cloth.

E. C. C. Stanford (England) in 1883 discovered that the viscous material of certain seaweed could be extracted and precipitated, but the first patent for a process to shape such material into filament form was issued to Sarason (Germany) in 1912. Beginning with the work of J. B. Speakman, N. H. Chamberlain, and Johnson, about 1939, efforts to develop alginate fibers have been concentrated in England. Methods for successfully spinning and using the fibers obtained are credited to this trio.

The steps in producing calcium alginate fibers are, briefly, (1) collecting, drying, and milling the seaweed; (2) treatment with a solution of sodium carbonate to produce a thick, gelatinous mass of sodium alginate; (3) filtration; (4) bleaching with sodium hypochlorite; (5) spinning on a viscose spinning system; and (6) coagulating in a bath containing small amounts of calcium chloride, hydrochloric acid, and a cationic agent to prevent filament adhesion. Other metals may be substituted for calcium, with the resultant fiber not so alkali-sensitive, but they are not practical for other reasons.

Calcium alginate has two notable properties; it is fire resistant, and it quickly dissolves in very weak alkaline solution, even in washing with ordinary soap. Alginate fibers are the most hygroscopic known. They have fair strength when dry but become steadily weaker with increasing humidity, until their strength is practically nil when they reach saturation. Treatment with synthetic resins or some other chemicals improves their resistance to alkalies.

The very high sensitivity to alkaline solutions determines the uses for this fiber, which are unique. Alginate fibers are spun with wool or other fibers, or used as core yarns, woven or knitted into fabrics, then dissolved out in finishing, leaving fabrics of a sheerness that would be impossible or impracticable to make otherwise. Alginates are used in background fabrics for laces, embroideries, etc., then are washed out after the processes have been completed, leaving an open-mesh lace or embroidery structure which has been easily handled by the lace-making and embroidery machines because of the alginate background fabric. Alginate yarns are also used as spacing yarns for open-patterned fabric and are then removed by washing in the finishing process. During World War II alginate camouflage nettings, because they are impervious to infrared rays, were used successfully to

hide military objectives in the United Kingdom from enemy radio detection devices.

Recently some new interest has been shown in the use of alginate as a carrying yarn or structure in hosiery and fabric mills and as a surgical dressing; alginate acts as an agent to arrest bleeding as well as to form an absorbable film over the wound.

Opinions vary on the possibilities for developing a desirable alginate fiber on large scale. Certainly there is no dearth of raw material. With the present abundance of other fibers, however, there seems little reason to expect that much more will be done about alginate fibers than is presently being attempted. But some new discovery may be made that will change the picture entirely!

FOR FURTHER READING

American Dyestuff Reporter.

Hollen, N. R., and Saddler, J.: *Textiles.*

Joseph, M. L.: *Introductory Textile Science.*

Labarthe, J.: *Textiles: Origins to Usage.*

Linton, G. E.: *Natural and Man-made Textile Fibers.*

Mark, H. F., Atlas, S. M., and Cernia, E.: *Man-Made Fibers: Science and Technology.* Volume I.

Mauersberger, H. R. (ed.): *American Handbook of Synthetic Textiles.*

Mauersberger, H. R. (ed.): *Matthews' Textile Fibers.*

Mauersberger, H. R. and Schwarz, E. W. K.: *Rayon and Staple Fiber Handbook.*

Modern Textiles Magazine.

Moncrieff, R. W.: *The Man-Made Fibres.*

Rules and Regulations under the Textile Fiber Products Identification Act. Federal Trade Commission Public Law 85–897.

Sherman, J. V. and Sherman, S. L.: *The New Fibers.*

Textile Chemist and Colorist.

Textile Research Journal.

▰▰▰▰▰▰▰▰▰▰▰▰▰▰▰▰▰▰▰▰▰▰▰▰▰▰▰▰▰▰▰▰

THE THERMOPLASTIC MAN-MADE FIBERS

acetate, nylon, modacrylics, nytrils, olefins, polyesters, rubber Sarans, vinals, vinyons, spandex

Acetate was the first thermoplastic man-made fiber, nylon was next, and now we have a great many such fibers with more still ahead. In addition to the acetates and nylons, this group of fibers at present includes the acrylics, modacrylics, nytrils, olefins, polyesters, rubbers (not true thermoplastic fibers), sarans, vinals, vinyons, tetrafluoroethylene, and spandex. The man-made mineral fibers are included in the Thermoplastic Class in Table 12 but are excluded in the discussions of this chapter because the temperatures at which they melt are so very much higher than those of the fibers included here that most of the statements made do not apply to them. The mineral fibers are included in Chapter 8.

The thermoplastic fibers are those that soften and become pliable or "plastic" with heat. Their softening points vary from quite low to very high. In the softened stage, this group of fibers may be shaped, pleated, embossed, or distorted, and unless the "setting" temperature is exceeded, the result is permanent. The thermoplastic fibers will also melt if touched with too hot an iron or other surface, if they are in contact with flames or hot air from blasts, or other sources at temperatures above their melting points. Hot cigarette ashes will melt them. The hot, melted material can

cause very severe burns, as does any other hot, syrupy material which tends to cling to the surfaces on which it cools.

These fibers, in common with other man-made fibers, must be stretched to orient the molecules in order to increase fiber strength, tenacity, and sometimes their dimensional stability. During the processing, spinning, and drawing operations, in which orientation of the molecules has occurred, the linear molecules are under considerable strain which, if released during washing and steaming, may result in considerable shrinkage and perhaps in puckering of the fabric. Heat treatments have been devised for relaxing such strains in the thermoplastic fibers. Heat-setting or heat treatment is used for some, but not all, of the thermoplastic fibers to achieve dimensional stability.

The Chemstrand Corporation, in its *Technical and Sales Service Manual*, has made these statements concerning heat-setting of nylon:

. . . Heat-setting causes a rearrangement and fixation of the internal molecular structure of nylon. Internal stresses are relieved and the fibers tend to permanently assume the structural arrangement in which they are held during the setting treatment. The degree of set imparted will depend on the severity of the setting conditions, which are determined by the tension involved and temperature and time of the treatment. . . .

Normally nylon yarn will tend to shrink when it is subjected to a heat-setting treatment. When shrinkage of the yarn is prevented, the maximum contraction force exerted by the yarn is approximately 0.4 gm/den in either steam or dry heat. If a greater force is applied, it is possible to stretch the yarn. In this manner, many of the properties of nylon can be appreciably altered by stretching or relaxing the nylon material during heat-setting. Stretching of nylon yarn at high temperatures will result in a reduction in elongation and denier and an increase in tenacity, providing the nylon is not damaged or degraded in the process. Relaxation at high temperatures will have the opposite effect.

The reasons given for heat-setting nylon are to stabilize the twist in yarns; to remove residual shrinkage from yarns, cords, ropes, and fabrics; to increase wrinkle resistance; to set the "grain" in fabrics; to remove edge curl of knitted fabrics; to obtain washable pleats; to obtain variation in hand or drape; and to shape garments according to end-use requirements.

The heat-setting reasons and methods for nylon are generally applicable to the other thermoplastic fibers.

The thermoplastic fibers have a number of properties in common. They are relatively nonabsorbent and hygroscopicity is low; therefore they may be uncomfortable to wear in hot, humid weather, particularly if closely woven or knitted. They are easily washed and quick drying. They tend not to stain easily, and water-soluble stains and spots wash out rather

readily. The latter is not always true of grease or oil-borne stains, which are difficult to wash out of fibers in general. Because of low moisture absorption and low conductivity, or none at all, when conditions are right the thermoplastic fibers accumulate charges of static electricity with their accompanying annoyances. Most thermoplastic fibers have excellent wrinkle resistance, but a few do not. Because of low absorption, new classes of dyestuffs and new methods of dyeing have had to be developed for most of this group of fibers. Dyestuffs and methods that work for one of the group often work for nearly all the other thermoplastic fibers. Seam fraying is about the same problem it is with silk and other man-made fibers; in some instances, however, seam edges may be heat sealed (in commercial production of garments) on thermoplastic-fiber fabrics.

The thermoplastic fibers, as seen through the microscope, all have the same longitudinal appearance as other man-made fibers with no distinguishing characteristics for the different fibers. Although cross sections vary among types of fibers, it has become impossible to positively identify most of the specific types by cross sections alone. More and more fibers or their modifications resemble at least one other fiber in microscopic appearance. With special spinnerets designed to give specific shapes, identification by means of cross sections becomes ever less certain.

All these fibers are immune to attack by moths, mildew, mold, or other organisms, and all are said to be nonallergenic to human beings.

Pilling has been a problem with several of the thermoplastic fibers, usually the stronger ones. The DuPont Company, in a bulletin titled *Dyeing and Finishing "Dacron" Polyester Fiber,* has given this description and explanation of Dacron pilling which is also applicable to other fibers:

"Dacron" polyester staple in many fabrics, including blends with other fibers, has a tendency to pill or form fuzz balls on the fabric surface. . . . Pills are formed when fibers of "Dacron" tangle with themselves or lint on the surface of the fabric. The abrasion and working action that a fabric receives during wear, washing, and dry cleaning raises a surface fuzz. This fuzz upon reaching a critical length will start entangling with adjacent fibers and lint, eventually producing pills. The "Dacron" fibers which anchor a pill are so strong that normal abrasion in wear will not break them away.

Static electricity also tends to cause the picking up and retention of lint and dirt, which may be held in the pills, giving a garment a soiled, rough appearance. Staple fabrics are more subject to pilling than filament fabrics because of the great number of exposed fiber ends. Texturizing processes for filament yarns, which permit their use in place of staple yarns for which pilling has been a problem, have overcome this difficulty in many instances.

With these common characteristics and explanations in mind, we shall be interested, primarily, in differences among the fibers and fiber groups.

THE ACETATES

Acetate

Acele[a]	Celaloft[c]	Celatress[c]	Loftura[d]
Avicolor[b]	Celaperm[c] *	Celaweb[c]	Type F[c]
Celacloud[c]	Celara[c]	Chromspun[d] *	Type K[c]
Celacrimp[c]	Celarandom[c]	Estron[d]	
Celafil[c]	Celatow[c]	Estron "SLR"[d]	

[a] Trade name granted to E. I. duPont de Nemours & Co., Inc.
[b] Trade name granted to FMC Corporation, American Viscose Division.
[c] Trade name granted to Celanese Corporation.
[d] Trade name granted to Eastman Kodak Co., Tennessee Eastman Company Division.
* Solution dyed.

The early history of general developments applicable to acetate is largely covered in the history of rayon since acetate was classified as a rayon in the United States until 1952. Acetate is usually described as a cellulose-base fiber or cellulose derivative, because its basic raw material is cellulose from cotton linters or wood pulp. But acetate has been so changed chemically that its characteristics are very different from those of cellulose. The textile world is divided in its opinion whether acetate is or is not a truly synthesized fiber. It shall be considered as one here.

The acetates are the first family of man-made thermoplastic fibers in point of time, and may yet be second only to nylon in the amounts produced; nylon production first surpassed acetate in 1956. How rapidly other fibers are overtaking acetate in amounts produced, if they are doing so, cannot be known at this time; nor are their present relative positions known, because the fibers are lumped together in reporting. At present there are only two members of the family—acetate and triacetate. Acetate is the oldest of the man-made thermoplastic fibers and triacetate is one of the newest.

Acetate is defined for the Textile Fiber Products Identification Act as ". . . a manufactured fiber in which the fiber-forming substance is cellulose acetate. Where not less than 92% of the hydroxyl groups are acetylated, the term triacetate may be used as a generic description of the fiber." The only triacetate fiber at present being manufactured is Arnel, the fiber to be explored after our study of acetate. Its history will often be apparent in the history and processing of acetate.

Since acetate was the first of the thermoplastic fibers, it has borne the brunt of the consumer's dissatisfactions and frustrations while learning to care properly for such heat-sensitive materials. Part of the current apathy toward, or dislike for, rayon may be associated with this early experience too, for many older consumers have not yet learned to distinguish between

acetate and rayon. The lesson on behavior of heat-sensitive fibers has been so well learned, however, that today there are relatively few complaints concerning garments that were ruined because too hot an iron was used, with the result that the fabric fused or glazed, or disappeared completely where an iron had been set down upon it. Many people still erroneously associate thermoplasticity with rayon, and many irons are still marked "rayon" at the low temperature setting.

The possibility of an acetylated cellulosic fiber began with the preparation of cellulose acetate by Schutzenberger in 1869; however, no attempt was made to spin a fiber from the material. In 1894, Cross and Bevan, who were working with the acetate compound as well as with the viscose rayon process, discovered that certain chemicals (zinc chloride or sulfuric acid) would serve as catalysts to speed up the formation of cellulose acetate, thus making it commercially feasible, and that the resultant compound could then be put into solution with chloroform to make a desirable "dope" for a protective coating for cloth and metals. E. Bronnert (Germany) made the first acetate filaments in 1899. The early fibers were the completely acetylated form of cellulose—triacetate—which could be precipitated at that time only in highly volatile and hazardous chloroform, and which were practically undyeable.

Cross and Bevan gave their information to A. D. Little, Morck, and W. H. Walker in the United States, who were also experimenting with viscose rayon. The American group perfected the first acetate fiber, for which they received a patent as "artificial silk" in the early 1900's. An important development, the kneading process still used in the production of acetate, was patented by Eichengruen and Becker in 1901.

In 1903, G. W. Miles discovered that by treating the triacetate to cause saponification, it could be made soluble in acetone, a much more feasible and less expensive solvent than chloroform for large-scale production. From this start, the present processes for partial de-acetylation of triacetate to make the acetone-soluble acetate were developed.

The Lustron Company, in 1914, started a factory and commercially produced a limited quantity of acetate fiber, but the venture was unsuccessful, probably because the acetate was the triacetate form, with the disadvantages listed previously.

World War I interrupted fiber work with cellulose acetate, which was then in demand as dope for coating the fabric wings and fuselages of biplanes—the only airplanes of that day. This was the beginning of the air age, and before the war ended there was a great demand for acetate dope for this purpose. Consequently, under the direction of the Dreyfus brothers of Switzerland, factories were established for its production. In the meantime, monoplanes with metal wings and fuselages were developed, replacing

fabric-covered planes within a few years' time, and this, together with the end of hostilities, found the factories with large supplies of dope and facilities for its manufacture on hand. Attention was again turned toward producing a fiber from the acetate dope.

In 1924, the Celanese Corporation of America completed a plant for production of acetone-soluble acetate, which then came on the market in 1925. At about the same time, the British Celanese and Chemical Manufacturing Company, working with the dyestuff industry, developed dyestuffs and methods for dyeing the new fiber. Their efforts, although very costly at the time, have paid off in that the same dyestuffs and methods have served to dye other thermoplastic man-made fibers.

Acetate was thus the fourth man-made fiber to be produced commercially. Acetate was considerably more expensive than the rayons until 1934, but has since been produced at very little higher cost. It is more of a luxury fiber in feel and use than is rayon, and is not so easy to produce because large volumes of the chemicals used must be recovered; for these reasons it has never been produced in the same quantities as rayon, particularly since the development of high-tenacity rayons.

PRODUCTION AND ECONOMICS

Acetate is produced by four companies in the United States and in 32 companies in other countries in various parts of the world. Figures for acetate are commonly reported with rayon, even though separate figures may be given for each fiber.

Table 16 shows data on the production of acetate fiber, in filament and in staple form, since 1940. Although the production of acetate is much less than for rayon, it has maintained a fairly steady part of the market. With

TABLE 16. United States Production of Acetate (Millions of Pounds and Percent)[a]

Year	Filament		Staple and Tow		Total
	Pound	Percent	Pound	Percent	
1940	133.0	92.7	10.5	7.3	143.5
1945	174.9	81.7	39.3	18.3	214.2
1950	326.6	73.6	117.0	26.4	443.6
1955	230.1	79.9	57.8	20.1	287.9
1960	228.2	79.2	60.0	20.8	288.2
1965	391.2	87.9	54.0	12.1	445.2
1968	439.9	89.8	50.0	10.2	489.9

[a] Compiled from *Textile Organon*, February 1964 and February 1969.

the development of texturizing processes, acetate filament yarn production has gone up at the expense of staple length fiber and has now reached the highest peak in its history.

According to *Textile Organon* for June 1968, a total of 788 million pounds of acetate filament was produced in the world in 1967 of which ten countries produced 93.8 percent. These countries were the United States (54.1%), the United Kingdom (9.3%), Japan (7.4%), the USSR (6.1%), Italy (4.8%), Canada (3.9%), Mexico (2.8%), France (2.1%), Brazil (2.0%), and Belgium (1.3%).

Acetate staple and tow produced in 1967 amounted to 76 million pounds of which the following seven countries produced 98.6 percent: the United States (65.8%), Canada (14.5%), the United Kingdom (5.3%), France and West Germany (3.9% each), and Mexico and Japan (2.6% each.

PROCESSES

The production of acetate begins with purified cellulose from cotton linters or wood pulp, as do the rayons. Successful production of acetate, however, depends on efficient recovery of some of the expensive chemicals used, or the acetate process would be prohibitive in cost compared to rayon. Recovery of chemicals was not necessary for any of the rayon processes; they use only the cheaper chemicals in large amounts.

In addition to purified cellulose, the production of acetate requires glacial acetic acid, acetic anhydride, sulfuric acid, acetone, water, and, if it is delustered, titanium dioxide. All these materials must be very pure, colorless, and free from traces of metals that might discolor the fiber. Throughout processing, wherever possible, materials from different batches are blended to insure constant uniformity of the fiber.

With improvement in processing and efficiency, the amounts of the various raw materials required to process a pound of fiber, and the amounts recovered of certain of these raw materials, vary somewhat from time to time. An idea of the quantities of some of these materials used at the start and actually consumed per pound of fiber may be gained from the following figures:

Raw Material	Amount Required for Process, Pound	Amount Consumed, Pound
Purified cellulose	0.67	0.67
Acetic anhydride	1.60	—
Glacial acetic acid	4.00	0.70
Sulfuric acid	0.05	0.05
Acetone	3.00	0.30

Part of the acetic anhydride and part of the glacial acetic acid are recovered as weak acetic acid; and much of the acetone is recovered—the amount depending on the efficiency of the particular plant. About 10 pounds of water are required to process a pound of acetate, and about 0.02 pound of titanium dioxide to produce a pound of delustered acetate.

The purified cellulose is pretreated by moistening with acetic acid in order to start reaction before the acetylation proper begins. The acetylators, in which most of the reaction takes place, are huge closed-system mixing tanks equipped with stirrers and jacketed to permit circulation of liquid or air around them so that temperatures can be controlled at ranges of 35 to 120°F.

The acetylator is prepared for a batch by putting in specific amounts of acetic anhydride, glacial acetic acid, and sulfuric acid, mixing thoroughly, and cooling to 45°F. Then the moistened cellulose, in amounts of 200 to 300 pounds, is added gradually, with constant kneading by the stirrer blades; the temperature is held below 68°F for an hour, and then held below 86°F for the rest of the acetylation period of 5 to 8 hours. During this time the cellulose, which has the chemical structure shown in Chapter 4, picks up acetyl groups (CH_3CO) in replacement for the OH groups, thus forming cellulose triacetate. This is called *primary acetate* and is the chloroform-soluble type discovered so many years ago. Frequent testing is necessary to determine when acetylation is complete and the right degree of viscosity has been reached to give the initial strength of fiber desired. During acetylation, the fibrous structure of the cellulose has disappeared, and the mixture has become a semitransparent, acrid-smelling, viscous fluid, sometimes described as having the consistency of molasses. Although sulfuric acid is called a catalyst and does speed reaction, it is entirely consumed in the process and is not recoverable; thus it does not function as a true catalyst, which stimulates action in which it is not itself involved.

From the acetylator, the viscous triacetate is run into tanks containing water and weak acetic acid, in which a higher temperature is maintained than in the acetylator. The mixture is allowed to stand for 20 to 50 hours for partial deacetylation. In this period, the weak acid encourages replacement of some of the acetyl groups with OH from water, as they originally were in cellulose. When the action has gone about one-fourth of the way to complete reversion to the original form, the process is stopped and the product is called *secondary acetate*. This is the acetone-soluble type.

At this stage the viscous solution is run into water, which precipitates the secondary acetate as white, crumblike flakes. The flakes are washed thoroughly in huge vats in order to remove and recover all remaining acetic acid, whirled in centrifuges to remove the water, dried, and stored until wanted for spinning into fibers.

Spinning of acetate is a dry-spinning process—the first such process developed for a man-made fiber. The acetate flakes are dissolved in acetone, placed for a few hours in vacuum tanks to remove air bubbles, and then forced by pressure to metered pumps where specific amounts of the viscous acetate are supplied to the spinnerets. Each spinneret is at the top of a very long, narrow, closed shaft (or chimney), which has an opening at the center bottom for drawing the filament fibers, and which is equipped with an air intake at the bottom and an air outlet near the top of the shaft (see Figure 7-1). Warm air circulates upward through the shaft, and as the filament is forced from the spinneret and drawn downward to the bobbin beneath the shaft, the warm air evaporates the acetone from the acetate, which is a dry filament by the time it reaches the bottom of the shaft. The acetone-vapor-laden air is removed at the top air valve for reclamation of the acetone. The whole system must be closed because of the flammability and volatility of the acetone.

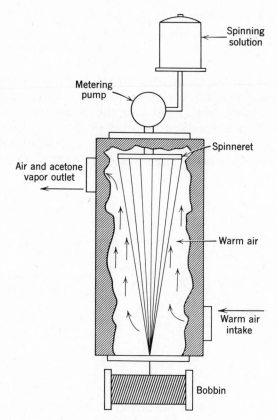

FIGURE 7-1.   Diagram of the dry-spinning system of acetate.

The difference in speed between the winding of the bobbins and the emergence of the filaments from the spinneret draws the fibers, helping to control diameter, orient the molecules, and increase fiber strength. The present high-tenacity fiber made from acetate, you will recall, is Fortisan, which has been saponified by the removal of the acetyl groups by alkali, and thus has lost its acetate nature and become a rayon. There seems to be no reason why acetate itself could not be produced in high-tenacity yarn without being subjected to saponification, if such a fiber were desired.

When drawn from the spinneret, acetate is a finished fiber, needing no further processing except lubrication as it is wound on the bobbin, unless staple length fiber is desired. In this case the filaments are cut in even lengths, according to the system on which they are to be spun, or in the lengths of other fibers with which the acetate fibers are to be blended. Staple-cut fibers are given crimp to facilitate blending, then are lubricated and baled.

If dull acetate is desired, titanium dioxide is added to the spinning solution. Black acetate has been made for years by adding black pigment to the spinning solution. A more recent practice is the production of other solution- or dope-dyed colors.

A diagram of the chemical structure of triacetate is shown in this chapter in the discussion of Arnel. Since no one is quite sure just how de-acetylation takes place, the position of the remaining acetyl groups of acetate is not definitely known. It is believed that the acetyl groups form side chains, which account for the stability and wrinkle resistance of acetate. A possible chemical structure of secondary acetate has been theorized thus:

PROPERTIES

Acetate has the characteristic cross section that is also possessed by Arnel and Fortisan. In regular types of acetate, the cross sections resemble

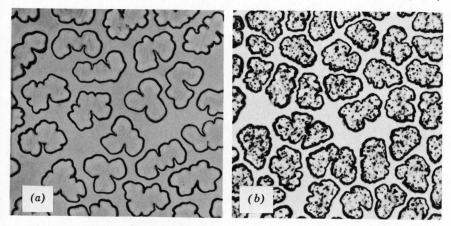

FIGURE 7-2. Cross-section photomicrographs of (a) acetate, and (b) Arnel. (Courtesy E. I. duPont de Nemours & Co. Inc.)

three- to five-petaled flowers or clover leaves. Figure 7-2a is a photomicrograph of bright acetate and Figure 7-2b is of delustered Arnel.

Acetate has a soft, smooth, cool, pleasant feel, rich appearance, and excellent draping characteristics, most of which are important in determining its uses. Sometimes a slight acetic acidlike odor can be noted, especially during pressing. Acetate produces a luxurious hand for both soft and crisp fabrics. Luster can be controlled to any desired degree.

Acetate is pure white in color, and yellows only slowly with age and use compared with silk, wool, and rayon. It has better resistance to light deterioration than the fibers thus far studied, except for Fortisan. The bright fibers usually have better sunlight resistance than do the delustered fibers, as is true of other man-made fibers. A new, light-resistant, dull-luster acetate (Estron SLR acetate-dull) for decorative fabrics was announced early in 1963 by the Eastman Company. This new dull acetate is said to have better resistance to light degradation than bright acetate and also to be more thermally stable than other acetates, that is, not to be so prone to changing length with changes in temperature and humidity.

Acetate can be made in any diameter or length desired, but it has not been commercially produced in diameters of less than 1.5 deniers; its softness and suppleness at this size apparently make a finer fiber unnecessary. The largest percentage of acetate is used in filament rather than in staple form.

Acetate melts or burns, depending on the weight and construction of the fabric. Lightweight sheer acetate fabrics flame almost like cotton or

rayon, leaving black, syrupy, melted material at the edges. Heavier fabrics tend to melt along the edges and curl rather than to flame and burn rapidly. After cooling, the curled black edge is very hard and rigid and cannot be crumbled with the fingers. All acetates turn black along the burning area and the residue is black. They burn with a penetrating, acrid odor. A British company is said to have produced a new acetate that is virtually flame resistant by adding a halogen compound to the spinning solution. The process should also be applicable to Arnel.

The absorbency, swelling, and hygroscopicity of acetate are lower than for other fibers we have studied. These properties account in large measure for its dimensional stability, resistance to staining and soiling, quick-drying characteristics, and ease in removing soil and stains. Moisture regain is 6 to 6.5 percent. Acetate shows some tendency to accumulate charges of static electricity, but not to the degree of the less hygroscopic man-made fibers. It is considered a good electrical insulative material.

The specific gravity of acetate is 1.32, about the same as that of wool, and, as presently produced, it is comparable to wool in its range in strength with a breaking tenacity range of 1.2 to 1.5 grams per denier. Acetate is considerably weaker wet than when dry. Elongation is about 25 percent and increases when the fiber is wet. Acetate has good resilience and good elasticity (at low loads), which make it quite resistant to creasing and a good fiber for blending or mixing with crease-prone fibers to give more desirable fabrics.

Acetate, being thermoplastic, is heat-sensitive. It begins to soften at a fairly low ironing temperature, sticks at a little higher temperature, and then melts at cotton or linen ironing temperatures. Since it was the first fiber that could be heat-set and could also be made in crisp fabric, acetate soon took over the moiré and taffeta fields which it still dominates. Its low cost has permitted it to be used for fabrics which previously could be afforded only by those who could buy silk. As was mentioned earlier, because of its thermoplasticity, acetate fabric will soften and glaze if the iron temperature is a little too high. Extra pressure exerted on seams causes yarn to fuse and melts holes. Acetate fabrics usually do require ironing, but they iron easily and ordinarily require little or no pressing between cleanings or washings. Whether acetate should be washed or drycleaned is determined by the nature of the fabric, the types of items made from it, and the trimmings used. Acetates should be pressed on the wrong side so that iron marks or glazing will not be apparent, and they need not be ironed to complete dryness. Boiling water dulls and may damage acetate.

Acetate is dissolved by some rather common solvents and is softened by others; therefore chemicals used on it must be chosen with care. Since

acetone is the solvent for producing the fiber, acetates will dissolve in acetone; solubility in acetone is the commonly used method for identifying the fiber quickly. The acetone test alone will not be sufficiently discriminating as other acetone-soluble fibers come into common usage. Acetone is the main ingredient of most nail polish removers and is commonly used in some spot removal fluids; labels need to be checked carefully before using such substances on acetate or fabrics that might contain acetate. Acetate is also soluble in glacial acetic acid and in phenol of the concentration used for identifying nylon. Although many drycleaning solvents contain acetone, cleaners in the United States no longer use solvents that affect acetate fabrics; this is not always true in other countries.

Strong alkalies cause saponification of acetate, converting it to regenerated cellulosic fiber. Mild alkalies and acids have little effect on the fiber but may affect the dyestuffs.

Because of its low absorbency, acetate had been difficult to dye until the new series of dyestuffs and methods referred to earlier were developed especially for it. It also is not receptive to resin treatment. A few colors, especially blues, in some types of dyestuff have been subject to gas fading, with the result that blues and sometimes other colors have turned pink. Perspiration also has sometimes caused a great change in some colors, although the fiber itself is not damaged by perspiration. Poor light- and perspiration-fast dyes are still used at times for lining materials and such fabrics. Solution dyeing has overcome some of the gas- and perspiration-fading difficulties. Fluorescent dyes can be applied to acetate with no loss of brilliance, a fact utilized for military safety and sportswear purposes.

USES

Acetate is the fiber most used to produce heavy, luxurious satins (such as bridal satins), taffetas, sharkskins, and other such fabrics, both knitted and woven, requiring body or body with soft drape. It is much used for lingerie fabrics, particularly tricot knits. In many fabrics, acetate warp and viscose filling are used to take advantage of the properties of both fibers; such combinations are often found in crepes and satins.

Acetate finds widespread usage in dresses, blouses, lingerie, bathing suits, other sportswear, and gloves for women; in sportswear, ties, and robes for men; and in linings for all sorts of garments from babies' snowsuits to men's and women's coats and suits, and in sleeping garments for all members of the family. Ribbons and other trimming materials are often acetate.

Acetate has wide use in textile furnishing materials for glass curtains,

drapes, blankets, bedspreads, and comforters, and more recently, it has had some use in rugs.

For certain military and industrial electrical insulative materials acetate has replaced silk. It is used for cargo parachutes, flares, and for all sorts of fluorescent-dyed fabrics for signals, safety garments, targets, and identification, because of its brilliance which aids in easy detection, and its weather and mildew resistance. A special high-impact acetate was developed for cargo parachutes during World War II. Many millions of pounds of acetate have been used in recent years for cigarette filters.

Acetate is frequently blended with other fibers in fabrics for suits, slacks, sportswear, dresses, blouses, and home furnishing fabrics. It often improves the texture, drape, and wrinkle resistance of a fabric, or gives interesting color effects or luxuriousness.

The place of acetate in the world of fibers seems assured because of its desirable qualities, the availability of raw materials needed for its manufacture, and its inexpensiveness. It has remained relatively unchanged over a period of a great many years, except for some instances of improved strength and improved color fastness. Apparently it satisfies certain of the fiber needs just as it is. No doubt if changes are desired, they can and will be made.

Arnel (Triacetate)

Arnel (trade name) was announced as a new fiber in October 1954 by the Celanese Corporation of America. It is the completely acetylated triacetate, called primary acetate in the discussion of acetate development and processing. Although known since about 1900, and produced commercially in limited amounts by the Lustron Company from 1914 to 1924, the fiber was not successful in its early years.

In relation to the early failure of triacetate fiber which resulted in its disappearance from the market for forty years, A. F. Tesi, then of the Celanese Corporation, in the *American Dyestuff Reporter* for July 30, 1956 (p. 512), has said

You may say that it was ahead of its time; however, there were other reasons for its failure. The process for making the fiber was quite inefficient, the solvents used were hard to handle, and the engineering know-how for spinning this type of fiber was meager indeed. Also, the fiber was not commercially dyeable. In addition, the textile consumer of the time had not been educated to demand the wrinkle-resistance, quick-drying, low-shrinkage, easy-to-care-for characteristics of the hydrophobic fibers.

Triacetate fiber is produced by only one company in the United States at present. It is produced in the United Kingdom under the trademarks Tricel and Courpleta, and in Canada as Trilan and Arnel. No data are generally available on the amounts of Arnel manufactured in the United States, the ratio of staple to filament fiber, or the proportions used for differing purposes. This picture is typical of all new fibers; the amounts produced are so small in relation to the established fibers as to be almost meaningless in terms of commercial production figures.

PROCESSES

Arnel is produced, presumably, in the same way as secondary acetate to the solvent stage in preparation for spinning, except that the deacetylation step is eliminated. Methylene dichloride is the solvent used now in place of the chloroform of earlier days; it is available in large quantities, is not much more expensive than acetone, and is easy and safe to handle. The cellulose units of completely acetylated triacetate are believed to have this structure:

Dry-spinning of the fiber is the same as for acetate. An antistatic agent is sprayed on the filaments as they are wound on the bobbins to facilitate later processing. Arnel to be made into staple lengths is cut and crimped as it leaves the spinning cabinet.

Heat treatment is considered to be the most important step in imparting to Arnel the properties that differentiate it from acetate. Heat treatment for Arnel is carried on after the fabric has been woven or knitted, and preferably after it has been dyed. Just what happens to the internal structure of Arnel during this process is not yet known.

Heat treatment of Arnel accounts for different properties at different temperatures; that is, by controlling the temperature only one, two, or all

the changes in properties may be obtained. At 356°F and upward, dyed fabrics become increasingly washfast, insofar as color is concerned, and less subject to ozone fading because the dye begins to penetrate to the interior of the fiber. At about 390°F dimensional stability, wrinkle resistance to ironing damage begin to improve. At about 460°F resistance to glazing and hot-bed pressing occurs. Properties obtained at lower temperatures may be obtained simultaneously with those at higher temperatures when the latter are used. A temperature of 425°F or higher is most often used. Differences in heat treatment temperatures undoubtedly account for some of the variability in Arnel fabrics.

Silicone resins usually applied before heat treatment are cured during the treatment; such resins help to prevent adhesion between fibers during the softened stage and give a soft hand to the fabrics. A finish which can be similarly applied to give a harsher hand for certain suiting fabrics and sportswear fabrics has not yet been found.

PROPERTIES

Arnel has the same appearance as acetate and Fortisan when viewed under the microscope (see Figure 7-2). It thus cannot be differentiated from them by this method. Arnel 60, available since 1960, has a round cross section and dull-appearing surface. It has higher wet modulus than Arnel with some of the advantages inherent in greater wet stability.

Arnel is similar to acetate in appearance and in many other properties; it has the same density (1.33), about the same strength, elongation, and abrasion resistance, with somewhat better wet strength in relation to dry, and higher wet elongation. It burns about the same as acetate; its light resistance is similar, and it has a somewhat higher resistance to gas fading. Its drape and hand resemble those of acetate. Absorbency is much less for Arnel than for acetate, and its moisture regain is only 3.2 percent, considerably lower than for any other fiber studied so far. Decreased absorbency and hygroscopicity mean increased propensity to build up static electrical charges, with a shock to the wearer when such charges are dissipated; they also mean lint attraction and other disadvantages which we have discussed as common to the thermoplastic fibers.

Arnel is a completely washable fiber, fast drying, wrinkle resistant, and so dimensionally stable that shrinkage is no problem; it can usually be pressed with an iron at the temperature used for cotton. Boiling water does not damage the fiber or cause glazing.

Since so few data are available on the performance of Arnel in use, a study made at Cornell University, of filament and staple Arnel woven

fabrics, is of special interest. M. Gebhardt* reported (1959) that two Arnel fabrics made into twelve blouses and worn over a period of sixteen months by six women were actually stronger at the end of the study than the new fabrics. Garments did not stain readily, and most stains were easily removed in regular washing, or by pretreatment with a synthetic shampoo followed by regular washing. Wrinkle resistance was excellent throughout the study. Although all the blouses required ironing after washing, they were easy to iron and required no additional pressing between wearings. Machine washing was as satisfactory, or more so, than hand washing in all respects except that deeper wrinkles resulted; such wrinkles were no more difficult to remove in ironing than the shallower wrinkles from hand washing.

Arnel is a white fiber. It can be dyed with some of the dyestuffs used for acetate and those used for other thermoplastic fibers. Special dyeing processes developed for other thermoplastic fibers are followed. Slight yellowing during heat treatment may be disguised with a blue tint.

Arnel is dissolved by methylene dichloride, a fact that may be used to distinguish between acetate and Arnel in fiber identification. Arnel is somewhat more resistant to damage by dilute acids than acetate, but it is subject to damage by concentrated acids and alkalies. It is not saponified by alkali as is acetate. The usual bleaches apparently have no harmful effect on Arnel, but many do not bleach it either; oxalic acid will bleach out metal stains.

Since Arnel is an unreactive fiber, finishes are deposited on the surface rather than reacting with the fiber. This may lead to less permanent finishes than with reactant fibers. Arnel can be drycleaned safely with cleaning solvents used in the United States; but trichlorethylene, used in some European countries, may cause swelling and spotting and should be avoided.

USES

Arnel has gained wide acceptance in fabrics made entirely of Arnel and also in blends with other fibers, particularly for the lightweight type of fabrics used for summer wear, for travel, and for sportswear. Arnel knitted fabrics are popular in women's dresses. Arnel-cotton blends are popular in cord and seersucker types of fabrics, although they do wrinkle badly in washing and must be ironed and do sometimes muss in wear. Arnel is being blended with other fibers for drapery fabrics. Modified Arnel which can be printed by ordinary methods is being developed.

* Margaret E. Gebhardt, master's degree thesis, "Wear, Care, and Laboratory Performance of Spun and Filament Fabrics of One Hundred Per Cent Arnel."

THE NYLONS

A.C.E.[a]
Anso[a]
Antron[b]
Ayrlyn[c]
Barbara[c]
Blue C [d]
Cadon[d]
Cantrece[b]
Caprolan[a]
Celanese Nylon[e]
Chadolon[f]
Chemfit[d]
Chemlux[d]

Chemstrand [d]
Cordura[b]
Courtaulds[g]
Crepeset[h]
Cumuloft[d]
Diane[c]
Dymetrol [b]
Enka[h]
Enkalene[h]
Enkaloft[h]
Enkalure[h]
Enkasheer[h]

Enkatron[h]
Firestone Nylon[i]
Firestone Nytelle[i]
Hazel [c]
Hyten[b]
Lowland [h]
Monosheer[h]
Nomex[b]
Nylon by Enjay[j]
Nypel [a]
Phillips 66 [k]
Poliafil [c]

Qiana[b]
Qulon[l]
Ruvea[b]
S-3 [m]
Sooflex[m]
Speckelon[d]
Spectrodye[h]
Superflex[m]
Touch[a]
Tri-Dye[a]
Twisloc[d]
Vylor[b]

[a] Trade name granted to Allied Chemical Corporation Fibers Division.
[b] Trade name granted to E. I. duPont de Nemours & Co., Inc.
[c] Trade name granted to Rohm and Haas Company.
[d] Trade name granted to Monsanto Company, Textiles Division.
[e] Trade name granted to Celanese Corporation, Textile Fibers Marketing Company.
[f] Trade name granted to Chadbourn Gotham, Inc.
[g] Trade name granted to Courtaulds North America, Inc.
[h] Trade name granted to American Enka Corporation.
[i] Trade name granted to Firestone Synthetic Fibers & Textiles.
[j] Trade name granted to Enjay Fibers & Laminates Company.
[k] Trade name granted to Phillips Fibers Corp., Subsidiary of Phillips Petroleum Co.
[l] Trade name granted to Beaunit Corp., Beaunit Fibers Division.
[m] Trade name granted to Soo Valley Company.

Nylon

Nylon is often considered to be the first truly man-made fiber, since it was the first fiber to be synthesized from materials none of which had previously been fibrous in nature. The DuPont Company, in a pamphlet titled *Fibers by DuPont*, says:

And yet the real importance of nylon is simply that for the first time man had gone back to the elements to create a molecule tailored specifically for use in a fiber. For the first time, man had stopped trying to imitate a worm, and had struck out with his own intelligence and initiative to create a fiber that was meant to make a stocking, or a garment instead of a cocoon. For the first time, man was free from the capriciousness of animal and vegetable raw materials for his textiles.

The discovery of the process for nylon was the breakthrough in long-chain polymerization in the textile field. This led to the synthesizing of

most of the many new fibers that have appeared on the market since nylon was first introduced, and to the promise of others still to come.

The discovery of a process for a new fiber and the new name *nylon* given to the fiber were announced in 1938. Nylon was first made available to the public in some ladies' experimental hosiery, offered for sale in a store in Wilmington, Delaware, in October 1939. They were an instantaneous success because there was a great need for a beautiful and durable fiber for hosiery. Ladies' nylon hosiery then was offered to stores all over the country in May 1940, and about 64 million pairs were purchased by consumers during the first year they were available. But the whole development program took much longer and was not as easy as these facts seem to imply.

The history of nylon starts at the DuPont laboratories in Wilmington, Delaware, in 1928, when Wallace H. Carothers, a brilliant young chemist, was allowed to explore freely any leads he wished in fundamental research, by which means it was hoped that basic facts underlying physical and chemical phenomena might be discovered. Such facts are essential to the development of new products and their utilization. Carothers had no particular interest in textile fibers at this time. With his team of helpers, he became most interested in exploring polymerization processes in which small molecules build up into ever-larger, long-chain molecules, processes that were quite new at the time and that were being pushed by the petroleum industry in their search for better and more powerful fuels for the new high-speed, high-power air and automobile age just dawning. Once the secret of nature's polymerization processes was really understood, it was only a question of time until man could cause polymerization of other molecules in products not found in nature.

It was soon discovered that by using very high temperatures, sometimes high pressures, and often catalysts to speed up reaction, certain molecular chains could be made to hook together end to end to form longer chains. By controlling the process in various ways, the chains could be built up, theoretically at least, to any desired length. Within two years, Carothers and his team discovered the possibility of creating new fibers through their work with the new giant molecules. Carothers' interest then turned to producing a fiber by polymerization, a process heretofore entirely unrelated to the textile field. In a few more years of concentrated work such a chemical compound was discovered; then when the process for cold-drawing was developed, the way was opened for success. Nylon was the result. Since polymerization is discussed briefly in Chapter 3, we shall not go into it any further here. (Please refer to Chapter 3).

As soon as it became apparent that nylon would be accepted immediately by the consuming public, facilities were built for expanded produc-

tion; but, until the last decade, demand has exceeded production capacity for nylon, despite continued expansion of facilities and the entry of a number of other manufacturers into the field. Increasing and changing end-uses and changes in yarn processing account for continuing shortages in some types and diameters of yarns.

At the beginning of hostilities with Japan, in 1941, silk supplies were "frozen," and all nylon production, including that from facilities which were rapidly expanded throughout the war, was diverted to the United States government for military purposes. Government control continued for awhile after hostilities ended in August 1945. Some of the nylon rejected for military use found its way into limited quantities of much-needed hosiery. Rejected parachute cloth, unsuited for most apparel, found its way into men's shirts. This material was tightly woven, allowed no air through, and was very uncomfortable to wear in warm and humid weather. The misuse of nylon fabric in this way was an important factor in its rejection for such purposes; much sentiment against nylon shirts still persists in the United States.

After the war ended most nylon production was again turned toward civilian uses—at first most of it was needed for women's hosiery. Experiments in weaving and knitting soon led to production of a wide range of knitted and woven nylon fabrics for apparel, house furnishings, and industrial uses.

PRODUCTION

Nylon is a generic name—which might more properly be "polyamide"—applying to a great number of related products which are being produced, or theoretically can be produced, from other materials similar to those used for nylon 66, the most common nylon fiber today. The "66" refers to the six carbons in each of the components finally used in manufacturing this type of nylon. Although the DuPont Company did not establish a trade name for their new nylon fiber, now that the patent has expired and a number of companies are producing nylon a great many trade names are being used. Caprolan (nylon 6) is produced by a different formula than the "66" nylons.

Nylon has been defined for the Textile Fiber Products Identification Act as

. . . a manufactured fiber in which the fiber-forming substance is any long chain synthetic polyamide having recurring amide groups ($-\overset{\overset{\displaystyle O}{\displaystyle \|}}{C}-NH-$) as an integral part of the polymer chain.

TABLE 17. United States Production of Nylon (Millions of Pounds and Percent)[a]

Year	Nylon					Total (Pounds)		Nylon (Percent)	
	Filament		Staple			Noncellulosic	All	Noncellulosic	All
	Pound	Percent	Pound	Percent	Nylon	Man-made	Man-made	Man-made	Man-made
1961	442	92.5	36	7.5	478	750.9	1846.1	63.7	25.9
1962	561	91.8	50	8.2	611	972.9	2245.0	62.8	27.2
1963	630	91.2	61	8.8	691	1156.0	2504.8	59.8	27.6
1964	736	91.4	69	8.6	805	1406.7	2838.5	57.2	28.4
1965	846	90.4	90	9.6	936	1776.9	3303.9	52.7	28.3
1966	961	90.1	105	9.9	1066	2068.7	3587.7	51.5	29.7
1967	945	89.9	106	10.1	1051	2333.7	3721.8	45.0	28.2
1968	1183	89.8	134	10.2	1317	3187.5	4781.8	41.3	27.5

[a] Compiled from *Textile Organon* for June 1968 and June 1969, excluding glass fibers.

Nylon is now produced in 34 plants in the United States and in 188 plants in 31 other countries. Not all countries manufacture nylon 66, which forms the bulk of nylon production in this country.

As new fibers become "of age" and are produced by a number of manufacturers, and as their market accounts for a substantial part of the total fiber supply in the United States, data are released on specific fibers so that it is then possible to see how their growth has taken place. This has now occurred with nylon. Until recently no production figures were released—just reports of producers' shipments. Data have now been released that go back to 1961. Table 17 has been compiled from these data.

In 1940 only 2.6 million pounds of nylon were produced; this was 83.9 percent of all the noncellulosic man-made fibers produced in the United States that year. The rest was not specified as to fiber but probably included a small amount of the casein fiber Aralac and some glass fiber. Nylon production had reached 90.1 million pounds in 1950 and was still 74.0 percent of the total noncellulosic fiber production. In 1955, nylon production reached 230.9 million pounds but it was beginning to share the noncellulosic market with the first of other such man-made fibers then, and this has increasingly been true, as can be noted in Table 17.

Several trends become apparent as you study the table. For instance, filament fibers have always predominated over staple although the percentage of staple has slowly but steadily increased a little. Nylon has been a pretty steady percentage of all the man-made fibers produced in the United States (last column in table) but as a percentage of the noncellulosic fibers it is decreasing consistently (next to last column)—the trend we noted that had already begun in 1950. A quick glance at such data makes one wonder if one set or the other is wrong. Can you give any reasons for such a seeming discrepancy? The explanation is that although the man-made fiber industry is growing, as can be seen from the various tables, the noncellulosic part of the industry is growing at a faster rate than the cellulosic part or the man-made fiber industry as a whole.

Also, you will notice that in 1967, for the first time, nylon production decreased. It will be interesting to see if this was something that happened just that one year or if it is the beginning of a trend. Have you any guesses and reasons for them? All the changes noted are taking place very rapidly when the fact is considered that Table 17 is a year-to-year report of data.

PROCESSES

Nylon is composed of carbon, hydrogen, oxygen, and nitrogen, as are the protein fibers, but because it is not made up of amino acids its properties are not like those of protein substances. In chemical structure, it is believed to be composed of long, straight-chain molecules with neither

side chains nor cross-linkages. Thus the chains pack closely together in the fiber.

Although nylon is often described as being made of coal, air, and water, the actual synthesis depends on compounds far removed from these substances. Nylon 66 is produced from an acid and a diamine, which have in turn been produced from other materials, actually going back to petroleum or coal tar derivatives. A great many different diamines and acids could be used for nylon production—their cost, amounts available, or methods of handling may determine whether or not they will eventually be used for this purpose. Nylon 6 is produced in the United States and nylon 9 (from soy oil) has been the subject of experiments. Before Qiana was announced there was speculation that the new fiber that DuPont was known to be working on was a nylon 4.

Nylon polymerization is typified by the condensation reaction of adipic acid and hexamethylene diamine. The molecules of the two substances hook together alternately (copolymerization), that is, a molecular unit of acid, then one of diamine, then acid again, and so on indefinitely, with elimination of water. The following formulas demonstrate the polymerization of a unit of nylon; many such units make up the nylon molecular chain, and many such chains make up the fiber. The process is controlled carefully to stop polymerization within a narrow range, or the chains would become too long to possess the characteristics desired in a textile fiber.

$$HO-\underset{\underset{O}{\|}}{C}-CH_2-CH_2-CH_2-CH_2-\underset{\underset{O}{\|}}{C}-OH \ + \ H_2N-CH_2-CH_2-CH_2-CH_2-CH_2-CH_2-NH_2$$

Adipic acid   Hexamethylene diamine

Heat

Elimination of H_2O

$$HO-\underset{\underset{O}{\|}}{C}-CH_2-CH_2-CH_2-CH_2-\underset{\underset{O}{\|}}{\underset{H}{C}}-\underset{H}{N}-CH_2-CH_2-CH_2-CH_2-CH_2-CH_2-\underset{H}{N}-H$$

Monomer of nylon 66

Further polymerization

$$\left[\underset{\underset{O}{\|}}{C}-CH_2-CH_2-CH_2-CH_2-\underset{\underset{O}{\|}}{\underset{H}{C}}-\underset{H}{N}-CH_2-CH_2-CH_2-CH_2-CH_2-CH_2-\underset{H}{N}\right]_n$$

Nylon 66 repeating unit

From polymerization to cold-drawing of the fibers, after which they are ready for use as filaments or for cutting to staple lengths, there are

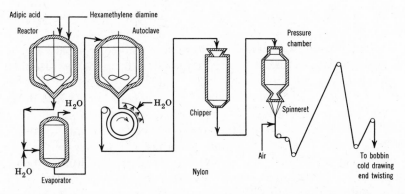

FIGURE 7-3. Flow chart of production of nylon. (Courtesy E. I. duPont de Nemours & Co. Inc.)

several steps in the production of nylon. Figure 7-3 is a flow chart of the steps involved but does not include cold-drawing. We shall begin with the acid and amine ready for use, and not go into the processes or sources for obtaining them. Some of the references for further reading go into these processes, if you wish to explore them, as do a number of books on organic and high-polymer chemistry.

The acid and the diamine in measured amounts are put into a huge kettle equipped with a stirrer, which mixes them thoroughly, forming a salt; then the mixture and some water are fed into an evaporator where the solution is evaporated to a desired concentration of the salt. The concentrated salt solution is fed into a jacketed autoclave where a sequence of high temperatures and pressures induces copolymerization of the two materials to molecular chains of the desired length, with acid and diamine alternating as described before. The water evolved in the process is removed from the autoclave by evaporation. Nitrogen is bubbled through the autoclave continuously to insure that air does not get in and expose the newly formed nylon to contact with oxygen. From a slot in the bottom of the autoclave the polymerized molten nylon resin is extruded in the form of a thick, white, translucent ribbon; a spray of water cools the ribbon and causes it to harden as it is carried away from the autoclave on a casting wheel. The ribbon has an appearance similar to white taffy and is quite hard. Delustrant may be added to the polymer before extrusion, and dyestuff (pigment) is added in some instances.

The next step is to break the ribbon up into small pieces in a chipping unit, ready for forming into fibers.

The spinning process for nylon is "melt-spinning"—different from anything we have thus far encountered. The whole process, from

feeding the chips onto the hot grid to forcing the molten nylon through the spinneret, is carried on in a closed cylinder in an atmosphere of nitrogen rather than air, for the cylinder and spinneret must be kept heated at a temperature above the melting point of the nylon, and at such temperatures nylon tends to become yellow if exposed to oxygen.

Nylon chips from a number of batches are blended before feeding into the spinning chamber. Within the spinning chamber is a coiled grid, said to resemble the heating coil of an electric stove. The chips flow into the hopper of the spinning chamber by gravity and fall onto the grid; as they melt, they flow through a sand filter at the bottom of the chamber to metered pumps which measure the viscous, melted nylon and force it through the spinneret. As the molten filaments emerge into the cool air below the spinneret, they solidify and are carried through a conditioner where steam or moisture prevents further stretching at this time and facilitates formation of filament cakes or winding on bobbins. The nylon fibers may, when cold, be subjected to drawing immediately, or this may be done at a later time.

Cold-drawing is a process that gives to the nylon some of the properties for which it is most noted, that is, great strength, toughness, abrasion resistance, and elasticity. Drawing is carried on as for other fibers, by passing filaments over rollers which revolve at different, controlled speeds. Nylon is drawn three to seven times its original length. Drawing orients the molecular chains in the direction of the fiber axis, lines the chains up parallel to each other, and permits a high degree of crystallinity of the fibers. Crystallinity, as noted previously, tends to give strength and a rigid structure to the fibers. Despite drawing, the nylon fiber still retains greater elasticity than most other fibers. After drawing, nylon may be given an oil or an antistatic spraying, twisted, and heat-set before being wound on cones or bobbins for weaving, knitting, or lacemaking.

If staple length fibers are desired, the filaments (or tow) are cut after the cold-drawing process, the fibers are given a crimp which is heat-set, and they are baled for handling.

Heat-setting is necessary to stabilize nylon in shape and dimensions. Nylon may be stabilized as yarn, as woven or knitted fabric, or as knitted garments. As an example of the latter, hosiery is heat-set on preboarding machines that have the leg shapes of newly purchased hosiery. Different times and temperatures are used for different purposes, that is, a few seconds are sufficient for lightweight fabrics, whereas as many as 20 minutes under considerable pressure are required for pleats, and perhaps 2 hours are necessary for heavy fabrics. Setting may be done with hot water, steam, or hot dry air. Careful control is necessary to attain the desired effects without causing degradation.

Some new types of nylon have been developed in recent years that differ considerably from the regular, or more usual nylon. Three of these—Nomex, Qiana, and Cantrece—we shall look at after we have considered the properties of the familiar types of nylon. In addition to new types of nylon, a new cross-sectional shape has been developed of which DuPont's Antron is an example. This shape is probably derived from a triangular or trilobed spinneret with the difference in processing during drawing that such a shape would require.

PROPERTIES

Although the cross section of the older types of nylon fibers are all smooth, even, translucent circles, Antron has a trilobal cross section. Both shapes are shown in Figure 7-4. The trilobal shape is said to be less translucent than the round-fiber nylon and produces fabrics with a softer, more pleasing hand. The other properties described are those applicable to nylons other than the new high-temperature Nomex, which is described separately.

Nylon has a somewhat cool, clammy feel in filament form; some people like this feel and others dislike it very much. Nylon is a lustrous, white fiber, transparent to translucent, which can, in common with other man-made fibers, be made in varying diameters, lengths, and degrees of strength, abrasion resistance, and luster. Its translucency has led to dissatisfaction with nylon for a number of uses; texturing processes have improved opacity to some extent. Nylon is both tough and pliable.

Nylon does not flame readily but burns slowly or fuses and drops off

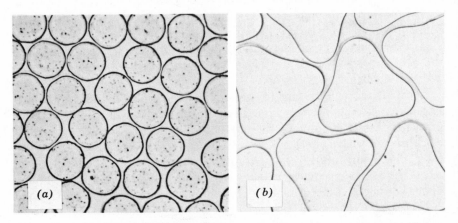

FIGURE 7-4. Nylon cross-section photomicrographs: (a) regular nylon; (b) Antron nylon. (Courtesy E. I. duPont de Nemours & Co. Inc.)

if flame is applied to it. It burns or melts with the odor of cooking green beans or celery, and, as it burns or melts, forms a waxy roll along the edge which becomes hard and tough as it cools. Regardless of the color of the nylon fabric, the curled, waxy edge is a light tan color after burning. Although nylon is often described as nonflammable, the fusing and dropping off may present almost as great a hazard in many ways. Finishes may change the flammability potential of nylon as well as of other fibers.

Nylon is potentially one of the strongest of the fibers; it has a breaking tenacity of 3.0 to 6.0 grams per denier in regular tenacities and 5.9 to 9.2 grams in high tenacities. Only glass and Fortisan are stronger in comparable filaments. The wet strength of nylon is about 85 percent of dry strength. Elongation is 18 to 37 percent and is about the same wet or dry. True elasticity of nylon is higher than for most fibers other than wool, and it also exhibits creep if stretched beyond its true elasticity.

Nylon has a specific gravity of 1.14—somewhat lower than that of any other fiber; thus good covering power with light weight has been one of its outstanding features. Absorbency is low and moisture regain is only about 4 percent. This fact, with the circular, close-packing shape of regular nylon fibers, may make it uncomfortable for summer wear in many fabric constructions. The low hygroscopicity also accounts for the tendency to accumulate static electricity. Nylon is somewhat rigid and does not drape as attractively as acetate, silk, or soft wool; this is somewhat less true of Antron nylon.

Nylon's low absorbency makes it quick drying and rather easily washed. Although it does not stain readily, it tends to pick up color, grease, and soil in laundering with other garments; therefore white and pastel nylons should not be laundered with colored or badly soiled garments. Controlled machine washing is recommended rather than hand washing, unless design or trimming needs more delicate care to maintain whiteness of nylon.

Nylon is not affected by cold temperatures but loses strength and yellows at sustained high temperatures. Pressing temperatures must be kept low to prevent softening, glazing, or melting and eventual discoloration. Softening and melting occur within a very narrow temperature range; an ironing temperature of 270°F is considered safe for nylon.

Nylon possesses fair wrinkle resistance and crease recovery—considerably better than untreated cotton, linen, and rayon but considerably poorer than Dacron and wool. It is important to avoid wrinkling while handling, especially in washing, if a good appearance is to be maintained with little or no pressing. Nylon has excellent abrasion resistance; because of this and its strength and elasticity, it is considered a very durable fiber.

Nylon is degraded by exposure to light; continued exposure to ultraviolet light leads to considerable loss in strength in a short time. It is less

sensitive to light degradation than silk but more sensitive than Orlon, Dacron, Fortisan, and glass. Bright nylon is less subject to light degradation than delustered nylon.

Nylon is not chemically reactive to soap, alkalies, or alcohols but is sensitive to acids. It is dissolved by concentrated nitric acid, by formic acid, and by 90 percent carbolic acid (phenol). It is little affected by bleaches; they are relatively ineffective in whitening discolored nylon. Nylon can be dyed with dyestuffs used for acetate and by some other dyes, and usually the colors can be made satisfactorily permanent. Nylons are sometimes resin treated to stabilize the weave, or treated with silicones to improve softness or water repellency, but they do not accept finishes readily because of their low absorbency. Nylon is unaffected by drycleaning solvents. Acid and alkaline perspiration have little or no effect on the strength of nylon.

USES

The apparel uses of nylon are widely varied and include items for all members of the family. Hosiery, lingerie, sleepwear, sweaters, fabrics for blouses, dresses, coats, shirts, and linings utilize large amounts of nylon. Ribbons, laces, braids, and other trimming materials are often made of nylon.

The textile furnishings field utilizes nylon in many decorator fabrics, including rugs, upholstery, drapery, and curtain fabrics, some for sheets, webbing for furniture, and nonwoven fabrics.

The industrial uses for nylon include tire cord, heavy-duty ropes and cordage, brushes, hose, belting, tapes, parachutes, sewing thread, fishnets, luggage, sails, electrical insulation, and other items.

In the military services nylon goes into parachutes, cord for airplane, truck and jeep tires, ropes, parachute shroud lines, tapes, sleeping bags, glider tow ropes, blood plasma filters, netting, hammocks, flying suits, tents, and innumerable other supplies.

Texturizing processes that make nylon more opaque and permit use of filament rather than spun yarns for lingerie, sweaters, and other goods have enabled nylon to regain some markets. Specially textured nylon is the most used yarn in the currently fashionable "stretch" fabrics and articles of wearing apparel for both sexes. Textured yarns account for roughly half the large amount of nylon yarn being made into carpets and rugs. Rubberized nylon tanks which can be towed behind boats or carried on flatcars have been used by the oil industry for some time, and with disposable film innerlinings such tanks are now being used for transporting other fluids, such as orange juice. When empty these tanks can be rolled into compact bundles for reshipment or for storage. Much nylon is still

going into tires, and nylon does not seem likely to lose all this market to the polyester or even newer fibers for some time to come. Some of the new nylon knitted fabrics are embossed and calendered to resemble leather in appearance while retaining the softness and pliability of a knit; some of this fabric has been used for dresses and for bathing suits. The space exploration coveralls of Figures 1-1 and 1-2 (Chapter 1) were made of nylon twill fabric.

An unusual new use of nonfilament nylon is in shutters for houses, offered in a limited geographical area. They are finished with an acrylic coating in a number of colors and have the general appearance of wood. It is surmised that these are being used to test the feasibility of nylon structures as exterior building materials.

Nomex

Nomex, an aromatic polyamide, was announced by the DuPont Company under the designation HT-1 in the early 1960's and went into full scale commercial production in early 1967. According to the DuPont *Technical Bulletin* N-228 (October 1968), in reference to industrial applications:

"Nomex high-temperature-resistant nylon staple and tow were developed to fill the need for a fiber that would retain strength, flexibility, and resistance to abrasion and stretch at continuous operating temperatures up to 500°F. The ability of Nomex fiber to do this, coupled with its good resistance to chemicals and its low flammability, makes it ideal for such industrial applications as protective clothing, laundry textiles, ironingboard covers, dust-filter bags, leader fabrics, and sewing threads.

Little additional information has been published since Leroy K. Mc-Cune reported in *Textile Research Journal* for September 1962 (p. 762), that

When HT-1 is exposed to excessively high temperatures its behavior is markedly different from that of other organic fibers. HT-1 can be ignited only with difficulty by direct exposure to flame, and the fire is rapidly self-extinguished as soon as the igniting source is removed. In addition, HT-1 does not melt but instead starts to char at temperatures in the neighborhood of 400°C. These fire-resistant and nonmelting characteristics can be particularly useful in the design of protective clothing to meet a variety of exposure conditions.

In addition to its resistance to high temperatures, HT-1 possesses a useful balance of other properties, including strength, toughness, dimensional stability, and resistance to chemical and solvent attack.

The new high-temperature nylon is so sensitive to ultraviolet light degradation, however, that it needs to be protected from direct sunlight;

protective sheathings and coatings are being investigated. It is expected to remain a more expensive fiber than the other nylons.

Nomex is produced in both filament and staple length fibers and in a paper-type structure, the latter especially for electrical insulation. Nomex has been used in space uniforms, in U.S. Navy flight suits, and in a number of military uses. Protective coveralls were developed for racing car drivers but no report has been given as to the extent to which they have been accepted and worn. Nomex suits coated with reflective aluminum film have possibility for firefighter clothing.

Most Nomex has been used in white or one of the two solution-dyed military colors because it was otherwise undyeable. Now, however, a chemical company that has succeeded in dyeing other fire retardant fabrics claims to be able to dye Nomex with several types of dyes without changing its important properties.

In *Daily News Record* for January 2, 1969 appeared the announcement that Pan American Airways, Inc., had placed an order for 25,000 yards of Nomex fabric to upholster seats in its coming 362-passenger Superjets. The article stated:

> The aircraft upholstery is the first such application of Nomex nylon by Du-Pont. Up to the present time, according to DuPont, it has been used primarily as an industrial fiber to give safety in clothing for racing drivers, military aviators, firemen, welders and steel workers.
>
> DuPont says that Nomex will not support combustion, has passed all proposed tests for flammability, and does not melt. In the event of fire, the company says, generation of smoke is minimal, and the material acts as a thermal barrier and prevents the involvement of the seat cushioning in the combustion process.
>
> The company also says that Nomex has the durability of conventional nylon and is superior in its ability to retain shape after repeated laundering.

Qiana

Qiana, registered trade name of the DuPont Company for a new silk-like polyamide fiber formally announced on June 27, 1968, has created more of a sensation and made many more headlines than did Nomex. There was much speculation for at least two years before the announcement of Qiana because it was known that a new high-fashion-potential fiber of some type (known then as Fiber Y) was in the offing. Some guessed that a nylon 4 was to be announced; others that an entirely new generic type might be forthcoming.

Pilot plant amounts of Qiana began to be produced in 1967 and sufficient fiber had been produced and made into a number of types of

fabrics for a limited trial in garments in late 1968. Some Parisian designers collaborated with DuPont by producing a few garments in their collections from the new fabrics. DuPont considered the fiber to be a potential success and Qiana was then announced to the world as plans for commercial production got under way. As this is written (early 1969) Qiana, although not yet available in the United States, will be available in women's high quality apparel for spring, 1969. Initially it will be an expensive fiber, priced as high or higher than silk.

Although some silk producers have stated that they do not expect Qiana to be a real competitor to silk, others are much concerned. Whether significant or not, almost immediately after the announcement of Qiana the price of silk dropped on world markets. Although the designers who used Qiana in their collections seemed disappointed that the new fabric was not much different from silk in the way it could be handled and in appearance, the nonwealthy consumer who will eventually own dresses, lingerie, or other items made of Qiana will most likely be pleased because of Qiana's other properties in addition to its beauty, light weight, and texture if it lives up to its billing.

According to *Daily News Record* for November 4, 1968:

DuPont's Qiana almost came a cropper on the Champs Elysees.

After all the work, after the countless millions spent in dollars and man-hours; after all the preparation and publicity and secrecy, the unrest in France this summer almost wrecked DuPont's plans to introduce its new nylon in the couture.

DuPont—giant of the Brandywine—was forced to cart its precious fabric by station wagon to plants in Switzerland and Italy for dyeing and finishing, because the French plants were inoperative.

But that's almost the end of the story.

The Qiana story is one of well-organized, methodical procedures which to many might sound dull and boring. Certainly the sweat and tears of thousands of items being discarded after various stages of development are not calculated to produce cheers.

Success in this field is a result of homework, not guesswork.

An *American Dyestuff Reporter* news report (July 15, 1968, p. 22) quoted Dr. Wallace E. Gordon, a DuPont vice president, as saying that Qiana represents an entirely new body of technology in man-made fibers; that it is unique in terms of ingredients, fiber chemistry, process technology, molecular structure, aesthetics, and performance. It has, however, the same chemical linkages as conventional nylon.

Qiana is said to be light in weight, soft, drapable, wrinkle resistant, dyeable in fast colors, dimensionally stable, strong, drycleanable, machine

washable and dryable, nonyellowing, and breathable. It can be woven or knitted into any type of fabric.

Although Qiana will initially go into women's garments, it is expected also to appear in the men's wear field in shirts, ties, and such items. There is even speculation that it may eventually be used in automobile tires.

Touch,* a modified nylon 6, may be similar to Qiana. It is said to have a "crisp, dry, silklike hand," moisture absorption, wicking action, porosity, and some loft without texturing. *Touch* will not be generally available before 1970, but some of the first fabrics are appearing in blouses, dresses, separates, and some men's wear in spring, 1969.

Cantrece, a Bicomponent Fiber

Cantrece is the name given to a nylon that has been used primarily for ladies' sheer stretch hosiery, but that has potential also for knitted and woven lightweight-bulk fabrics. Cantrece is a bicomponent nylon made up of two different types of nylon fused in the spinnerets to produce a fiber made up (as seen in cross section) half of one type of nylon and half of the other. When drawn, finished, knitted or woven, and subjected to heat or steam treatment, the two types of nylon shrink differently, causing the fiber to crimp or curl. The effect attained varies with how the yarn is used—whether stretched out as in hosiery, or filling in bulk to give soft covering power such as is desired in sweaters.

We shall digress from our study of specific fibers to explore briefly the procedures for obtaining two-component fibers, also known as conjugate fibers. Cantrece nylon and Orlon Sayelle acrylic are examples of bicomponent fibers. Fiber E, a rayon produced for a time, although considerably different from Cantrece and Sayelle, also belonged to this group. Source, a new biconstituent fiber, is somewhat different and is discussed elsewhere in this chapter under the heading Polyamide/Polyester.

Analysis of the structure of wool which has a natural crimp that results in soft three-dimensional bulk sparked the inspiration for bicomponent fibers. The crimp was noticed to disappear or to be reversed when the wool was wet or undergoing certain treatments, but to return to its original shape as it dried. This behavior was shown to be due to two slightly different types of cortex in bilateral position running the length of the wool fibers. The more sensitive (greatest swelling and shrinking) component took the shortest route as it dried, pulling the fiber into a crimped or helical shape somewhat like this sketch.

---

* Trademarked fiber of Allied Chemical Corporation, Fibers Division.

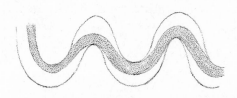

Man's first successful attempts to imitate this two-component structure of wool was with viscose rayon in a process where a thick amorphous skin and a crystalline core were obtained. The skin could be made to coagulate thickly primarily on one side of the fiber by means of cross currents in the coagulating bath, or in other ways. Fiber E, which appeared briefly on the market in carpets and upholstery fabrics, was an example of this type of crimped fiber.

Fibers other than the rayons depend on a two-component spinning system. The procedure for these fibers is the same as for single-component fibers as far as the spinneret except that two different fiber or fiber-variation systems must be set up in close enough proximity to feed into the same line just at the entrance to the same spinneret. The spinnerets are often different in shape and structure than single-component spinnerets; their shape may determine the way in which the mixtures merge at their point of contact as well as the fiber shape. Cross-section shapes of some of the bicomponent fibers produced to date are sketched here.

Cantrece   Orlon Sayelle   Fiber E

Drawing has an important influence on the resulting fiber and its characteristics. Fibers produced by melt spinning are probably easiest to combine. When subject to heat, chemical, steam, or water treatment—depending on the components—the more sensitive fiber shrinks as does the one part of the wool cortex; its contractions cause the fiber to crimp or curl. Since length is taken up by the crimp, allowance must be made for such shrinkage in planning garments, fabrics, or other items that are to be subjected to the crimping treatment after the item is knitted or made. Cantrece hosiery crimp is developed and set during preboarding. Sometimes crimp is developed during dyeing.

Bicomponent yarns are used for stretch hosiery, sweaters, and lingerie. One of the most important uses is for carpet yarns. There are many other possibilities for such fibers.

THE ACRYLICS

Acrilan[a]	Creslan[b]	Spectran[a]
Anywear[a]	Nomelle[c]	Weatherbright[d]
Chemstrand [a]	Orlon[c]	Zefkrome[d]
Colacril [a]	Orlon Sayelle[c]	Zefran[d]

[a] Trade name granted to Monsanto Company, Textiles Division.
[b] Trade name granted to American Cyanamid Company.
[c] Trade name granted to E. I. duPont de Nemours and Company, Inc.
[d] Trade name granted to Dow Badische Company.

Acrylic is defined for the Textile Fiber Products Identification Act as "a manufactured fiber in which the fiber-forming substance is any long chain synthetic polymer composed of at least 85 percent by weight of acrylonitrile units ($-CH_2-CH-$)."

$$\underset{\displaystyle CN}{\overset{\displaystyle |}{}}$$

The acrylics are synthesized by addition polymerization, with one entire unit of acrylonitrile hooking to the end of the next entire unit, and no condensation products to be disposed of. It has been theorized that about 2000 such units hook together, in random or parallel arrangements, to form the pure acrylic fiber. Because of difficulties in dyeing the pure acrylic fibers, most of those now being produced incorporate small amounts of any of a number of other materials (such as methyl methylacrylate, vinyl acetate, or vinyl pyridine) in the chains; consequently, acrylic fibers are now usually copolymers.

There is a dearth of acrylic fiber data, and those available refer to the acrylics as a group without indicating the proportions of the total reached by the various family members. Data also include the fibers now known as modacrylics, since they are produced in too small amounts to be separated from acrylics in published materials. Predictions made for this group of fibers were very favorable. W. A. B. Davidson, in a discussion accompanying the *Textile World 1957 Man-Made Fiber Table,** wrote

There are extremely optimistic estimates as to the future of acrylic fibers in the United States. For one, the President's Material Policy Commission predicts

* By permission from *Textile World*. Copyrighted 1957, McGraw-Hill Publishing Company.

that consumption of the acrylics alone in 1960 will hit 325-million pounds and by 1975 it will reach a whopping 1,200-million pounds.

That this prediction was not fulfilled is evident from the figures in Table 18, although the acrylics have made a very substantial growth.

Since the processes for these fibers are covered by still-valid patents, little definite information is publicly available concerning materials used, processing, and drawing. Literature supplied by some of the producers, however, gives a good idea of the general procedures followed.

Acrylonitrile, a product of the petroleum or natural gas industry, is the basic material from which all the acrylic fibers are polymerized. It may be obtained in any one of several processes, the most common one being through reaction of ethylene oxide or acetylene with hydrogen cyanide (hydrocyanic acid). A newer process is reported to make use of propylene and ammonia. Acrylonitriles are usually manufactured in industries other than those in which the fibers are produced.

Acrylic fibers are lightweight with good covering power, warm and pleasant to the touch, resilient and crease resistant, with medium strength and elongation. They are not very reactive with acids, but alkalies tend to cause yellowing. Pilling has been a problem with staple yarns of some of these fibers. They are the most woollike of the man-made fibers, to date.

Static electricity seems to be an inherent problem of some of the acrylic and modacrylic fibers, especially when relative humidity and temperature of the atmosphere are low. Persons who are very sensitive to static electricity and who are using acrylic fiber blankets have complained of the crackle of static; they have further complained that the blankets cling to other bedding; and when the bed is made or changed, the blanket clings to the person handling it, with stinging discharges of electricity wherever it touches the skin and whenever attempts are made to pull it loose. Sparks are visible in the dark whenever the users disturb the blankets on their beds. Mothers have sometimes complained of electric shock when they pick up their babies who are wrapped in such blankets. Acrylic blankets, however, have largely replaced woolen ones on the market.

In a study of blankets made at Cornell University,* Orlon and Acrilan acrylic blankets were satisfactory in retaining dimensions and in insulative quality when washed either by a soak method in an automatic machine or by a four-minute agitation wash period. Although these blankets were dried on racks, later experiments have demonstrated that they may be satisfactorily dried in a dryer if the temperature can be controlled to "medium" or "low" and if they are removed from the dryer as soon as

* Ann Fahnestock, "Changes in Physical Properties of Selected Blankets as Related to Various Cleaning Methods; and Consumer Reaction to the New Blankets in Use," Cornell University master's thesis (1958).

TABLE 18. United States Producers' Shipments of Acrylic Fibers (Millions of Pounds)[a]

Year	Acrylic Fiber[b]			Total Noncellulosic	Total Man-made
	Pound	Percent (Noncellulosic)	Percent (Total)		
1948	0.1	0.2	—	65.6	1,120.3
1950	0.9	0.7	—	121.7	1,268.6
1955	54.6	14.8	4.3	368.5	1,261.9
1960	116.0	17.4	11.4	667.3	1,020.7
1965	344.4	17.3	10.0	1,992.2	3,433.5 [c]
1968	467.1	15.5	9.3	3,063.4	5,030.6 [c]

[a] Compiled from *Textile Organon*, February 1968 and 1969.
[b] Includes modacrylic fibers but does not include acrylic filament which was reported as part of a group of fibers designated as "other."
[c] Includes glass fiber.

they are dry. Cleaning by a commercial firm which used a blanket dry-cleaning method on them was less successful in retaining the original properties than was washing. Insulative quality, which is a factor in warmth, was much more satisfactorily retained with washing than with drycleaning.

Acrylic and modacrylic fibers have been very popular in psychedelic stuffed animals in recent years, and a modified acrylic plastic has been perfected in Europe for contact lenses. Acrylic plastic shields to replace glass for automobile headlights have been developed in the United States. They are said to permit more efficient lighting with less glare than glass shields.

Orlon

Orlon is the result of research on polymerization of acrylonitriles which began about 1940 at the DuPont laboratories. Although the linear nature of the polymers was soon recognized, with the possibility this implied for a new fiber, it was a number of years before a suitable solvent could be found for this chemically inert material. Promising solvents were found to warrant authorization of a pilot-scale plant in 1944, and by 1948 results were so good as to lead to a choice of the name Orlon for the new fiber, some of which was made available on an experimental basis in limited usage. Acrylonitrile served military purposes during World War II, and early work with the acrylic polymer indicated that it would have military value, but the war ended before Orlon was ready for trial. Full-scale commercial production of the fiber began in 1950 and has been greatly expanded since that time. Public acceptance of Orlon has been rapid and extensive.

Development of suitable dye procedures for Orlon took still longer, so that early Orlon was available only in pastel colors. Although a number of dyestuffs and procedures have now been developed, some dyers are still unable to produce fast-color Orlon in the deep or bright color ranges. Pilling of Orlon staple was also a problem but has now largely been overcome by the use of textured filament yarns. Orlon is synthesized by the method which is typical for the acrylic group of fibers. It does not have side chains, but there are believed to be numerous hydrogen bonds between adjacent chains in the fibers, accounting in large measure for its stability and inertness to chemical reaction. That the processes for Orlon seem to be simpler than those for many of the other man-made fibers is suggested by the diagrammatic sketch shown in Figure 7-5. The inference may be misleading, however.

Specific amounts of acrylonitrile, a catalyst to stimulate polymerization, and water are mixed thoroughly in a reactor kettle where temperature and

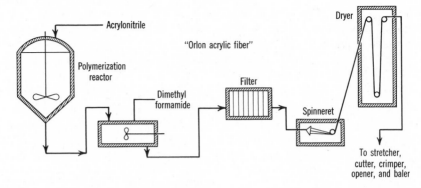

FIGURE 7-5. Flow chart of production of Orlon. (Courtesy E. I. duPont de Nemours & Co. Inc.)

time are carefully controlled in an atmosphere of nitrogen rather than air. The polymer precipitates as a solid, which is said to be filtered from the reaction mixture, pressed through perforated plates, and then cut into bits resembling broken-up noodles. The resulting bits are dried before being dissolved, to insure uniform moisture content and a more uniform product.

The broken-up or pulverized polymer is dissolved in dimethyl formamide and, when correct conditions of viscosity are reached, is filtered, forced by metered pumps through the spinnerets, and dry-spun, whether in air or in some other gaseous medium has not been disclosed. Wet-spinning presumably could be used instead of dry.

The fiber is hot-drawn to several times the original length, presumably through passage over heated rollers which revolve at different speeds. Filament yarns are then ready for bobbins or cones; staple length fibers are crimped, cut, and baled.

Orlon does not require heat-setting to obtain dimensional stability and wrinkle resistance but may be heat-set for durable pleats or creases.

In 1959 a process was announced by DuPont for synthesizing Orlon as a bicomponent fiber, now trade-named Orlon Sayelle. In this process each Orlon fiber is made up of two distinct longitudinal segments with different potential for shrinkage when heated. With heat treatment one segment shrinks more than the other, causing the fiber to assume the spiral or corkscrew shape characteristic of curly hair. When it is wet, the segment which has shrunk most now swells most and thus straightens the fiber, but the corkscrew shape returns upon drying. Orlon Sayelle looks, feels, and acts very much like wool. It must be handled carefully when wet to avoid stretching it out of shape.

PROPERTIES

In cross section Orlon has a distinctive dog bone or dumbbell shape, and Orlon Sayelle a lobed effect very similar to the cross sections of acetate, Arnel, and Fortisan (see Figure 7-6).

Filament Orlon bears more resemblance to silk than to any other fiber, and staple Orlon is wool-like in a number of properties. Orlon has a warm, dry feel that is pleasant to the touch. It is opaque, which, combined with the low specific gravity of 1.17, gives it good covering power with very little weight. It is a good insulator and thus may combine warmth, bulk, and light weight. It has semi-dull luster and is white in color.

Breaking tenacity of Orlon is 2.2 to 2.6 grams per denier, a medium strength. Its wet strength is 95 percent of its dry strength. It has excellent stretch resistance. Because of wet strength and resistance to stretching, Orlon does not require special handling when wet, except for knit goods which may be distorted because of the nature of knitted fabrics, and Orlon Sayelle which may be distorted rather easily when wet because of its bicomponent structure. Orlon is tough and has good elasticity; its elongation is 17 to 45 percent. It has good flex resistance, abrasion resistance, and very good wrinkle resistance and crease recovery. Its dimensional stability in laundering is excellent, but white Orlon tends to yellow in steam processing. If pressing is necessary, a cool iron set at "synthetic" or lower is recommended.

Absorbency of Orlon is low, and moisture regain is only 1 to 2 percent; hence it is quick drying and also subject to static electricity accumulation.

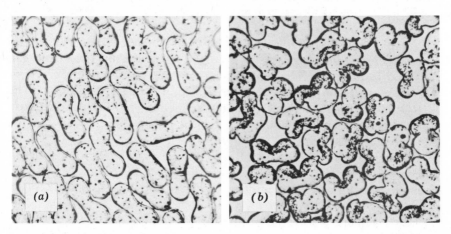

FIGURE 7-6. Orlon photomicrographs: (a) regular Orlon; (b) Orlon Sayelle. (Courtesy E. I. duPont de Nemours & Co. Inc.)

It is dimensionally stable under extreme changes in humidity. Pilling was a widespread problem, in sweaters particularly, during the early production of Orlon.

Orlon is outstanding in its resistance to weathering, industrial fumes, and ultraviolet degradation; for this reason it is ideal for outdoor use or in areas where exposure to one or more of these factors is a problem.

Orlon burns about like cotton, rayon, and acetate, leaving a residue similar to that of acetate. Some Orlon fabrics sputter as they burn, that is, the flame almost dies out momentarily, then flares up and resumes burning, with continuous alternate dying down and flaring up. The manner of burning can be dangerous if consumers are unaware of this possibility. Orlon does not ignite easily, however, so it cannot be considered more hazardous than many other fibers in similar uses.

Although Orlon was initially difficult to dye, several classes of dyes may now be used with varying degrees of success insofar as color fastness is concerned. Pressure dyeing methods are often used.

USES

In the apparel field Orlon has taken over a considerable part of the sweater market and is being used alone or in blends in many types of knitted goods. Dress, blouse, suit, and coat fabrics make use of Orlon. Much washable fleece coating material has been made from Orlon because of its bulk, warmth, and light weight, and it is currently one of the fibers most often used in making simulated fur coats. Permanently pleated, washable skirts of a blend of Orlon and wool have sometimes been very popular. Printing of Orlon sweaters and jersey fabrics has been quite successful.

In the textile furnishings field Orlon is of special value for curtain and drapery materials because of its light resistance, but it seldom can be found in those fabrics. Orlon blankets are warm, light, and fleecy, but Acrilan seems to be more generally available in blankets than Orlon. The first Orlon carpet yarn (Type 37) was announced by the DuPont Company in November 1959; Orlon 33, a bicomponent fiber, is now on the market for carpets.

Among listed industrial uses for Orlon are sails, filters for chemicals, awnings, outdoor furniture, convertible tops, marine cordage, tents, tarpaulins, sewing thread for outdoor fabrics, tobacco nettings, and signal fabrics.

Orlon is more satisfactorily cared for by washing than by drycleaning, especially in knitted garments which tend to shrink and to discolor in drycleaning. Informal observation of the effect of drycleaning and of hand washing on several dresses of 80 percent Orlon–20 percent wool jersey led

a group of women in New York State to conclude that hand washing was preferable. No shrinkage occurred when garments were washed and dried by methods commonly used for wool sweaters, whereas those that were drycleaned shrank so much that in some instances they were no longer wearable by their owners.

Acrilan

A patent for Acrilan was registered by the Chemstrand Corporation in 1951, and some staple fiber was ready for the market in 1952. Difficulty was encountered in some uses in which fibrillation, a kind of splintering of the yarns, occurred with abrasion (rubbing type) wear. The plant was shut down while processing machines were altered to overcome this difficulty, and the now successful fiber reappeared on the market in 1954. Acrilan has been widely accepted by the consuming public and plant capacity is being increased.

PROCESSES

Materials other than acrylonitrile used in processing Acrilan have not been revealed, although steps involved have been described. The processes are about the same as those for Orlon. Acrilan is a copolymer of acrylonitrile and vinyl acetate, although some other substances may replace a part of the latter material. The producer has stated that the polymer is a white powder which is centrifuged and then dried in a heated revolving drum, after polymerization. The spinning solvent has not been revealed but is believed to be dimethyl acetamide. Acrilan is wet-spun with equipment similar to that used for spinning rayon, with coagulation of the fiber taking place in a bath of unrevealed chemical nature. Since coagulation could presumably be carried on in any of several mediums, it is possible that the coagulating bath is varied experimentally from time to time.

Drawing to about three and a half times its original length is accomplished by means of dryer-rollers set to revolve at different speeds. Drawing temperatures are not specified. After drawing, the fiber is crimped, cut into staple lengths, and baled for shipment, or sold as tow to be cut at the factory where used. No filament Acrilan is being produced at this time.

PROPERTIES

The properties of Acrilan are, for the most part, quite similar to those of Orlon. Acrilan is much more readily dyed than pure acrylic Orlon and can be handled by conventional dyeing methods and equipment.

The strength, absorbency, hygroscopicity, light weight with warmth,

and high covering power are similar to those properties in Orlon. Acrilan does not have the cashmerelike softness of Orlon and is less resistant to sunlight and weather. It has excellent wrinkle resistance and crease recovery. Acrilan fabrics often have a rather crisp, springy, woollike hand.

Acrilan has a specific gravity of 1.17, breaking tenacity of 2.0 to 2.7 grams per denier, wet strength about 90 percent of dry, elongation of 17 to 30 percent, and moisture regain of 1.2 to 1.6 percent.

Acrilan is a light beige in color, and although it can be bleached white, light exposure tends to cause color change. Fluorescent whiteners seem to be more satisfactory than bleaches and are used for white fabrics or with dyes for pastel colors. Acrilan is semi-dull but may be delustered further by adding delustering pigments.

Dry heat tends to discolor Acrilan at temperatures a little lower than for Orlon. Washability and care required are about the same as for Orlon; boiling water causes high shrinkage. Charges of static electricity on Acrilan, in some instances at least, are apparently in the same direction as electrical charges on wool, so that these materials repel each other. In contrast, Orlon apparently has an opposite charge and clings to wool and even to cotton.

Acrilan does not ignite readily and does not sputter as it burns, but it does burn, although somewhat less readily than cotton and rayon. Once a flame is generated, burning may be intense.

In cross section Acrilan is almost circular with irregular scalloped edges (see Figure 7-7).

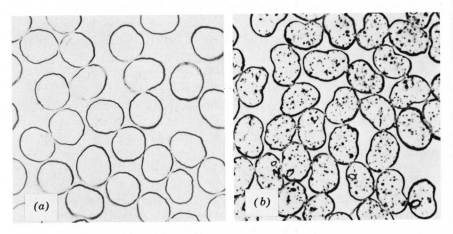

FIGURE 7-7. Photomicrographs of Acrilan: (a) regular; and (b) Acrilan 16. (Courtesy E. I. duPont de Nemours & Co. Inc.)

USES

Acrilan is popular for blankets, for knitted goods such as sweaters and jersey fabrics, and for permanently pleated fabrics. It is used in blends for lightweight woollike suit, dress, and sportswear fabrics. A fast-growing field is for carpets and rugs, which are much like wool in appearance and resilience, resistant to soiling and spots, and easily cleaned; they are also durable. Because of its dyeability, a great range of decorator colors are available in Acrilan carpeting at prices comparable to wool prices or less. One of the big motor lodge chains has adopted Acrilan blankets for all its lodges.

Creslan

Creslan first appeared on the market in late 1959 after a plant for production on a commercial scale was completed. Preliminary work was carried on as early as 1952 on fibers X-51 and X-54, forerunners of Creslan, and most available data are based on these fibers, assuming that Creslan resembles them in many ways. Creslan is produced in both staple and filament length fibers.

Creslan is a copolymer of acrylonitrile with small amounts of some other chemical compound, possibly acrylamide. The processing is assumed to be essentially the same as for Orlon and Acrilan, except that spinning is a wet-spinning process with coagulation taking place in a frigid bath. How the frigid temperature is obtained and maintained, and what the drawing and stretching temperatures are have not been published. The filaments are crimped, cut into staple lengths, and baled for shipment.

Creslan is much like Orlon and Acrilan in combining light weight with warmth and high-bulking power. It has the same specific gravity, 1.17. Breaking tenacity of Creslan is 2.0 to 4.2 grams per denier. Creslan is said to be more readily dyed than the acrylics which preceded it. Other properties are about the same as those of Orlon and Acrilan. In cross section, Creslan is round with a thick skin or double outer ring structure visible.

Uses of Creslan are similar to those for Orlon and Acrilan. Sweaters and other knitted goods, fur-like fabrics, blankets, and other items for which bulk, warmth, and light weight are desirable are fields for this fiber. It may appear in blends with wool, rayon, cotton, and in special types of wash-and-wear garments. Creslan is being promoted for rainwear, suits, jackets, dresses, and children's outerwear. The producer allows the fiber trademark only on those products that meet specified performance standards.

A Cornell study* of Creslan blankets made by traditional and new

* Anne J. Kinsel, "Comparison of Woven and Tufted Creslan Blankets in Laundering and in Use," Cornell University master's degree thesis (1963).

tufting processes followed most of the procedures of an earlier study (Fahnestock). The new Creslan blankets performed satisfactorily and were warm and attractive. With washing, the tufted blankets assumed a wrinkled appearance believed due to the wrinkling and shrinkage of the cotton core fabric. This problem no doubt can be solved by using a different core fabric.

Zefran

Zefran, on which work began in the late 1940's, went into commercial production in 1958 and was available in a limited array of apparel offered in carefully selected stores in the fall of 1958. The manufacturer chose this method of introducing the new fiber in order to control end-uses, which, when uncontrolled, have sometimes led to public aversion for an otherwise excellent new fiber.

Zefran is composed of acrylonitrile and limited amounts of other substances; both materials and processes are secret. Personnel from the Dow Company have said that although Zefran is made of materials which might be expected to copolymerize, the way in which the substances have been induced to join in the molecular chains is unique. This results in a chain backbone structure of acrylonitrile with the other substance hooked on as a side-chain-type tail. The tail material is highly dyeable and absorbent, resulting in a Zefran fiber with some of the advantages of both the thermoplastic and the nonthermoplastic fibers. At present Zefran is available only in permanently crimped staple lengths.

Zefran resembles the other acrylics in most of its properties, although the unique molecular-chain structure results in some differences. Its specific gravity is 1.19, its breaking tenacity ranges from 3.3–4.2 grams per denier, and wet strength is about 95 percent of dry strength. It is slightly less heat sensitive than the acrylics which preceded it. Elongation is about 30 percent and moisture regain is 2.5 percent. It is wrinkle resistant, dimensionally stable, and washable, as are the other fibers of this group. Zefran is white in color and has a round cross section; the yarn is not adaptable to texturizing processes at this time. Zefran can be heat-set and is said not to pill. It is soft, warm, comfortable, and drapable. Because of its absorbent tail, Zefran can be dyed by conventional methods with most of the dyestuffs used for other fibers, and it can be bleached with chlorine bleaches. Flammability and hole-melting propensities are said to be similar to these properties for wool.

In its first year on the market Zefran was made into fabrics for high fashion, and sale was limited to these prestige garments in fashionable stores. Some 100 percent Zefran sweaters have been offered for sale, but most of the fiber has gone into blends with wool for suit fabrics and with

rayon or with cotton for dress fabrics. Zefran is expected to find a market in most types of textile fabrics—from those for work and play clothes to drapery and upholstery materials—and for heavy industrial fabrics. Some Zefran ribbon-knit dresses have been very satisfactory examples of what this fiber may do in wear, cleaning, and in holding its shape.

Other acrylics fit into the general descriptions of those discussed here.

THE MODACRYLICS

Dynel [a]   Verel [b]

[a] Trade name granted to Union Carbide Corporation.
[b] Trade name granted to Eastman Kodak Company, Tennessee Eastman Company Division.

Until the Textile Fiber Products Identification Act was passed, the modacrylic fibers were classed as acrylics, to which they are closely related. According to the FTC rules, a *modacrylic* fiber is ". . . a manufactured fiber in which the fiber-forming substance is any long chain synthetic polymer composed of less than 85% but at least 35% by weight of acrylonitrile units ($-CH_2-CH-$), except fibers qualifying under category (2) of

$$\underset{CN}{|}$$

Paragraph (j) of Rule 7." The exception is fibers that come under the definition of "lastrile" defined under the generic class *rubber* as containing at least 10 percent by weight of acrylonitrile units.

Dynel

Dynel was announced in 1949 and came on the market soon after. Dynel was originally a generic name, but it is now being used as a trade name. Dynel and Verel are staple fibers and so much like the acrylics that we shall not spend much time on them.

PROCESSES

Dynel is a copolymer of 40 percent acrylonitrile and 60 percent vinyl chloride, processed in very much the same ways as the acrylics. Polymerization takes place in an autoclave under controlled heat and pressure. The polymerized resin is precipitated as a fine white powder and is then dried. Acetone dissolves the Dynel resin; air is exhausted in a vacuum tank before spinning. The viscous solution is forced by metered pumps through the spinnerets, and the fibers are coagulated in a water bath. After drying, the filaments are hot-drawn to as much as thirteen times their original length

to orient the molecular chains within the fiber and to give the desired properties. Dynel is commonly sold as tow, or crimped and cut in staple lengths and baled. Fabrics are later heat-set to relax strains and tensions within the yarns in order to give stable forms and dimensions.

PROPERTIES

Dynel is one of the most heat sensitive of the commercially available fibers. It shrinks away from a hot iron or steam press and may darken. Heat resistance of Dynel is now said to be improved. Blending with other fibers improves heat resistance of Dynel by shielding it somewhat.

Dynel has a specific gravity of 1.30, the same as wool, and has good covering power and insulative ability with fairly light weight. Its breaking tenacity of 3.5 to 4.2 grams per denier is better than that of wool and is similar to that of the acrylics. Wet strength is 85 to 95 percent of dry strength. Elongation is 30 to 40 percent, moisture regain 0.4 percent. It has excellent wrinkle resistance and resilience and dimensional stability. Hot water delusters Dynel, which has a rather crisp, springy hand.

Dynel may be made in any desired diameter, and hand may vary accordingly from soft to stiff. It is creamy white in color. Sunlight may whiten it, but long exposure may cause darkening. It has about the same resistance to light deterioration as cotton. Dynel may be heat-set in permanent pleats or shape, and high temperatures may be used to give stiffness and rigidity, as in straw-like summer hats.

Dynel shrivels, blackens, and burns in a direct flame but is self-extinguishing when the flame is removed.

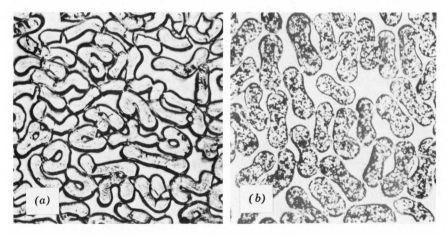

FIGURE 7-8. Photomicrographs of (a) Dynel, and (b) Verel. (Courtesy E. I. du-Pont de Nemours & Co. Inc.)

The cross sections of Dynel are like irregular ribbons or broken noodles in shape (see Figure 7-8).

Dynel is resistant to most chemicals but is dissolved by acetone and other ketones. It can be dyed readily with a number of dyestuffs in a wide range of colors. It may also be solution dyed. It is resistant to perspiration and to salt-water deterioration.

USES

Dynel is used for apparel and household furnishings, such as dresses, fleece coats, suits, sleeping garments, sportswear, men's summer hats, blankets, draperies, and furlike rugs. A large proportion of popular simulated fur coats are part or all Dynel. Chemical-resistant clothing is one of its most important industrial uses, which also include chemical filters, air and furnace filters, felts, bagging and nets, paint roller covers, and many other items. Boat blankets of double construction with Dynel on one side and vinyl on the other are being promoted as warm, water repellent, mildew and fire resistant, and washable. Dynel is used in making wigs and for doll hair which may be washed, combed, set, and, in some instances, redyed.

The Union Carbide and Carbon Corporation, in recognition of its heat sensitivity, has given instructions for pressing and ironing Dynel in a widely circulated pamphlet titled *Dynel Staple Fiber General Information*. However, because many household irons cannot be set at the low temperatures advised and others do not hold constant at these low settings, a communication from the company advises that pressing 100 percent Dynel with household irons should not be attempted. The instructions are said to be satisfactory for fabrics in blends that have been especially designed for specific amounts (usually 8 to 35%) of Dynel. By substituting "Dynel-blended" for "all-Dynel" the instructions are as follows:

Wrinkles disappear from Dynel[-blended] fabrics under ironing with little effort and at low ironing temperatures. Too high ironing temperatures, however, will cause Dynel to stiffen and shrink. To preserve the beauty and luxurious hand of Dynel fabrics, these pressing and ironing instructions must be closely followed:

When ironing Dynel[-blended] fabrics, the lowest iron setting and a dry cover of cotton cloth or other fabric should be used. If no cover cloth is used, an iron with a lower than "rayon" setting is necessary. Dynel[-blended] fabrics can be steam-pressed at reduced pressures, and wrinkles can be removed by jet-steaming, but steam irons, mangles, or hot-head presses should not be used.

A new use for Dynel is in moldable fabric—heat-molded to three-dimensional shapes but retaining their fabric characteristics. Such molded

fabrics are useful for radio and TV grilles, and perhaps automobile upholstery.

Verel

Verel, announced in 1956 and commercially available since late 1965, is a copolymer made up chiefly of acrylonitrile combined with other unspecified materials and processed by unrevealed methods. The fact that Verel is available in stabilized and unstabilized forms leads to the conclusion that it may be heat treated to relax tensions for dimensional stability, although this apparently is not essential to obtain a sufficiently oriented fiber for many uses. Processing may be assumed to be similar to that for the acrylics and for Dynel.

Verel is produced in three degrees of stability, apparently by varying the heat treatment and methods or extent of drawing, and in two degrees of flammability, probably by adding different chemicals.

PROPERTIES

The cross sections of Verel have the shape of peanuts in their shells (see Figure 7-8). In some instances they may be difficult to distinguish from the cross sections of Orlon.

The outstanding property of Verel is its relatively high moisture regain (3.5 to 4%), which is higher than that of most thermoplastic fibers and should make this fiber more comfortable to wear and somewhat less subject to static electricity problems. Drying speed should be similar to that of nylon unless the irregular cross section permits more water to be held within the fabric compared with round, closely packing nylon fibers. Type FR Verel is said to be extremely flame resistant.

Verel is a white fiber which can, if necessary, be bleached with sodium chlorite plus oxalic or formic acid; peroxide and ordinary chlorine bleaches discolor the fiber.

The specific gravity of Verel is 1.37, similar to that of wool, acetate, and rayon. It has a breaking tenacity of 2.5 to 2.8 grams per denier, medium elasticity, elongation of 33 to 35 percent, and a soft hand similar to that of wool. It has good wrinkle resistance and resilience and low pilling tendency. A maximum safe ironing temperature is 300°F. Above this temperature the fabric softens and, when cool, becomes stiff. Verel has good resistance to weather deterioration. It can be permanently heat-set in curl, crimp, or pleats.

The chemical resistance of Verel is said to be high. It is said to be easily dyed and soil and stain resistant.

The differing degrees of stability enable fabric manufacturers to combine the different types of fibers and to control yarn texture by treatment

with boiling water, since shrinkage varies greatly in such treatment. One result is the simulated fur fabric with so-called "guard hairs." Thermosetting resins cannot be used on Verel; they stay on the surface and make the fiber stiff and boardy.

USES

Verel is finding a considerable market in furlike pile fabrics for coats, coat linings, collars, and other trim. It has also been promoted in carpets and in fluffy harem rugs.

Verel is commonly blended with Acrilan for rugs, often in the proportions Acrilan 80 percent–Verel 20 percent. This combination is considered safer than all-Acrilan which has sometimes been deemed dangerously flammable.

THE POLYESTERS

Avlin[a]	Fortrel [e]	Quintess[h]
Blue C [b]	Fortrel 7 [e]	Shapespeare Wonder Thread[i]
Chemstrand [b]	Grip[b]	Trevira[j]
Dacron[c]	Kodel [f]	Vycron[g]
Encron[d]	Lowland [d]	Wellene[k]
Enka[d]	Puff Stuff [g]	Xtra-Tuf [g]

[a] Trade name granted to FMC Corporation, American Viscose Division.
[b] Trade name granted to Monsanto Company, Textiles Division.
[c] Trade name granted to E. I. duPont de Nemours & Co., Inc.
[d] Trade name granted to American Enka Corporation.
[e] Trade name granted to Celanese Corporation, Celanese Fibers Marketing Co.
[f] Trade name granted to Eastman Kodak Co., Tennessee Eastman Co. Division.
[g] Trade name granted to Beaunit Corporation, Beaunit Fibers Division.
[h] Trade name granted to Phillips Fiber Corp., Subsidiary of Phillips Petroleum Co.
[i] Trade name granted to Soo Valley Company.
[j] Trade name granted to Hystron Fibers, Inc.
[k] Trade name granted to Nichols & Co., Inc.

Polyester has been defined for the Textile Fiber Products Identification Act as "a manufactured fiber in which the fiber-forming substance is any long chain synthetic polymer composed of at least 85% by weight of an ester of a dihydric alcohol and terephthalic acid (p—HOOC—C_6H_4—COOH)."

Polyester fibers, new on the American scene in 1953, are among the fastest growing fiber groups, and new developments in durable press and other blends as well as all-polyester uses give promise of still faster growth for this group of fibers.

There are as yet no data available on all polyester fibers produced in the United States. The rapid growth since 1959 when enough was produced in the world to make reporting the totals practicable can be seen in Table 19. Polyester staple and tow are now beginning to appear in data on pro-

TABLE 19. World Production of Polyester Fibers (Millions of Pounds and Percent)[a]

| Year | The Americas | | Western Europe | | All others | | Total |
	Pound	Percent	Pound	Percent	Pound	Percent	Pound
1959	89	48.9	62	34.1	31	17.0	182
1961	111	36.2	106	34.5	90	29.3	307
1963	222	38.6	199	34.6	154	26.8	575
1965	416	41.3	333	33.1	258	25.6	1007
1967	771	46.5	471	28.4	417	25.1	1659
1968	1171	49.4	692	29.2	509	21.4	2372

[a] Compiled from *Textile Organon*, June 1968 and 1969.

ducers' shipments, but filament polyester figures are lost in a group of fibers labeled "other" which also includes acrylics. Since only a limited amount of acrylic fiber is produced in filament form, it is reasonable to assume that such figures largely represent the polyesters. On this basis, the following data taken from *Textile Organon* for February 1969 are of interest (exports included):

Producers' Shipments of Polyester and Certain Other Fibers*

Year	Staple and Tow	Filament
1964	177.5	63.6
1965	290.4	77.2
1966	372.1	94.8
1967	563.4	144.8
1968	636.8	—

* Figures refer to millions of pounds. Acrylic filament is included as well as polyester.

When the figures for 1967 here are compared with those for the Americas in Table 19, and allowing for some discrepancies due to the method of gathering and reporting data, it is obvious that most of the polyester is produced in the 20 plants of the United States. There are,

however, 23 polyester plants scattered through nine other American countries. The 78 plants in the rest of the world are located in 21 countries on all continents. It is largely through the influence of this group of fibers that wash-wear, durable press, and other easy care fabrics and garments have become a reality rather than a dream. These developments are discussed in Chapter 13.

Polyester fibers are outstanding in their wrinkle resistance, their ability to be permanently pleated, creased, or shaped, and their dimensional stability when properly heat-set.

Most of the following discussion on Dacron, the first of these fibers produced in the United States, is also true of the other polyesters which are all similar in chemical structure.

Dacron

In his early work on polymerization of long-chain molecules while concentrating on those suitable for textile fibers, Dr. Carothers worked with the polyester raw materials, but later he turned to the polyamides as being more promising, and, with his research team, succeeded in synthesizing and perfecting nylon. British chemists, who were following this work closely, became interested in the polyester possibilities, and by focusing their attention on this group of materials between 1936 and 1941, successfully developed Terylene, named for the chief ingredients in its manufacture. Although work with polyesters was still being carried on in the DuPont laboratories, after the announcement of the British success in 1946, the DuPont Company purchased patent rights in the United States, and, with some modifications in processing, put the new fiber on the market in 1953 as Dacron. Other European countries also purchased patent rights from the British and are producing the fiber under other names. Dacron and Terylene are essentially the same fiber.

PROCESSES

Dacron is manufactured from two plentiful and inexpensive starting materials, ethylene glycol (an alcohol known to automobile owners as a permanent antifreeze for radiators, a by-product of the petroleum industry) and terephthalic acid (an acid with benzene ring components). Although details have not been published, the processes are similar to those for nylon.

The process is an ester interchange copolymerization between the glycol and terephthalic acid, which results in straight-line molecular units of polyethylene terephthalate as are shown by the following chemical reactions:

$$CH_3-O-\overset{\overset{\displaystyle O}{\|}}{C}-\!\!\!\left\langle\right\rangle\!\!\!-\overset{\overset{\displaystyle O}{\|}}{C}-O-CH_3 + 2HO-CH_2-CH_2OH$$

Methyl terephthalate Ethylene glycol

$$HO-CH_2-CH_2-O-\overset{\overset{\displaystyle O}{\|}}{C}-\!\!\!\left\langle\right\rangle\!\!\!-\overset{\overset{\displaystyle O}{\|}}{C}-O-CH_2-CH_2OH + 2CH_3OH$$

Hydroxyethyl terephthalate Methanol

A great many (perhaps 80) units of hydroxyethyl terephthalate hook together end to end in a straight chain reaction, with elimination of water. The Dacron unit has this chemical structure:

$$\left[-\overset{\overset{\displaystyle O}{\|}}{C}-\!\!\!\left\langle\right\rangle\!\!\!-\overset{\overset{\displaystyle O}{\|}}{C}-O-CH_2-CH_2-O-\right]_n$$

Dacron

According to R. W. Jackle of Celanese Fibers Company, in an article in *American Dyestuff Reporter* for December 6, 1965 (p. 112) the method used to manufacture the polyester fibers is basically as follows:

Para-xylene is oxidized to form terephthalic acid which is then reacted with methanol to form dimethyl terephthalate. The dimethyl terephthalate and ethylene glycol are brought together under pressure to form polyethylene terephthalate, which in the final stages of manufacture is quenched in water to form solid sheets which are cut into chips for easier handling. These chips are remelted, the molten polymer filtered and extruded through a spinnerette (this is referred to as melt spinning), quenched in air and wound on a suitable takeup package as undrawn yarn or tow. The spinnerette consists of many small holes. The number and size of the holes determine the final total denier and denier/filament. At this time, the yarn or tow is drawn several fold and the filament yarn is then packaged on 3-pound or larger draw-wind (O-twist) or draw-twist packages, or with suitable modifications, entangled for Rotoset yarns. The staple is crimped, heat treated at 85–150°C, cut as desired and baled in 400–500 pound bales.

Further on in the same article Mr. Jackle said,

In summary, polyester is a fiber that will be in ever-increasing demand because it makes possible fabrics of such superior and wanted properties as durability with minimum weight, high strength and abrasion resistance, appearance retention (wrinkle resistance, crease retention) ease of care, and dimensional stability. Polyester fibers have the best balance of performance characteristics of any natural or man-made fiber produced in the world today.

The resulting fibers are hot-stretched to orient the molecular chains within them. Cold-drawing may be used for coarse yarns or for those in which uniformity of diameter is not essential. Dacron has a high degree of crystallinity.

Dacron fiber is produced in filament, tow, and staple lengths. Fabrics (and some yarns) are heat-set to relax tensions, set yarn twist, and obtain dimensional stability and unsurpassed wrinkle resistance. Heat-setting can be done with dry or steam heat; the former is preferred because of some depolymerization of the molecular chains in steam. Dacron is produced in both bright and dull luster. Continuous processing is being perfected.

PROPERTIES

In microscopic appearance, Dacron is similar to nylon, although it may appear to be less translucent. Dacron 62 has a trilobal cross section very similar to that of Antron nylon and also to that of cultivated silk (see Figure 7-9). A burning test, however, quickly distinguishes between the three fibers. There are other types of Dacron with other special properties.

The most outstanding properties of Dacron are its excellent resistance to wrinkle and creasing, both when dry and when wet, unsurpassed crease and pleat retention, and excellent dimensional stability. Dacron is usually considered to be our most wrinkle-resistant fiber. Dacron 62 is silklike in many properties, and fabrics made from it are much like similar silk fabrics, having many of the desirable properties of both silk and polyester.

Dacron is an opaque white fiber with high strength and elongation, good abrasion resistance, toughness, resilience, elasticity, and stretch

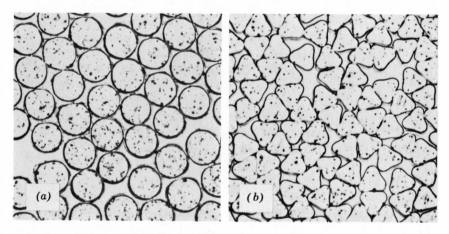

FIGURE 7-9. Photomicrographs of Dacron: (a) regular; (b) Type 62. (Courtesy E. I. duPont de Nemours & Co. Inc.)

resistance. It is among the strongest of the fibers and has an elongation of 20 to 48 percent. The specific gravity of Dacron is 1.38; it has breaking tenacity of 2.8 to 5.2 grams per denier in regular fibers and 6.0 to 9.5 in high-tenacity fibers. Because of its strength it can be drawn to very fine diameter for very sheer or lightweight fabrics. It has a rather crisp hand. Moisture regain is only 0.4 percent, so Dacron fabrics do not absorb, do not soil or stain easily, and are easily washed and quick drying. They are subject to static electricity and to pilling, although new yarn processes have improved the latter tendency. *Wicking* is a property that helps to make Dacron comfortable to wear in hot weather, even though it is non-absorbent. Wicking is the ability of a fabric or fiber to pick up moisture and have it travel along the fiber, although not actually absorbed by the fiber. Thus moisture is carried from the skin of a wearer outward, where it evaporates. Several other fibers exhibit this property to a more limited degree than Dacron; part of the coolness of untreated linen is due to wicking as well as to absorbency. Wicking, however, can work both ways. In a rainstorm moisture may be carried from the outside in, particularly if the clothing underneath is absorbent, resulting in a normal-looking exterior but uncomfortable wet clothing underneath.

Dacron melts and drops off when exposed to flame, or rolls, with a black, waxy edge forming along the affected area. It is often self-extinguishing. Dacron does not flash-burn.

Dacron has good light and weathering resistance; it ranks next to Orlon in this respect.

Dacron melts at 480°F, so if pressed a low-temperature setting must be used. An ironing temperature of 250°F is considered safe for staple fiber Dacron and 275°F for filament Dacron. Heat with pressure may cause glazing.

Dacron has good resistance to most weak acids even at boiling temperature and to strong acids at room temperature, but it is disintegrated by concentrated sulfuric acid. It has good resistance to weak alkalies but is degraded by strong alkalies at high temperatures. Drycleaning solvents do not affect Dacron, nor is it affected by bleaches. Dacron is more difficult to dye than many fibers, but it can be satisfactorily colored with at least three classes of dyes, including the acetate dyestuffs. It has less tendency to discolor with heat than nylon and the acrylics.

Kodel, Fortrel, and Vycron

In September 1958, Eastman Chemical Products, Inc., announced the development of their new polyester fiber Kodel, which was supplied for a limited yardage in apparel fabrics in early 1959 and went into full-scale commercial production in 1960.

The specific gravity is 1.22 compared with 1.38 for Dacron, heat-setting is not necessary for dimensional stability, and it may be safely ironed at temperatures as high as 425°F. Breaking tenacity is 2.5 to 5.5 grams per denier, moisture regain is only 0.2 percent, and elongation is 27 percent. Other properties are about the same as those of Dacron.

It is claimed that Kodel fiber has better whiteness retention than other polyesters because some part of its structure is designed to convert ultraviolet rays of sunlight and artificial light into visible energy.

Fortrel is produced under the license granted by the DuPont Company before the patent rights had expired on Dacron; it is assumed that Fortrel is essentially the same as Dacron in all respects.

Vycron was announced in June 1959 and was available in commercial amounts in late 1959. It is being made in filament, staple, and tow, which are heat-set, and in direct-spun yarn, which is not heat-set. The latter can be woven or knitted, then shrunk 7 to 10 percent to give tight construction for rainwear, tents, and similar items. Heat-setting is needed following the weaving or knitting.

Vycron is said to be different from other polyesters in chemical constitution and structure and to have high strength, excellent dyeability, outstanding resistance to pilling, and the other properties common to the polyester fibers. The specific gravity of Vycron is 1.36, breaking tenacity 5.0 to 8.0 grams per denier, elongation 35 percent, and moisture regain 0.6 percent, so it would seem to be very similar to Dacron. Other polyesters are similar to those discussed.

USES

The polyesters have a wide and ever-growing range of uses, in woven and knitted structures, as 100 percent polyester textiles, or in mixtures or blends with other fibers. They appear in the most delicate chiffons and in cord for heavy duty tires where high strength, toughness, stability, and durability are demanded. Figure 7-10 is a photograph of an air-inflated, synthetic-rubber coated, Dacron radome that houses a Telstar tracking station; it is typical of many such structures serving many purposes. No doubt you have had considerable experience with the polyesters, at least in the apparel field.

Apparel uses include clothing for all members of the family of both sexes and all ages, and for all seasons. Garments range from undershirts for babies to lingerie, pajamas, dresses, skirts, slacks, suits, sportswear, rainwear, sweaters, and the full range of permanent or durable press and soil release fabrics and garments.

Polyesters are used for curtains and draperies, as filler for pillows, comforters, and cushions, for blankets, for tablecloths, for carpets and rugs,

FIGURE 7-10. Air-inflated radome of Dacron coated with hypalon synthetic rubber. This structure shields a Telstar tracking station. (Courtesy Bell Telephone Laboratories.)

and in blends with cotton for no-iron sheets and pillowcases, and other items.

Industrial and military uses include filler for sleeping bags, marine nets, ropes, cordage, sails, fire hose, filters, sewing threads, conveyor belts in food and other industries, and many other uses. Polyester cord tires for automobiles are now available and there are even polyester cord bicycle tires. A line of polyester seat belts has been developed which are said to elongate 15 percent less than nylon and to be less bulky and thus neater, and to roll easier on take-up reels.

Dacron is being used by the medical profession in specially constructed flexible tubing to replace areas of damaged human arteries, trachea, and such structures, and as open-mesh material to reinforce damaged body tissues. Such mesh is said to act as a latticework through which the body's own tissues grow; it apparently lasts indefinitely with no ill effects. A very interesting, illustrated article titled "Surgery on Blood Vessels" (*Scientific American*, April 1961) discusses this use of Dacron tubing. The Duke of Windsor has a knitted Dacron tubing in place of a part of his aorta. A new medical use that was reported in *Daily News Record* for November 21, 1968, was attributed to Dr. W. V. Sharp, head of a research team at Akron City Hospital. The article said:

The use of a polyester velour fabric developed by Goodyear Tire & Rubber Co. as a replacement for damaged blood vessels is being tested (on dogs) at Akron City Hospital.

"While corrective procedures have been available for the larger arteries— over one-fourth inch in diameter—this is the first indication that surgeons may be able to replace sections of the smaller arteries and veins, which make up most of the vascular system," Dr. Sharp said.

He said the major problem in perfecting small diameter artificial blood vessels has been their tendency to cause rapid clotting of blood.

The Goodyear material has biolectric properties closely resembling those found in human tissue. The Electrolour blood vessel has numerous closed loops lining its inner wall. This is fashioned into tubes, one-eighth of an inch in diameter and about one inch in length.

The outside of the tubes then are sprayed with biolectric polyurethane to simulate human blood veins and arteries.

Currently Goodyear researchers are working on adapting the material for heart valves and artificial booster hearts but the long range hope is that it will serve as a replacement for small veins and arteries for persons suffering from hardening of the arteries and other arterial diseases.

POLYAMIDE/POLYESTER BICONSTITUENT FIBERS

Source

Source, the trademark fiber of Allied Chemical Corporation, Fibers Division, is the first of a new group of fibers that are produced from two generic fiber systems. Source is formed with a core, or matrix, of polyamide and an outer sheath of thousands of fibrils of polyester that are parallel to the length of the matrix and embedded in its surface. The polyester fibrils are so fine they cannot be seen with the unaided eye. The cross section of such fibers is represented by this sketch.*

Source fibers produced thus far are 70 percent polyamide and 30 percent polyester but the proportions can be varied over a range of 90 to 10 percent of one fiber with the reciprocal percentage of the other. Either

* Some recent data indicate that the fibrils may be dispersed throughout the matrix.

fiber could serve as the matrix, depending on the effect desired. Properties would vary with which position was occupied by each fiber.

Properties of the new fibers depend upon the proportion of each constituent but properties do not all change in direct ratio to the changes in proportions. Moisture regain, for instance, is directly related to the proportion of each constituent, but modulus and response to texturing improve with even very low proportions of polyester. Thus no hard and fast list of properties can be defined for the new fibers; they could, theoretically, fall lower than the constituent having the lower values but may well be better than the higher values of the constituent having the higher values—a halo effect that is not uncommon in fiber blends.

Some of the advantages of the new fibers, as seen by its producers, are: the ability to be dyed essentially as nylon; a rich, satiny, polished rather than a shiny appearance; unusual optical properties of fiber ends—the effect being described as similar to refraction and reflection of certain gem stones; and the possibility of selecting the properties desired and proportioning the components to achieve these properties.

Source fibers were first produced and tested as carpet yarns. Some of the new carpets were introduced by leading carpet manufacturers at the Chicago Home Furnishings Market in June 1968. A broad market in apparel, home furnishings, and industrial uses is foreseen.

In an interview with W. J. Polett, vice president of the producer's marketing division, the *Modern Textiles Magazine* for July 1968 (p. 48) reported that he said,

> The fiber embodies a unique concept in technology—the result of years of research and development—and opens the door to a new generation of fibers. The aesthetic values of the fiber help establish a new era in the marketing of carpets.

Source carpets are said to be outstanding in performance with excellent resilience and high ratings for abrasion resistance and dyeability. Tires of the new type fibers would be expected to resist the flat-spotting characteristics of nylon.

The biconstituent method of producing fibers should have application to several fiber systems.

THE NYTRILS

Nytril is defined for the Textile Fiber Products Identification Act as ". . . a manufactured fiber containing at least 85% of a long chain polymer of vinylidene dinitrile ($—CH_2—C(CN)_2—$) where the vinylidene dinitrile content is no less than every other unit in the polymer chain."

Darvan

Darvan was the first and only one of these fibers in the United States. It was the trademark for the nytril fiber originally manufactured by the Goodrich Rubber Company. The Celanese Corporation of America now has purchased the trademark, patents, and world rights to produce Darvan. The fiber is produced in West Germany under the trade name Travis by a company owned jointly by Celanese and a German firm.

The basic structure of this class of fibers was first produced in 1947, and Darvan was introduced under the trade name Darlan in late 1955. Its name was changed to Darvan in 1958. Its importance is due to the possible new class of fibers it introduced, whether or not Darvan itself is ever produced in commercial quantities.

PROCESSES

Darvan was a copolymer of about equal amounts of a vinyl cyanide, called vinylidene dinitrile, and vinyl acetate, which copolymerize in the molecular chains. The process, as inferred from patents issued to the original company, included polymerization in a reactor kettle at about 115°F temperature, precipitation of the polymer, drying, and subsequently dissolving for spinning with dimethyl formamide. Spinning was accomplished by forced pressure through the spinneret into a coagulating water bath. The filaments were heat-stretched and drawn, given antistatic treatment, sometimes crimped, and cut into staple lengths for use. The high degree of stability, even in boiling water, suggests that Darvan was heat-set at high temperature during processing.

PROPERTIES

Cross sections of Darvan were somewhat similar to those of Dynel (see Figure 7-11a).

The specific gravity of Darvan was 1.18, similar to the acrylic fibers. It was creamy white in color, soft, and warm to the touch. Its strength and elasticity were medium. Elongation was 30 percent, and it was resilient and wrinkle and shrink resistant. Darvan flamed and burned about the same as the cellulosic fibers. Moisture regain was 2 to 3 percent. Pilling was said not to be a problem. Darvan had excellent weather resistance. It was less heat sensitive than the acrylic and modacrylic fibers.

Darvan was less chemically resistant than the acrylics and modacrylics but was not damaged by any of the common cleaning solvents. Although the original fiber was very difficult to dye, new modifications overcame much of the initial difficulty. It could be bleached with hypochlorite but not with hydrogen peroxide.

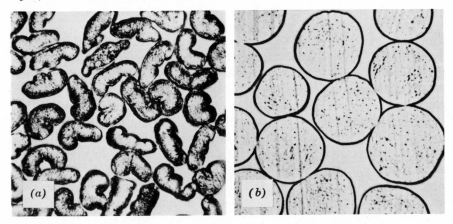

FIGURE 7-11. Photomicrographs of (a) Darvan, and (b) Saran. (Courtesy E. I. du-Pont de Nemours & Co. Inc.)

USES

Darvan was used largely in pile fabrics for simulated fur coats, but it has potential for washable sweaters and other soft knitted goods, and in blends for many types of fabrics. It, too, offers possibilities in the wash-wear field.

THE SARANS

Anovor[a]   Saran by Enjay[b]   Rovana[a]

[a] Trade name granted to Dow Badische Company, but not in use at present.
[b] Trade name granted to Enjay Fibers & Laminates Company.

Saran, the generic name for a class of fibers, is defined for the Textile Fiber Products Identification Act as ". . . a manufactured fiber in which the fiber-forming substance is any long chain synthetic polymer composed of at least 80% by weight of vinylidene chloride units ($-CH_2-CCl_2-$)."

Saran patents are owned by the Dow Badische Company and have been licensed under different trademarked names to a few other companies but it is being produced at present by only the Enjay Company. Saran is produced in both fiber and film form; no doubt you are familiar with the film.

Vinylidene chloride has been known since about 1840, and its ability to polymerize since the early 1920's. The first commercial vinylidene chloride polymer was introduced as saran monofilament, a plastic, by the Dow Company about 1940.

PROCESSES

Ethylene, obtained in the cracking of petroleum, and chlorine, obtained by electrolysis of sea water, are the basic and inexpensive raw materials for vinylidene chloride. Any one of several materials can be used as copolymers, but vinyl chloride is the best for a textile fiber. *Harris' Handbook of Textile Fibers* gives the following chemical structure for the copolymer, which is an addition polymer, but not an alternate arrangement of the two materials since smaller numbers of vinyl chloride units than of vinylidene chloride units are combined.

$$\left(CH_2-\underset{\underset{Cl}{|}}{\overset{\overset{Cl}{|}}{C}}\right)_{6n-9n}\left(CH_2-\underset{\underset{Cl}{|}}{CH}\right)_n$$

Vinylidene chloride, vinyl chloride, and a catalyst are mixed in reactor kettles and heated to obtain the basic resin powder. The resin is then melted by application of heat, extruded through heated spinnerets, and coagulated in a water bath in such a way as to cool it before crystallization can occur. The latter step is termed *quenching*. From the quenching bath, saran fiber is immediately stretched to about four times its original length to orient the molecular chains within the fiber, to increase strength and toughness, and to give fibers the desired fineness. Saran is produced in filament or staple lengths—staple fibers have crimp similar to wool and possess several of the properties of wool. Properties of the fiber can be controlled by the degree of crystallization permitted; crystallization is affected by the amount of heat supplied during or after stretching. Pigments are added to the melt before extrusion if color other than the pale yellow of the fiber is desired.

PROPERTIES

Saran is a smooth fiber with round cross sections (Figure 7-11b). It is heavy, with specific gravity of 1.70. Strength, toughness, and elasticity are controlled by the stretching process. Breaking tenacity is 1.2 to 2.3 grams per denier. Elongation is 15 to 25 percent. Saran does not absorb at all, so wet and dry strength and elongation are the same. Abrasion resistance is good. Saran is stain and soil resistant and can be easily cleaned by washing. It is weather and sunlight resistant, although it may darken in color with exposure. Saran will soften and char when exposed to a flame, but it will not support combustion; its softening temperature, however, is low.

Saran is unreactive toward all common chemicals except concentrated ammonium hydroxide; it cannot be dyed.

USES

Saran is utilized for rain apparel, accessories, furnishings, and industrial items. In its various forms it is used for auto upholstery and seat covers, luggage, filter cloths, carpets and rugs, wigs and doll hair, outdoor furniture, upholstery and drapery fabrics, rope, braid, dust mops, handbags, grille fabrics for radios, television sets, and phonographs, paint rollers, insect screening, shade cloth, brushes, and numerous other things. In monofilament form, especially in coarse diameters, saran is considered by most consumers to be a plastic. In Japan, artificial turf is being produced from saran face yarns in a polypropylene backing. Although artificial turfs are becoming very common for football fields in the United States, the companies who produce the turfs tend to evade identifying the fibers used. One grasslike carpeting, named "Sassygrass" has a saran pile attached to a woven olefin backing with a secondary backing of rubber. Difficulties have been reported with some of the turfs—some color change and some breaking of fiber are said to have been observed. Installing and keeping up the artificial turfs is said to be less expensive than upkeep of a normal grass turf.

THE OLEFINS

Amco[a]	DLP [b]	Nypel [i]	Polytwine[l]
Amcostrap[a]	Floterope[a]	Patlon[j]	Poly-Weve[m]
American[a]	GC [e]	Poly Bac[j]	Pro Pex[j]
Beamette[b]	Herculon[f]	Polycrest[k]	Radiant Twine[l]
Chevron[c]	Lambeth[g]	Polyex[l]	Vectra[n]
Crowelon[d]	Loktuft[h]	Polyloom[c]	Voplex[o]
Dawbac[b]	Marvess[h]	Poly Needl Bac[j]	

[a] Trade name granted to American Manufacturing Co., Inc.
[b] Trade name granted to Dawbarn Division, W. R. Grace & Co.
[c] Trade name granted to Chevron Chemical Co.
[d] Trade name granted to Crowe Rope Co.
[e] Trade name granted to Golden Crescent Manufacturing Co., Inc.
[f] Trade name granted to Hercules, Inc., Fibers and Film Department.
[g] Trade name granted to Lambeth Rope Co.
[h] Trade name granted to Phillips Fiber Corp., Subsidiary of Phillips Petroleum Co.
[i] Trade name granted to Allied Chemical Corp., Fibers Division.
[j] Trade name granted to Patchogue-Plymouth Division.
[k] Trade name granted to Uniroyal Fibers & Textiles.
[l] Trade name granted to Columbian Rope Co.
[m] Trade name granted to Langston Bag Co.
[n] Trade name granted to Enjay Fibers & Laminates Co.
[o] Trade name granted to Vogt Plastics.

Olefin, according to the definitions for the Textile Fiber Products Identification Act, is "a manufactured fiber in which the fiber-forming substance is any long chain synthetic polymer composed of at least 85% by weight of ethylene, propylene, or other olefin units, except amorphous (non-crystalline) polyolefins qualifying under category (1) of Paragraph (j) of Rule 7." The exception refers to synthetic rubber.

Fifty-three plants in the United States for production of olefin were listed in *Textile Organon* for June 1969 and 27 trademarked names were listed, but it is not known to what extent the various producers listed are actually producing an olefin fiber or seriously preparing to do so in the near future. A total of 91 olefin plants are located in other countries around the world.

TABLE 20. United States Producers' Shipments of Olefin Fiber (Millions of Pounds)[a]

| | Olefin | | | Total | Total |
Year	Pound	Percent (Noncellulosic)	Percent (Total)	Noncellulosic	Man-made
1957	3.4	0.7	0.3	495.5	1,116.5
1960	13.2	2.0	1.3	667.3	1,020.7
1963	29.1	2.6	2.1	1,121.9	1,366.6
1965	60.5	3.0	1.8	1,992.2	3,433.5
1968	191.1	6.2	3.8	3,063.4	5,030.6

[a] Prepared from data in *Textile Organon*, February 1969.

Table 20 shows olefin shipments by United States producers for five years beginning with 1957, the first year for which these data were reported. Although production has increased during this time, the total output is rather small considering the number of producers. Herculon, which is produced in the United States (Hercules Powder Company), has been on the market in carpets and rugs since 1962.

These fibers are characterized by their waxiness—often associated with the name *plastics* to which this group of fibers belongs. Three types of fibers, depending on molecular chain structure and composition, are included in this classification; they are branched polyethylene, linear-chain polyethylene, and polypropylene. All three are long-chain paraffins with many properties in common and need not be differentiated for our purposes. The straight-chain polyethylene type is the most promising for textile uses in many ways.

PROCESSES

The olefins described as polyethylenes are polymerized from many ethylene (C_2H_2) units. The polypropylenes (C_3H_6) are by-products of the petroleum industry. Both types have been used for many years for plastic articles and films, but fiber uses are relatively new.

Development of olefin fiber is credited to Professor Natta of the Milan (Italy) Polytechnic Institute, who made some basic discoveries in 1954, including a method of extrusion, which led to the successful production of Meraklon fiber.

According to Efraim Z. Cohen, in an article "Meraklon Polypropylene Fibers," published in *American Dyestuff Reporter* for August 1962 (pp. 43–46):

Meraklon fiber is extruded from the isotactic polypropylene polymer, a white powder-like substance, in the melt-spinning system. The extruded fibers, still in the molten state, solidify on air-cooling. The fibers then pass through a finishing process which includes stretching and various heat treatments.

The melt-spinning process has been employed for many years in extruding synthetic fibers such as nylon, Dacron, polyester, etc., but in the case of Meraklon, a special study of the rheological behavior of the molten polymer was required. This study developed a system of extrusion revolutionary in comparison with existing spinning methods such as those used for polyethylene terephthalate and nylon. This main innovation consists of special screw conveyors for melting the polymer and feeding the metering pumps, and specially designed spinnarets or jets.

PROPERTIES

Olefins have a specific gravity of 0.90 to 0.96. Breaking tenacity varies from 1.0 to 8.0 grams per denier, according to type, with the propylenes strongest. They do not absorb water at all. They burn slowly and tend to melt and drop off in a flame. They are chemically inert and odorless. Until 1962, adding pigments to the melted polymer before extrusion was the only way of coloring the olefins. Although dyes have been developed for polypropylene fibers, the color range is extremely limited and it is apparent that no group of dyes or procedures are thus far completely satisfactory in the full range of the colors offered, particularly in relation to lightfastness. Modifications necessary to permit dyeing are so expensive that they take olefins out of the inexpensive class of fibers in which they had been expected to fall. These difficulties, however, are likely to be overcome as these or similar difficulties have been for other fibers. If subjected to a dead load over a period of time, the fibers creep to a longer length and never recover to original length. The polypropylenes are brittle at low temperatures and are sensitive to ultraviolet light deterioration, but they

have better spinning qualities, less waxiness, and better resilience than polyethylene. Since olefins do not require plasticizers, they remain unchanged indefinitely in storage.

Ultraviolet light sensitivity and poor immunity to light degradation are serious shortcomings of the olefins, particularly in the home furnishings field for such items as draperies, upholstery, curtains, and carpets, and rugs that consumers expect will give long service. Their propensity to melt at very short exposure to heat could also lead to considerable dissatisfaction and difficulty.

Olefin fiber has met with considerable consumer acceptance in carpets and rugs. Their price varies with quality and method of construction but has, in general, been comparable to cotton, rayon, and the cheaper qualities of Acrilan and nylon carpeting. Indoor-outdoor carpeting is being widely used in all types of public buildings (including schools), around swimming pools, in kitchens, bathrooms, on patios, and in many other places. Nylon and saran are also used, but to a lesser extent than olefin fibers. Such carpets may be flocked on a nonwoven backing—the cheapest type—or tufted into a woven backing. Pile height can be varied, as can thickness. The resiliency of such carpeting is said to be good.

Olefin fibers are used for filters, automobile seat covers, outdoor furniture, marine ropes, screening, shoe webbing, three-dimensional padding and insulative fabric, and electrical insulation.

Ladies' sheer hose of 14-denier olefin fiber were introduced in the markets in mid-1963. Although no report of their acceptance has been found, some dissatisfaction has been heard concerning their imperfect and slow recovery from elongation in wear—garter marks were not even removed in washing. Whether this difficulty is common to all such hosiery or was true of only a limited number is not known.

THE VINALS

Vinal is defined for the Textile Fiber Products Identification Act as "a manufactured fiber in which the fiber-forming substance is any long chain synthetic polymer composed of at least 50% by weight of vinyl alcohol units ($—CH_2—CHOH—$), and in which the total of the vinyl alcohol units and any one or more of the various acetal units is at least 85% by weight of the fiber."

No vinal fibers are commercially produced in the United States at present, but it is being produced in 10 plants in other countries; Japan, where the fiber was developed, has the majority of the world's vinal plants. Raw materials are said to be cheap and plentiful, making it of special value in Japan for rainwear, umbrellas, fishing nets, and such uses.

The DuPont Company, in 1952, was issued patents for two types of vinals, but neither is being produced at present.

THE VINYONS

Avisco[a]   Voplex[b]

[a] Trade name granted to FMC Corporation, American Viscose Division.
[b] Trade name granted to Vogt Plastics.

Vinyon, according to FTC definition for the Textile Fiber Products Identification Act, is "a manufactured fiber in which the fiber-forming substance is any long chain synthetic polymer composed of at least 85% by weight of vinyl chloride units ($-CH_2-CHCl-$)."

Vinyon fiber is also produced in four other countries. Avisco, the oldest of these fibers in the United States, is assumed to be typical of the group.

Avisco Vinyon is a copolymer of vinyl chloride and vinyl acetate in which the vinyl acetate plasticizes the vinyl chloride. Polymerization is accomplished by high temperature in the presence of a catalyst. The resulting resin is dissolved in acetone, filtered, deaerated, and forced by metered pumps through the spinnerets. Spinning is similar to that of acetate and Arnel with coagulation in a current of warm air. Vinyon must be stretched to orient the fibers. It may be delustered by adding titanium dioxide.

Vinyon has low strength, high extensibility, and water resistance and is subject to static electrical problems. It does not support combustion. It has good chemical resistance but is dissolved by acetone and other ketones. It is very heat sensitive, softening at 170°F.

Vinyon is used primarily for bonding and heat sealing of other fibers in making bonded (nonwoven) fabrics, felts, and certain types of papers. It is sometimes woven with other fibers in carpets to make embossed designs. Treating the woven or tufted carpet with heat causes the Vinyon to shrink, thus producing the design.

RUBBER

Lactron[a]   Lastex[a]

[a] Trade names granted to the U.S. Rubber Company.

Although rubber is not a true thermoplastic fiber, it is heat sensitive and requires much the same care as the thermoplastic fibers; therefore it is placed with them here. Rubber and spandex fibers and yarns are com-

monly called elastic or "elastomeric" fibers or yarns in contrast to textured "stretch" yarns. An excellent description of an elastomer appeared in articles in the *American Dyestuff Reporter* by E. M. Hicks, Jr. (January 7, 1963, p. 33), and William Kirk, Jr. (September 16, 1963, p. 59), as follows:

An elastic fiber is one which, by virtue of its chemical structure, is characterized by a high-breaking elongation (in excess of 100 percent and usually 500 to 800 percent), a low modulus of extension (about 1/1000 that of hard fibers such as Dacron polyester), and both a high degree and rate of recovery from a given elongation. Recovery is essentially instantaneous and complete. It is intended by this definition to exclude fiber assemblies such as Helanca-type yarns which owe their stretch properties to a physical change in the spatial configuration or crimp of individual filaments. Also excluded are undrawn conventional "hard" fibers which exhibit high elongation but possess little or no recovery from such deformation.

Rubber, as defined by the rules for the Textile Fiber Products Identification Act, is

A manufactured fiber in which the fiber-forming substance is comprised of natural or synthetic rubber, including the following categories:

1. A manufactured fiber in which the fiber-forming substance is a hydrocarbon such as natural rubber, polyisoprene, polybutadiene, copolymers of dienes and hydrocarbons, or amorphous (non-crystalline) polyolefins.

2. A manufactured fiber in which the fiber-forming substance is a copolymer of acrylonitrile and a diene (such as butadiene) composed of not more than 50% but at least 10% by weight of acrylonitrile units ($-CH_2-CH-$). The
$$\underset{CN}{\mid}$$
term "lastrile" may be used as a generic description for fibers falling within this category.

3. A manufactured fiber in which the fiber-forming substance is a polychloroprene or a copolymer of chloroprene in which at least 35% by weight of the fiber-forming substance is composed of chloroprene units

$$(-CH_2-\underset{\underset{Cl}{\mid}}{C}=CH-CH_2).$$

PROCESSES

According to Moncrieff in *Man-Made Fibres*, 1967, (p. 69):

Rubbers are composed of molecules which are of a shape too awkward to form stable orderly (crystalline) arrangements, but which will, under tension, temporarily adopt such arrangements. When the tension is released, the molecules return to their random arrangement.

In 1925, scientists at the U.S. Rubber Company discovered that the

raw rubber liquid could be extruded as a round thread of almost any desired fineness and then cured to maintain this shape.

Latex, the milky sap of the rubber tree, is mixed with specific quantities of unrevealed chemicals, to prevent air and light deterioration, extruded through fine porcelain tubes, which perform the same functions as spinnerets for the other man-made fibers, and then vulcanized in a special vulcanizing oven. Radiation is being used in place of vulcanizing for curing some rubber products; whether it is applicable to thread is not specified. We shall discuss Latex as typical of all rubber yarns.

The rubber fibers form the core for Lastex yarns. They can be dyed in pastel colors. After curing, the rubber fiber is put through a bath of fine talc to facilitate handling.

In the process of covering the core with cotton, rayon, nylon, or other fiber yarns, the elasticity and resiliency of the resulting Lastex yarn can be controlled to varied degrees of stretch and recovery. These processes result in elastic yarns fine enough to be knitted, woven, and made into lace on conventional machines.

PROPERTIES

Lastex yarn is highly elastic. Properties of absorbency, comfort, and hand depend largely on the fiber used in covering the rubber core. Lastex is heat sensitive and will be deteriorated at high temperatures, therefore it should not be dried in a dryer or by direct heat. It is completely washable; mild detergents are advised.

USES

The many uses for Lastex include women's foundation garments, elasticized shoe fabrics for shoes for both sexes and all ages, elastic hose, tops of men's socks, surgical bindings and hose, swimsuits, stretchable trimming, and shirring yarns for machine shirring.

THE SPANDEXES

Elura[a]	Lycra[d]	Unel [f]
Fulflex[b]	Numa[e]	Vyrene[g]
Glospan[c]		

[a] Trade name granted to Monsanto Company, Textiles Division.
[b] Trade name granted to Carr-Fulflex Inc.
[c] Trade name granted to Globe Manufacturing Co.
[d] Trade name granted to E. I. duPont de Nemours & Co., Inc.
[e] Trade name granted to American Cyanamid Company.
[f] Trade name granted to Union Carbide Corp., Fibers and Fabrics Division.
[g] Trade name granted to Uniroyal Fibers and Textiles, Division of Uniroyal, Inc.

Spandex is defined for the Textile Fiber Products Identification Act as "a manufactured fiber in which the fiber-forming substance is a long chain synthetic polymer comprised of at least 85% of a segmented polyurethane."

Since Lycra was the first of these fibers we shall study it as typical of its generic class.

Lycra, known in the early experimental stages as Fiber K, was introduced commercially on a limited scale in November 1959 from pilot plant production and from regular plant production in 1961. It has taken over large sections of the fiber and yarn market formerly held exclusively by rubber. It is here considered to be typical of the spandex group of fibers.

PROCESSES

The production of Lycra is said to be the most complex of any fiber produced thus far by the DuPont Company. Chemically, polyurethane is produced by interaction of glycol and diisocyanate, as represented by the following formulas:

$$(HO-R-OH)_n \quad + \quad (O{=}C{=}N-R-N{=}C{=}O)_n$$

Glycol   Diisocyanate

$$\left[\begin{array}{ccccc} O & H & & H & O \\ \| & | & & | & \| \\ -C & -N-R-N & -C-O-R-O- \end{array} \right]_n$$

Polyurethane

The segmented structure is a result of each molecular chain being synthesized in the form of alternating hard and soft sections. The soft sections are the elongatable areas that allow elastic stretch and recovery. The hard areas give form to the structure and tie the chains together. When in the relaxed state, the molecular chains are in tangled disorder, but when stress is applied they disentangle and orient themselves parallel to each other. Upon relaxation of the stress they return immediately to the tangled, disordered state. Polyurethane may be extruded in fiber form as in the spandexes, or in foam form, discussed in Chapter 10.

PROPERTIES

The cross sections of Lycra are often described as "coalesced multifils," that is, although each fiber has a distinct dog bone cross-sectional shape, each is always attached to several of its neighbors. Figure 7-12 is a photomicrograph of the cross sections of Lycra fibers.

Lycra is a white, dull-luster fiber with breaking tenacity of 0.6 to 0.8

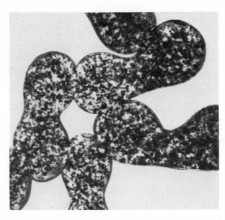

FIGURE 7-12. Photomicrograph of Lycra cross sections. (Courtesy E. I. duPont de Nemours & Co. Inc.)

grams per denier,* and high breaking elongation of 500 to 610 percent. It can be dyed satisfactorily. Other properties are specific gravity 1.0, moisture regain 0.3 percent, good abrasion resistance and flex life. Although strength is rather low, because of its combination of normal tenacity, high elongation, and low specific gravity, sheer lightweight fabrics with excellent "power" are possible. Lycra can be used covered or bare. Because of its dyeability the bare Lycra fibers can be dyed the same color as other fibers with which it has thus far always been combined.

Lycra yellows with heat and light exposure, sticks at a temperature of 347°F, and melts at 482°F. It can be satisfactorily machine washed and dryer dried at temperatures below its sticking temperature. Lycra is soluble in boiling dimethyl formamide. It is made in a range of deniers from 70 (fine) to 1120 (coarse).

Most Lycra thus far is covered with other fibers rather than used bare, perhaps because of its cost, although it may eventually be more economical bare because of the cost of covering. Nylon, rayon, acetate, and cotton are fibers commonly used for the cover yarns. Covered Lycra, in relation to the temperatures it can withstand and other such properties, may be limited by the cover fiber.

* According to Mark, Atlas, and Cernia in *Man-Made Fibers: Science and Technology*, Volume III (p. 411), "Such figures appear low in comparison to most other synthetic fibers. However, it should be realized that these data are computed on the basis of the relaxed and unstretched yarn. Due to the high elongation of the spandex fibers, the unit stress at the moment of break is in the same range as for conventional fibers."

USES

Lycra spandex fibers and yarns are used successfully in all apparel and home furnishing applications for which rubber is suitable, with additional uses for which rubber is not suitable, that is, stretch fabrics of yarns spun from staple length Orlon and Lycra fibers.

Lycra and the other spandex fibers have taken over a large share of rubber's traditional place in the foundation garment and brassiere industries. They are also being used for swimsuits and support hose and in elasticized fabrics designed to fit over contours of furniture, seats, etc. The spandex fibers are too new for the potentialities to be clearly defined. Rubber and spandex stretch fabrics and garments are discussed in Chapter 15.

TETRAFLUOROETHYLENE AND OTHER HIGH TEMPERATURE FIBERS

BBB	Pen-2,6
PBI	Teflon[a]

[a] Trade name granted to E. I. duPont de Nemours & Co., Inc.

Modern industrial and military needs have led to great interest in recent years in fabrics that can resist deterioration at very high temperatures. The space programs' need for high temperature fabrics and apparel has led to concentrated efforts to develop suitable organic fibers for such fabrics. Inorganic materials such as glass and metals meet the temperature requirements but often do not have other properties desired. Most of the discussion of inorganic materials appears in Chapter 8. In this chapter we shall look briefly at Teflon, and the other promising materials known at present as PBI, BBB, and Pen-2,6.

Teflon

Teflon, trademark for the tetrafluoroethylene fiber of the DuPont Company, is not covered by the rules for the Textile Fiber Products Identification Act, since it was expected to have industrial uses only. It is produced as a textile fiber, however, as well as in molded forms. It was the first fiber of its class and is the only fiber of its type produced in the United States.

Teflon consists of long-chain carbon molecules in which all available bonds are saturated by fluorine; there are no side chains. The molecular chains pack tightly together to make a smooth, strong fiber.

Teflon is heavy (specific gravity 2.2), originally dark brown in color but now is produced in white. It has round cross sections, and a soft, slippery hand. It is exceptionally resistant to heat and chemicals. Strength is rather low (0.6 to 1.9 grams per denier is its breaking tenacity) and elongation medium, but it has high impact resistance. Although some other fibers are superior to Teflon in flex-abrasion resistance at ordinary temperatures, as temperature rises (up to 500°F) or under chemical conditions, Teflon's flex-abrasion resistance and lack of brittleness are much superior to those of other fibers. Because of its low coefficient of friction, Teflon gears, bearings, packings, and such items do not require lubrication.

Teflon is not flammable but melts at high temperatures. The only known solvents for Teflon are perfluorinated organic liquids at temperatures above 570°F, but it is affected by certain fluorine and chlorine gases at high pressure and temperature and by alkali metals. Prolonged exposure at temperatures of 400°F or lower do not degrade Teflon. Above this temperature special precautions must be taken to remove toxic breakdown products, although it continues useful at temperatures up to 570°F. Teflon can be heat-set.

The usual uses of Teflon are largely industrial, for such things as packings, filters, tapes, gaskets, laundry fabrics, special conveyor belts, protective clothing, and antistick surgical bandages.

With space exploration, however, Teflon has gone glamorous. After the Apollo fire in January 1967 in which three astronauts died, the coverall-type space suits were all made of Beta glass reinforced with metallic patches at knees and other vulnerable spots to protect the glass from abrasion. Some of the Gemini astronauts wore these suits on a space trip and found them not too uncomfortable or unwieldy for limited wear. However, there was a continuing problem of abrasion, and analysis of the spacecraft after recovery disclosed bits of glass fiber everywhere within the craft. This was considered a great danger to proper functioning of all the delicate equipment. For the Apollo moon-orbiting flight of December 1968, astronauts Borman, Lovell, and Anders had lighter-weight coveralls of Beta glass coated with Teflon. This apparently was satisfactory. All Teflon fiber is going into military and space uses at present but has potential for a great many civilian uses. Teflon is expensive, but will eventually be less expensive as production facilities are increased.

Protective suits have been put into use for handlers of rocket and missile fuels and for handlers of other volatile substances and explosive mixtures in some of the DuPont plants. These suits are made up of layers of fluoroelastomer, Teflon fiber, and a fluorocarbon film laminated in a sandwich form.

Other High Temperature Organic Fibers

PBI is the designation by which polybenzimidazole, an attractive, golden-bronze fiber, is known. Silklike in appearance, coveralls made of this fiber have been displayed by the U.S. Air Force at various times and places. Both the DuPont and the Celanese companies have worked with the Air Force on development of PBI.

The molecular units of PBI are aromatic compounds, as shown in this chemical structure.

PBI

Walter H. Gloor of Wright-Patterson Air Force Base, in a report in *American Dyestuff Reporter* for June 17, 1968 (pp. 59–60), said

Of the polymers investigated as high-temperature fiber-formers, polybenzimidazole has had the largest amount of effort devoted to it, and is in the most advanced state of development. . . . PBI polymer is formed by the melt condensation of diphenyl isophthalate and diaminobenzidine. Fiber is dry spun from solution in dimethyl acetamide. Typical yarn properties are 5 grams per denier and 15–20% ultimate elongation. Strength retention after one minute air exposure at 850°F is approximately 40%. A comparison of loop strength and elongation versus temperature for PBI and Nomex is shown in. . . . Nomex is clearly superior up to approximately 450°F, with the advantage being to PBI above that temperature. PBI has also demonstrated a superiority to Nomex in sunlight and accelerated ultraviolet tests. After 200 hours' exposure in a Fade-Ometer, PBI retained 58% of its original strength, Nomex 23%.

Inflammability is an important fabric consideration in many applications, although ignition characteristics are not directly related to other aspects of high-temperature performance. In a direct comparison with several other fibers, PBI was found to be superior both in difficulty of ignition and burning rate.

BBB, poly(bisbenzimidazobenzophenanthroline) was listed by Mr. Gloor as another promising fiber. It is an orange-colored fiber formed by condensation of 1,4,5,8-naphthalene tetracarboxylic acid and 3,3-diaminobenzidine. He said,

The fiber is formed by wet-spinning from solution in concentrated sulfuric acid into a bath containing 70% or less of acid. Following washing and neutral-

ization of the yarn, drawing is accomplished at temperature in the 1000–1100°F range.

The highest tenacity obtained to date on BBB yarn is 4.5 gm/den. Breaking elongation at this strength level is about 4%. Strength retention at high temperature is superior to any other polymeric fiber reported to date. BBB retains 60% of room-temperature tenacity when tested at 1100°F and indications are that usable strengths exist well above 1200°F. These comments are based on one-minute air exposures at the indicated temperatures.

Preliminary Fade-Ometer testing indicates excellent ultraviolet resistance.

Pen-2,6, poly(ethylene 2,6-naphthalene dicarboxylate) which they use as a thin Mylar film, is considered by NASA researchers to be a promising polymer. *Chemical & Engineering News* for May 17, 1965 (p. 38) said of PET poly(ethylene terephthalate) to which they compared PEN,

. . . This polymer has been used in a number of aerospace programs, including the Echo and Explorer inflatable satellites. In PET, the benzene rings are important. They protect the polymer from ionizing radiation by acting as energy sinks, which dissipate absorbed radiation energy as heat and light. The close electronic interaction of the two ester groups acting through the short ethylene segment appears to produce "weak links" along the main polymer chain, according to the NASA workers.

A number of other promising materials are in various experimental stages and some undoubtedly will prove valuable, although these fibers are very expensive at this time. Benefits of such research eventually filter down to consumers, sometimes not as the same type product but as a result of things learned along the way, termed "spin off" by researchers.

ANIDEX

ANIM/8[a]

[a] Trade name granted to Rohm and Haas Company.

Anidex is the first new generic class of fibers authorized (as of October 31, 1969) by the FTC since the initial classes were established by the Textile Fiber Products Identification Act. Anidex fibers are elastomeric fibers with a different chemical base than rubber and spandex. "Anim/8" is the first trade-named fiber in the new class; it is the result of fifteen years of research by the Rohm and Haas Company.

Anidex has been defined for the FTC as "a manufactured fiber in which the fiber-forming substance is any long-chain synthetic polymer composed of at least 50% by weight of one or more esters of a monohydric alcohol and acrylic acid."

F. W. Tetzlaff, vice-president of Rohm and Haas, in the *American Dyestuff Reporter* for November 17, 1969 (p. 25), said this of the new Anim/8 fiber:

The extraordinary chemical resistance of Anim/8, its textile hand and ease-of-care properties will qualify it as the first really practical elastomeric fiber in textiles. Its chemical structure is such that it is impervious to two problems inherent in the use of spandex and rubber: white fabrics, as well as color and print fabrics made with Anim/8, can be chlorine bleached; repeated washing and drycleanings do not impair its resiliency.

The new fiber is expected to be used as a minor component in blends with other fibers, imparting stretch without obscuring the characteristics of the other fibers. A future in textile furnishings as well as in apparel is projected.

FOR FURTHER READING

American Dyestuff Reporter

Hollen, N. R., and Saddler, J.: *Textiles.*

Joseph, M. L.: *Introductory Textile Science.*

Labarthe, J.: *Textiles: Origins to Usage.*

Linton, G. E.: *Natural and Man-made Textile Fibers.*

Mark, H. F., Atlas, S. M., and Cernia, E.: *Man-Made Fibers: Science and Technology,* Volumes I, II, and III.

Modern Textiles Magazine.

Moncrieff, R. W.: *Man-Made Fibres.*

Peters, R. H.: *Textile Chemistry,* Vol. I.

Textile Chemist and Colorist.

▰▱▰▱▰▱▰▱▰▱▰▱▰▱▰▱▰▱▰▱▰▱▰▱▰▱▰▱▰▱▰

THE MINERAL FIBERS: NATURAL AND MAN-MADE

Chysotile crocidolite [handwritten]

Do not burn
Melt at very high temps
Glass + Asbestos - inert to chem. attack
All inorganic - not typical of long chain Molecu [handwritten]

Three minerals are used as textiles: one, asbestos, is a natural fiber; two, glass fiber and metallics—of which the latter might better be called a textile material than a true fiber—are man-made. This group of fibers behaves differently from all others we have considered, and the natural and man-made have some characteristics in common. They do not burn, and if they melt, do so only at very high temperatures much above those ordinarily encountered by textile fabrics. Two fibers, glass and asbestos, are inert to chemical attack. All have specialized uses and are not used interchangeably with most other textile fibers. All three are inorganic; hence they tend to be somewhat simpler than the organic fibers, and their structure is not typical of the long-chain molecule organic fibers. In addition to the mineral fibers, we shall look briefly at some new, herein unclassified fibers, possibly the forerunners of new classes of "exotic" fibers.

THE NATURAL MINERAL FIBER ASBESTOS

Asbestos is the only naturally occurring mineral fiber. It is fibrous rock, called by French Canadians *pierre à coton* (cotton stone), and has been

- only naturally occuring mineral fiber
- fibrous rock
- non-burning [handwritten]

famed for centuries for its nonburning qualities, sometimes used to mystify and frighten those unfamiliar with it. It seems from earliest times to have been regarded as a textile fiber. A number of interesting legends concerning the use of asbestos have come down through history from many countries. These legends describe such varied uses as wicks for the lamps of the vestal virgins, sleeve ruffles for the Chinese, the funeral dress of kings, napkins, and a tablecloth for Charlemagne.

Since Canada is the world's leading producer of fibrous asbestos, the tales surrounding its discovery and use in Canada are of special interest to us. A. S. Rossiter, in *Matthews' Textile Fibers* (p. 1044), has given the following account:

The first discovery of asbestos in Canada is said to have been made at a place later known as Webb's Ledge, in Shipton Township, Province of Quebec. The owner, Charles Webb, regarded the field in which it was located as only waste land. Webb's Ledge was the present site of the town of Asbestos and of the large mine located at that point. In 1877 a forest fire laid bare the rocks in Thetford and Coleraine Townships, and a French Canadian, named Fecteau, is credited with being the first to observe the prevalence of the fiber veins. But two brothers, Alfred and Robert Ward, must be given the credit as the *practical* discoverers, for they at once turned over their discovery to their brother-in-law, Andrew S. Johnson, who in turn started a mine, which by 1878 had produced 50 tons of the mineral and is currently operating.

Although asbestos was known in Canada, as previously stated, as early as 1850, and was discovered "commercially" about 1860, there is proof that it was spun and woven (possibly by Indians) as early as 1724. The proof of this is the story of Benjamin Franklin's purse, told by Franklin himself in his autobiography. One of the earliest surviving letters of Franklin was written to Sir Hans Sloane on June 2, 1725, and mentioned the asbestos purse. In this letter Franklin told Sir Hans that he had been in the northern parts of America and had brought from thence a purse made of the stone asbestos. It appears that Sir Hans was a lover of curiosities, and, since Franklin was at that time in London, he got in touch with Franklin and bought from him a number of curious articles, among which was the asbestos purse. Since Franklin had arrived in London on December 24, 1724, he must have acquired the purse at least 6 months earlier; therefore it can safely be assumed that the purse was made during or before the year 1724—136 yr earlier than the date generally regarded as the date of discovery of asbestos. The purse is in the British Museum at Bloomsbury, near London. The purse is a small closely plaited bag in a fairly good state of preservation, with a thread running through the top. It was probably the first known asbestos textile in America.

There are a number of types of asbestos in the world, only two of which, chrysotile (serpentine) and crocidolite (amphibole), the latter often called "blue asbestos," have textile significance.

FIGURE 8-1. Asbestos-veined rock. (Courtesy Canadian Johns-Manville Company, Ltd.)

Asbestos fibers have formed in narrow veins, in an unknown manner and in past ages, in fissures and cracks of certain types of rocks in various parts of the world. The fibers are usually across the fissures, from wall to wall, but occasionally are found lying parallel to the fissures. A photograph of a rock with asbestos veins may be seen in Figure 8-1, and a photograph of the fibrous asbestos by itself in Figure 8-2. The composition of chrysotile asbestos has been described by C. A. Carrol-Porczynski, in his book *Asbestos* (p. 12):

Chemically, chrysotile is a hydrated basic silicate of magnesia, its approximate constitution being represented by the formula $3MgO \cdot 2SiO_2 \cdot 2H_2O$. The

amount of water varies from about 12.5 to 15.5 per cent, and there is usually a small amount of carbonate present. Part of the magnesia may be replaced by iron or aluminum; small amounts of calcium and manganese may occur in the actual fibrous crystals. In addition, iron is very frequently found as magnetic oxide, in close association with the crystals.

Magnesium carbonate, present as dolomite and brucite, is also often associated with the fibres.

All the different types of asbestos vary in chemical composition, primarily in amounts of the different metallic compounds present. The lavender-blue color of crocidolite asbestos is due to the presence of ferrous oxide.

Asbestos is largely mined in open-pit or bench mines, although there is some underground mining in which a process called "block-cave" is used. The asbestos-veined rocks are blasted free. The broken mass is then sorted into free asbestos, bare rock, and asbestos-veined rock. The latter must then be crushed to free the fiber masses, which appear somewhat like chunks of colored glass, and the asbestos, which has been more or less

FIGURE 8-2. Asbestos, showing how the fiber can be stripped from the glasslike chunks. (Courtesy Canadian Johns-Manville Company, Ltd.)

reduced to small masses of fibers, freed from the crushed rock by a blowing or vacuuming process, or by a wet-separation method.

Canada has established a classification system for grading chrysotile asbestos that has been adopted in other chrysotile-producing countries. An asbestos grading machine has also been developed there. Grades are based on fiber length. Only those grades with fibers ⅜ inch and longer are considered suitable for making textiles. They are often, if not usually, blended with a small proportion of cotton or rayon to give strength and better processing qualities.

Canada (Quebec and Ontario provinces) ranks first in world production of asbestos fibers, followed by the Union of South Africa, Russia (probably), with only small amounts coming from the United States. Vermont, Arizona, and California have sizable deposits. Production figures for asbestos have little meaning since such figures usually lump all types together and those for textile uses cannot be distinguished. Although total world production is small compared with most other textile fibers, its importance is much greater than the amounts imply because of its noncombustible qualities which enable it to be put to unique uses. Prices vary widely for different kinds and qualities of asbestos, and in different years. The United States is the largest asbestos consumer, primarily for industrial purposes.

Under the microscope, asbestos fibers appear straight, smooth, and needle-shaped. They seem to be capable of indefinite division into finer and finer fibrils, which are now believed to be tubular rather than solid in structure.

The specific gravity of purified chrysotile asbestos is about 2.2; length varies from a fraction of an inch to more than 2 inches for the common cross-vein varieties, and to as much as 11 inches for the parallel-to-vein varieties, which usually cannot be sufficiently freed from other materials to be used for textile purposes. Strength of chrysotile fibers is considered good, and of crocidolite fibers high. Asbestos does not burn or melt, but relatively short periods of high temperature (over 600°F) will decrease its strength. It is absorbent and has wicking ability, a desirable property for this fiber.

Most asbestos in the glass-like solid mass is green in color, varying from light to dark in different deposits, but there are yellow deposits and the lavender-blue of crocidolite asbestos. When separated into fine fibers the color is usually a greenish or grayish white, although the yellow types and the lavender-blue types continue to show their characteristic colors. Asbestos dyes readily, but color is likely to be spotty and to have poor fastness.

Since asbestos is acid and alkali resistant, it is important for production

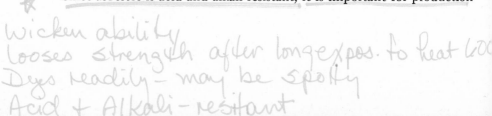

equipment, for filters for chemicals, and for other purposes in industries where chemicals are used.

Asbestos is used for flameproof clothing of many kinds for laboratory, industrial, and military purposes, with limited civilian use also. It goes into all types of protective equipment for fire fighting, fire screens, fire blankets, insulation for steam and other hot pipes, brake linings, insulative building materials, tapes and braids for electrical uses, and hundreds of other items where non-combustibility is essential. Asbestos is sometimes used with glass fiber in making decorative fabrics for curtains and draperies for hospitals, theaters, libraries, schools, and other buildings where the public assembles.

Uses

THE MAN-MADE MINERAL FIBERS
GLASS

Aero ROVE [a]	NUF [e]	Ultrastrand [h]	Unistrand [e]
Beta[b]	Pittsburgh[f]	Unicure[e]	Unitape[e]
Fiberglas[b]	PPG [f]	Unifab[e]	Vitro-Flex[c]
Garan[c]	Rovcloth[g]	Uniformat [e]	Vitron[c]
Garanmat [c]	Rovmat [g]	Uniglass[i]	Vitro-Strand [c]
Modiglas[d]	Textilmat [g]	Unirove[e]	

[a] Trade name granted to Glass Fibers Products, Inc.
[b] Trade name granted to Owens-Corning Fiberglas Corp.
[c] Trade name granted to Johns-Manville Fiber Glass Inc.
[d] Trade name granted to Modiglass Fibers.
[e] Trade name granted to Ferro Corporation.
[f] Trade name granted to PPG Industries, Inc.
[g] Trade name granted to Fiber Glass Industries, Inc.
[h] Trade name granted to Gustin-Bacon Manufacturing Co.
[i] Trade name granted to Uniglass Industries.

Glass is defined by the FTC, in relation to the Textile Fiber Products Identification Act, as "a manufactured fiber in which the fiber-forming substance is glass."

The United States is the leading producer of glass fiber, followed by four European countries reporting as a group (Sweden, Belgium, West Germany, and Netherlands), Japan, France, Italy, and East Germany. The United States produces considerably more glass fiber than all the other countries combined.

Glass fiber production data in the United States appeared with other data first in 1940 (see Table 4, Chapter 2). *Textile Organon* now includes a limited amount of consumption data too. Both appear in Table 21. Of

TABLE 21. Glass Fiber Production and Consumption in the United States (Millions of Pounds and Percent)[a]

Year	Production Total Man-made	Production Glass Pound	Production Glass Percent	Consumption Glass Pound
1955	1715.8	75.8	4.4	76.9
1960	1882.7	177.0	9.4	148.2
1965	3586.2	282.3	7.9	268.2
1968	5181.4	399.6	7.7	383.7

[a] Compiled from *Textile Organon* for February 1968 and March 1969.

the total glass used in broad woven goods a little less than half goes into household textiles and the rest into industrial textiles.

Fiberglas

Fiberglas was the first of the glass textile fibers and is still the fiber most widely used and about which most information is available.

A. Marzocchi, in an article in the *American Dyestuff Reporter* (May 10, 1954, p. 329), said that glass fibers are inorganic polymers based on silicon rather than carbon, and

The silicon is in its oxide form as a silicon dioxide network and, unlike polymers in other textile fibers, is completely cross-linked, that is, polymerization has occurred linearly as well as at right angles to the linear direction. A completely cross-linked carbon polymer is unsuited for fiber formation, but in this case a structure having no definite melting point but a long softening range is prepared by dissolving various metallic oxides within the silica network, thus lowering the melting point and yielding a solution which is mobile at high temperatures of about 2000°F. Cooling of this melt results in a gradual increase in viscosity until a rigid structure is produced. It is this range of viscosity and the fact that glass can be deformed at these intermediate temperatures, which makes glass fibers possible.

Textiles as a group depend on a linear polymerization of the monomer for flexibility. Since the glass polymer is completely cross-linked, flexibility is attained by attenuating the filaments to very small diameters. Thus, we might consider each fiber, regardless of length, as a single silica molecule with a slightly degraded structure caused by the metallic oxides in its network. As a result of this the filaments have low stretch (3–4%) with complete elasticity.

The use of glass fibers, drawn out by hand from molten glass rods into long, thin strands, has been known for centuries and they have been used in spun glass decorative objects almost as long as the processes for glass-

making have been known. Such fibers, however, were limited in amount and utility. They were also too coarse in diameter for the flexibility demanded of textile fibers.

In a pamphlet *Fiberglas Yarns for the Textile Industry,* by the Owens-Corning Fiberglas Corporation, these statements appear:

> The Venetian artisans of the Middle Ages attenuated fine glass rods for many decorative purposes including "spun glass" ornamentation on goblets and vases, but it was not until the 19th century that any textile results were achieved. In the Columbian Exposition of 1893, Edward Drummond Libbey exhibited a glass dress and other articles woven of silk and coarse glass yarns. However, the coarseness of the fibers, lack of drapeability and poor tensile properties doomed this effort to failure.

Making of glass textile fibers has developed largely since 1936 and 1937, when the processes were developed for mechanically drawing the fibers out into fine enough filaments to enable the yarns made from them to be folded, woven, and knotted without breaking. The perfected processes permitted the drawing of filament and of staple length fibers.

PROCESSES

Glass for textile fibers is made from about the same ingredients as any other glass: sand (silicon dioxide), boric oxide, lime (calcium oxide), oxides of aluminum, sodium, potassium or other metals, and a small amount of soda ash (sodium carbonate). Sand is the principal ingredient; it is both very cheap and very heavy, so shipping costs tend to fix the location of glass factories. Sand suitable for glassmaking must be high in silica and low in iron and other undesirable impurities, the sand particles small and preferably fairly uniform in size, and also preferably angular in shape. Although much sand of this type exists in many parts of the United States, the largest deposits now being utilized are located in Pennsylvania, West Virginia, and Illinois.

The various materials used in glassmaking all serve particular purposes: sand and boric oxide are the basic materials for textile glass formation, making up more than half the total mixture; soda ash acts as a flux to facilitate melting and mixing; calcium oxide and calcium carbonate give hardness and also facilitate melting and refining; aluminum oxide improves weathering qualities; and other oxides modify the glass in other ways. Choice of ingredients varies with the end-use for which the glass is intended.

The raw materials are all placed in a batch furnace at a temperature of over 3000°F, where the ingredients melt and form a colorless, transparent, homogeneous, viscous liquid, which is the molten glass. Until a few years ago, the molten glass has been dropped in small amounts to form

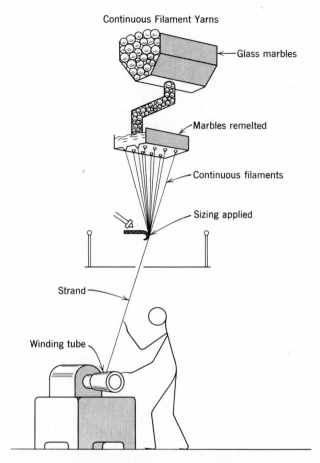

FIGURE 8-3 Schematic diagram of the formation of Fiberglas filament fibers from marbles. (Courtesy Owens-Corning Fiberglas Corporation.)

clear, greenish-colored marbles, and these were later melt-spun and drawn to form fibers. The marbles enabled easy detection of flaws and impurities and were easy to handle in subsequent operations. Recently a method has been perfected for drawing the fibers directly from the molten glass in the batch furnace, thus eliminating the marble-making and melting steps. Plants have been constructed for direct drawing of glass fibers. Use of marble melt will undoubtedly continue, too, for some years to come.

Formation of the fibers from marbles is fairly simple, as can be seen from the schematic diagram of Figure 8-3. The marbles are placed in a small furnace (hopper) in which a temperature of 2500°F is maintained,

above the spinneret device and winding equipment. As the marbles melt, gravity forces the molten glass to flow downward into the bushing box, the bottom of which has more than 200 tiny holes or orifices. The bottom of the bushing box with its holes serves the same purpose as a spinneret in other man-made fiber systems, but bears little resemblance to the usual spinneret. As the molten streams of glass emerge into the air, they begin to congeal, a sizing or other binder material is applied to prevent abrasion, and they are wound onto a tube; the tube rotates at a speed so much faster than the speed at which the glass leaves the bushing box that the still soft glass fibers are drawn out into filaments of much finer diameter than they had at the point of leaving the orifices. About two miles of filament per minute can be drawn from each bushing box by the winder.

The process for staple fibers is essentially the same, except that air blasts at regular intervals and at very great pressure pull the fibers down and pull them off in short lengths. They then pass through a lubricating spray and fall onto a rotating drum, forming a thin, gauze-like sheet which is gathered up and twisted just enough to form a thick, ropelike roving to be used in subsequent processes as spun or staple glass fibers.

Drawing the fibers into very fine diameter is essential in order to obtain the flexibility necessary for a textile fiber. A great number of these tiny flexible fibers combined into a yarn give the yarns and the fabrics made from them flexibility, pliability, and drapeability.

Glass fibers may also be texturized. Texturing is accomplished by subjecting filament fibers to an air blast which lifts the filaments and causes them to tangle before they are gathered together in a yarn.

A new, finer-diameter glass fiber than has hitherto been available was announced by Owens-Corning in 1963 under the trade name Beta. The filaments have a somewhat lower specific gravity and are more flexible than other glass fibers since decrease in diameter is reflected in increased flexibility. Such yarns are considered usable for knitting and suitable for blending with other textile fibers. Problems remain on methods of sizing, dyeing, and finishing such blended fabrics. Beta fibers are more resistant to folding damage than other glass fibers.

CORONIZING. Glass fibers and yarns are processed like other fibers and yarns, but glass fabrics require a finishing process called Coronizing. The first part is a heat treatment of from 5 to 20 seconds' duration at 1200°F in a muffle furnace. The treatment has three purposes: (1) burning off of the lubricant or binder applied in drawing, (2) relaxation of tensions due to yarn processing and weaving, and (3) setting the fabric in permanent size and shape in which it was made, with the crimp produced by the

weaving also permanently fixed. The third part of the process serves essentially the same purpose as heat-setting of the thermoplastic man-made fibers.

After leaving the furnace, the glass fabric must be given an abrasion-resistant finish; this is usually one of the thermoplastic resins which will form a protective coating around the glass fibers. Pigments are added to the resin bath for solid-color glass fabrics; then the fabric is again subjected to heat to cure the resin. If the fabric is printed, it is done after Coronizing, and the pigmented resin is set by a process similar to Coronizing.

PROPERTIES

Longitudinal sections of glass fibers look like clear glass rods, as do the other man-made fibers. In cross section, glass fibers are perfectly circular, with smooth edges, and a uniformity of appearance (see Figure 8-4). The outstanding properties of glass are non-flammability and heat resist-

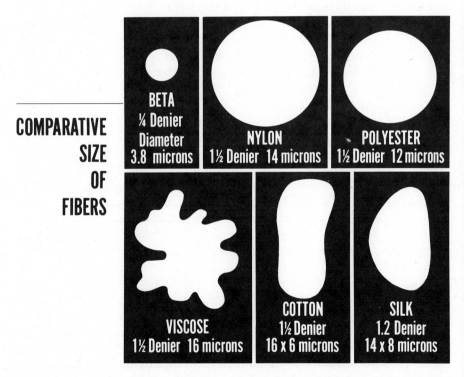

FIGURE 8-4. Comparative size of cross sections of Beta Fiberglas and several other fine-diameter fibers. (Courtesy Owens-Corning Fiberglas Corporation.)

Don't Burn
11 Conduct electricity

ance. It will not burn, although resins used in finishing may burn off if sufficiently high temperatures are reached. Glass fiber is a non-conductor of electricity.

Glass fibers for textile purposes are made in diameters of 0.00023 to 0.00028 inch, in staple fiber lengths of 9 to 15 inches, or in continuous filaments. Glass is the strongest of the fibers, with breaking tenacity varying from 9.6 to 19.9 grams per denier, and its strength is unaffected by moisture. It is brittle and lacks pliability, and although it is often described as "elastic," the word is not used in its customary meaning. Elongation is low at 2 to 4 percent. Glass is considered to have excellent resiliency because it resists compression; although its crease resistance is also said to be excellent, it may break if creased severely because of its brittleness.

Glass is nonabsorbent and nonhygroscopic; only a small amount of moisture (0.3%) is held by the resin finish, so that water held in the fabric when washed runs off very quickly, making glass one of the most rapid drying of the textile fibers. Glass fabric is water repellent unless interstices of the weave are large enough to permit penetration of water between the fibers or yarns. The specific gravity of glass fiber is 2.49 to 2.57, making it the heaviest of the textile fibers. This fact must be considered in handling large amounts of glass fabric. It may be necessary to use specially reinforced rods for floor to ceiling draperies of glass fabric, as well as for those used in buildings where the windows extend for more than one floor.

Bare glass fibers are subject to severe abrasion, and the fibers cut each other if they rub together. The resin treatment applied in Coronizing has improved the resistance of glass to abrasion and to self-cutting, but caution is still necessary in caring for glass fiber fabrics. The Owens-Corning Fiberglas Corporation recommends that "If used as draw or traverse draperies, hang just off the floor and slightly away from protruding window sills or other objects which cause abrasion and snag the fabric." Further suggestions are "Fiberglas should be cared for like fine lingerie: when washing do not scrub or wring; never dry clean or wash in washing machine; be sure to remove jewelry to prevent snags. When hanging Fiberglas be sure to thread curtain rod with thimble or other protective device." Glass fabrics should not be ironed.

Glass fibers are colorless, although their fineness makes them appear to be white. It is not practical to add color during the glassmaking stage. Why not? Color is usually added as pigment to the resins used after weaving but may be added in the final stage of Coronizing. Some new dyeing effects are being obtained by combining new textured yarns, Aerocor, with regular yarns. Because of the difference in surfaces, the pigmented resins give cross-dye effects. Glass fabrics are not affected by sunlight except as

the pigments used in dyeing may be more or less colorfast. They are very durable if not subjected to flexing, abrasion, twisting, and other distortions under strain. In several instances, however, it has been noted that sheer glass fiber curtains of ninon-type fabric have faded, split, and changed in texture after limited sunlight exposure; this seems not to have occurred in glass curtains of plain or bouclé marquisette. Although the reason for the failure of the ninon-type fabric is not definitely known, it may be that yarns of the type for such fabric contain too few fibers to support the fabric weight, or that sunlight has reacted with the finish in some way to cause the undesirable result.

Glass is resistant to acids (except hydrofluoric), alkalies, and other compounds likely to be found around the home, school, hospital, hotel, or other buildings where the public congregates. It is also resistant to insect, mildew, rot and mold, and bacterial attack.

Beta Fiberglas fabrics are machine washable but it is not advisable to wash them with clothing, nor is it advisable to use the machine for washing clothing without running it through the rinse cycle again to remove as much lint as possible. When washed together, bits of glass fibers become imbedded in the other fabrics. Clothing thus washed may be uncomfortable to some persons and may lead to skin irritations. It is not possible to remove the glass. It has been found that clothing washed with other coarser types of glass must be discarded.

Because some people who handle glass fibers or fabrics find glass irritating to their skin, and because there have been a great many complaints as a result of washing glass fabrics and clothing together, the Federal Trade Commission has made some rules concerning glass fabrics. Effective since January 2, 1967 glass fiber curtains, draperies, and fabrics for these items must carry labels which warn that skin irritations may result from handling or washing them. Warning against washing glass items with clothing, although apparently not a part of the rules, would seem to be advisable too.

USES

According to the end-use survey for 1967, reported in the January 1969 *Textile Organon*, some of the most important home furnishing and industrial uses of glass fibers, in millions of pounds, were: plastic reinforcement (180.2), drapery fabrics (56.7), electrical applications (18.2), paper and tape reinforcement (22.9), with a number of other uses in small amounts. Although it may be possible to use Beta glass for some apparel uses, the experiences with Beta coveralls in the space program would seem to make this seem impracticable for ordinary uses.

The time lag of the availability of data is well illustrated in the case of glass fibers. In 1968, much glass fiber was going into reinforcement in new types of tires for automobiles, trucks, and other vehicles, as well as a number of other uses. The Owens-Corning Fiberglas Company in 1968 was expanding facilities at other plants and building a new one primarily for the tire market. They predicted that by 1970 all new cars would be equipped with glass-fiber reinforced tires and that at least half the replacement tires sold would be of these types—a total of about 43 million pounds of glass fiber for this use alone.

Textile glass fibers are used largely for lovely and translucent curtain and drapery fabrics, to some extent for tablecloths, lamp shades, fireproof mattress and ironing board covers, and the fibers are used as dust filters in conditioning units in homes. Glass fabrics have wide use as decorative window fabrics in homes, schools, churches, banks, and other places of assembly, as stage curtains in theaters, wall drapery, etc. The trend toward buildings with one or more window walls has greatly stimulated the demand for curtains and drapery fabrics of glass fibers because of their beauty, noncombustibility, and resistance to light deterioration.

There are many industrial uses for glass fibers, several of them connected with the home building trades. Glass fibers are used in insulating electrical equipment, for safety fabrics for fire fighting, fire screens and blankets, insect screens, filters, as reinforcement for paper, plastics, and building panels, for strong fireproof tapes for parachutes, and for many other such items. Glass-fiber-reinforced plastics are used in making boat hulls and bodies of certain models of sports cars, for pipes for plumbing, and for inflatable domes over ice skating rinks and other sports structures. Much glass fiber is used as glass wool for insulation in buildings, and even for jacket innerlining. Glass fibers are not suitable for wearing apparel because the fiber ends tend to irritate the human skin; they are heavy, nonabsorbent, and lack the elongation necessary for clothing. Their abrasion resistance is also too low for clothing uses. As abrasion resistance and coloring methods are improved, and as they become less expensive (assuming that they will), there will undoubtedly be a great upsurge in many uses, not only in public places but also in homes. Blending and mixing with asbestos give safety fabrics of improved pliability, drapeability, and dyeability, and may become more important for many uses than at present.

Because light can be transmitted from end to end of glass fibers, the whole field of optics may be affected. Transmission of images, coding and code unscrambling, and even better internal examinations of patients by medical doctors are possibilities. The new electronic starlight scopes utilize such fibers.

The Apollo teams have Teflon-coated Beta glass coveralls for outer-wear, and a number of the Indianapolis 500 racing car drivers in 1968 wore Fiberglas coveralls.

METALLICS

Metallic, as defined by the FTC, is "a manufactured fiber composed of metal, plastic-coated metal, metal-coated plastic, or a core completely covered by metal."

Metallic fibers, along with other "inorganic" fibers, are making news today because of the great interest in uses undreamed of a few years ago. Apparel and home furnishing types of aluminum metallics are produced under several trademarked names in the United States. A few of the inorganic fibers also have trade names. We shall consider the regular metallic yarns in some detail and then the new metallics briefly.

Metallics are yarns, and not fibers in the usual sense of the term, but they are considered in fiber groupings because they replace or supplement fibers in yarns for textile purposes. Gold and silver have long been used in textile fabrics; the use of some of the less precious metals such as aluminum and copper is of relatively recent origin.

One of the earliest accounts of how metals were used as yarns or threads in weaving fabric is the account given in the *Bible,* of the making of garments for Aaron to wear in presiding at the altar in the tabernacle in the wilderness. Exodus 39:2 says

And they did beat the gold into thin plates, and cut it into wires, to work it in the blue, and in the purple, and in the scarlet, and in the fine linen, with cunning work.

Adele Weibel, in *Two Thousand Years of Textiles* (p. 7), has given this interesting account of the history of the use of metallic yarns in apparel:

. . . Darius the Achaemenid wore a mantle on which two golden hawks were pictured as if pecking at one another. These were probably embroidered, possibly as a development from the Achaemenid custom of sewing thin gold plaques on costumes. But textile fragments with inwoven gold, wire beaten into flat strips, have been discovered in Crimea. They can be dated to the third century B.C. The early Roman Empire deemed such luxury vainglorious and likely to incite jealousy. Verrius, the tutor of princes Gaius and Lucius, grand-sons of Augustus, told his charges how Torquinius Priscus, fifth legendary king of Rome, first to celebrate a triumph after the Etruscan fashion, appeared there clad in a golden tunic, and Josephus has a similar tale about Herod

Agrippa, who wore a mantle woven of silver, wonderful to behold in the rays of the evening sun. Both men were eventually assassinated.

Records of gifts to the churches and monasteries list fabrics with gold, but presumably the fabrics have long since been burned and the gold reclaimed. The burial mantle (408 A.D.) of Maria, wife of the Emperor Honorius, is said to have had 40 pounds of gold reclaimed from it when her tomb was opened at the time old St. Peter's was torn down to be replaced with the present church.

Some of the less expensive metallic yarns were made by wrapping thin, fine strips of metal around a linen core yarn. About 1000 A.D., a process for applying thin leaf gold to animal membrane replaced flattened gold wire in Europe. It was less expensive, softer, lighter, and more pliable, but not so beautiful or durable. This process was used for only a few centuries.

China and Japan used metallic yarns made of flattened gold and silver wire in brocades many centuries ago, and gold and silver have long been used in making the beautiful fabrics for expensive, handwoven saris in India and Ceylon. When the saris wear out, it has been a common practice to ravel out the metallic yarn very carefully and to use it again in weaving new fabric. Sometimes the yarns have been melted down and the metals reclaimed for other purposes.

Almost the same methods as these continued to be used until recent times. In America, fabrics with metallic yarns were imported from Europe. As late as 1929, Helen Bray, in *Textile Fibers, Yarns, and Fabrics* (p. 5), said

> The metallic threads are made by drawing out gold, silver, copper, etc., into threads often heating them until soft. Pure metallic threads, however, are rarely made at the present time. Gold threads are made by covering fine silver wire with a layer of gold, and silver threads by covering fine copper wire with silver. The imitations are made by covering linen threads with a fine film of gold or silver. The metallic threads are used in decorative fabrics.

Gold was the only really satisfactory metallic yarn because it did not itself tarnish or discolor other yarns. Gold, silver, and copper, however, were all expensive, heavy, sometimes odorous, often discolored by contact with the body or from perspiration, and were harsh and uncomfortable to the touch. Metallics have always been used to add richness, luxuriousness, glamor, or glitter to fabrics. They have been used by church and royalty alike, but today they are available to almost everyone because of modern yarn developments and relatively low costs. A few years ago metallics were being used so widely in all types of items—from rugs, upholstery, and even bath towels to exotic fabrics of evening clothes,

and at all price levels—that finally a sort of revulsion set in on the part of many people and many items were rejected as being gaudy and cheap-looking.

With the development of man-made fibers and their twin transparent films from the same basic formulas, as well as the development of processes to smelt and refine aluminum, a new metallic yarn industry has grown up in the United States since 1946, although the old methods are still practiced in most other countries. Aluminum, the basic metal used, is much cheaper, softer, lighter in weight than the more precious metals, and supposedly does not tarnish or cause discoloration. We have today not only the gold, silver, and copper colors of old, but also a rainbow array of metalized colored yarns to serve all sorts of purposes from apparel and furnishing textiles to car upholstery and glamorous packaging materials.

PROCESSES

American metallic aluminum yarns are made by bonding or laminating transparent plastic film and aluminum foil or film, holding the layers together with adhesives, which are the trade secrets of each of the companies which produce the yarn. The assemblage is called a "sandwich" because of the way it is made. Some yarns have five layers, others only three. The five-layered sandwich is most common. It consists of a layer of thin aluminum foil or of aluminized film in the center, a layer of adhesive on each side of that, then a layer of transparent film on the outside of each layer of adhesive. Figure 8-5 is a diagram of such a sandwich. The three-layered sandwiches have aluminized film, adhesive on one side of the film, and a layer of transparent film beyond it; these metalized yarns are usually, if not always, silver in color.

If a silver color is desired, clear adhesives and colorless transparent films are used with the foil or aluminized films. For gold and the many other colors now available, pigments are usually added to the adhesives. Different colors may be added above and below the aluminum layer, giving an iridescent effect. Sometimes colored transparent film is used,

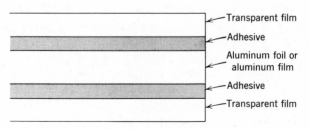

FIGURE 8-5. Diagram of five-layered metallic yarn "sandwich."

or even film that has been printed in a pattern of different colors to give a varied-color yarn.

The metallic center of the laminates may be either of two types of material. The older and more commonly appearing center is a very thin, pure, aluminum foil, rolled to a thickness of only 0.00045 inch and polished mirror bright on both sides. The other and newer center layer is metalized polyester film. In making the newer type of center the metal, usually aluminum, is vaporized and applied under high vacuum in extremely small amounts to the transparent film. The new process makes an extremely high-luster film layer, which is used with one or two other layers of transparent film, usually polyester, so that this sandwich is made of the same materials throughout, except for the adhesive. Metlon with Mylar and Reymet are made in this way. Because of the small amount of metal, this type of laminate does not interfere with electrical operation of the machines, as the foil type sometimes does.

Presumably, any type of transparent film that has the desired qualities could be used with either type of metalized center layer. The transparent films originally used were cellophane, acetate, and—after World War II —acetate butyrate. All these films are sensitive to heat at 200°F. This type of film may be used for unsupported yarns but is more often plied with a regular textile yarn for added strength and other properties needed in processing or weaving and finishing. Mylar, developed in 1954, is a tough, pliable, and heat-resistant (350°F) twin to Dacron polyester fiber. It may be used with foil or with aluminized Mylar. Mylar is more often used in unsupported yarns than in supported, although it may be used in either.

Whichever type of metallic source and transparent film is used, the laminate is made in widths of 20 to 54 inches, then cut into widths of $\frac{1}{8}$, $\frac{1}{16}$, $\frac{1}{32}$, $\frac{1}{50}$, $\frac{1}{64}$, $\frac{1}{80}$, $\frac{1}{100}$, or $\frac{1}{120}$ inch, depending on the end-use for which it is intended. The resulting strips may be used as monofilament yarns or cut into staple lengths for spinning, and they may even be given a crimp, although straight monofilament yarns are most common.

An estimated 5 million pounds of metallic yarns were produced and used in the United States in 1957, and probably even more was used in the next year or two when metallic yarns appeared in all types of decorative and home furnishings textiles and car upholstery. Now the fashion for glitter everywhere has subsided for the time being.

PROPERTIES

Since metallics are not fibers, microscopical appearance has no significance to us.

The laminated metallic yarns are all lightweight, non-tarnishable, and

relatively inexpensive compared with yarns of the precious metals. All are bright. Strength varies with the type of film and the width of the yarn. Acetate and acetate butyrate laminates are quite weak, do not knot or tie easily, and may tear in such distortion. Usually these yarns are plied with another textile fiber for weaving, knitting, and most other types of processing. Polyester films are considerably stronger than acetate films and may be used unsupported for knitting, weaving, and processing, even, it is said, on the power looms and knitting machines. Polyester films tie and knot more readily than acetate films.

Polyester film metallics have considerable elasticity, resiliency, and elongation. All these properties are lower for acetate films of the different types, but overstretching during weaving, knitting, or finishing is said to cause irreparable harm in all types. All metallics are sensitive to abrasion and flexing.

Heat resistance of acetate films is low; therefore such yarns must be processed at low temperatures, and fabrics containing them must be washed and ironed at low temperatures or delamination and melting of the acetate layers will occur. The polyester types of metallic yarns can go through regular processing, including wet- and dry-finishing and dyeing, without harm. Polyester-film-decorated shoes are said to withstand vulcanizing without harm to the metallic yarn, and the yarn is said to be able to withstand bleaching and commercial laundering processes. Dry cleaners are advised to turn articles and garments with metallic yarns inside out when cleaning and pressing; this would probably be a good home practice too.

Although metallic yarns are protected from action on the metals by the film laminates, the cut edges are vulnerable to attack by any agent that might attack the aluminum. Once delamination has begun, damage can progress rather rapidly. Perchlorethylene solvents can be used safely on both types of metallic yarns, but trichlorethylene should not be used on acetates, nor should other solvents such as acetone and glacial acetic acid, which will dissolve acetate. Polyester metallics can be cleaned in any of the regularly used drycleaning solvents.

Metallics are insect, moth, mildew, and rot resistant and are completely nontoxic.

USES

In the textile furnishings field, metallics have appeared everywhere: in carpets and rugs, upholstery and drapery fabrics, slipcovers, tablecloths and placemats, towels, curtain fabrics, bedspreads, shower curtains, and even in sheets and pillowcases.

In the apparel field, there are few items for women in which metallic

yarns have not appeared: dresses, blouses, coats, suits, shoes, handbags, belts, millinery, and in a great variety of yard goods of wool, cotton, rayon, and many other fibers, in laces, braids, and embroidery. The men have not been forgotten either; metallics have appeared in men's shirts and suits, socks, ties, suspenders, garters, and decorative insignia. Metallics also appear in rainwear and umbrellas, beachwear, swimsuits, ecclesiastical garments, and sundry small articles.

A large amount of metallic yarn has sometimes gone into automotive upholstery, which is considered an industrial use. Metallics appear in radio and television set grills, theater curtains, and eyeglass frames. They are used by the military services for radar scrambling and braid for uniforms.

OTHER INORGANIC FIBERS

A whole field of new inorganic materials, as well as the organic materials discussed in Chapter 8, have been developed on at least an experimental basis as the result of the need for new fibrous materials today. These materials must meet the rigorous requirements associated with space travel and exploration, rocketry, and other developments of our technological age. Many are very expensive at this time.

High-temperature-resistant fibrous fabrics are needed for deceleration balloons, shielding devices, space and high-speed vehicle parts, personnel and equipment parachutes, and many other such uses. The fibers must not only withstand temperatures of 1500 to 2000°F without being destroyed, but they must also retain a high percentage of their original functionality for a reasonable period of time. It has been noted that these very high temperatures are often not those to which a fabric will be exposed in use, necessarily, but are due to the area where such items are stored in flight— usually in the tail section where exhaust of engines is very hot. They must usually have high strength and high impact resistance, not be readily degraded by ultraviolet and other types of radiation or by other atmospheric conditions, pack well in limited space and unpack readily with slight effort and no sticking, and be as light in weight as possible.

A group of *metallic alloys* has been developed for some uses where properties different from any of the individual metallic components are needed. For the most part, other materials now available seem to be more suitable for extremely high temperature uses, but some of the alloys such as Chromel, René 41, Elgiloy, Hastalloy, Iconel, and Karma have valuable industrial uses.

A very fine *steel* wire has been developed which can be used as a textile fiber in making steel fabric that is tough, flexible, and durable.

Some of this or a similar wire is being used experimentally in carpeting to reduce accumulations of static electricity, a phenomenon most unpleasant to many people. Even small amounts of wire are effective in reducing static buildup, and in use such carpets do not seem to be less durable than comparable carpets without wire in the pile. They are also said to resist airborne soiling.

The Brunswick Corporation has a plant at Muskegon, Michigan for production of metal fibers. According to *Chemical & Engineering News* (March 21, 1966, page 48),

> The metal fiber is strong, resists high temperatures and chemicals, and possesses electrical and thermal conductivity and dimensional stability. The problem in making textile fibers from metals, however, is to make the fibers fine enough to give them adequate flexibility. For instance, nylon has a Young's modulus of about 500,000; stainless steel has a rating of 29 million. Thus it is necessary to reduce the diameter of stainless steel filament to about 12μ to give it the flexibility of a 3-denier nylon filament.

Steel fiber can be woven and knitted. Many uses have been suggested for steel fiber—from reinforcing belts for tires, cargo nets, filtration fabrics, and such, to space uses.

Graphite (carbon) fibers are produced by the Carborundum Company, and under the trade names *Thornel-25* and *Thornel-40*, by Union Carbide Company. Such fibers are considered ideal reinforcing materials for both resins and metals that are to be used in aerospace, hydrospace, and aircraft —structures where maximum strength and stiffness with minimum weight are needed. These fibers are said to be the strongest and stiffest material for their weight ever produced. Weaving fabrics from such fibers was first successfully accomplished in 1967 by Fabric Research Laboratories, Inc., of Dedham, Massachusetts.

The Carborundum Company, in 1968, announced the development of a silicon carbide-coated graphite fiber which is said to be more resistant to oxidation at high temperatures and more versatile than uncoated graphite. This company also produces a boron nitride fiber, silicon carbide whiskers, alumina-silicon fiber, and Fiberfrax (ceramic). The company makes glass-backed ceramic body armor such as protective vests and other clothing for active war zones.

The FMC Corporation has developed a process for making continuous inorganic filament fibers in which the inorganic materials are spun with cellulosic materials, then the cellulose is removed by ignition, leaving an inorganic fiber of alumina, silica, silica/carbon, or other such material. Fibers made by this method are said to be porous. They can be produced on rayon-production equipment.

An interesting comment appeared in *Chemical & Engineering News* for November 21, 1965 (p. 23), which has relevance to this discussion and the future of these fibers. It says

Dr. Epremian admits that the graphite filament will never compete with glass fiber in uses where glass performs well. The graphite filament costs too much. Development quantities are available from the Fostoria plant at $500 a pound. Glass fibers sell for from 32 cents a pound for commercial grade to $3.75 a pound for aerospace uses. However, the graphite filament is cheaper than boron fibers, which sell for $1500 to $6000, depending on purity.

Some of these new materials have already been utilized in special types of protective clothing for civilian occupational uses. As an example, according to *Daily News Record* for March 7, 1968:

In recent months, telephone company utility workers in Ohio, aircraft workers in Washington, coal miners in Kentucky and speleogists in southern France all have been able to perform their duties better because of a new apparel designed to protect them against the hazards of their particular jobs.

Developed by Fyrepel Products Co., Newark, O., a suit made of Union Carbide Corp.'s electrically conductive cloth is now being worn by utility crews of the American Power Service Corp. and its Buckeye-State affiliate, Ohio Power Co. The two utility firms sponsored development of the suit.

Manufactured under the Voltex name, the Fyrepel ensemble, of hooded jacket, trousers, gloves and socks, is made of fabric woven from carbon yarn and Beta glass fiber.

The outfit protects the wearer from the effects of the intense electrical field surrounding extra-high-voltage transmission lines . . . Essentially it acts as a conducting medium to drain off electrical energy discharge.

* * *

In wearing the suit, the lineman is actually brought to the same voltage as the line, thereby eliminating the high-voltage danger. The Beta fiber serves to insulate the carbon yarns from each other.

FOR FURTHER READING

Alderfer, E. B., and H. E. Michl: *Economics of American Industry.*
American Dyestuff Reporter.
Carrol-Porczynski, C. Z.: *Asbestos.*
Mauersberger, H. R. (ed.): *Matthews' Textile Fibers.*
Modern Textiles Magazine.
Moncrieff, R. W.: *Man-Made Fibres.*
Scientific American.
Textile Chemist and Colorist.
Textile Research Journal.

▄▄▀▀▀▄▀▀▀▀▄▀▀▄▀▀▀▀▀▄▀▀▀▀▀▄▀▀▀▀▀▄▀▀▀▀▄▀▀▀▀▄▀▀▀▀▀▀

YARNS AND YARN PROCESSES

Yarns play an important part in determining the characteristics of the great variety of fabrics of all types that serve every kind of purpose. Not only the nature of the fibers from which the yarns are made is important, but also the ease and variety with which the fibers can be made into yarn, and the yarns into fabric by the various construction methods. Also of importance are their susceptibility to various treatments and their reaction to finishing processes. Much of the variety, beauty, and texture of fabrics is due to yarn differences.

Not all fabrics need yarns for their construction, but by far the greater part of the fabrics used in the world are made by processes that require the fibers to be made into yarns as an intermediate stage.

Yarn, as defined by Committee D-13 on Textile Materials of the American Society for Testing and Materials* in *Standard Definitions of Terms Relating to Textile Materials* (1967), ASTM Designation D123-69a, is

A generic term for a continuous strand of textile fibers, filaments or material in a form suitable for knitting, weaving, or otherwise intertwining to form a textile fabric. Yarn occurs in the following forms:

* This organization is generally designated simply as ASTM and will be so designated hereinafter. Other citations refer to the same edition.

(a) A number of fibers twisted together,
(b) A number of filaments laid together without twist (a zero-twist yarn),
(c) A number of filaments laid together with more or less twist,
(d) A single filament with or without twist (a monofilament), or
(e) One or more strips made by the lengthwise division of a sheet of material such as a natural or synthetic polymer, a paper, or a metal foil, used with or without twist in a textile construction.

Yarns may be made, and all the steps necessary to ready them for fabric construction may be carried out, in the plants where the fibers are processed or produced. There are also separate groups of mills whose sole business is yarn processing; they produce neither fiber nor fabric. Yarn processing is sometimes the first series of operations in the plants where fabrics are produced.

The steps necessary for making fibers into yarns vary considerably for the different fibers because of the differences in raw state from which processing starts. Discussion of its raw state and processing unique to each fiber or fiber group is presented in the section in which each is discussed in detail. The basic facts are summarized briefly here.

Raw cotton is the tightly packed baled cotton as it comes from the gin with seeds removed, but still containing considerable foreign material such as bits of leaves, twigs, and dirt. Raw wool is the fleece as received from the sorting rooms. It contains the wool grease, suint, and other foreign materials acquired while on the sheep, such as burs, other vegetable matter, dirt, branding paint, tick-repellent dip, etc. Pulled wool, in addition, has on the root ends the chemicals used in its removal.

Raw linen is the flax fibers after retting and removal from the stems; scutching was discussed in the section on linen fiber, Chapter 4. Raw silk has been removed from the cocoons and has been reeled into skeins for handling but still retains the gum (sericin). Silk is already in a continuous strand, except for waste silk, so it requires relatively little work to make a yarn.

The man-made fibers in the raw state are the form in which they have come from the fiber-producing processes; further steps depend on whether they are in staple or filament lengths. Staple length man-made fibers must go through a number of the same steps as natural staple length fibers, although fewer operations are sometimes required. Filament man-made fibers require about the same processing as silk. All man-made fibers come from their production systems clean and free from foreign materials, so that unless something has happened to them in the interim, they do not have to be opened, cleaned, scoured, or degummed as do one or another of the natural fibers.

PROCESSING OF YARNS

In making fibers into yarns there are two types of processes: general, which are common to many yarns, and texturizing, to obtain special textured effects, extra bulk, stretch, or a combination of these properties in the fabrics made from them.

There are many large, intricate machines for yarn making; often there are several different machines for a single process. Somewhat different types of machines are required for wool, linen, cotton, and silk. The manmade fibers can often be processed on the equipment for the natural fibers they most resemble in length. Many of the machines in use are little changed from the days of the Industrial Revolution, but some are very new and different. There is a trend toward continuous-process, automated machines in the newer factories, or as replacements for the old.

Detailed discussion of yarn processing together with excellent pictures may be found in the *American Cotton Handbook*, Volume I; there are also many pictures in *Wellington Sears Handbook of Industrial Fabrics*. We shall take a very brief look at the processes here.

General Processes

The general processes include opening, picking, cleaning, blending, tinting, degumming, scouring, bur picking, carbonizing, carding, combing or hackling, drawing, spinning, winding, throwing, quilling, slashing, and rewinding. No fiber goes through all these processes.

DEGUMMING

Degumming is the removal of the sericin from raw silk. The silk is soaked in warm soapy water until the gum is dissolved or softened and then is passed between parallel plates set closely enough together to remove any adhering gum or other matter. From degumming, short fibers are carried through many of the processes for other short fibers and become spun silk.

SCOURING

Scouring is the method used since ancient days to remove grease, suint, dirt, and other foreign material from the wool fiber. It consists of a series of washes with soap and soda ash and several rinses at varying temperatures. Scouring operations vary for different types and qualities of wool. A chemical solvent in a closed system has been used in recent years in a few plants instead of soap and water and is said to result in a more open mass of soft-textured fiber. The high cost of installing and maintaining this method is said to be the reason why it is not more widely used. A freezing

process, in which wool was kept at low temperatures until the grease solidified and could be beaten out, was successful in producing an undamaged fiber, but it did not clean well enough to eliminate the need for some scouring and therefore has been abandoned. This method was known as "frosted" wool.

BUR PICKING AND CARBONIZING

These are also processes for wool. They are methods for removing bits of burs, sticks, and other vegetable matter remaining in wool after scouring. If not removed, the bits of vegetable matter damage equipment, interfere with spinning and other processing operations, or cause uneven dyeing or other undesirable effects, thus affecting the quality and appearance of the finished product. Needless to say, bits of burs left in wool can be very irritating to human skin.

Bur picking is a series of mechanical actions in which the wool is carried over toothed rollers where the opening operations continue and then is passed over a rack. A combination of centrifugal force and air currents removes much of the vegetable matter.

Carbonizing is the process of removing vegetable matter (such as burs, twigs, straw, and seeds) picked up and held in the fleece during the time it was growing on the animal. Carbonizing is usually done after scouring by treatment with weak sulfuric or hydrochloric acid, or with salts that become acids when heated. Heating to 200 to 220°F causes charring of the acid-treated vegetable matter without harming the wool. The wool is then passed between heavy rollers that crush the carbonized matter, which can be shaken or beaten out. Vegetable matter may be less satisfactorily removed by mechanical means.

OPENING AND BLENDING

These two steps, carried on simultaneously, are necessary for cotton and wool and may be used for other staple length fibers. The steel bands holding together the bales of cotton must be cut, and the tightly packed cotton lifted out in quantities that can be opened up into fluffy masses in early operations. Wool comes from the scouring rooms, or after bur picking or carbonization, already fairly well opened. Man-made fibers are baled under much less pressure than cotton and are therefore easily opened. All groups must have large masses and clumps of fibers broken up. This is *opening*.

Blending, as the name indicates, is the mixing of fibers from different bales, bags, or suppliers to insure uniformity of a large output of yarn. For successful blending, fibers must be of approximately the same length, diameter, density, and moisture content. Why are these similarities essen-

tial? Blending is not considered necessary, nor is it advised, for man-made fibers that are to be made into yarns composed of only one fiber and type, but it is necessary if fibers of different nature or type are to be used together in yarns.

Blending is accomplished either by laying approximately equal amounts, or exactly weighed amounts, of the fibers from the various bales or bags in thin layers, one on top of the other. The layered mass is then carried through the next processes, in which the masses are picked up vertically through all the layers and mixing is begun. Or, instead of layering, a machine process may be used in which weighed amounts from each source are put into a hopper from which mixing is carried on by means of blowers and rotating funnels. Blending is also done by combining slivers.

Carding, combing, and drawing all continue to contribute to the thorough blending of the fibers.

TINTING

Tinting is the adding of a nonpermanent color to one or more types of fibers in a blend in order to identify the fiber or fibers in further processing. This step is necessary to check the uniformity of the blend at various stages of yarn processing, and to identify fibers in the waste, which also has commercial value. Such tints are not removed until the final bleaching or in preparation for dyeing fabrics or garments.

PICKING AND CLEANING

These steps continue, through an additional machine, the opening and removing of trash and such materials. A great deal of cleaning occurs in the opening, shaking, beating, and other mechanical movements to which the fibers are subjected as they move along. Much of the heavier type of foreign matter drops out in these treatments. At the end of the picking operation, the fibers are spread out in sheet form, collected in a batting on a roller, and removed as a "lap" ready for carding. Fibers still remain largely in small tufts at the end of picking.

CARDING

The object of carding is to separate completely the individual fibers from each other and to put many in a parallel arrangement; at the end of the process, a continuous, gossamer-thin sheet of uniform thickness is delivered to a funnellike gadget that forms the sheet into a continuous, soft, inch-thick strand called a "card sliver." During carding, further opening and cleaning of the fibers occur, and short and tangled bunches of fibers are carried off as waste (noils).

COMBING

Combing is a process used to produce yarns for a limited number of fabric types in which smooth yarns of long fibers, and with considerable twist, are used. Worsteds and voiles are examples. Combing results in still further elimination of short fibers and quite thorough straightening of all fibers that remain, so that all are lined up parallel to the strand length. The continuous strands which leave the machine resemble card slivers but are smoother and more lustrous. Several slivers may be combined and drawn into a "roving" similar in size to a card sliver.

DRAWING, SPINNING, AND WINDING

Carried on together, these are various parts of the same process. From two to six card slivers, or rovings, are fed into the machines together, to insure further uniformity and to facilitate further blending and paralleling of the fibers. Drawing is similar to the processes with which you are already familiar for drawing (stretching) the man-made fibers in orienting the molecules, but is, of course, for a different purpose. It is accomplished by several sets of wheels rotating at different speeds to draw the strands out, pulling some of the fibers past others in order to make a continuously thinner strand. Spinning inserts a small amount of twist as drawing progresses and is necessary in order to hold the fibers together—the shorter the fibers the more twist required.

Winding on bobbins, spools, or other holders is necessary to take up the slack in yarns as they are drawn and spun.

This series of steps must be seen to be appreciated! It does not seem possible that several strands the size of slivers or rovings could eventually come out so very fine that they will be used in making the very softest, finest fabrics.

THROWING

Throwing is to filament fibers what drawing, spinning, and winding are to staple length fibers. Combining a sufficient number of filaments to give the size of yarn desired, adding twist, winding onto holders of the type needed for fabric construction, lubricating, and giving an antistatic treatment may all be a part of this operation.

The further steps of slashing and quilling are sometimes considered a part of yarn processing and are carried on where the yarns are produced. *Slashing* is the adding of sizing material, such as starch, to warp yarns in order to give them body, smoothness, and strength to withstand the stresses of loom or knitting machine operations. This treatment is not

necessary for filling yarns, which do not have such stresses. *Quilling* is filling of the small spindles or "quills" that fit inside weaving shuttles.

Texturizing Processes

The texturizing processes discussed here are primarily those applicable to the man-made fibers, and particularly to the thermoplastic fibers. The history of such yarns is said to be tied to man's search for a substitute for wool; textured yarns are also a result of attempts to overcome the transparency and slipperiness of thermoplastic filament yarns and the pilling tendency of spun yarns.

Since the first processes developed were for nylon and are still much used for this fiber, the name nylon will often appear in the presentation, although the processes are equally applicable to many of the other thermoplastic fibers. It is possible to obtain similar results on certain of the non-thermoplastic fibers by applying thermosetting resins, followed by curing in the desired shapes.

Texturizing imparts a permanent curl, loop, or crimp to the individual filaments, so that when they are recombined the yarns are more or less fuzzy appearing and have stretch, bulk, or both to a more limited degree. Textured yarns do not have free fiber ends to pull out, roll up, and pill. Textured nylon yarns are more opaque, have a different appearance and feel, are warmer and more absorbent, and have better covering power than the corresponding regular nylon filament yarns. The texturing operations result in filament yarns that can be used in the same way as staple fiber spun yarns, and they thus eliminate some of the steps in converting staple fibers to yarns.

The texturizing process is of considerable importance to the nylon market. In 1962 approximately one-fourth of all the filament nylon produced in the United States was textured. Chemstrand Corporation engineers, in an article "Textured Nylon Yarn" in *Modern Textiles Magazine* for August and September 1959 had predicted that by 1961 textured nylon would account for 50 million pounds of nylon per year. The actual production figures reported for 1961 were twice that. Carpets and rugs alone used only a little less than the 1959 prediction.

In October 1968 it looked as if the textured yarn market might reach 200 million pounds by the end of the year for apparel alone, and a total of more than 300 million pounds was predicted for 1971. Nylon, polyester, and acetate were sharing most of the increase with polyester making proportionately larger gains than the other fibers. Increased use of knits in the men's wear field was expected to account for much of the predicted increase. When the amount of textured yarns going into home furnishings and industrial uses are added, the growth of such yarns truly seems to be

enormous. Textured yarns have fairly well solved the pilling difficulties of Orlon and other man-made fiber sweaters and have been a factor in the return of acetate to the carpeting field.

More textured yarns with crimp are produced at present than are made by other texturizing processes. Crimp may be of different shape and depth, depending on the process used, and the results achieved vary. A zigzag crimp of this shape /\/\/\/\ is characteristic of yarns that have been forced into a heat-setting stuffer box, where they must fold up in zigzag shape because there is excessive yarn for the space. Textralized and Spunized are the registered trademarks for these yarns of the Joseph Bancroft & Sons Company and the Spunize Company of America, respectively. Ban Lon is a trademark for some of the end-use products made of Textralized yarns. Figure 9-1a is a photomicrograph of a yarn textured by this method. Zigzag crimp gives bulk but not stretch.

The original crimp process was Helanca, registered trademark for the stretch yarn of the Heberlein Patent Corporation. Stretch yarns are characterized by great elongation under stress and immediate recovery when the force is removed. Such yarns enable garment manufacturers of certain items to fit nearly all sizes of individuals with two or three garment sizes. This yarn has deeper, rounder crimp of this general shape ՄՄՄՄ . It is made by a twist–heat-set–untwist process which is not continuous in operation and thus requires much handling of the yarn. In the conventional Helanca process, yarns are twisted beyond the desired final twist, heat-set with the excess twist, untwisted completely, then retwisted according to the final product desired. During the time they are completely untwisted, the filaments separate and kink up separately; then with retwisting they make a stretch yarn which can be pulled out to several times the finished yarn length. Since all heat-set twist is in the same direction, the result is a *torque* yarn, which means that when the fiber hangs free it twists and distorts in the direction in which the twist was set. In contrast, *no-torque* fibers or yarns hang relatively straight. In order to balance and make a nondistorting item, some yarns are set with Z twist and others with S twist; then the final yarn is composed of plies of Z and S filaments which balance each other, or the fabric may be woven of alternating Z and S twist yarns. The S and Z twists are explained on page 289. Figure 9-1b is a photomicrograph of a conventional Helanca yarn. A continuous-process false-twist method is often substituted for the twist–heat-set–untwist method.

Other crimped-stretch yarns are Superloft, registered trademark for the stretch yarn of the Universal Winding Company, and Fluflon, trademark for stretch yarn of Marionette Mills, Inc. These yarns are made by the false-twist process, which permits the yarns to go right on through continuous processing with less handling than is required for the twist–

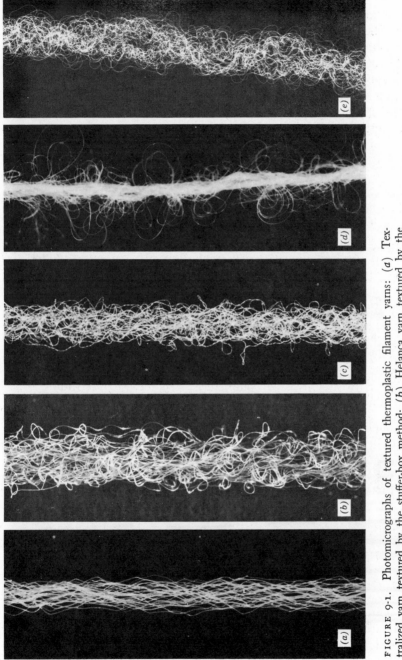

FIGURE 9-1. Photomicrographs of textured thermoplastic filament yarns: (a) Texturalized yarn textured by the stuffer-box method; (b) Helanca yarn textured by the twist-heatset-untwist method; (c) Superloft yarn textured by the false-twist method; (d) Taslan yarn textured by the looped method; and (e) Agilon yarn textured by the curled method. (Photographs a, b, c, and d courtesy Chemstrand Corporation. Photograph e courtesy Deering Milliken Research Corporation.)

heat-set–untwist method; the effect is about the same. The Helanca name may now be used for false-twist yarns. False-twist yarns are torque yarns and must be balanced by using Z and S twist yarns. Figure 9-1c is a photomicrograph of a stretch yarn crimped by the false-twist method.

Another method for making a bulky yarn is the looped method ～～～～ used in the Taslan process, registered trademark of the DuPont Company. In a pamphlet titled *Taslan,* this company has said

> The processed yarn is characterized by many tiny loops in the individual filaments of the basic yarn. These loops occur inside as well as outside of the yarn. Only a few of the filaments in the yarn are looped at any one point. Between each loop of any single filament there are relatively long straight sections. Because the loops are placed at random, each loop in the yarn is firmly anchored by adjoining filaments.

This type of yarn has bulk but does not stretch. In Figure 9-1d it is shown in a photomicrograph.

A fifth type of texturing is called a "curl" or "coil" because the yarn in softened, pliable condition is wound around a knife edge which gives it a continuous spiral curl ～～～～ which uncurls without distorting, making a no torque yarn. This is a stretch yarn. Agilon is the registered trademark for the Deering Milliken Research Corporation yarn produced by this method. Figure 9-1e is a photomicrograph of this type of yarn.

In addition to the yarns just described, there are several yarns made first as stretch yarns and then treated to remove part of the stretch and increase the bulk. Trademarks are registered for these yarns as follows: Saaba, of the Universal Winding Company, and Helanca SS and Helanca SW, of the Heberlein Patent Corporation. Tycora yarn is any textured

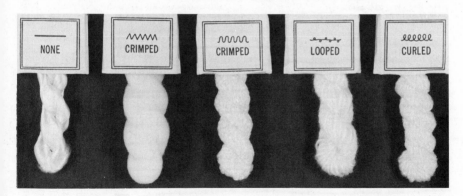

FIGURE 9-2. Equal lengths of nylon yarn when regularly processed and when textured by various processes. (Yarn samples courtesy Allied Chemical National Aniline Division.)

yarn of the Textured Yarns Company, Inc., and does not necessarily refer to any specific process or fiber.

Figure 9-2 demonstrates the difference in bulk and appearance of nylon yarns textured by the different methods compared with the same length of regular nylon yarn.

In addition to the textured yarns, another group, called "hi-bulk" yarns, are made by combining filaments of high-shrinkage potential with other filaments of low-shrinkage potential in the same yarn. Then the yarns are put through washing, steaming, or whatever medium will cause the shrinkage of the high-shrinkage yarn. A permanently bulky, non-stretch yarn results.

A newer texturizing process than those thus far described is a knit-deknit process. Filament yarns with zero twist (or almost zero) are knitted into fabric by a plain knit process, heat set to stabilize the loop structure, then raveled. These yarns separate into individual kinked or crimped filaments which are then lightly twisted, producing a textured yarn.

A report on textured yarns by Raymond Jelly which appeared in *Modern Textiles Magazine* for July 1968 included data on fibers, processes, effect, and such. When this article was written 59 United States companies were producing textured yarns—some confining their work to one fiber and one process while others used a number of different fibers and processes. Fibers and numbers of companies texturing them were: nylon 59, polyester 40, acetate 22, triacetate 19, olefin 10, rayon 3, acrylic 2, polyamide/polyester 1, triacetate/nylon 1, and glass 1. The false-twist process was used almost five times as frequently as the nearest other processes—stuffer-box and knit-deknit (used equally often).

It is also interesting to note which fibers were textured by the different processes. All the different processes were used for nylon. Polyester was textured by false-twist, stuffer-box, knit-deknit, air jet, and curl or coil processes; acetate and triacetate by false-twist (nearly all), knit-deknit, and air jet; olefin by stuffer-box, false-twist, knit-deknit, and an unspecified special process; rayon by air jet; acrylic by stuffer-box and an unspecified method; polyamide/polyester by false-twist and stuffer-box; triacetate/nylon by false twist; and glass by air jet.

The yarns were textured for all the various purposes including: stabilization only, bulk, stretch, bulk and stretch, bouclé and other types of special texture. Quite a number were identified as carpet yarns.

According to B. L. Hathorne in *Woven Stretch and Textured Fabrics*, torque crimp processes give maximum stretch, torque crimp (post-treated), stuffer-box, and edge crimp give maximum softness, while air jet processes give bulk with stability and crispness, and special texture effects such as bouclé, chenille, and nub.

Stretch yarns are used for such things as swimsuits, tights, socks, stockings, gloves, underwear, leotards, girdles, and sportswear and lounge apparel; and sometimes for rugs.

Bulk yarns are used for woven and knitted fabrics for blouses, shirts, dresses, sweaters, underwear, leotards, hose, girdles, brassieres, rugs, carpets, and automobile upholstery, to list only a few things.

A *Modern Textile Magazine* article in the August 1959 issue (pp. 37–38), made statements concerning the values of texturing which are still valid. It said

Some of the advantages of fabrics knitted and woven from textured yarns of nylon are as follows: They simulate the characteristics of fabrics constructed from hi-bulk spun yarns and give certain additional plus values such as non-pilling, absence of broken filaments, and greater durability. They combine the high abrasion resistance, strength and toughness of nylon with bulk, comfort, high thermal insulation, and satisfactory moisture absorption properties.

In many cases their use enables garment manufacturers to produce stretch-to-fit items. This is more economical to both manufacturer and seller in that both parties can work with smaller inventories and thereby cut costs.

Their texture can be varied from one of unusual softness to one of firm crispness depending on the method and conditions under which the nylon has been textured.

The fabrics are extremely durable; they are easy to wash and dry rapidly.

The fabrics do not felt and can be made dimensionally stable.

Fabrics—woven and knitted from textured yarns of nylon feel warmer than do fabrics constructed from regular nylon. This is because regular un-textured nylon removes body heat faster than textured nylon due to its greater area of surface contact with the skin.* Both laboratory and wear tests have shown that fabrics woven and knitted from textured yarns of nylon have similar surface characteristics to fabrics constructed from spun yarns, in that both type fabrics have a lower real area of contact with the skin.

Finally it should be mentioned that fabrics knitted and woven from textured yarns of nylon have tremendous versatility—because of their ability to stretch, to bulk, to look like spun yarns, and to give warmth without undue weight.

CLASSIFICATION OF YARNS

Yarns may be classified in a number of ways—according to how they are constructed, direction of twist, count or size, their use as warp, filling, knitting, or other purpose yarns. We shall consider two classifications, one according to ply and the other according to yarn structure.

* See explanation in discussion of wool.

Classification According to Ply

Ply refers to the number of individual strands that make up a yarn and the manner in which they are put together. The terms commonly used are single, ply, and cord.

A *single* (or *one-ply*) yarn is a yarn which, if untwisted, will separate into the individual fibers from which it was made. ASTM defines a single yarn as

The simplest strand of textile material suitable for operations such as weaving, knitting, etc. A single yarn may be formed from fibers with more or less twist; from filaments with or without twist; from narrow strips of material such as paper, cellophane, or metal foil; or from monofilaments. A yarn which is either twistless or can be rendered twistless in a single untwisting operation. When twist is present, it is all in the same direction.

A *plied* or *folded* yarn is a yarn made up of two or more single yarns twisted together. Upon untwisting, the ply yarns will separate into single yarns, which in turn can be untwisted to separate into fibers.

A *cable, cord,* or *hawser* yarn is made up of two or more ply yarns twisted together. Which name is used depends on whether the twist alternates in direction from singles to ply to cable, or whether two are the same one following the other. Figure 9-3 is a diagrammatic sketch showing all three types of yarn.

Single yarns are used for a greater percentage of fabrics than are other types. If, for example, you ravel yarns from sheeting, gingham, chambray, flannel, batiste, satin, or a majority of other fabrics, you will find yarns that fit the single description. Ply yarns are used for extra strength in heavy work and industrial fabrics, or for sheer fabrics such as voile. Cord yarns are used for strength in heavy industrial fabrics and sometimes in very sheer dress fabrics made of exceedingly fine fibers. Can you find examples of these?

Classification According to Yarn Structure

According to structure, yarns may be classified, in general, as self-blended, blended, elastomeric, fancy, and textured. We have already discussed textured yarns. The other four structures are described by ASTM (D123, 1969) as follows:

Yarn, Self-Blended, n.—A single yarn spun from a blend or mixture of the same fiber species.

Yarn, Blended, n.—A single yarn spun from a blend or mixture of different fiber species.

Yarn, Elastomeric, n.—A non-textured yarn which can be stretched repeatedly at room temperature to at least twice its original length and which

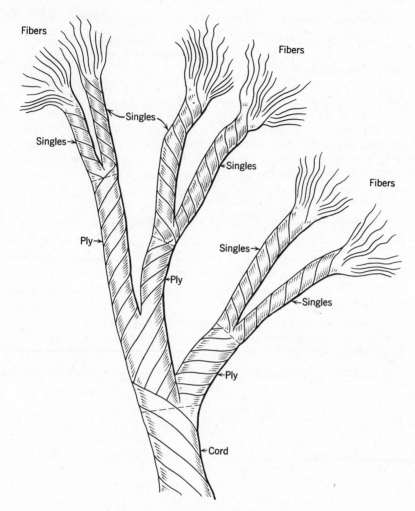

FIGURE 9-3.   Diagram of single, ply, and cable yarns.

after removal of the tensile force will immediately and forcibly return to approximately its original length. The elastic properties of the yarn are produced by the use of filaments, or a core, made from polymers having a special chemical composition of molecular structure, for example, filaments made from spandex, or from cut or extruded rubber.

Yarn, Fancy, n.—A yarn that differs significantly from the normal appearance of a single or plied yarn due to the presence of irregularities deliberately produced during its formation. In single yarns, the irregularities may be due to the inclusion of knots, loops, curls, slubs, and the like. In plied yarns, the

irregularities may be due to a variable delivery of one or more of its components or to twisting together dissimilar single yarns.

The fancy yarns have long been known as "novelty" yarns. They create opportunities for unusual pattern, texture, or other surface effects and are interesting to analyze. Such yarns are much used in producing rough-textured fabrics for items such as coats, suits, and upholstery. Plied yarns of this type have been produced for long ages, usually by plying two or more yarns under different tensions, using different-sized yarns together, or yarns with differing amounts of twist, loops, or other such variations. A third fine yarn is often used to secure the texture produced by the two main yarns. Since textured yarns made by processes other than heat-setting are well covered in literature, we shall not examine them further here. But you will be interested to examine yarns textured by different processes and the fabrics made from them—long-used processes that result in yarns such as corkscrew or spiral; covered, coated, or striped; ratiné, gimp, truffle, diamond, or chain; knot, spot, node, or nub; snarl or spike; and loop, curl, or bouclé. Slub yarns, although classed as complex, are single yarns which vary in twist and diameter along their length. Chenille yarns are not made like other yarns. A cloth "blanket" with widely spaced warp yarns is woven; then the filling is cut between the warp yarns and brushed in the desired direction, or left unbrushed, to form the "caterpillar" chenille yarn.

The type of weave or knit and amount of twist influence texture too.

YARN TWIST

The purpose of yarn twist is to hold the fibers together in order to make yarns strong enough for weaving, knitting, or other construction, for durability in wear, and to give the type of surface desired in the fabric. Some twist improves strength, but overtwisting decreases strength and will in itself break the yarn if carried to extremes. This is especially true in staple yarns made up of short-length fibers in which twisting causes stresses on the fibers lying in different directions within the yarns. The different fibers also vary in the amount of twist they can be given without impairing other properties.

The amount of twist given a yarn depends on the uses for which it is intended. *Warp* yarns are usually given considerable twist and are ordinarily simple or blended yarns so that they can withstand the rigors of weaving and present as frictionless a surface as possible. A zero-twisted warp yarn must be a filament yarn of considerable strength. *Filling* twist may vary from zero of satins to the high degree of twist essential to cause

kinking for crepe fabrics. Since little or no strain is placed on filling yarns in weaving, they may be very fragile or any type of novelty or textured yarn. *Knitting* yarns have little twist because soft texture is ordinarily desirable. Yarns may be given a hard (great amount of) twist for such fabrics as worsted twills, where the face of the weave is to be visible.

Although the direction of twist in yarn is of concern primarily to fabric producers, we are interested in some of its uses. Production of textured yarns was mentioned earlier. Direction of twist is defined by ASTM as S or Z as follows:

> The direction of twist in yarns and other textile strands is indicated by the capital letters "S" and "Z."
>
> Yarn has S twist if, when the yarn is held in a vertical position, the visible spirals or helices around its central axis conform in direction of slope to the central portion of the letter "S," and Z twist if the visible spirals or helices conform in direction of slope to the central portion of the letter "Z."
>
> Where two or more yarns, either single or plied, are twisted together, the letters "S" and "Z" are used in a similar manner to indicate the direction of the last twist inserted.

In other words, S twist is a clockwise-twisted yarn and Z twist yarn is counter-clockwise-twisted. Figure 9-4 illustrates S and Z twist yarns. There is no advantage of one type over the other; the only time direction of twist really matters is in the construction of ply, cord, and balanced texturized yarns, and in construction of certain fabrics, such as crepes, in which

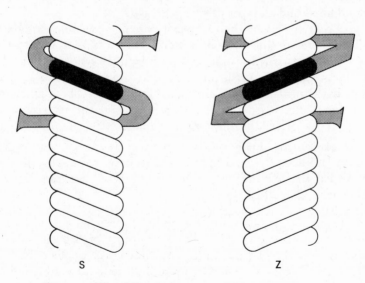

S   Z

FIGURE 9-4.   Diagram of S and Z twist yarns.

tightly twisted filling yarns of alternate and equal numbers of S and Z twist yarns form the pebbles of the crepe and prevent distortion and twisting of the fabric.

The singles making up a ply yarn may be twisted in the same or in the opposite direction to the twist of the ply, depending upon the effect and end-use for which it is intended. For example, in making carpet yarns that will resist abrasion and not "pick" easily yet that will be desirably soft in texture, ply yarns twisted in the same direction as the singles from which they are made perform better than alternating the twist direction from singles to ply.

YARN NUMBER, COUNT, OR SIZE

Yarn number, also sometimes known as *yarn count* or *yarn size*, refers (roughly) to diameter and (specifically) to linear density. The great variation in the practice of numbering yarns made of the different fibers is probably the most confusing aspect of yarns to a great many people. A movement to have all yarns numbered or sized by one system is gaining momentum and probably will be adopted sooner or later. Chief objection comes from the mill men who would have to learn a new system. International adoption of the Tex system has a good chance.

In the Tex yarn numbering system, yarn numbers are the weight in grams of 1000 meters of yarn. The same units of length and weight are used for all fibers and all types of yarn.

To give a brief idea of the complexity of the yarn numbering systems still in use: there are four separate systems, each based on different units, and with variations within some of the individual systems. Two systems are the more commonly used; one based on weight per unit length and the other based on length per unit weight. Weight per unit length is a direct system that is used for silk, some jute, and the man-made fibers. Numbers are based on the number of deniers (0.05 gram) that a 450-meter length of yarn weighs. As the diameter of the yarn increases, the number increases.

Length per unit weight is an indirect system; as the diameter of the yarn increases, the number decreases. This system is commonly used for asbestos, cotton, glass, linen, woolen, and worsted yarns. It is based on the number of units of varying yardage required to weigh 1 pound and varies as follows: for cotton and spun silk, the number of 840-yard hanks; for glass, the number of 100-yard lengths; for linen and woolen, the number of 300-yard hanks; for worsted, the number of 560-yard hanks; and so on. A simpler system would certainly seem to be desirable!

FOR FURTHER READING

American Society for Testing and Materials: ASTM *Standards on Textile Materials.*

Hadfield, J. W.: *Linen Flax Fibre Production in New Zealand.*

Hamby, D. S.: *The American Cotton Handbook,* Vol. I.

Hathorne, B. L.: *Woven Stretch and Textured Fabrics.*

Kaswell, Ernest W.: *Wellington Sears Handbook of Industrial Textiles.*

Linton, S. E.: *Applied Basic Textiles.*

Mark, H. F., Atlas, S. M., and Cernia, E.: *Man-Made Fibers: Science and Technology,* Vol. I.

Mauersberger, H. R.: *American Handbook of Synthetic Textiles.*

Modern Textiles Magazine.

Potter, M. D., and B. P. Corbman: *Fiber to Fabric.*

Strong, J. H.: *Foundations of Fabric Structure.*

Von Bergen, W.: *Wool Handbook,* Volume 1.

FABRIC CONSTRUCTION

The history of fabrics is almost as ancient as the history of man himself. Felt, tapa cloth, braids, and woven fabrics, using the basic weaves known to us today, were perfected before the first historical records were kept. Lacemaking had been developed and lace was much used by the time of the Roman Empire. Knitting is usually considered to be a relatively new fabric construction method, although Egyptian and Arabian artifacts of the third to ninth centuries A.D. give evidence that knitting processes were well developed at that time. Bonded or webbed fabrics, foams, and plastic films are of recent origin.

Fabrics, according to construction methods, may be grouped into three classes: (1) fabrics in which neither fiber nor yarn is used, (2) fabrics made directly from fibers, and (3) fabrics made from yarns or from yarns combined with other materials such as bamboo strips and other adaptable materials. The third group is far more important than the others and will command most of our attention. With few exceptions, however, the methods are old and well covered in literature and will receive only brief descriptions.

A *textile fabric* is defined by ASTM (D123 1969) as follows:

Fabric, Textile, n.—A planar structure consisting of interlaced yarns or fibers.

"*Fabric, Bonded,*[a] n.—1. A structure consisting of a web of fibers held together with a cementing medium which does not form a continuous sheet of adhesive material.

2. A layered fabric structure wherein a face or shell fabric is joined to a backing fabric, such as tricot, with an adhesive that does not significantly add to the thickness of the combined fabrics.

Fabric, Braided, n.—A structure produced by interlacing several ends of yarn in a manner such that the paths of the yarns are not parallel to the fabric axis.

Fabric, Knitted, n.—A structure produced by interlooping one or more ends of yarn or comparable material.

Fabric, Laminated, n.—A layered fabric structure wherein a face or outer fabric is joined to a continuous sheet material, such as polyurethane foam, either by the flame bonding method or by an adhesive, and this in turn normally, but not always, is joined on the back with a backing fabric such as tricot.

Fabric, Nonwoven,[b] n.—A textile structure produced by bonding or interlocking of fibers, or both, accomplished by mechanical, chemical, or solvent means and combinations thereof. . . ."

Fabric, Woven, n.—A planar structure comprising two or more sets of yarns interlaced in such a way that the elements pass each other essentially at right angles and one set of elements is parallel to the fabric axis.

In addition to these types we shall consider other methods of producing fabrics or materials which substitute for fabrics as defined by ASTM.

FABRICS REQUIRING NEITHER YARN NOR FIBER

This group of fabrics is considerably less important to the textile field at present than the other two groups. Included are tapa cloth, paper, and unsupported plastic sheets, often called plastic films, and polyurethane foams.

Tapa

Tapa cloth was and still is used in some tropical areas, particularly certain islands. Tapa is made by pounding together several layers of a thin, lacy, inner bark of a specie of mulberry tree. Tapa cloth resembles a crepey paper in texture and appearance. It has apparel uses.

Tapa fabrics are a creamy or light tan color and usually are decorated by the natives of the islands where they are produced. Designs vary greatly in type, size, and intricacy. They frequently are applied in an all-brown color made from natural substances, but may be executed in a combination of

"[a] Note.—In this context, a thin layer of foam is considered an adhesive when the cell structure is completely collapsed by the flame method.
[b] Note.—The term does not include paper, or fabrics which are woven, knitted, tufted, or those made by wool or other felting processes."

several lovely colors. Designs and colors are often unique to the people of a specific island or area and serve to identify their work wherever found.

Paper

Paper, although not ordinarily considered a textile fabric, is used as a fabric for a number of textile furnishing and apparel purposes. Many items belong in the disposable class. Have you tried one of the disposable paper dresses or other articles? If so, how did you like it? Would you be interested in a variety of such items in your wardrobe? A few manufacturers here and abroad predict a large market for cheap paper undergarments. Many paper items are planned purely for "fun" but others serve more utilitarian purposes. Have you seen the pictures of the paper wedding planned a few years ago with the dresses for all the feminine members of the party so-called "paper"?

Considerable experimental work has been done with a soft crepey paper for apparel and textile furnishings; sometimes the paper is reinforced with rows of stitching to add strength and toughness, and many others are backed by a very open scrim—often made of nylon. Many of these materials really should be called laminates. The paper is frequently printed in colorful designs. In the 1968 presidential campaign, both major parties had gay dresses made up with party symbols and national colors as decorations. If really good-looking apparel is to be made, however, the cost of designing and construction remove the garments from the cheap class; if they are of this type many persons are unwilling to pay the price then discard them after wearing them once or a few times.

Paper, often the reinforced type, has been successful in draperies, laboratory uniforms and coats, examination gowns in doctors' offices, protective "bibs" in dentists' offices, tablecloths, napkins, and such uses. Civil Defense has emergency paper blankets stockpiled in nearly every area of the United States. Have you seen them? Perhaps they have been used during an emergency in your area.

Paper may be cut into strips, wet-twisted to form yarns, and woven or knitted as other yarns. These yarns are used for mesh bagging for fruits and vegetables, cord, "fibre" rugs, automobile seat covers, and seat cushions; and for hats, handbags, and other such items. The paper yarns have considerable strength and are durable in many uses.

Films

Plastic films are made from the dope for man-made fibers, or other similarly viscous material, by extruding it in flat, continuous sheets of film instead of through spinnerets. These fabrics vary from very thin, transparent wrapping films, such as cellophane and Saran Wrap, to medium weight

such as are used for drapery materials, vinyl coats, boots, for example, to very heavy fabrics that resemble leather or heavy woven upholstery fabrics. The materials we think of as "films" are unsupported by any fibers or fibrous structure. Many raincoats, umbrellas, rain bonnets, shower curtains, drapery fabrics, and some of the cheaper upholstery plastics are of this type. Many plastics, however, that are used for clothing or upholstery fabrics are extruded on a woven or knitted base fabric, thus become "supported" films or plastics which are much more durable than unsupported films. It becomes a question of when to consider materials "coated fabrics" or "supported films."

Films vary from the thinnest of unsupported, transparent cellophane to soft, beautifully patterned, colored, and textured supported upholstery fabrics that are much used for good quality furniture for home, business, school, for transportation upholstery, wall finish in public places, and many other such uses.

Polyurethane Foams

Although foams are not at present being used alone for textile purposes, such use has been projected and seems logical. Since polyurethane foams do not really fit elsewhere, we shall consider them briefly here.

Polyurethane foams are essentially the same as spandex except that instead of being extruded in fiber form the polyurethane "batch" is mixed with a large volume of air in the kettles and then is run out as a "log" or "bun" which cures quickly in the familar foam structure. It is then sliced to the desired thickness, although it may be extruded as a thin flexible sheet, if this is preferred. The flexible sheet has the potentiality of being used as a fabric. The size of the air cells, foam thickness, and appearance can all be controlled within close specifications. Foams can be dyed and printed; they are an excellent insulative material and are soft, elastic, resilient, and strong. Foam-fabric laminates were popular for raincoats used as all-weather coats until carelessly produced, poorly laminated products ruined a promising market. Backing for tufted carpets is a rapidly growing use for both latex and urethane foams; they are also used as rug pads as well as for furniture cushions, mattresses, and such items. Rigid foams for building insulation are a new and promising construction material; they can be foamed right in place and are said to adhere and be highly efficient insulative structures. Such foams eliminate need for several conventional materials, thus lower building costs. These foams are also used for appliances, refrigerator cars and trucks, and even to waterproof and insulate underground telephone cables and their connections.

FABRICS MADE DIRECTLY FROM FIBERS

Fabrics made directly from fibers are felt, bonded (or web) fabrics, and sprayed-fiber fabric.

Felt

The first wool fabric made by ancient man is believed to have been loose matted fibers that were collected from wild sheep and pressed into solid masses, making a sort of felt.

Felting is discussed briefly in Chapter 5 (p. 116) in relation to wool. It is noted that under the right conditions of temperature, moisture, and pressure, wool scales will open up somewhat and the fiber will settle toward its root end, becoming shorter and thicker in the process. These actions, combined with motion or agitation, cause the fibers to mat together and to interlock in such a way that they cannot again be separated. Recent research reports indicate that felting, in addition to the factors already described, is partially due to the perfect elasticity of the wool fibers, which, under such conditions, tend to curl up into perfect coils. The curling adds to the intertwining and interlocking of the fibers.

Wool is the only fiber that will felt. A highly felting wool, however, may entrap and hold as much as 80 percent of other fibers in the fiber mass; often varying percentages of other fibers are blended with wool in making felt. Short-length fibers of new, reprocessed, and reused wools, except for those treated to prevent felting or on which scales have been destroyed, are all satisfactorily used for felt, as are noils up to 1½ inches in length; longer fibers tend to mat but not felt.

Modern methods of feltmaking, although carried on by complicated machine processes, accomplish the same results in essentially the same way as ancient felting methods. Wool or other fibers for felt are prepared as for other processing through the carding steps; after that the processes differ. Heat, moisture, and pressure are supplied throughout subsequent steps. The first part of the process is called *hardening*, and it is intended to mat the fibers together sufficiently to withstand the fulling process which comes next. In *fulling*, the matted fabric is eased through a fulling mill with curved, bowllike sides that tend to ease the mat into the bottom, as the surface is pounded with wooden-headed hammers. An acid or some other fulling agent is added to speed up the felting process and to increase the body of the fabric. Fulling takes from a few minutes to 10 or 12 hours, depending on the thickness of felt desired. Felt may be made in any thickness from a fraction of an inch up to 3 inches; a 3-inch-thick felt may require at the start a 3-foot-thick card lap of fibers. By the end of the fulling process, the individual fibers cannot be pulled out from the mass.

In addition to fiber felts, woven felts are made for certain industries in which a very uniform width and thickness of felt is essential, such as in papermaking, fabric printing and finishing, for belts, and for industrial blankets, such as Sanforizing blankets. The fabrics are coarsely woven at many times the desired finished width and then are napped and felted by the same processes as fiber felts.

After felting, felts go through many of the finishing processes common to other fabrics.

Felt is a thick, warm fabric with low elasticity and pliability, so it is not suited for many apparel uses, although widely used for hats, boots, and house slippers. Felt has many home and industrial uses because of its excellent insulative qualities against both sound and vibration and its water resistance. It is used to line walls of broadcasting studios, for control of vibration in pianos and other musical instruments, and for myriads of other items. What uses can you recall?

Bonded Nonwoven Fabrics

Bonded (or web) fabrics, often called *nonwovens*, are made of fibers that have been laid down in a sheet or lap and are held together by an adhesive (bonding agent), or by a high enough percentage of thermoplastic fibers to soften and hold the other fibers in place when heat and pressure are applied. The method of laying down the fibers and holding them together determines the classification as to type. This type of fabric has attained acceptance largely since 1950.

A new type of bonded fabric, called "spunbonded" has been developed for thermoplastic fibers in recent years and is included here. Figure 10-1 is a photograph of bonded nonthermoplastic and a spunbonded thermoplastic fabric showing the appearance of such fabrics under magnification. Laminated fabrics, too, are often called "bonded"; we shall consider them as a separate class in this section of this chapter.

Rayon is the fiber used in the greatest percentage in bonded fabrics; others are glass fiber, cotton, asbestos, acetate, nylon, the acrylics, cotton, Dacron, Dynel, and sometimes wool. Both bright- and dull-luster fibers are used. End-uses determine which fibers are chosen and also the texture and other properties that will be attempted.

The web may be laid down with fibers that are fairly well lined up in parallel arrangement from carding and combing processes, that are in random directions in a combination of carding and suction delivery to form a lap, or that lie in layers at right angles to each other. The latter two methods are said to give equal strength in length and width directions, and the first to give greater strength in length than across.

Bonding is accomplished by means of coating or impregnating resins

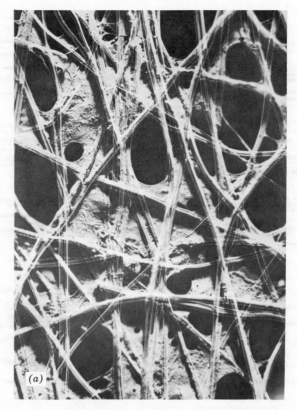

(a)

and other adhesive solutions, including starch, thermoplastic powder, thermoplastic fibers, or by gelatinized fibers.

Bonding adhesives may be sprayed on, or the web may be saturated by immersion in the solution. The bonding agent may cover the whole field or be put on at intervals; sometimes the adhesive bonding agents are pigmented and put on in pattern. Pressure and heat supplied by steam, electronic devices, or infrared units bond the fiber and the adhesive. Bonded fabric may be embossed and/or printed in color.

Bonded nonwovens are used for disposable, semidurable, and durable items. Some of the fabrics are sold under trade names, for example, "Key-bak" for Chicopee's 100 percent rayon, "Novonette" for Kendall's combination thermoplastic and nonthermoplastic, "Frontera" for Tennessee Chemical's sculptured nonwoven, and "Pellon" for Pellon's series of bonded interfacing fabrics. Disposable uses include a newly perfected line of flushable, biodegradable diapers that are expected to be competitive in price with diaper service, panties, swimsuits, hospital operating gowns and shoe covers, headrests in public vehicles, sheets and pillowcases for motels,

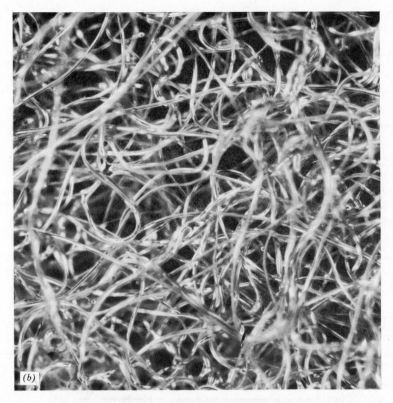

FIGURE 10-1. Photomicrographs of nonwoven bonded fabrics: (*a*) viscose bonded with viscose dope; (*b*) spunbonded polyester. (Courtesy Fabric Research Laboratories.)

hotels, and camps, to name a few. Semidurable items include garments that can be worn a few times and dry-cleaned, pressed, and perhaps washed, draperies, tablecloths, bedspreads, and such. Durable are the interfacing materials for coats, suits, dresses, heading for draperies, and such uses that need to take whatever the shell fabric will take in terms of length of life, method of cleaning, and color stability; also headliners for automobiles and other vehicles, and such uses.

Much research goes into these products, as illustrated by this statement attributed to Mr. Kaslow of the Pellon Corporation (*Modern Textiles Magazine*, November, 1968, p. 22) in relation to their new multidirectional, all-bias interfacing for knitted fabrics. He said

. . . These new interfacings, the result of five years of research, will shrink compatibly with any fine knitted shell, have the same drape, resilience, wash-

ability, wet and dry recovery and the ability to be dry cleaned. They are available for either sewing or for fusing operations.

The future of many of the nonwovens, which have thus far failed to meet predictions, will depend on whether they can be tailored to specific end-uses, can maintain a quality suitable to the end-use, can compete with the materials for which they might be substitutes, and whether some of them can be made so satisfactory and convenient that the consumer will buy them even at a price disadvantage; such is anticipated for the new diapers. One problem is the fact that clothing items to substitute for dresses, uniforms, or other garments with design and style features are about as expensive to produce in these as in more durable materials, thus they cannot at present anyway, be sold for the hoped-for low price. The problem of immediate or eventual disposal of many such fabrics may become a very real problem if such items are widely adopted.

International Paper Company has recently announced plans to produce a line of nonwoven fabrics for hospital use under the trade name "Confil" by agreement with a West German firm. This fabric is to be manufactured from short textile fibers (1¼ inch or longer) and wood cellulose pulp.

Spunbonded fabrics are made up of continuous filament thermoplastic fibers (primarily polyester thus far) extruded and separated in random order and direction with a low binder content. Because of their thermoplasticity they can be fused, molded, embossed, or any of several other heat-effected treatments. They are said to exhibit good performance in tear and breaking strength and to have good flexibility. These bonded fabrics are expected to be used as base fabrics for coating, for stiffening and reinforcing, for protective coverings, and many industrial uses. "Remay" is the trade name for DuPont's spunbonded polyester, and "Tyvek" their spunbonded olefin.

Needle-Punched Web Fabrics

Needle-punched web fabrics, also called "needle-loomed" and "needle-felt" nonwovens, go through the same steps as bonded nonwovens through the laying of the web; the quality of the web is perhaps more critical than for the usual adhesive bonding. All fibers may be needle-felted but cotton and asbestos present special frictional difficulties. Fabric properties vary with the fiber type, size of needle, depth of penetration, speed of operation, and whether a small amount of adhesive is used. Fibers 1½ to 7 inches in length are most commonly used.

The process was described by W. J. Kennedy in *Modern Textiles Magazine* for July, 1966 (p. 53). He said

The needle felting art, like many parts of the textile industry, has a long history. Felts were produced in ancient times and needle felts have been produced for many years. The process of needling is merely a method of entangling filaments to such a degree that the fiber-to-fiber friction is sufficient to hold the structure together and create a fabric. The needle loom forms a fabric by forcing the fibers to entangle as a result of multiple penetrations of barbed needles.

* * *

A web of loosely arranged fibers is prepared by any of the conventional processes. . . . With the fibers in position, the needle board descends and the barbed needles pass through the web, causing fibers to be forced from the upper surface of the batting through the web. As the needles complete their stroke, many of the fibers from the top surface are oriented completely through the web, thus tending to hold the two sides of the web together as if it were stitched. As the needles withdraw some of the top fibers are drawn back, but some of the fibers on the bottom are also brought to the surface. By repeating this process a sufficient number of times, the fibers become so intermingled and entangled that the web is given strength resembling that of a conventional fabric. . . .

Needle punch processes have captured a large part of the rug cushion business and now are sharing with the tufting process the burgeoning indoor-outdoor carpet market, especially that part in which olefin fibers are used. Needle punching can be carried through to a prepared scrim or foam backing, thus making carpets possible. Needle punch processes are also used for blankets; horse blankets and saddle pads; padded dashboards, headliners and backing for vinyl fabrics for automobiles; and even in some types of shoes.

Mechanical Bonded Fabrics

Mechanical bonding is a new process which is carried out on three different types of Mali machines; the machines were first developed in 1956 in East Germany. Each machine produces a different type of fabric, none of which is really a bonded or web fabric in the usual meanings of the terms. The following descriptions were published in an article titled "A Forward Look at Nonwoven Fabrics," by F. M. Buresh in *Modern Textiles Magazine* for November 1963 (p. 51):

. . . The three models known as Malimo, Malipol and Maliwatt produce fabrics by a combination thread-laying and sewing and knitting technique. . . .

The Mali technology involves three separate basic principles requiring three different types of equipment. The Malimo makes a fabric with characteristics similar to woven fabrics including a warp and filling. The construction makes the fabric ravel-free and more tear-resistant than other fabrics. Warp ends are

laid on top of the filling threads; both filling and warp are connected with a third interlacing system which uses a sewing thread. Warp and filling are under considerable less tension than in a loom which permits the use of yarns with less twist; also slashing of warps is not necessary.

Depending upon the counts used in each of the three systems (warp, fill and sewing thread) fabrics with a knit or woven look can be created; however, all have woven properties. Interesting new effects as well as stripes can be created by the use of colored yarns in one or more of the three systems.

The Malipol machine is a different model using a backing fabric of either a woven or Malimo structure which is presented to similar needled elements. The use of pile sinkers on one side of the fabric causes the sewing or pile yarn to form a pile of the desired height. These one-sided pile fabrics will not pull or shed since the pile yarns are knit onto the back. Products of the Malipol machine include fabrics for outerwear, coatings, blankets and carpets. . . . The machines and the fabrics seem to be much closer to knitting and weaving than to nonwoven fabrics.

The third machine, however, called the Maliwatt, is closer allied to nonwovens. The name of the machine is derived from Mali plus the German word for a batt of fiber: "watt." In this process a fiber web or batt is presented to the machine where the sewing elements use a sewing thread to compact and interlace the card web or batting into a nonwoven fabric for a variety of uses.

This process may be classified as a form of *mechanical bonding* of fiber webs to form nonwoven fabrics. The bonding material here is a great number of parallel seams. This procedure has the advantage of preserving the natural fluffiness of the textile fibers as opposed to the loss of this feature in a saturated fabric. The material is said to handle well for further processing, such as coating, laminating or latex application for use as a stiffener, as well as dyeing and napping.

The machine itself consists of three units: the sewing and knitting machine with feeding mechanism for the roll of web which is conveyed through the sewing process on a flexible belt; a swinging bobbin creel and feeding device for the sewing threads, and a unit for folding down the finished fabric. The type of stitch is the conventional or locked chain stitch applied longitudinally 7.2 mm apart.

With the Mali processes it may be possible to use poorer quality fiber and yarn than are required for knitting and weaving. The fabrics are as yet less soft and drapable than those which are woven or knitted. They have probably been overrated for apparel uses but may have possibilities as upholstery fabrics. These fabrics have too little price advantage to insure much of a market in the near future.

Sprayed-Fiber Fabric

Sprayed-fiber fabrics were announced by Arthur D. Little, Inc., in 1959. Viscous, quick-coagulating fluid is sprayed by considerable air

pressure from a spray gun, and the resultant fibers are collected on a per-forated surface. A nonsupported, porous mat of coherent fibers results. Natural rubber seems to give promise for this type of fabric. Uses for such fabrics are purely speculative.

Laminated Fabrics

The laminated group of fabrics is often called "bonded" and is probably recognized by most consumers by this term. These fabrics are made up of at least two layers of material of some sort, held together by heat fusion, some sort of an adhesive, stitching, or chemical tacking.

This type of fabric began to assume importance in apparel with lining materials that were laminated to a thin sheet of polyurethane foam by fusion. The idea was then applied to fabrics for all-weather coats, and for a variety of woven fabrics ordinarily sold for dresses, coats, and other such uses. They gave warmth and water-repellency with light weight and crease resistance but tended to be bulky. A flood of poorly fused, unsuitable cheap fabrics more or less killed the market because of delamination and excessive shrinkage. Apparently it has been assumed (with insufficient testing) that the shell fabric would maintain the original dimensions of the foam layer; instead, the foam assumed the dimensions of the shell fabric as it changed. So the properties of the shell or face fabric determined the final product. The idea, however, is still a valid one when properly used as it often is for foam-backed table mats and upholstery materials. Foam is considered to be very good material for stabilizing knit goods. Unstable foam color and reaction with chlorine have limited some potential uses.

The most widespread use of the principle now is in the laminating of two different fabrics, particularly of wool or woollike fabrics or knitted face fabrics with an acetate tricot lining fabric. Again, poor quality fabrics threaten the market. There are many consumer complaints of delamination in dry cleaning or laundering. Although some producers of these fabrics have set standards for their own operations in choice and quality of face and backing fabrics, bonding adhesives (if needed), and procedures to be followed, there are no industry-wide standards. The industry is considering setting and policing such standards.

R. G. Strassel, in *Modern Textiles Magazine* for August 1968 (p. 22) indicated that use of acetate tricot backing material had grown from about 25 million yards in 1964 to about 400 million in 1967. He said further

Why acetate tricot? This relatively weak fabric—polyester and nylon fibers are stronger—with a low melting point would not seem the ideal fabric to kick off a million-dollar industry.

But acetate tricot has advantages. It's inexpensive. It was used for ladies' underwear, and when the idea of bonding a lining to a face fabric was first put forth, acetate tricot was the logical choice. Despite its low melting point (tricot gets sticky at 350–375 degrees, softens at 400 and melts at 500 degrees) it is well within the heat limits needed for bonding. Acetate is a smooth fabric, and its microscopically small fibers give it a flat, unbulky look.

Tricot is a knitted fabric, an essential quality in bonding. Two woven fabrics, bonded together, only fight each other. Woven fabrics are rigid and are good for outer or face fabrics. The knit linings have more "give" and can respond to the stresses of the face fabrics. Of all knitted fabrics, tricot has the softest hand without sacrificing durability.

Bonded fabrics, of course, have advantages over unbonded fabrics. They impart shape retention and are practically wrinkle-free; they're more durable than conventional fabrics, are easy to sew; are drapable without losing shape (knit apparel with bonded linings are proving highly successful); are relatively easy to produce (actual bonding operations are not complicated. The adhesives used and the techniques employed are the all-important factors); bonded fabrics make less work at the factory level, reduce costs, they can be either washed or dry cleaned, depending on the face fabric.

No doubt you have had experience with garments or fabrics made up of such materials. What has been your experience? How have you liked them? Where else have you seen such materials used? Greatest potential growth other than in the apparel field is believed to be in industrial uses such as seat covers, protective covers, tentings, insulation, and so on.

Included in the laminated classification also would be such things as quilted fabrics in which a face and backing fabric with a fiber layer between are held together by stitching. Sleeping bags, down comforters, as well as apparel fit this classification. An example is the snowmobile suits made up of a closely woven nylon windbreaker fabric shell, soft lining fabric, and polyester fiberfill insulation between, all held together by rows of stitching through the whole assembly, and said to keep the wearer warm in weather as cold as 50 degrees below zero.

FABRICS MADE FROM YARNS

This group of fabrics is not only the most important of the classes listed, but weaving alone is more important than all other methods of fabric construction combined. Fabrics made from yarns or yarns in combination with other long, thin materials include braids, knits, nets, laces, and woven goods.

FIGURE 10-2.   Diagram of a three-strand braid.

Braid

Braids are narrow fabrics made by diagonal interlacing of one set of strands by a method often called "plaiting," in which individual strands form a zigzag pattern as they crisscross one another, and no two adjacent strands make complete turns about each other. At least three strands are required for braiding; braiding several strands resembles the interlacing for plain weaving. Figure 10-2 is a diagram of a three-strand braid that shows the path taken by each strand.

Braids may be made from yarn, narrow fabric such as ribbon or tape, from straw, leather, and many other materials. Braiding gives a strong, pliable tape or cord. Braids may be made flat or tubular, and plain or fancy; the tubular braids often enclose a core which may be rigid for uses that require a firm cord, or elastic for a stretchy cord. Plain braids are used for shoelaces, parachute cords, tapes of many types, electrical cord coverings, wicks, fishing lines, and trimmings. Fancy braids are used primarily for trimmings. The armed services use considerable amounts of braid of various types.

Braiding machines were invented in the eighteenth century. Because each strand must be manipulated separately, braiding machines are large

and complicated; this is the factor which limits braided fabrics to narrow widths.

Net

Net is an open-mesh fabric constructed from threads or yarns on special bobbinet machines, on raschel knitting machines, or by hand-tying. Fish nets may have been the first fabrics made by this method. A true net has four- to six-sided openings with interlacing or knotting at each corner where the threads cross one another. The manner of interlacing at each corner holds the mesh open and in correct position. The meshes vary in size from the coarseness of fish nets to the fineness of the net background in the finest laces and in tulle. Net with a design added becomes lace. The first bobbinet machine was patented in the early nineteenth century by John Heathcoat in England.

True nets are of two types, explained in the *American Handbook of Synthetic Textiles* (p. 690), as follows:

The most common is the "twist-lace" in which one set of warp ends, wound upon shuttle bobbins and mounted in carriages, go through and twist around a second set of ends, usually of like total number and wound upon one or more beams in warp formation. This is classed an "intertwisted" structure. Other examples of nets are the "inter-knotted" structure, or fish nets, made by hand and on so-called "netting machines." The net types must not be confused, however, with the open-work fabric structure produced for 200 years or more on knitting machines.

In addition to fishing nets, nets are used for many other purposes, such as for loading and unloading marine supplies and freight, for bagging, for safety nets, and for many industrial uses. You are familiar with the apparel and textile furnishing uses for nets.

Lace

Lace is a fabric of decorative design on an open-mesh background, ordinarily made from threads rather than from yarns. Similar designs on regular fabric backgrounds are known as embroidery. Lace may be made by hand or machine, but most lace today is machine made, and much of it is inexpensive enough to be used for adornment of clothing at all price levels. The first machine lace was made in 1809.

Linton, in *Applied Basic Textiles* (pp. 99–100), in relating the history of lace, wrote:

The term "lace" comes from the old French *las*, by way of the Latin *laquens*, which means a noose, or to ensnare—rather well adapted to lace. A single yarn can produce a plaited or braided fabric or article, since it will

interlace, entwine, and twist in several directions to produce a porous material or lace. It should be kept in mind that one yarn may be used to make a lace, and that the action is like that of several yarns entering the machine; this action is used in knitting as well.

A crude form of meshed cord for ornamentation was used in Peru over four thousand years ago. Ancient Egypt used a form of lace to cover mummies. In the days when Rome was at its height, the term 'lace' merely implied the cord which holds by being tied or interwoven; in time, however, lace came to mean the openwork fabric made of interwoven threads. Today, such threads may be made of cotton, linen, silk, metal, lastex, rayon, acetate, nylon, wool, and similar fibers or filaments. The threads can be braided, plaited, twisted, interlaced, or looped to make some type of material.

Lace was well known in the early Christian era, and lacemaking took on impetus through the Middle Ages, chiefly in Europe. The work was done in convents and monasteries. By the sixteenth century, Flanders, France, and Italy had good lace industries; and it may be stated that lacemaking in the modern sense began around the year 1500.

*   *   *

By the end of the century, fashions and styles changed considerably with the advent of the industry in many centers in Europe. England, France, and Italy began to use lace in dress in many ways. As lace became more plentiful, the vogue for it grew, and all classes of people began to wear it. Lace was now a mark of distinction and prestige. The rich and the poor had something in common, but not for long. Laws were passed by the various countries which forbade the use of lace by the common people. This irksome edict caused a furore throughout Europe. In due time the laws were finally repealed through the valiant efforts of a Jesuit, Father Regis. For his work he is the patron saint of the lace industry to this day.

And so, although we tend to think of lace as being feminine and dainty, it certainly has not always been so considered.

Rayon and Synthetic Textiles for November 1951 (p. 33) introduced an article on lace in this way:

The lace and embroidery manufacturing trades are important to the textile producing and marketing industries far out of proportion to the quantities of yarn which they consume, or in terms of any other measurement of mere volume. For lace is to fabric what whipped cream is to a cake—the fluffy decoration that sells the whole thing.

Lace is usually considered to be fragile in comparison with fabrics made by methods other than netting, although some lace is quite sturdy and durable. It is often made by embroidery machines (Schiffli, Leaver, and Nottingham) with the design being developed on a previously constructed net background. By some methods, the background may be formed along with the design. Raschel knitting machines develop back-

ground net and design simultaneously and are apparently the cheapest means for producing lace in this country. Lace may be handmade by crocheting, knitting, tatting, or embroidery methods. Machine laces vary in width from ¼ inch for delicate edgings to more than 100 inches for

(d)

FIGURE 10-3. Four widely known types of lace: (a) Valenciennes; (b) Cluny; (c) filet, and (d) Alençon.

some all-over lace fabrics. Lace may be made of any of the commonly used fibers, including the metallics.

Handmade laces of different types, known as bobbin, needlepoint, or pillow lace, each include laces with distinguishing characteristics that have been given names in order to signify their type, often the name of the city famed for a particular lace. The machine-made laces of today are often

given the same names as the famous handmade laces that have similar distinguishing characteristics. Names of some of these particular types of lace are Chantilly, Valenciennes, filet, Cluny, Alençon, Irish crochet, Rose Point, Venetian Point, Torchon, Duchesse, Mechlin, Maltese, Honiton, and Teneriffe. The first four types, three of which may be seen in Figure 10-3, are widely known and produced by machines today. Beautiful handmade laces may be seen in many museums and in private or other collections, but they are not widely available today because of their scarcity and expensiveness.

Chantilly is a delicate lace much used as 36-inch-wide all-over lace for bridal and evening gowns. It is also used for wide flounces or tiers. It is scalloped along one edge and is characterized by distinctive scroll and floral designs, sometimes with baskets or vases of flowers, on a fine net background. The design may be outlined with a heavier thread or cord. *Alençon* lace is quite similar in appearance to Chantilly; the design is always outlined in heavier thread and often has dots in the net between the larger designs.

Valenciennes or *Val* lace is that most commonly used for narrow edgings and to trim lingerie. It has diamond- or round-mesh background with simple flower designs (usually) and a picot edge.

Filet is square-mesh lace with the squares filled in to make the design.

Cluny lace is coarser and sturdier than Chantilly, Val, and Alençon and is not made on a net background. It has open space between the parts of the patterns which are largely circle or paddle-wheel effects. *Torchon* is an even heavier and coarser lace, much used at times for decoration of household articles.

Lace has many uses, ranging from the trimming on babies' garments and the simplest to most exotic lingerie, to all-over lace dresses, blouses, lingerie, curtains, tablecloths, and even shoes. Some types of women's foundation garments are knitted Lastex lace.

Knitting

Knitting is probably the most familiar of all methods for producing fabric, considering the popularity of hand knitting among women of all ages today, and particularly among college-age women. G. A. Urlaub, in *American Handbook of Synthetic Textiles* (pp. 690–691), has given both a brief history and definition of knitting in a few concise sentences. He said

Making fabrics by knitting is a modern art. Despite examples of knitting found in museums, earliest records of the art date from the late 15th century. It was originally practiced by the sailors and inhabitants of the sea lands of Spain, Northern England and Denmark. Hand knitting has not changed from the use of pointed or hooked-end needles to form loops of yarn into fabric, but the mechanical adaptation thereof went far beyond the handicraft theories.

In fact, the knitting machine is considered by this author among the world's primary inventions.

Knitting, in its simplest form, consists of forming loops of yarn with the aid of thin pointed shafts* and drawing other new loops through those previously formed. This "interlooping" and the continuous formation of more loops into each other produces the knitted fabric structure. In machine knitting, a multiplicity of needles, needle holders, and yarn feeds replaces the pins, hands, and fingers of hand knitting.

Knitting mills generally produce only one type among four general classes of products—hosiery, underwear, outerwear, or yard goods. They may produce a variety of both warp and weft knitted fabrics or garments in their specialty, or they may be so highly specialized as to produce only one specific item, such as ladies' full-fashioned hosiery.

There are two basic types of knitting processes, *weft* or *filling knit*, and *warp knit*, each with its special knitting machines, types of fabrics, and often of garments. Filling knit is more elastic than warp knit and is used for nearly all hosiery, sweaters, much underwear fabric, and jersey fabrics. Weft knit may be made on circular or flat-bed knitting machines; warp knit, except for certain milanese fabrics, is made on flat-bed machines and is intended primarily for wide fabrics. Flat-bed knitting machines somewhat resemble looms in size and general appearance except that they have rows of needles along the front bar and do not have the series of harnesses and heddles noticeable on looms.

Filling or weft knit, of which hand knitting is typical, often uses only one yarn at a time; it is picked up and carried in loops from side to side horizontally in flat knitting or around and around in circular knitting. In knitting tubular fabric, however, a process has been developed that permits the knitting of a number of yarns simultaneously from many feeds, with each feed furnishing a row of loops (see Figure 10-4). Tubular fabrics are often knitted for entire or parts of specific garments such as T-shirts, underwear, seamless hosiery, socks, and for jersey and some outerwear fabrics; since the machines are built with the needles in a circular (closed) arrangement, different machines are needed for tubular fabrics of very different diameters. Factories that produce tubular knit fabrics often carry on all operations necessary for completing the garments. This diversified activity necessitates their having cutting, sewing, and finishing departments, generally considered to belong to the needles trades.

Warp-knitted fabrics often have hundreds of separate yarns being knitted vertically at a time, usually one yarn for each needle, all of which are looping at the same time, and without the special interlooping operation between rows, each yarn would make a separate "ladder" of loops

* The needles.

FIGURE 10-4. A circular knit machine. Fabric rolls down inside the cage as knitted. (Courtesy the Singer Company.)

unconnected to its neighbors. The yarn is warped on a beam as for weaving; each warp end must be drawn into its needle in preparation for knitting. Tricot knit fabrics form the bulk of fabrics produced by warp-knit processes, although raschel, milanese, and special run-resistant and no-run fabrics of lace or mesh knit, each with its own method of intertwining the loops of the different rows, are also made by warp-knitting methods (see Figure 10-5). Tricot may be one-, two-, or three-bar; two-bar tricot is made with two guide bars and two warps and is more stable and heavier than one-bar tricot made with only one warp. Three-bar tricot is used largely for fancy patterned fabrics. Much more fabric can be knitted in a given time by a warp-knitting machine than by a weft-knitting machine

with the same number of needles and using the same type and size of yarn. Why should this be true?

Flat-knitted fabrics in widths of 80 to 168 inches are usually sold to the garment cutting industries rather than being made into garments at the mills where they are knitted; articles made from the narrower flat-knitted fabrics, however, are often completed at the mills. Full-fashioned hosiery, for example, are usually completed at the mills where they are knitted on special small flat-bed weft-knit machines, and other garments such as sweaters are often completed at the knitting mills.

Knitting machines can be adapted only to the types of knitting for which they were specifically designed; that is, filling-knit machines cannot be used for warp knitting, nor can warp-knitting machines make filling-knit fabrics. Although fancy knitting can be made on both warp- and filling-knit machines, once the pattern has been set up little change can be made without reestablishing an entirely new procedure; then there is variability only within a limited range. Knitting machines are less adaptable to variations in pattern than are looms in weaving.

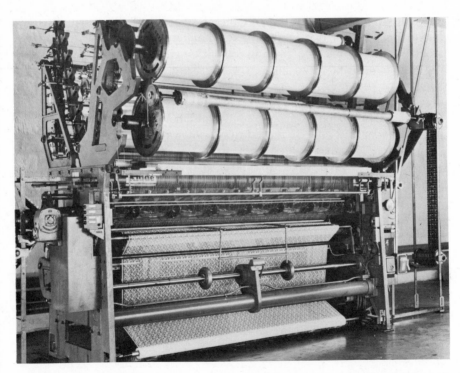

FIGURE 10-5. Raschel lace warp knitting machine. (Courtesy Cocker Machine & Foundry Company.)

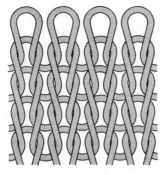 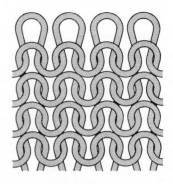

Face side of jersey   Reverse side of jersey

(a)   (b)

FIGURE 10-6. Diagram of plain weft-knitted fabric: (a) "knit" side, showing wales; (b) "purl" side, showing courses.

Machine knitting is considered to have three basic stitches—plain, rib, and purl—with an additional variant of the rib stitch, called *interlock*. Hand knitting has two basic stitches, knit and purl, that are really the stitches basic to machine knitting too, although purl has a different meaning to machine and hand knitters. Since hand knitting is already familiar to many of you or can be seen readily, the hand knitting stitches are herein described.

In *knit* stitch loops are picked up and new loops are pulled toward the knitter or the face of the fabric. In *purl* stitch the loops are picked up and new loops are pulled away from the knitter or toward the back of the fabric. It is possible, of course, to use either the knit or purl side as the face of the fabric; hosiery worn inside out displays the purl side as the face of the fabric. The most common type of knitting, called *plain knit* by both hand and machine knitters, has all loops pulled toward the front; jersey is a common fabric made by plain knitting methods. Plain knitting results in clearly visible rows of vertical loops or *wales* on one side of the fabric, and of horizontal ridges or *courses* on the reverse side. Figure 10-6 shows the front and back of a plain knitted fabric; the appearance of the front is typical of the knit stitch and the back of the purl stitch. In most hand knitting, one row is knitted and the next is purled in order to have all loops pulled toward the face; this is not necessary in circular hand knitting or weft machine knitting where the knit stitch can be used continuously.

Rib knit is a regular alternation of knit and purl stitches or group of stitches; this results in a ridged fabric in which the similarly knit rows

pull closer together and have considerably more elasticity than plain knit fabric. In machine knitting, ribs are knitted by groups of needles set at different angles to each other. Rib knit is used for cuffs, neck-bands, collars, waistbands, or other areas where close fit needs to be combined with elasticity.

Garter stitch alternates one knit with one purl row on the face of the fabric, resulting in a fabric that looks the same on the front and back sides. The garter stitch of hand knitting is the purl stitch of machine processes. Garter stitch is sometimes used for button and buttonhole bands, for neckbands, and as trimming on knitted garments.

Fancy patterns are made by combining knit and purl stitches with variations obtained by using different colors or kinds of yarns, by slipping certain stitches, by knitting two or more stitches together at intervals, by special looping of the yarns, by crossing some stitches over others (cable knit), by bringing in additional yarns for certain patterns, etc.

Yarns for most knitting must be smooth, even in diameter, pliable, elastic, strong, and soft for most end-uses. They are usually two-ply or more. Any fiber can be knitted that can be made into yarns meeting knitting requirements; even glass fiber has been knitted successfully. Textured yarns are also used for knitting and are very popular for dresses, suits, coats, and sweaters.

Gage is a term which supposedly refers to the number of needles on a unit length of the knitting machine for a particular fabric, but there is no common agreement on the unit length except for full-fashioned hosiery. The FTC has ruled that gage shall mean the number of needles used for a 1½-inch width of the knitting bar in the knitting of full-fashioned hosiery. Seamless hosiery gage has practically the same meaning, although stitches are tighter in the ankle region and thus give a different number than in the upper leg area. Gage, however, means little except when considered with denier, the fineness of the yarn. Why is this true? A number of hosiery manufacturers have recently discontinued the use of gage in hosiery descriptions.

Double-knit fabrics, made by a circular knitting method, have made a fabulous growth in the apparel field in the past few years, and their market seems to be both growing in volume and expanding to include additional end-uses.

The process of double knitting was well described by V. J. Lombardi in an article "The Expanding World of Circular Knitting," in *Modern Textiles Magazine* for September 1961 (pp. 62–63):

A double knit, broadly defined, is a jersey construction knitted on a machine equipped with two sets of needles so that, in effect, the cloth is a

"twice knitted" fabric in which, by the action of the double set of needles the two sides of the cloth are interlocked., The resulting fabric is heavier than single-knit cloth; one surface has a fine ribbed appearance, and the reverse the texture of a fine birdseye or diamond effect. The heavier, double knit construction makes the fabric more dimensionally stable than plain jersey and permits it to be cut without curling on the edges.,

Knitted fabrics are more pliable and elastic than fabrics constructed by other methods; thus they are especially adaptable for form-fitting garments such as hosiery, undergarments, foundation garments, sweaters, and sleepwear. We noted that much inexpensive lace is raschel-knitted; simulated fur fabrics are successfully made on raschel-knit machines and comprise a large share of that market. Pile carpeting has also been knitted successfully. Knitted garments require little or no pressing but may be distorted by their own weight if left on hangers for a long time. Wool, acetate, nylon, triacetate, acrylic fibers, cotton, polyester fibers, and combinations of fibers have been used the most often, but possibilities include all fibers and even paper yarns. Thermal knitted cotton blankets began appearing on the market in 1962 and are also available in acrylic fibers in limited areas.

With advances in knitting processes, particularly in double knitting, growing use of knitted fabrics in the apparel field has been phenomenal. Until 1968 the effect was most apparent in apparel for women, children, and infants, with only a relatively few white dress shirts for men made by knitting (tricot). Of course, knitted sports shirts and sweaters have been popular for years for casual wear. But the turtleneck shirt fashion and the availability of double knit fabrics in a variety of fiber types initiated what may prove to be a revolution in men's wear. Because double knits can be handled as easily as wovens—though somewhat differently—in garment factories, and some of the double knits—polyesters in particular—can be given durable creases, such fabrics are now going into tailored suits, jackets, and slacks for men. You may have noted the promotional campaigns in fashion magazines, *Daily News Record, Men's Wear Daily,* and elsewhere.

These are expected to be used as are other tailored garments. Don Gay, manager of knitwear marketing services for DuPont, as reported in *Daily News Record* for December 2, 1968, has gone so far as to make these predictions:

By 1972, knits will have approximately 25 per cent of the men's tailored slacks and sport coat market and about 10 per cent of the suit market.

The growth in knitted fabrics will not be at the expense of wovens but will stimulate growth of the total tailored outerwear market. Because of knits, the industry will grow in size, in fashion excitement and in profits for fiber producer, knitter and apparel manufacturer.

Mr. Gay's predictions appear to be supported by other producers of fibers that may predominate in this market.

Other developments in knits that may affect many types of uses are: suitable weight circular and raschel knits for many garments and other uses, development of fabrics for specific end-uses, special surface appearance and textures such as the leather look, variation in texture, luster, and hand, new blends of fibers, whiter yarns for printed knits, laminated knits—especially those with high-wet-modulus rayon face and acetate back, and, of course, increased dimensional stability.

Weaving

Weaving is a method of producing cloth by interlacing two or more sets of yarns, at least one warp and one filling set, at right angles to each other. The *warp* is also called *ends*; and the *filling* is also called *picks*, or *weft*. The warp runs from front to back of the loom and lengthwise in a woven fabric. Extra warp yarns at each side form a *selvage* during weaving. Filling yarns run across from side to side, or from selvage to selvage.

The machine for weaving is a *loom*, of which there are several types, varying in complexity. All looms, from the most primitive to the most modern, operate on similar principles. A diagram of a simple two-harness loom set up for weaving a plain-weave fabric is shown in Figure 10-7. A study of this diagram will help to understand the weaving process.

Essential parts of the loom include the *warp beam*, on which the warp yarns are wound; the *cloth beam*, on which the cloth is wound as it is woven; *harness frames* which carry the heddles, and which move up or down to form the weaving shed; *heddles*, each with an eye in the center, through which the individual yarns are threaded, usually one yarn to a heddle; the *reed*, which keeps the warp yarns separated, helps to determine cloth width, and acts as a beater; and *shuttles* or *bobbins* for carrying the filling yarns across from side to side.

In preparation for weaving, the warp yarns are measured and wound evenly on the warp beam according to the number of warp yarns needed for the entire width of fabric. Each warp yarn, in consecutive order, is drawn through the eye of the correct heddle on the correct harness frame, according to the pattern to be woven, and then is carried through the correct opening in the reed to the front of the loom where all the warp yarns, when the threading is completed, are evenly tensioned and tied to the cloth beam apron. Each warp yarn must run straight from cloth beam to warp beam without being crossed with any other yarn; this is essential for raising and lowering the different harnesses to form a *shed*. During weaving, the harnesses are raised and lowered in an order determined by the pattern; as one harness (or group of harnesses) is raised, the other (or

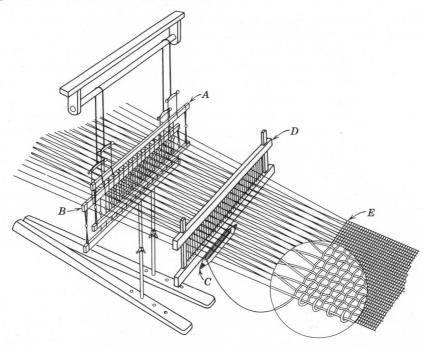

FIGURE 10-7. Diagram of two-harness loom set up for plain weaving. A and B, harness frames, each carrying a set of heddles; C, filling shuttle, passing through shed made by raising A and lowering B harness frames; D, reed or beater; and E, plain woven fabric made on the loom. (Courtesy National Association of Wool Manufacturers, and *Applied Textiles*, 6th edition, George E. Linton.)

others) is lowered, causing a separation of the warp yarns as the heddles are carried up or down with the frames, thus forming a shed. The shuttle carrying the filling yarn goes through the shed from one side to the other, and the yarn left by its passing is beaten forward by the reed against the tied-in knots at the cloth apron or against cloth already woven. The harnesses then change position, a new shed is formed, and the procedure is repeated over and over. As power loom weaving proceeds, the warp beam automatically unrolls a little warp at a time, and the cloth beam takes up the finished cloth at almost the same speed, maintaining an even tension on the warp yarns. Looms may have two to twelve harnesses with hundreds of heddles on each harness frame.

There are many types of looms, including those with Jacquard heads for elaborate figure-weave patterns, and those with special attachments for gauze or leno weaving. There have been many improvements in looms in the past few years, resulting in smaller, lighter-weight, faster, quieter-

operating, and more efficient machines. There are circular looms for weaving tubular fabrics. Shuttleless looms are now used in many places and water jet looms are the newest innovations. Some of these do not form regular selvages but require other type of side finishing; since a well-made selvage facilitates handling of fabric through finishing processes, lack of a conventional selvage may be a limiting factor in the use of such looms. Another development, called three-dimensional weaving, is a method of manipulating sets of warp and filling yarns so that shaped objects can be woven, such as shaped, seamless, reinforcing fabrics for missile nose cones, for seamless square laundry carts, etc.

WEAVES

Weaves are classified according to the method of interlacing of the warp and filling yarns, and the number of sets of warp or filling yarns required. The weaves most often identified are plain, twill, satin, gauze or leno, figure, pile, and double. All except pile and double weaves and some types of figure weave may be made with only one set of warp and one set of filling yarns. In addition to these distinct types of weaves, infinite combinations and variations are possible, making practicable many variations in fabric caused by weave alone.

Plain, twill, and satin weaves are often considered basic, as other weaves are largely combinations or variations of these. The weave interlacing pattern may be developed by either the warp or the filling yarns; for the sake of uniformity and clarity we shall use diagrammatic figures in which the filling threads do the interlacing.

PLAIN WEAVE

Plain weave is the simplest type of weave. It is shown on the loom diagram of Figure 10–7. In making plain weave, the filling yarns is carried over one warp yarn and under the next alternately across the width of the fabric $\left(\dfrac{1}{1}\right)$ Figure 10–8 is representative of the appearance of a plain-woven fabric. This weave gives the maximum number of interlacings, but not the most closely woven fabric because the frequent interlacing limits packing of the yarns and therefore how closely the yarns can be beaten against each other. Although much plain-weave fabric is smooth-surfaced and flat, the characteristics vary with the character of the yarns used and their spacing. Plain weave is the least expensive method of weaving. Why would you expect this to be true?

A few fabrics made by plain weave are batiste, voile, taffeta, crepe, muslin, broadcloth, handkerchief linen, chambray, and most ginghams.

Variations of plain weave are *ribbed* fabrics, in which heavier yarns or

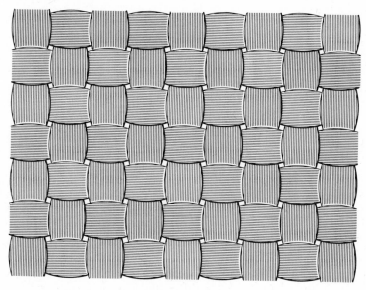

FIGURE 10-8. Diagram of a plain-weave fabric ($\frac{1}{1}$).

groups of yarns are used in one direction, such as in bengaline and faille. Another variation is *basket weave*, in which two or more yarns are handled together in weaving, as though they were one. Oxford cloth and monk's cloth are examples of basket weave.

TWILL WEAVE

Twill weave is identified by the parallel diagonal ridges on the face of the fabric. At least three yarns are required for a pattern. In a three-yarn twill, the filling (or warp) is carried over two and under the third warp (or filling yarn) $\left(\frac{2}{1}\right)$; this pattern is repeated in exactly the same way all across the fabric. Each succeeding filling yarn progresses one warp yarn to the right (or left) from the "under" yarn of the row before, then repeats the over two, under one across the row. The result of the simplest twill interlacing is shown in the diagram of Figure 10–9. There are many variations possible in twills in which more yarns are used per pattern. It is interesting to see what variations of twills can be worked out on squared paper or by interlacing strips of yarn or paper.

Because the filling yarn floats over at least two warp yarns in each repeat of the pattern, resulting in fewer interlacings that in plain weave, more yarns can be packed into a given area than with plain weave because they

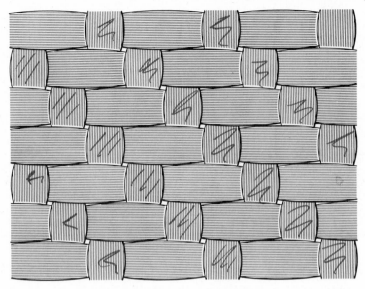

FIGURE 10-9. Diagram of a $(\frac{2}{1})$ filling-faced twill-weave fabric.

can be pushed up against each other more tightly. More yarns could result in a stronger fabric, under favorable circumstances. What would be the limiting factor?

Some typical twill-weave fabrics are denim, gabardine, serge, surah, covert, whipcord, middy twill, chino, and many flannels.

SATIN WEAVE

This weave requires at least five yarns to a pattern in which the interlacing goes over all except one of the yarns and under only one, forming floats on the face of the fabric. Thus a five-shaft satin would go over four and under one $\left(\frac{4}{1}\right)$. Satin must have a regular pattern for the interlacing of the yarns, as do all other weaves, but the interlacing for true satin must not be on adjacent yarns in different rows so that a twill ridge is formed. Twills with long floats that form a satin-like face, however, are often used for so-called satins for rugged uses, such as athletic uniforms. Figure 10-10 demonstrates a five-shaft satin weave; this is a sateen in which the filling yarns form the floats. Diagrams usually show a satin in which the warp yarns form the floats; by turning your book 90 degrees to either right or left, you will see how the typical satin weave diagram looks.

In order to fulfill the requirements of a satin, the interlacing must be

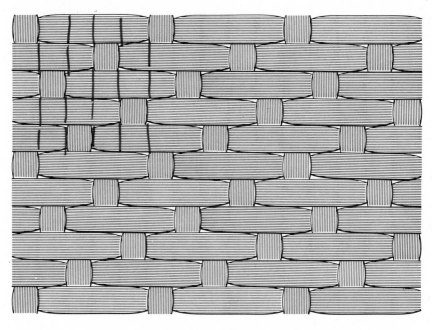

FIGURE 10-10. Diagram of a ($\frac{4}{1}$) filling-faced satin-weave fabric.

planned according to the number of yarns per pattern, so that the interlacing progression from one row to the next is not a factor of the total, nor
are the divisions factors of each other. For example, if an eight-yarn satin
is desired, and the first row is interlaced over seven and under one, the
progression for the interlacing in the next row, whether moved to right or
left, cannot be two or four as these numbers are factors of eight, and two
is also a factor of four. A progression of two or four would result in a repeat in the same row before the pattern has been completed and other rows
would not be caught down at all. An eight-shaft satin could have a three- or
five-yarn progression between rows. Trying out such patterns on squared
paper helps in understanding what happens and why not all progressions
work.

A smooth, lustrous surface is the object of satin weave. Very rich satins
may have as many as ten to fourteen yarns per pattern. Yarns with a minimum amount of twist, and usually highly lustrous, are used for the yarn
forming the floats on the face of satin. Since each yarn is caught down
only once in a repeat of the pattern, the long floats snag and rough up rather
easily. Because of the infrequent interlacing, great numbers of yarns can

be packed into a little space, and the satin, although usually considered a luxury fabric, may be very strong and durable.

Warp yarns usually form the floats in satin, but sometimes the floats are formed by the filling yarns as in the cotton fabric known as sateen. Satins are usually made from silk, acetate, nylon, or highly mercerized cotton; filament yarns are used wherever possible.

Satins made with lustrous, low-twist yarns in one direction and tightly twisted crepe yarns in the other direction produce crepe-back satin fabrics.

Satins are much used for evening dresses, bridal dresses, for shoes, lingerie, trimmings, ribbons, and sometimes as coats. What other uses can you mention?

GAUZE OR LENO WEAVE

This weave produces open or sheer fabrics of good stability. A special leno attachment for the loom is required. The warp yarns are arranged in pairs, with wider spaces between pairs than between the yarns of the pair. Between filling shots the warp yarns of each pair exchange places, and after the next shot they return to their original positions, thus forming figure 8's around the filling yarns. Figure 10-11 is a diagram of this weave.

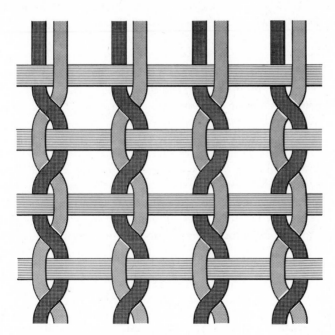

FIGURE 10-11. Diagram of a leno-weave fabric.

Marquisette is probably the best-known fabric made by this method of interlacing, although leno weave is also used for some sheer dress fabrics and as a decorative stripe or figure in novelty fabrics. Fabrics made by this weave should not be confused with nets, or with surgical gauze, which is either made by plain weave or knitted.

FIGURE WEAVING

Figure weaving is of two types: one type requires only one set of warp and one set of filling yarns, and the same yarns, by changes in the weave, produce both the design and the background; the second type uses the conventional warp and filling yarns for background but brings in a third set of yarns, which may be either warp or filling, for the design.

In the first type of figure weaving, simple designs, such as those for some dobby chambrays or shirting madras, may be made with as few as four harnesses on a regular loom; on the other hand, the elaborate figures of damasks and brocades require the use of the Jacquard-equipped loom, by means of which each warp yarn in the pattern can be handled independently of all others. Figure 10-12 is a photograph of a figure-weave fabric produced on a Jacquard loom. Combinations of plain, twill, and satin weaves are often used to form the design, and plain or satin weaves often form the background weave. When satin weave is used as a background, the satin weave in the design is often on the opposite set of yarns, that is, the satin floats run in the opposite direction. Simple diagramming is not effective in showing this method of interlacing and the weaves following; examining fabric made by the weaves is more meaningful than a complicated diagram would be.

The second type of figure weaving brings in an extra set of yarns just to form the design; the design yarns do not enter into the background between designs but are carried as floats between the figures and will eventually be clipped close to them. Plain or leno weaves are most often used as background weaves for these fabrics. Dotted swiss and dotted marquisette are examples of this type of figure weave.

The design may be put in by shuttles, which carry the yarns across from selvage to selvage in the filling direction, or the design yarns may be carried in the warp direction. When the design yarns are cut between the designs, two cut ends are left for every yarn in the design. By taking hold of such yarns one by one they can be pulled out, leaving no design in that spot. This commonly used method produces a design called *clipped dot* or *clipped spot* (see Figure 10-13). In another method, called *tied-knot* design, small shuttles are provided for each design in the width of the fabric. These shuttles just come up and through the shed for the width of their own design pattern, then drop down until the next design shed opens, then

repeat their action so that only one yarn is carried back and forth to make a specific design and only one yarn thus is carried from one design to the next in the row. When the yarn is cut between figures, there are left just two cut ends for a design. Tension exerted on one of these ends pulls the

FIGURE 10-12. An all-gray figure-weave fabric woven on a Jacquard-equipped loom. Pattern and apparent difference in color are due to change in the weave.

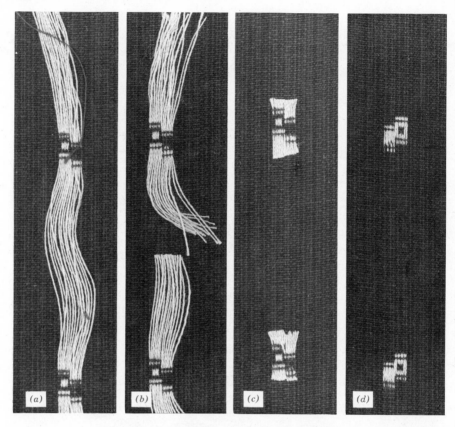

FIGURE 10-13. Clipped-dot figure-weave fabric representing stages in clipping of the design. Row (a) shows the long floats between the designs on the back of the fabric, (b) the first clip, and (c) the completely clipped design. (d) is the face side of the same fabric. (Fabric sample courtesy Victor Lobl, Dan River Mills, and *Modern Textiles Magazine*.)

yarn tighter rather than pulling it out. Such design can sometimes be found in imported dotted swiss fabric.

PILE WEAVE

Traditional pile weave requires three sets of yarns, two of which are the regular warp and filling yarns, and a third which is caught into the background for anchoring, but whose purpose is to form loops or cut pile on the surface of the cloth. Pile yarns may be put in to form an all-over pile surface, such as in velvet, velveteen, and the simulated fur fabrics; or they may be woven in to form a pattern such as corduroy, or the elaborate pile

patterns of Jacquard weaving exhibited by some types of upholstery and dress fabrics popular in past years, by some carpets, and in some terry towels. All-over pile surface may be straight pile, curled, or have other treatments, or may be cut to different height to make sculptured design. Pile weave gives depth to the fabric, creating a luxurious, soft texture.

A "new" process for pile fabric construction, called "tufting," is a revival of a hand method of producing pile fabrics in Colonial America; it was revived soon after 1900 as a cottage industry for making bedspreads in the highlands of the South. When these found a ready market, efforts in the early 1930's were directed toward perfecting simple tufting machines, and the process was extended to the making of robes, bath mats, and similar products. With success of wide-fabric tufting methods, the process became adaptable for production of carpets and rugs in 1950 and in 1967 accounted for 87 percent of total yardage of carpet and rug shipments in the United States. The total of all types was 482,600,000 square yards, up more than 51 percent from 1953 shipments.

Machines are now being used which operate continuously, using a myriad of controllable needles to produce any desired pattern.

Tufting requires an already constructed core fabric, often called "scrim," through which loops are inserted by means of a needle-punch process. As the needles are pulled back, the loops remain on the surface of the core fabric; loops may be cut or not but are opened out (fluffed or "bloomed") or are napped to hold the pile in place. Loops may be napped on one or both sides of the fabric.

Cotton yarns were used for the early bedspreads and for the first carpeting, but today many fibers are used for tufting. Tufting is said to be ten to twenty times faster than traditional pile weaving and is thus less expensive. Although no fabrics such as velvets and corduroys have as yet been produced by tufting, furlike coating fabrics have been produced. Blankets are being made by the tufting process which may revolutionize the blanket industry as it has the carpeting industry.

DOUBLE WEAVE

This weave requires five sets of yarns—a warp and a filling each for two separate fabrics which are woven simultaneously, and a fifth set, which alternates between the two fabrics, binding them together, sometimes lightly throughout the fabric and sometimes only at the edges. The fifth set of yarns may be put in very densely and then cut in the center to form two lengths of pile fabrics. Velvets are often made in this manner. Double-woven fabrics are often double-faced, such as double-satin ribbon and some reversible coating materials. This weave is not much used and is often more expensive to produce than other weaves.

Fabrics made of three sets of yarns, such as blankets and napped-back lining materials (which are made with two sets of filling yarns), although often called double woven, are really only double-faced or "backed" cloths. Sometimes a separate classification is given for this type of fabric.

In addition to the weaves described, there are many fabrics, often classed as novelty, made by combinations or variations of these weaves. It would be impossible to describe, or even to list all the possibilities for such different interlacings. The weaves described in detail can be distinguished quite readily, although the pattern of interlacing can often be determined only after considerable experience in analyzing weaves.

FOR FURTHER READING

American Dyestuff Reporter.

Baity, E. C.: Man Is a Weaver.

Denny, G. G.: Fabrics.

Hamby, D. S.: The American Cotton Handbook, Vol. I.

Joseph, M. L.: Introductory Textile Science.

Kaswell, E. R.: Wellington Sears Handbook of Industrial Textiles.

LaBarthe, J.: Textiles: Origins to Usage.

Linton, G. E.: Applied Basic Textiles.

Linton, G. E., and J. J. Pizzuto: Applied Textiles.

Mauersberger, H. R.: American Handbook of Synthetic Textiles.

Modern Textiles Magazine.

Potter, M. D., and B. P. Corbman: Fiber to Fabric.

Press, J. J.: Man-Made Textile Encyclopedia.

Textile Chemist and Colorist.

Textile Research Journal.

Von Bergen, W.: Wool Handbook, Volume 1.

FABRIC FINISHING

Fabric finishing covers those processes that fabric undergoes after it is fabricated by weaving, knitting, felting, or other methods in preparation for use by garment manufacturers or, in some instances, directly by the ultimate consumers. Many finishing processes have interesting histories which we do not have time to follow here but which are well worth exploring.

Finishing becomes ever more complicated with the appearance of new fibers, new finishing processes and chemical compounds, and new ways of combining fibers into fabrics. Many new machines for new processes or combinations of new and old processes have replaced the old and familiar equipment; all the machines are complicated, although much of the finishing is simple in principle. The trend today is toward continuous processing, so that lengths of fabric are sewed together end to end and move as a continuous belt or web of fabric through one process after another. Finishing has become, more than ever, a business for highly trained technicians and workers.

Although wool, some cotton, and silk fabrics are often finished in the factories where they were woven or knitted, and many of the large mills that handle other fabrics now include the full range of finishing operations that carry them through all processes ready to be made into garments or

other items, a large proportion of fabrics are still finished in mills other than where they were fabricated. Mills whose purpose is such finishing are known as *converting* mills, and the mill men as *converters.* Fabric is often not attractive as it comes from the looms, knitting machines, felting machines, etc. It is known as *gray* (or *greige*) goods, a term which has grown with usage to mean any unfinished fabric, and not just those in need of bleaching—probably the original meaning of the term. Except for industrial uses, fabrics are rarely sold and used in the gray state.

Most finishing, as is much fabric production, is carried on in small mills, although there are large organizations too. A vertically integrated mill carries on all processes from spinning and weaving or knitting through to the final pressing and packaging ready for the garment manufacturer or the consumer. Such vertical integration, however, may be carried on in a series of buildings or mills, and not under one roof. Horizontal integration is organization of similar processes under one management. There is a trend toward both types of integration as mills build modern new plants with much more use of mechanization.

Finishing processes vary for different fibers because of the differences in their properties and the way they are affected by chemicals, mechanical action, and heat. The kind and amount of finishing also depends on the construction of the yarn and of the fabric, the overall purpose of the finishing process, and the end-uses for which the fabric is intended. Woven fabrics are relatively sturdy and can withstand a greater variety and intensity of finishing operations than knitted fabrics, which become distorted in shape quite easily, or lace, which is relatively fragile. Successful fabric finishing implies the preservation or improvement of as many desirable characteristics as possible and holding of damage or deterioration to other properties at zero or a low minimum.

Two reasons are usually given for finishing fabrics: to enhance aesthetic qualities or to improve service qualities. F. Fortess, in the *American Dyestuff Reporter* for July 28, 1958, has given an excellent list of five objectives for finishing, as follows: (1) to improve aesthetic qualities, (2) to impart specific functional properties not inherent in fiber or fabric, (3) to improve easy-care characteristics, (4) to improve durability by improving certain service qualities, and (5) to permit adaptation of present fabric constructions to changing market needs. What would each of these objectives involve?

The fact that fabrics are finished with these objectives in mind, and usually for fairly specific end-uses, does not insure quality. Nor does it guarantee that the fabric will be used for the type of end-use for which it is made and finished. There is little to prevent a garment manufacturer,

or anyone else who wishes, from using fabrics in ways that are not desirable, or unscrupulous finishers from using certain finishing processes to cover up a poor fabric. A poor fabric cannot be made good through finishing, but a good fabric may be made poor by improper finishing. Although there are many finishing processes, no fabric goes through all processes and some go through very few.

Fabric-fiinishing processes are categorized in different ways: physical and chemical, wet and dry, temporary and permanent, for appearance or for function. We shall divide finishes into three groups: (1) general processes used for many fabrics to improve appearance, serviceability, or both; (2) processes designed primarily to change appearance or surface texture, and for which any change in function or serviceability is largely incidental; and (3) processes designed to give special functional or serviceability properties not inherent in the fiber or fabric, and in which any change of appearance is incidental. Finishes are not necessarily mutually exclusive; sometimes two or more goals are obtained simultaneously. Improvement in one property, however, must often be gained at the expense of another. Improved crease recovery, for instance, may result in decreased breaking and tear strength.

A number of finishing processes are covered in relation to specific fibers in sections where the fibers are discussed or in relation to yarn processing. Others, such as applying color and design, are covered in Chapter 12.

GENERAL PROCESSES USED IN FINISHING MANY FABRICS

This group of finishing processes may vary considerably for fabrics made of different fibers and by different construction methods. Cotton and linen, for example, can withstand considerable strain and tension in both wet and dry processing; most fabrics made of the other fibers cannot withstand great tension without permanent damage. Some fibers can be processed at high temperatures with either wet or dry heat; others are ruined by any type of high heat. Judicious choice of processes and conditions for a process are essential for successful finishing.

The group of finishing processes that are used for all or many types of fabrics include cleaning, bleaching, drying, shrinkage control, heat-setting, inspection, repair, singeing, shearing, brushing, softening, sizing, weighting and fulling, tentering, dyeing, and mercerizing. These finishes may sometimes be applied in conjunction with, or before or after, finishes in the

other groups. Heat-setting is discussed in Chapter 7, weighting in Chapter 5, and mercerizing in Chapter 4. The finishes in the various groups are not discussed in the order of use, which may vary.

Cleaning

Cleaning includes all methods by which waxes, pectins, soil, lubricants, warp sizing, and other foreign substances remaining on the fibers, or picked up in fabrication, are removed in preparation for other finishing processes. It also includes any final cleaning necessary to prepare the fabric for the consumer. Some fabrics are cleaned two or more times during finishing.

Cleaning processes may be scouring and washing with soap or other detergents and water at any temperature, drycleaning with any of the various solvents, kier boiling, and enzyme treatment for removal of sizing, starches, etc. Bleaching, when necessary, is usually carried on in conjunction with scouring or washing.

Bleaching

Bleaching is the process of making goods whiter. Man-made fibers are usually white or are bleached in manufacture before going through the spinnerets. Linen is bleached to varying degrees of whiteness, depending on end-use requirements. Wool and cotton vary in color and need to be bleached to insure evenness of color, whether left white or subsequently dyed. Cotton also contains occasional black flecks that require bleaching. Bleaching may destroy microorganisms on the fabric and also increase its absorbency.

Bleaching is a chemical process, usually of oxidation, in which color is removed by means of chlorine or sodium compounds, or by hydrogen peroxide, depending on the fiber. Sulfur compounds have sometimes been used for reduction reaction bleaching of wool and other protein fibers, but this reaction is temporary because exposure to oxygen gradually restores the original color.

Optical bleaches are much used for white fabrics at present. These compounds do not really bleach but give a whiter effect because they change light ray reflections, causing more blue light to be reflected. This effect is accomplished by means of fluorescent colorless dyes that convert invisible ultraviolet rays to visible light. The kind of light source under which such fabrics are viewed affects their appearance. Considerable difficulty has been experienced with poor light fastness of the fluorescent dyes used for this purpose. The dazzling white appearance of such dyed fabrics in sunlight may be very different when seen in other light. There is evidence that decomposition of the fluorescent dyes is accompanied by tendering of the fabrics; the

greater the concentration of the chemical, the greater the degree of degradation.

Drying

Drying not only removes moisture but also ordinarily includes provision for removal of folds, creases, and wrinkles, whether by pressing, tension, or blowing, Many fabrics are dried as many as four times during processing, and different methods may be used at successive stages of finishing.

Possibly the oldest method of drying is by means of calender rolls between which opened-out fabrics are passed. One roller of firm, heavy metal is heated and acts as an iron; the other, soft-covered with paper or cloth blanket, serves as the ironing board. If the rollers rotate at different speeds, a shine may be developed on the face of the cloth. A series of several rollers may be used. Calenders are used for a considerable amount of finishing, particularly of cotton, but thermoplastic fibers and resins and other special chemical finishes have been instrumental in stimulating the development of additional drying means for many fabrics.

Drying may be done in a drying cabinet built over tentering frames or other machines that hold fabrics in shape or dimensions, or that carry the fabric through without tension in a series of deep loops on special frames. Hot dry air currents or jets, steam, infrared light, or electric devices may be the sources of heat. Tubular knitted fabrics must be turned inside out after removal from the knitting machines and washing; they are then passed through a closed, heated tubular canvas passageway where much moisture is removed and then are pressed flat between tentering rollers. Final drying must be done on tenter frames for all fabrics.

Overdrying results in harsh-feeling fabrics, so both temperature and humidity, as well as time, are carefully controlled.

One of the machines developed for tricot-knit fabrics, but also used for woven goods, is a cloth-covered perforated cylinder dryer on which an open-mesh blanket holds the fabric by means of suction. Air is pulled through the goods to the inside of the cylinder where it is exhausted. Shrinkage is controlled by the blanket.

Shrinkage Control

Shrinkage control may be obtained more or less satisfactorily by one of three methods, depending on the fiber, fabric, and end-use for which it is planned. One method is compressive shrinkage, one is heat-setting, and the other is stabilization by treatment with thermosetting resins. Heat-setting is discussed in Chapter 7 (p. 178). Please read this section before proceeding.

Sanforization* of cotton and the newest rayons, decating, and London shrinkage of wool are examples of compressive or relaxation shrinkage. In this type of preshrinkage, the overstretching distortion of fabric during weaving or other processing is removed by dampening the fabric and drying it in a sufficiently relaxed condition to remove such tensions or distortions. A guaranteed minimum shrinkage is a part of some patented processes for this type of shrinkage.

Thermosetting resins are being used with varying degrees of success on wool, some rayons, cottons, linen, and sometimes on mixtures or blended fabrics. The resins are applied in a liquid state, the fabric is pinned or clipped to the desired dimensions on tenter frames, and then the resin is heat cured. This type of shrinkage control is effective, if correctly applied, for as long as the resin remains on the fibers as cured, but success is dependent on susceptibility of the fibers to such treatment, amount of resin used, efficiency of the curing process, and subsequent processing and care. Stabilization of dimensions by means of resin treatment has been very important in the present widespread popularity of cotton knitted fabrics for women's dresses.

Inspection

Sometimes called *perching,* inspection is examination of the fabric for the purpose of locating defects, faulty selvages, and other irregularities and marking them for repair. If such repairs are too extensive or too numerous, the fabric may not be completely finished or may be sold as not of first quality. For inspection, the goods are opened out and passed between the inspector and a source of light so that he can detect knots, holes, irregularities of weave, etc.; he also inspects for uneven dyeing and surface-visible irregularities. The inspector may clip dangling yarns and knots and remove specks.

Mending

Mending is done by highly skilled women and consists of any type of repair needed, as indicated by the inspector. Such repair is often spot reweaving with needles and yarn, in high-quality goods.

Singeing

Singeing is the burning off of fiber and projecting yarn ends and of other fuzz so that the fabric has a smooth, bare, even surface. It is accomplished by passing the opened-out fabric directly over gas flames or hot plates at a speed sufficient to permit the protruding material to burn but not to allow

---

* Patented process of Cluett, Peabody, & Sons, Inc.

the fabric itself to be scorched or burned. From the singeing apparatus the singed fabric passes over a wet surface that insures the quenching of any smoldering fibers or yarns. Singeing is said to be the most important process in preventing pilling of staple-yarn man-made fibers.

Shearing

Shearing is the process of cutting pile or nap to a uniform height, or, in some instances, cutting away all fuzz on the surface. Shearing machines are similar to rotary-blade lawn mowers in their operation. Pile fabrics may be sheared several times to insure maximum evenness of pile height. The blades for the first shearing are set to take off just the tip ends of the longest pile fibers, and subsequent shearings are each set closer to the fabric. Cut ends are removed by suction. Why do you think such caution in the shearing process is necessary? Fancy shearing in stripes, checks, or more elaborate patterns may be done with special shearing equipment.

Weighting, Softening, Sizing, and Fulling

These are processes for changing hand or feel of fabrics, to replace waxes, gums, or oils lost in finishing, and to increase flexibility and drape of the fabrics.

Weighting of silk is discussed in Chapter 5 (p. 130). Please refer to this section before proceeding. Softening is the addition of one or more various products to make the fabric softer and also, in many instances, to make it more absorbent. Softening agents include dextrin, glycerin, sulfonated oils, sulfated tallow, waxes, sulfated alcohol, soaps, and quarternary ammonium compounds. Sizing agents are used to give stiffness or body and may be any of a number of starches, gelatin, sugars, vegetable gums (such as tragacanth or arabic), casein, glue, albumin, cellulose derivatives, or resins. Warp sizing was mentioned as a yarn process in preparation for weaving. Fulling agents have the same effect on wool as sizing materials on other fabrics; the effect is used as a finish for wool goods as well as in felt fabrication. Some of these products are removed with wear or at the first washing or cleaning; others are durable.

Tentering, Crabbing, and Heat-setting

These are final processes by which warp and filling of woven fabrics are set at right angles to each other and pulled out to the dimensions at which they are to be dried as finished products. Crabbing is the term applied to wet-tentering of wool; heat-setting is used for most of the thermoplastic fibers. Pins or clips grasp the selvages and hold the fabric in place as it travels through the machine, releasing it at the end where it is folded or rolled for packaging. If the fabric is started through the process with warp

and filling yarns not at right angles, and this is not corrected at once, they cannot be straightened without considerable effort, and if printed in this condition, the print will be crooked after the fabric has been straightened. Washing or cleaning straightens fabrics unless they have been given a resin treatment; resin-treated fabrics cured "off-grain" cannot be straightened, but remain so as long as the resin remains on the fabric.

All fabrics are *weighed, measured, labeled,* and *packaged* at the end of other finishing. These terms are self-explanatory.

Although there is no set of procedures in general finishing common to all fabrics, cotton fabrics, except for those woven in color or to be given special finishes, go through a fairly well-standardized set of operations. An idea of the sequence may be gained from the following paragraphs written by L. D. Howell for the USDA Technical Bulletin 1210 (1959), titled *Changes in American Textile Industry* (pp. 168–169):

When gray goods are received at the finishing plant, they are made up into lots of perhaps 40,000 yards by sewing together the individual pieces or cuts shipped from the mill. The cloth is then passed in open width at high speed over gas flames to burn off loose fiber ends. It then goes through a quenching bath, which contains an enzyme solution that converts to water-soluble products the starch used in warp sizing. After steeping for a few hours in the enzyme solution, the cloth is washed and run into large cylindrical steel tanks or kiers, in which it is boiled under pressure with a caustic alkali solution. Next, the cloth is thoroughly washed and then bleached white by treatment with an oxidizing agent, usually sodium hypochlorite or hydrogen peroxide. At this stage, purification is completed, and the goods, after being dried, are ready for the final finishing operations.

If the goods are to be mercerized to increase their luster and dye affinity, the cloth is passed in open width through a concentrated solution of caustic soda and held briefly under tension to complete the mercerizing reaction. Then the caustic soda is removed by washing and neutralization.

If intended for sale in the white state, the cloth is next lightly starched or softened, calendered, sanforized to reduce residual shrinkage, folded, inspected, and packed. If it is to be dyed or printed, these operations usually follow mercerization. After that, the handling is substantially the same as for white goods.

Modern finishing practice has tended to the continuous processing of cotton goods by eliminating intermittent or batch treatments whenever possible. Along with this development has gone a more complete mechanization of plants substituting mechanical for manual operations. Although much progress has been made in this direction, with resulting improvement in uniformity of treatment and speed of production, the many types of processing required by the widely varied demand apparently will not permit the adoption of straight production-line methods throughout the finishing industry.

PROCESSES FOR CHANGING APPEARANCE OR TEXTURE

This group of processes includes, in addition to several processes for applying design to fabric, other processes such as napping, plissé, crepeing, mercerizing, Schreinerizing, beetling, heat-setting of pleats, puckers, or three-dimensional effects, ciréing, and glazing. Some of these processes may form a design if they are applied in such a way as to form patterns that meet a definition for design. The processes that usually add design, and that are discussed in Chapter 12, are embossing (p. 374), moiréing (p. 375), and printing (p. 365). Beetling is discussed in Chapter 4 (p. 85) and mercerization in Chapter 4 (p. 70). You will wish to read these sections before proceeding.

Napping, Raising, or Gigging

These are processes for pulling fiber ends free from the yarns into which they have been twisted so that the ends may make a fuzzy surface on the face of the fabric, as in canton flannel, or on both face and back of the fabric, as in blankets. The pulling must be done carefully so that the fibers are not broken or stripped from the yarns completely; in any case, the yarns are weakened by napping. Wool nap may be felted to the fabric surface and thus compensate for the weakening of the yarns, but felting cannot be done with other fibers. The purpose of napping is usually to give a soft, pleasing, air-entrapping warm fabric, but napping may also be used to obscure a poor fabric, to soften design outlines, or to blend colors. Nap may be raised to different heights, clipped evenly and left upright, brushed to lie in a given direction or pattern, or curled—limitations are imposed by the nature of the fiber.

Nap is raised by means of vegetable teasels or wire nappers. Teasels are the dried, tapered-cylinder flowers of a thistle that grows wild in several areas of the United States and is cultivated for the textile industry in Oregon and New York. Wire nappers are small cylinders covered with wire teeth. Whether teasels or wire nappers are used, they are set in rows on the surface of a large roller and are brought into gradual and gentle contact with the tautly stretched fabric. The nap must be raised gradually so that fibers do not break or pull out. This takes a long period of time. How would you distinguish between a napped and a pile fabric? It is important to be able to do so.

Schreinerizing

Schreinerizing is an imitation of mercerization for cotton, in which calendering is done with a roller engraved with fine lines that cross warp

and filling at an angle, increasing luster temporarily. It is cheaper than mercerizing and is used in fabrics for costumes or other temporary purposes. Schreiner-calendering is now used to increase the opacity of nylon tricot.

Heat-setting

This process—in its present connotation—includes establishing permanent pleats, the characteristic surface effects of seersucker and plissé, and the three-dimensional effects of fabrics such as Trilok.

Glazing and Ciré

Glazing gives a shiny, slick, more or less stiff surface to fabrics. The effect is achieved with resins for durable glazing, or with glue, shellac, or starch for temporary glazing. The glaze is developed with calender rolls set to revolve at greatly different speeds. Chintz is the most common example of a glazed fabric. Ciré is essentially the same process applied to silk or rayon with a wax used as the glazing material. Ciréing produces an extremely high, metallic gloss.

Plissé

Plissé is a crepe effect produced by printing cotton fabric in stripes or other patterns with caustic soda, then permitting the fabric to dry in relaxed condition, which shrinks the areas touched by the caustic soda. This shrinkage causes the surrounding areas to pucker, producing the characteristic crinkle-crepe effect. Such puckers straighten out with wear, or if ironed, but reappear when the fabric is washed again. The pucker tends to disappear permanently after a number of washings. Plissé is sometimes confused with seersucker. How can they be distinguished? A rapid acid treatment of silk gives the same effect.

PROCESSES FOR OBTAINING SPECIAL FUNCTIONS

This group of processes is relatively new as finishing goes, many having been developed during and since World War II, although a few have been used for many years. The Quartermaster Corps of the United States armed services has played a major role in developing a number of these finishes.

Although the term *permanent* is sometimes applied to certain finishes in this group, *durable* is a more accurate term. These are chemical finishes, for the most part; their durability depends not only on the initial com-

pound and how it is applied, but also to what type of fiber and fabric construction it is applied, and the subsequent use of the fabric and kind of cleaning it receives. For apparel and furnishings purposes, the chemicals used must ordinarily not have an adverse effect on dyes, other finishes, texture, or other properties and must not be toxic to human beings. There are differing degrees of durability for different products which are used for the same purpose and even for the same product used in varying amounts or cured differently.

Some of the finishes used for the same general purpose are described as *proof* and others as *resistant* or *repellent*. These, too, are differences in degree. The proof finishes are supposed to give absolute protection against the phenomenon for which planned, such as waterproof, flameproof, and mothproof. The resistant or repellent finishes give limited protection, sometimes full protection for a short time, and in other instances limited protection over a longer period of time. Examples of these are flame resistance, which slows down the rate of burning and reduces the danger of flaming enough for the person to have a chance to attain safety; or water-repellent coats which keep the wearer dry for a limited period of time and in limited types of rainstorms.

The problem with many of the chemical finishes is to achieve the function desired without affecting wear properties, appearance, or texture. Dyes, in particular, are likely to be affected. The effect of these chemicals on appearance may determine the usefulness of an otherwise excellent finish. Research has resulted in effectively obtaining several of these functional finishes simultaneously in one finishing operation. Results look promising in relation to several such combinations of finishes.

The special-function finishing processes include waterproofing and water repellency, mothproofing, wrinkle resistance and crease recovery, flame resistance and flame retardance, durable crispness, soil and stain resistance, mildew and rot resistance, abrasion resistance, and germicidal, antiseptic, thermal insulative, and antistatic finishes. This list is not exhaustive. The durable press-easy care finishes are discussed in Chapter 13.

Waterproof and Water-repellent Finishes

These two are among the best-known finishes in the functional group. Waterproof materials or finishes have been used for many years as rubber, rubber-coated, oiled-silk, plastic-film, and plastic-coated fabrics. Have you anything that fits into this class? The rubber and oiled-silk slickers of fishermen and lumbermen were among the first of these garments; they are widely used all over the world. Waterproof fabrics are made or finished so that they present a smooth, unbroken surface that is impervious to water and also to air. These fabrics make excellent windbreakers but can

also be very uncomfortable in hot, humid weather. They keep the wearer dry in all types of storm as long as there is no break in the fabric and the seams are waterproof.

Water-repellent fabrics are treated with wax-resin mixtures, aluminum salts, silicones, ammonium compounds, or other chemicals so that the fiber is coated by the compound, but the interstices produced by the weave or knit are not covered. The open interstices permit passage of air and will also permit passage of some water in a downpour, sometimes very quickly in a hard-driving rain. Fluorochemicals are the newest and best group of chemical compounds for this purpose. They impart both oil and water repellency—thus they may be effective in stain and spot resistance also. Water-repellent fabrics are more likely than the waterproof ones to be comfortable in warm weather. Fabrics used for general-wear coats, suits, work clothing, or other garments may be treated for water repellency so that no extra rain garments are required. Effectiveness of water-repellent garments depends on fabric structure, lining material, and cut of the garment too; an absorbent lining material may act as a wick and pull moisture through to the inside. Who would be interested in waterproof garments and who in water-repellent garments?

Effectiveness of a water-repellent finish following washing or dry cleaning, regardless of how good and durable the initial finish, depends on the completeness with which soaps or other detergents have been removed. It is probably impossible to remove all traces of soap or detergent with the most thorough rinsing possible, and the effect of haphazard or poor rinsing may be to nullify almost completely the effect of the finish. This is particularly true in dry cleaning. If you have a washable raincoat that is still good but is no longer effectively water repellent, particularly if it has a fluorocarbon finish, you may wish to try the following procedure:

If your coat needs washing, first put it through the regular automatic wash with warm water, a detergent, and a water softener (such as Calgon, for example). Put through regular rinse and spin cycles. Then run it through the whole procedure again, but the second time use only the softener and *no* detergent. Dry in a tumble dryer set at warm to hot temperature until almost dry—pull out of dryer before tumbling stops and place on a hanger. Touch up seams and where needed on the right side of the garment with an iron set for a temperature compatible with the fiber content of the fabric. If you do not have access to a tumble dryer, dry on a hanger and press on the right side before completely dry.

Mothproofing

Wool, hair, and fur of all types are subject to attack by some species of moths, usually called "clothing" or "webbing" moths, and by certain

species of carpet beetles. Moths are more prevalent in this country. These insects eat wool, hair, or fur for food; they will feast on wearing apparel, household textiles such as blankets and rugs, wool stuffing in upholstered furniture, wool scraps, or wool in fiber, yarn, or fabric wherever found; but they do not infest such fibers on the living animals. Since the insects are small and largely nocturnal in their habits, their presence may not be known until their ravages are discovered; often minor areas of damage will ruin a garment for further wear. Rather simple precautions will prevent infestation in moth-free wool items and well-built houses and closets. Old, open, decrepit, or heavily infested buildings can probably never be made safe, but garments and furnishings can be protected even in these places. Constant vigilance, however, is necessary.

The clothes moth has a four-stage life cycle very similar to that of the silkworm, and it is during the larva stage that it feeds on wool and does its damage. The larva builds a cocoon of fibers or anything else at hand for its dormant stage. Clothes moths are smaller than silk moths at all stages. Only the males fly. The female chooses obscure areas of seldom disturbed wool, preferably in dark, warm areas, to lay her eggs; the eggs are attached to the wool by means of an adhesive. Places often chosen are underneath areas of seams, inside cuffs and pockets, under rarely moved pieces of furniture, in boxes of scraps, and other such areas. Soiled garments are more likely to be chosen than clean, and soiled spots on otherwise clean garments; fine, soft wools are more likely to be attacked than coarse, harsh wools.

Mothproofing compounds of varying degrees of durability are available in different forms. Many of the compounds effective against moths are also effective against carpet beetles. Some compounds are for buildings and must be applied by professional exterminators because of their inherent danger to persons or property. Some can be applied by the consumer in the house, closets, rooms, or to garments. Some are applicable to fabric in finishing operations in the factory; these are labeled with a time guarantee, usually within limits of a specified cleaning method.

The most durable mothproofing compounds, for which there are at least two manufacturers, may be applied at the factory with the dye and are often guaranteed for the life of the fabric. There is some question how effective these compounds are with repeated washing or drycleaning of the fabrics.

Mothproofing preparations that contain fluorine compounds, naphthalene, DDT, and paradichlorobenzene have been found satisfactory for consumer uses within the limitations of their form of application. Such compounds are available in crystals, cake, spray, and aerosol bomb forms.

Crystals may be sprinkled among garments or folds of garments or

blankets in preparation for and during storage and are effective as long as any crystals remain, if kept in a tightly closed storage place. Their effectiveness is due to emanation of a gas as the crystals evaporate. Effectiveness of cakes or crystals placed in closets depends on the closet being kept tightly enough closed for the gas to penetrate all folds of the garments and areas of the space and to maintain this penetration. Plastic belts, etc., may be adversely affected by the gas.

The effectiveness of mothproofing sprays depends on the spray reaching every spot, including inside areas of seams and pockets, under collars, lapels, and cuffs. Some sprays leave a white deposit on the garments when dry. Sprays seem to vary in the length of time for which they are effective. Respraying is probably necessary after dry cleaning and certainly after washing.

When placed in tightly closed rooms or closets, aerosol bombs are effective in killing moths or already hatched larvae, but they do not destroy eggs, so the treatment should be repeated when additional larvae might be hatching. Once the gas is dissipated, there is no reliable protection against reinfestation. Such bombs, however, are good precautionary treatments for closets or other storage areas believed not to be infested—if they can be sealed tight during treatment—before storing clean, moth-free wools in them.

Wool items receiving constant or frequent use are not generally attacked by moths. In addition to precautionary (moth-preventive) storage, other aids to moth prevention are to keep wool items clean and free from spots and stains, occasional thorough brushing inside and out, occasional airing out of doors or in a well-ventilated room, preferably in sunshine, and storage in clean condition in seasons when the items are not used. Such storage places as cedar-lined closets and chests and garment bags may prevent moths from getting in, but may not prevent eggs that are already laid on the garments from hatching and the larvae from doing considerable damage.

Serious infestation calls for more drastic measures than have been discussed here.

Germicidal, Antiseptic, and Antibacterial Finishes

Germicidal and antiseptic finishes are those designed to make fabric medically protective against bacterial infection from cuts, abrasions, or other wounds, or to protect babies against diaper rash and other infections. Such finishes now come under the jurisdiction of the U.S. Food and Drug Administration and must be proved to be nontoxic, which is both expensive and difficult. The effectiveness of such finishes for general use is

questionable; it seems safer to depend on other, more conventional protective measures. Few compounds, according to medical research reports, hold out promise of effectiveness at low concentrations, and if used in concentrations high enough to be effective for a healthy adult, these finishes might be dangerous for a baby or an ill person. Such fabrics may have value in limited, special uses, such as for the armed services in time of combat or other danger.

Effectiveness of the antibacterial finishes changes with washing and cleaning, with part of their potency being expended in carrying out their function and with the passage of time.

The so-called "bacteriostat" finishes or additives inhibit growth of bacteria that cause perspiration odor in fabric; many laundries use bacteriostat finishes regularly on men's shirts and sometimes on other garments. The American Viscose Division of FMC Corporation has received a license for a bacteriocidal finish which can be incorporated into the spinning mixture for rayon and acetate; the purpose of the finish is to prevent the growth of odor-producing bacteria. Some acetate lingerie fabrics were being so finished as early as 1960. How prevalent the use of such finishes is has not been reported. Chemicals used for this type of finish are said to be non-irritating to human skin. The bacteriostat finishes are expected to gain wide public acceptance.

Flame Retardance or Resistance

The purpose of all flame-resistant or retardant finishes is to slow down burning or change its nature to allow time for human safety. Serviceability of all fabrics is destroyed or impaired by fire; the preservation of the service qualities of the fabric is not a purpose of this type of finishing. No finish is truly flameproof; it changes the nature of burning from flash to steady burning, charring, or glowing, perhaps; raises ignition time; or forms a self-extinguishing margin around a burning area. Few finishes are available that do not affect color, appearance, hand, or all three; all such durable finishes are expensive, and none is satisfactorily and equally durable through dry cleaning, laundering, and weathering. Modifications of cellulosic fibers, particularly phosphorylation of cottons, to make them less flammable have been successful but are too expensive for ordinary use. Flame-retardant compounds vary in their effectiveness on different fibers; a compound that will decrease the fire hazard of one fiber may make another dangerously flammable.

Despite the difficulties, progress is being made along several lines. For example, some effective and durable phosphorous-containing compounds such as THPC and APO-THPC and a new fiber reactive flame retardant for cotton have been developed. Further work needs to be done to improve

the hand of some finishes, to prevent yellowing, and to reduce adverse effects on breaking and tear strengths, as well as to reduce cost. A most promising new approach would include chemicals for two or more different finishes obtained simultaneously; durable press and flame retardance seem a very near possibility and at a reasonable cost. American Viscose Division of FMC Corporation put a flame retardant acetate fiber on the market in 1963, a semipermanent rayon fiber in 1966, and in December 1967 announced a permanently flame retardant rayon "Avisco PFR" which should be available now in at least limited quantities. Blends combining flammable with flame retardant or nonflammable fibers are being used for some items such as acrylic/modacrylic carpets and rugs, rayon/polyester or rayon/modacrylic blankets.

In response to a growing demand for something to be done about the dangerously flammable fabrics appearing on the market—to which have been attributed such holocausts as the Hartford circus tent fire, the Coconut Grove Nightclub (Boston) fire, the Winecoff Hotel (Atlanta) fire, in each of which scores to hundreds of lives were lost, in addition to many individual and small group tragedies—the Congress of the United States passed the first Flammable Fabrics Act. This law, enacted in 1953 and signed by President Eisenhower, became effective on July 1, 1954.

In recent years, with advances being made in building desired properties into textile fibers, with improvements in finishes and technology, and with the continuing long series of fatal but often preventable accidents, there has been a resurgence of interest in flammable clothing and textile furnishings that has enlisted medical, public health, textiles, space, military personnel, and representatives of consumers' groups in an attack on the problem. Data have been accumulated from hospitals and other sources which indicate that burning clothing leads to more severe and painful injury, more surgery, and longer hospitalization than other types of injuries. Highest incidence of severe and fatal burns are among young children, the aged, and the infirm who are dependent on someone else for help or rescue. As a result of the concern and realization that much could be done that presently was not being done, the Congress passed an amendment to the Flammable Fabrics Act which, on December 14, 1968, was signed into law by President Johnson. The amendment broadens the scope of the 1953 law and incorporates several new features.

The act, as amended, covers all articles of clothing and all interior furnishings. Clothing is defined as "any costume or article of clothing worn or intended to be worn by individuals," and interior furnishing as "any type of furnishing made in whole or in part of fabric or related material and intended for use or which may reasonably be expected to be used, in homes, offices, or other places of assembly or accommodation."

The definitions cover all kinds of fabrics made of all types of fibers by all construction processes, and also such related materials as paper, plastics, rubber, synthetic film, and synthetic foam used in such products.

The new features are a series of requirements for which the Secretary of Commerce has responsibility; certain of these will be delegated to the appropriate subdivisions under his jurisdiction. The new requirements are:

1. That the Secretary of Commerce and the Secretary of Health, Education, and Welfare together conduct a continuing investigation and study of "deaths, injuries and economic losses resulting from accidental burning of products, fabrics, and related materials."

2. Results of these studies must be reported to the Congress annually.

3. The Secretary is authorized to conduct and/or cooperate with other agencies or persons in research on flammability of products, methods of testing flammability, and on proper use of such tests.

4. The Secretary must appoint a nine-member National Advisory Committee that represents manufacturers, distributors, and consumers to serve as consultants for proposed regulations, and such matters.

5. Probably the most important, the Secretary has power, with assent of the Advisory Committee, to initiate proceedings for establishment of any regulations that the studies show are needed.

The provisions of the 1953 law and the test methods developed for it continue in force unless and until superseded by new regulations which, except when considered especially urgent, will not go into effect until 12 months or more after they are announced.

We shall now consider some of the major regulations developed for interpretation and enforcement of the 1953 Flammable Fabrics Act.

Dangerous flammability has been established by the FTC as the burning time in seconds by specified test methods, according to the class of material. The classes established are plain surface fabric weighing 2 ounces or more per square yard; plain surface fabrics weighing less than 2 ounces per square yard; raised surface fabrics that have dense cut pile of uniform short length or looped yarns; nitrocellulose fiber, coating, and fabric; garments made directly from yarns and meeting these specified fabric descriptions; and fabrics decorated with tufting, embroidery, appliqué, or other surface decoration. What examples can you name in each class?

The time test for burning varies for some of the classes, and the type of flammability for which tests must be made varies also. The latter includes fabric ignition and flash burning. The meanings of these two terms are very different; you need to understand both and their implications.

It has been difficult to determine satisfactory test methods and standards to cover all the wide range of fabrics, and although several research

groups have worked constantly on the problem, there is still considerable dissatisfaction with current standards and methods. With inclusion of interior furnishings, additional classes will have to be added or a whole new series of test methods may be developed. The standard test method for apparel fabrics has required that the fabric be tested at a 45° angle. A vertical strip test, however, has had widespread use for drapery and curtain fabrics (flame retardance tests) and may, with refinement, become the standard. Or new methods may be developed for all types of fabrics as this problem receives intensive study. The foams used for upholstery may require a separate test method.

Flammability is dependent on the kind of fiber, film, foam, plastic, or other material, type of fabric construction and its openness or tightness and weight, style of items and their decorative features and finishes, and nature of the immediate environment. How do each of these elements enter into the picture, and why? Glass and asbestos are the only fireproof fibers, though their finishes may burn; all others used for ordinary purposes flame, char, melt, or both melt and flame, with the attendant dangers. This is one of the properties covered in the study of individual fibers in this book; you can quickly turn to the various fibers and establish lists of fibers that are dangerously flammable, that are slow burning, that will melt, and that will be self-extinguishing. Some fabrics such as net and brushed nap sweaters flash-burn. Heavy fabrics may ignite slowly but burn vigorously when ignited, and some fabrics may char but not flame. Articles that are customarily washed or dry-cleaned are expected to meet the flammability standards after washing or dry cleaning.

An effective, temporary, home-applicable flame-resistant treatment for *cellulosic fibers only* can be made by using the following proportions of easily and cheaply obtained ingredients: 7 ounces borax (sodium borate), 3 ounces boric acid, and 2 quarts of hot water. Fabrics may be dipped in or sprayed with the solution. This treatment is durable to ironing or pressing but is removed with washing. Where and when would use of such a treatment be desirable?

It is heartening to note that in spite of predictions to the contrary, with the public interest in and publicity that accompanied agitation for enactment of the amendment to the 1953 law, by the time it became mandatory, steps were already being taken by manufacturers, finishers, and retailers to increase the kinds and supply of flame retardant fabrics and other items on the market, to be more concerned with aesthetic qualities of such products than in the past, and also for institutions and individuals to show interest in buying them. Of course, need for flame-retardant properties varies greatly with the end-use for which an item is destined. Although upholstered-furniture manufacturers and manufacturers of drapery and

bedding are not expected to be affected by the law for at least a year from the time of its enactment, many were already anticipating its requirements and moving ahead to meet them even before its passage was certain, hoping by acting early to win a good market for their products.

Wrinkle Resistance and Crease Recovery

These terms are self-explanatory and are different facets of the same thing. What do you understand their meaning to be? Because of the great interest in durable or permanent press and wash-wear fabrics, which are explored in considerable depth in Chapter 13, we tend to lose sight of the fact that the concepts of wrinkle resistance and crease recovery have much broader applicability than just to these classes of fabrics.

Fibers and fabrics vary greatly in their resistance to wrinkling and recovery from creasing. Fiber, yarn, fabric construction, and finishing processes all make a difference. Wool and polyesters are outstandingly satisfactory in this respect, untreated cotton and linen very poor, with all other fibers ranging between. Mixing and blending sometimes take advantage of natural wrinkle-resistant and crease-recovery properties; this is covered in Chapter 14. Knitted fabrics of all types have long been valued for resistance to wrinkling and quick recovery. Synthetic resin finishes for cellulosic fibers, first used for crease resistance and soon afterward for dimensional stability, were introduced by the Tootal, Broadhurst, Lee Company (England) in 1929. Use of these resins paved the way for cotton and the man-made cellulosic fibers to compete with the later-appearing but readily and widely accepted thermoplastic fibers, which got off to their fine starts largely because of their minimum-care properties.

Finishes used for wrinkle resistance and crease recovery are synthetic high-polymer resins. The resins are believed (if properly applied and cured) to form cross-linkages between molecular chains and also to increase fiber stiffness. Satisfactory performance and durability depend on suitable choice of resin for the particular fiber or combination of fibers, the method and concentration of resin application, correct curing procedures, laundry or cleaning procedures, and, particularly, whether or not chlorine bleaches are used. Some of these aspects are examined in more detail in Chapter 13.

Crease-resistant finishing is often accompanied by decreased breaking and tear strength and elongation, especially in cotton, by lower absorbency, by a tendency to accumulate static electricity, and by difficulty in removing greasy soil and stains, to mention a few changes. The maintenance of a fresh appearance over long periods of time, however, is generally considered to outweigh such disadvantages.

For cottons and practically no rayons—except underwear, lingerie, and hosiery—appear on the market for any end-use today that are not crease-

resistant finished. Although treated cottons ordinarily are so labeled, rayons often are not. In blends with other fibers where crease-resistant finishes are incorporated, they often are not mentioned.

Mildew and Rot Resistance

Under certain conditions, a number of bacteria and fungi cause mildew and rot to develop on textile materials. The right conditions may exist in mill storage areas. Finishes that increase absorption may also encourage mildew on material that is otherwise ordinarily mildew free.

Tropical and subtropical conditions of high relative humidity (above 75%) and warm temperature (above 80°F) favor development of these organisms. Cellulosic materials are most subject to attack, especially those containing starch or sizing materials, but no fiber is entirely immune if conditions are right. Wood and leather are also subject to attack. Conditions do not depend alone on geographical area or climate; they may be produced indoors or out almost anywhere in temperate or warmer climates. The microorganisms are present everywhere in air and soil, ready to grow when temperature and humidity are favorable. Mildew and rot are very great problems to the armed services operating in tropical areas. The life of tents was sometimes six weeks in the tropics in World War II, and of shoes less than half that long; similar problems have been encountered in Viet Nam.

Mildew can be readily recognized by its musty odor, taste, and discoloration of the fabrics on which it grows. Have you seen and smelled it? Compounds of mercury, formaldehyde, chrome, zinc, copper, and chlorine are considered to be effective in mildew-resistant finishes; not all can be used on apparel because some are toxic. Acetylation, cyanoethylation, and phosphorylation modifications of cotton are said to provide mildew resistance. Few finishes can be used without effect on fabric hand, color, or both.

Preventive measures are effective in many instances. These include thorough drying of clothing before storage or before putting the articles in clothes hampers; constant circulation of air through closets and storage rooms in mildew-prone locations; use of calcium chloride crystals to dehumidify storage areas, with drying out of crystals as frequently as needed; use of dehumidifying equipment in rooms and factories; and use of starch substitutes or plastic starches rather than ordinary starch.

The military services have been greatly concerned with mildew prevention treatment for sandbags, which they are using in ever greater numbers for many purposes that range from protection for living beings and for military installations to road and dam building. Olefin fiber is now much

used in sandbags because it does resist rot and mildew and is thus more durable.

Abrasion-resistant Finishes

These finishes cut down on rubbing-wear damage by coating fibers or fabric, or by lubricating in some way. Resin, rubber, and silicone finishes make fibers less subject to abrasion, although they are not usually applied for this specific purpose. Coronizing treatment for glass (Chapter 8, p. 261) is an example of an abrasion-resistant finish applied for this specific purpose. Results of experiments with nitrile latex are promising.

Thermal-insulative Finishes

Thermal insulation is aimed at maintaining warmth or, in reverse, at keeping out heat or cold. A sprayed-on metallic aluminum coating for lining fabrics is produced for this purpose. Such fabric, used as lining material for coats and jackets, is said to eliminate the necessity for heavy interlinings. Aluminum-coated fabric is also used as lining for window drapery fabric. Effectiveness varies with the quality of the finished fabric. Considerable metal may be lost in drycleaning, which should be reduced to a minimum running time. Washing may remove all the metal.

A new vacuum-plating process adapted from a metal-plating process may result in more permanent adhesion of fabric and metal than has been achieved thus far; this remains to be proved.

Permanent Crispness

Synthetic resin compounds are used in place of starches and gums to obtain durable crispness in cellulosic fabrics, primarily cottons. Although curing at high temperature is not considered essential, the permanency and hand appear to be better if the resins are heat-cured. Some combinations of starch and urea-formaldehyde resin are used successfully for these finishes. Acrylic polymers are also used as additions to or substitutes for starch; they are more transparent than starch solutions. Many resins applied for other purposes add stiffness to the fabric.

Soil- and Stain-repellency and Soil Release

Soils and stains that are difficult or impossible to remove have always been of concern to the persons responsible for laundering or cleaning apparel and textile furnishings. The problem has caused widespread concern to ever-increasing numbers of consumers since the introduction of resin finishes for cellulosic fibers about twenty years ago and the growing use of automatic home laundering equipment, which has been a corollary

development. The problems have been compounded as new resins and combinations of fibers have been used and as the concept of finishing has expanded to wash-wear apparel and, since 1964, to durable press fabrics and garments. Most of these are combinations of cellulosic and non-cellulosic man-made fibers (largely polyesters) from which oily soils are particularly difficult to remove.

Soiling and staining vary with types of fibers and fabrics, their finishes, whether soils or stains are air-borne, water-borne, oil-borne, or a combination, and whether such soils or stains rest lightly on the fabric surface or have been ground or forced in. Another phenomenon not yet completely clear is the fact that untreated cellulosic fibers tend to repel oily stains in air, but not in water, while the opposite is true for polyesters, so what happens in preparation for, or in laundering may have the opposite effect to that desired if one is not aware of this. Much soiling of white and light-colored man-made or blended fabrics has been found to be due to soil removed during the washing cycle and then redeposited on the fabrics during the spin cycles in automatic washing; the fabrics serve as filters to catch the dirt as the water is centrifuged through them in draining. Some manufacturers are redesigning the operations of their washers to prevent redeposition. Studies also show that a majority of the failures in removal of soil, as well as many stains, in laundering are due to underuse of detergent, defined to include both soaps and synthetic compounds, and also to insufficiently high water temperature. There is much good recent literature on soiling and detergency which we cannot explore here but which is available to anyone wishing to pursue this subject.

There are different types of problems involved in soiling and staining of fabrics, in finishing to repel soil and stains, and in releasing soil and stains that adhere in spite of any repellent finish that a fabric may have.

Soil- and stain-repellent finishes were first successfully developed for carpets and rugs for water-borne types of stains. A series of wax emulsions and aluminum compounds suitable for water repellency were of value as temporary finishes. The development of durable silicone finishes was a boon; these finishes form a flexible protective film around each fiber. Such finishes, however, are thus far not effective against oily type stains and may even increase affinity for them.

Several fluorochemical finishes are now available that repel both aqueous and oily stains and some of the newest finishes in this class are purported to facilitate release of both types of soil, too. R. E. Read and G. C. Culling, in the *American Dyestuff Reporter* for November 6, 1967 (p. 43) summarized the effectiveness of these finishes when they said:

Presently available fluorochemical finishes are intrinsically highly repellent, but they cannot make a fabric completely stainproof; they can, however, make

it stain resistant or repellent to liquid soils. The level of stain resistance observed in practice is dependent upon the level of fluorochemical used, the fabric color, construction, pattern, and the staining situation. However, a high level of fluorochemical on many fabrics produces a durable finish which also is essentially stainproof to many water-borne stains and which restricts most oil-stains to light spots at the points of contact. With the fluorochemical finish, such residues are readily removed by spot-cleaning without leaving a ring.

Soil-release finishes were developed as a result of the great difficulty in removing stains, particularly oily stains, from durable press fabrics. The first was a radiation process announced in 1966. Other finishes incorporate fluorochemicals or acrylics as a film-producing element. Soil-release finishes work any of several ways: they may change the hydrophobicity of a fabric, its electrostatic condition, or its surface energy, all of which play a part in determining whether the washing solution (not just water) can get to the fabric to "float" the soil or stain off the surface. According to the AATT Committee on Technology (*Modern Textiles Magazine,* April 1968, p. 65):

The principle being followed by most mills is to impart a hydrophilic water-wetting surface film on the fabric in a final washing step. This greatly facilitates the removal of most soiled spots by greatly increasing the ability of standard detergents and washing procedures to remove the soil.

Although 15 to 20 trade names (by February 1969) for soil-release finishes have been issued to various producers or finishers, not all are yet on the market nor are those on the market all equally effective. Some labels include the words "soil release" with the trade name of the finish; others have a trade name that clearly identifies them as such. Industry-wide standards are needed; this is now recognized by most of the producers who wish to protect their good names with consumers.

Antistatic Finishes

A number of antistatic compounds of different types are generally effective during mill processing but are not durable enough to reach the consumer. No successful durable antistatic finish has yet been proved, although a few have been announced from time to time. One was said to be hygroscopic so that absorbency was increased. Most antistatic products to date have discolored in cleaning, have been affected by chlorine in laundering, or have caused increased soiling.

The group of products available on the market as fabric softeners are effective temporary antistats; they must be replaced after each washing. Class experiments with softeners indicated that their action was due to deposition of wax which does tend to build up with a series of launderings

and retreatments. Thus, their effect is due not to increased absorbency but to the wax buildup.

A great many trademarks for specially finished functional fabrics for many of the purposes discussed have been registered. Since new names are constantly appearing, it is desirable for each person to keep a current list of those trade names in which he is interested.

FOR FURTHER READING

Alderfer, E. B., and H. E. Michl: *Economics of American Industry.*

American Dyestuff Reporter.

Edelstein, S. M.: "Series of Historical Developments in Dyeing and Finishing," *American Dyestuff Reporter*, Vols. 42–48.

Hamby, D. S.: *The American Cotton Handbook*, Vol. 2.

Kaswell, E. R.: *Wellington Sears Handbook of Industrial Textiles.*

Marsh, J. J.: *An Introduction to Textile Finishing.*

Mauersberger, H. R.: *American Handbook of Synthetic Textiles.*

Modern Textiles Magazine.

Moncrieff, R. W.: *Mothproofing.*

Textile Chemist and Colorist.

Von Bergen, W.: *Wool Handbook*, Vol. 1.

Ward, K., Jr.: *Chemistry and Chemical Technology of Cotton.*

▗▄▄ **12**

FABRIC COLOR AND DESIGN

Color and design are closely associated in many of the objects about us; the form and color of one object against the background of another form and color makes our world visible and meaningful. Although a large percentage of plain-colored fabrics have no design, a great amount of textile design is achieved with color to attain or to emphasize the design form and its details.

The history of man's use of color and design is most fascinating; color and design have been used by all prehistoric peoples in climates ranging from temperate to tropic in all parts of the world. In the colder climates there has been more limitation on color, but design has been achieved with little or no color.

COLOR

What is color? The physicist's definition of color is generally accepted, that is, that color is visible light, a phase of electromagnetic radiation. We see color as a result of the reflection of light rays. The white light of daylight is made up of light rays of many lengths, which, when separated by means of a glass prism, beveled mirror, or other such means, appears to the hu-

man eye as bands of color ranging from red through orange, yellow, green and blue, to violet. This band of brilliant pure color is known as the *spectrum*. There are light rays at both ends of the spectrum that are invisible to human eyes without special aids to bring the rays into the visible range. Ultraviolet and infrared are examples. There is evidence that birds, some insects, and perhaps animals can distinguish colors—to what extent is not known. Perhaps some of them can see a wider or different range of colors than we can!

The source of light influences the colors seen; that is, a light source cannot reflect color not contained in its own rays. This limitation accounts for a part of the variation in color appearance when a colored object is viewed under different types of lights. Light rays are differentially absorbed by objects, so that an object appears to be the color of the light ray or mixture of rays reflected. For example, a fabric that absorbs all colors of light rays except blue would reflect them and appear to the viewer as "blue." When all rays are reflected and none absorbed, the object appears to be white; when all rays are absorbed and none reflected, the object is described as "black." Black, however, is really complete absence of color and white a mixture of all colors of light rays.

Colored fabrics, then, absorb or reflect certain light rays. Dyestuffs enable a fabric to do this. We shall, however, use the commonly accepted meaning of color as being the dyestuffs themselves or as being a part of an object emitting the stimulus which causes us to see color. Colors we see vary, not only because of the hue, intensity, and light and dark value of the coloring matter used and the source of light under which we view it but also with the type of fiber, its size, texture of the surface to which it is applied and from which it is reflected, and undoubtedly, too, with the eye of the person who views it.

F. Fordemwalt, in "The History of the Development of Fast Dyes" (*American Dyestuff Reporter*, April 8, 1957, p. 244), has said:

There are certain aspects of the nature of man which cannot be explained. They are traits with which he has been endowed by his Creator. One of these is the perception of color. Why certain electromagnetic frequencies and certain combinations of frequencies when impinging on the eye should bring to man a pleasant reaction or any reaction at all for that matter is completely unexplainable. But the effects are real. We all experience them every day. They have been very real to man from the day he became a man, and life has been richer and more beautiful because of them. . . .

All peoples, until comparatively recent times, made use of whatever natural sources of dyestuffs were at hand, such as colored clays, berries, nuts, fruits, insects, roots, leaves, and scraps of certain metals when such

became available. Their first use of color was often to paint their bodies; then color was applied to whatever was used for clothing, to the walls of caves, and tents, and other dwellings, to pottery, and to other things which they had or with which they worked. Color was probably first used to ward off evil spirits, but aesthetic enjoyment and ritual appeal cannot have lagged far behind the first use.

Color symbolism developed in response to emotional reaction to colors. Black is believed to have been the first color identified; it was associated with darkness, mystery, winter, and death. Evil spirits were believed to be unable to see through it; hence it had "magic" protective properties. Color symbolism varied among primitive peoples, depending on their own environment and the sources of dyestuffs at their command. Red was universally associated with life, fire, and sun, but the symbolism, and thus the use of other colors, varied widely. As civilizations developed, meanings attributed to colors sometimes changed. The symbolism of particular colors is closely associated with the various religions of the world, and persists today; the color associated with one specific religion, however, is different from that associated with another specific religion.

We still make considerable use of traditional color symbolism of our culture, as evidenced in the Western world by the traditional white for brides, black for mourning, and red for gaiety. The theater, opera, and movies make extensive use of color to set the mood for their productions. Even in academic circles, the colors used on the gowns are symbolic. B. Brown, in an article "Ceremonial Use of Color" (*Rayon Textile Monthly*, April 1947, p. 128), has said:

. . . This regalia had its origin during the Middle Ages when classrooms were often so chilly and damp that extra clothing was necessary during lectures and debates which were the current form of instruction. Colorful hoods worn by present day recipients of college degrees still display colors of the Middle Ages, doctors of law wearing purple, the royal color of kings who once made the laws; doctors of divinity wearing scarlet, as a reminder of the crucifixion; doctors of philosophy wearing blue, the symbol of truth; doctors of medicine wearing green, the color of herbs used in healing; doctors of engineering wearing orange, suggesting strength and endurance; doctors of arts and letters wearing white, denoting integrity; while doctors of science wear golden yellow, a reference to gold which alchemists once attempted to recover from baser metals.

Brown has also said that "An inheritance from this symbolic use of color is that the average person can, without effort, name only about thirty of the million or more colors which are in use for a wide variety of purposes, and the colors named will invariably be those anciently used for symbolic reasons."

N. S. Knaggs, in an interesting historical account of dyes, "Dyestuffs of the Ancients" (*American Dyestuff Reporter*, August 27, 1956, p. 595), writes:

. . . As Man began to explore the surface of the earth in search of better food and lands, he discovered that other people were using dyes unknown to him and, in many cases, superior to his own. Thus commenced one of the earliest forms of industrial commerce—the trading or bartering of dyes. Cities sprang up and became centers of dye-making and trading. Notable among these was Tyre on the Phoenician coast, which achieved its prominence because the tiny seashell mollusk, source of the most famous of all purple dyes, Tyrian purple, was found near this ancient city.

Importance of Color

Its aesthetic appeal is one of color's greatest values. Since color is so closely tied to emotion, symbolism, and tradition, this appeal may be its most important attribute by far. Color choice can be highly individual and thus a means of creative expression, denied through many other outlets in our complicated society. Almost everyone has a favorite color and many have a color to which they are adverse. Do you have a favorite color? What is your reaction to it? To a disliked color? How does your feeling affect your use of these colors?

The psychological aspects of color are closely tied to emotion and aesthetics. Because of their emotional impact some colors are known as "stimulating" and others as "soothing." Color has sometimes been found a medium through which mentally disturbed persons can be reached; often their first positive reaction will be to color. Nearly all hospitals of all types make use of color in rooms and furnishings today because of its beneficial effect on the morale of the patients, and no doubt on the morale of persons who visit them there. It has been found that the colors used in markets, restaurants, and other places of business play a considerable part in the success of the business and in the type of clientele they attract. A red public telephone booth has even been found to cut down on the length of telephone conversations! Does the way you feel at any particular time affect the color of garment you choose and wear?

The safety function of color is very important in our modern, high-speed living—not just for red and green traffic signals, important as they are, but also because the variation in color all around us and of colored objects moving against a background of still different color enables us to see the objects. Have you ever tried to imagine what living in our modern age would be like if everything were one color, even a most beautiful color, with not even variation in light or depth of that color? Modern factories make much use of color for machines and to identify dangerous areas, on walls, and in many other ways. It has been found

that judicious use of color cuts down on fatigue and, on this count, also adds to safety. What is color blindness? What difficulties does it pose? One of the newest uses is to assign a color to the phonetic sounds of the English language in teaching beginners and illiterates to read.

Mr. Howard Ketcham, in an article in *Color Engineering* for April 1964 (pp. 18–21) titled "Color Environment and The Learning Process," has given a number of interesting examples of the physical and psychological effects of color and its importance. Among other examples were the following:

There is a relationship between sound, light and physical comfort to the learning process. Surprisingly color also has an effect on all three of these environments—acoustical, visual, and physical? Here are some examples.

Color "influences" apparent noise levels. Nine phonebooth-like structures were painted on the inside in the following colors: vermilion, chrome yellow, white, green, violet-blue, orange, black, purple and gray. A bell system was installed to provide an identical noise in each booth. Then 18 young people, free from any hearing defects, were asked to enter each booth in turn and indicate the color of the booth, on a score card, in which the noise seemed quietest and the color of the booth where the noise was loudest. The results of the scoring made on this test showed that the majority of the youngsters thought the noise sounded loudest in the white booth and quietest in the purple one.

As for color effect on visual apprehension, U.S. Army insurance adjusters were intrigued by results of one color study they made. They were examining records of parking accidents. They found that there were more claims for damaged fenders made when Army drivers parked between two *blue*-colored cars than when they parked between cars of any other color. They concluded that those accidents were caused by the greater apparent space between the two blue-colored cars.

And what about color's effect on physical comfort? One school cafeteria was embellished with blue paint on upper walls and dark blue ceramic tile on the lower walls. During the winter months a number of the girl students complained about the temperature in the cafeteria, saying it was too cold. The building superintendent was at a loss to understand the complaints since the entire school was under thermostatic control and there were *no* complaints from other areas in the school. So he decided to heat the cafteria with color. He put vermilion slip covers on the backs of all the chairs, and painted a bright vermilion band around the walls just above the tile dado. You could take one look at this previously cool room and see warmth all over it. The complaints stopped immediately.

Dyestuffs and Dyeing

Although through the ages hundreds of natural dyestuffs have been recorded, only twenty-four were commercially important; eight of these

were far more important than the others. They were cochineal, Tyrian purple, madder, indigo, saffron, safflower, woad, and logwood. Of these eight, only logwood is of commercial importance today; it is one of the best dyestuffs for obtaining a good black on silk, nylon, and perhaps other of the man-made fibers.

Cochineal was a red dye that was discovered and used by the Aztecs. It was obtained by crushing the bodies of tiny female insects that live on a specie of cactus. *Tyrian purple* was obtained from the tiny sea mollusks, *Murex brandaris* and *Murex trunculus*, as mentioned earlier, and was the most expensive of all, for 12,000 animals were required for a single gram of dye. Its use was often restricted to royalty, and the color produced came to be called "royal" purple. *Madder,* obtained from the roots of the plant *Rubia tinctorum*, was a widely used red dye. *Indigo,* obtained from steeped and fermented leaves of the plant *Indigofera tinctoria*, was a source of blue dye. *Saffron,* obtained from the stigmata of the plant *Crocus sativus*, was an expensive rich yellow dye that is still used in Asia for dyeing monk's robes. *Safflower* was obtained from the flowering head of the plant of the same name and, by varying the solutions from acid to alkali, produced a range of colors from yellow to red. *Woad*, obtained from dried and fermented leaves of the *woad* plant, was an important source of a dull blue. *Logwood,* from fermented wood chips of the tree *Haematoxifon campechianum*, was used for varying shades of bluish purple to black.

In 1856, William H. Perkin, a 17-year-old English boy and chemist's assistant, in additional research of his own outside regular hours, in a laboratory set up in his home, synthesized the first aniline dyestuff. This dye, a coal-tar derivative, was the beginning of our huge synthetic dyestuff industry today. Perkin was attempting to synthesize quinine, and although he failed in this, his curiosity led him to experiment with the dark, tarry mass that resulted. When he dipped a piece of white silk in a solution made from the coal-tar product, and it came out a purple color, he immediately recognized the possibilities his find implied. He sent some of the new dye off to a silk factory for confirmation of his opinion, and the first synthetic dye, aniline purple, was born. Perkin also developed the process for mordanting cotton so that such dyes would color cotton. He solved other problems concerning production of the dye and, with family backing, started a small factory that began selling aniline dyes commercially six months after his discovery. This discovery not only served as the starting point for the synthetic dyestuff industry, with its great variety of chemical compounds and colors of all degrees of depth, brilliance, and fastness, but also was the beginning of the many other coal-tar derivatives that are so important today. Sad to relate is the fact that others "cashed in" on his

discovery, and although Perkin received recognition for other important work when some of the discoveries were new, he did not receive the credit due him for synthesizing the first aniline dyestuff until he was an old man.

The first known instance of synthetic dyestuffs offered for sale for home dyeing were those patented in 1863 and advertised in this country in 1864 by Manley Howe and Henry R. Stevens of Boston. The bulk of synthetic dyestuffs today are not aniline dyes; these were but stepping stones to even better dyes.

There are now available a number of different classes of dyestuffs, none of which is equally effective in dyeing all fibers. Some dyes work especially well for protein fibers, others for cellulosics, some for certain of the thermoplastic fibers, and still others for a specific fiber in a group. The dyer, to be successful, must have great knowledge of fibers and dyestuffs and must be an excellent color matcher, as almost everything he dyes must match a color sample submitted in fabric, metal, leather, or perhaps on a color card. Most fabric colors are obtained by mixing proportions of various dyestuffs and colors, rather than by using one color in one dyestuff only. With the thousands of dyes and colors available, the dyer must choose those that are likely to give the same result, possibly when viewed under several light sources, and with as economical a use of dyes as possible, for dyestuffs are expensive.

The classes of dyestuffs, in addition to natural dyes already discussed, include acid dyes, basic dyes, sulfur colors, vat dyes, azoic or naphthol colors, mineral dyes, premetallized colors, acetate dyes, azo dyes, analine dyes, and the newest class, fiber reactive dyes. The latter dyes are reactive with cellulosic fibers, forming a chemical union with the fiber itself and, therefore, are very fast. Fastness is due not only to the class of dye, however, but also to other factors. Descriptions of the dye classes are largely meaningless except to dyers and chemists, but how they work is of general interest. No matter what the dye or method, the final step is "fixing" the dye or "setting" it. This is usually done by means of steam heat which may contain an acid or other chemical, but it may be by dry heat or by infrared light.

Dyes may be grouped as direct, developed, or mordant, and as pigment colors. Any one dyestuff, theoretically, could work one way on one fiber but differently on a chemically different fiber. *Direct* dyes are those that will dissolve in the dyebath and be taken up directly from the dyebath by the fiber. *Developed* dyes are those that are taken up from the dyebath, but the final color does not appear until further treatment of some sort, perhaps exposure to acid steam or some other chemical treatment. *Mordant* colors, not extensively used any more, are those that have no affinity for the fiber but have an affinity for another substance, usually a metal with

which the fiber will also combine. By adding such a metallic compound to the dyebath, both dye and metal are fixed on the fiber. *Pigment* padding presents a different problem. Pigments are very finely milled colored powders. They are diluted (dispersed) with various compounds (emulsions) to form pastes of the desired color and contain an adhesive to bind them to the fabric. Any pigment, theoretically, can be used as a dyestuff for any fiber; the problem is to find the adhesive with an affinity for the particular fiber that will be permanent enough for the end-use intended.

Dyeing, as so many other processes, has undergone many changes in recent years. In addition to new fibers that challenge the dyer, blends and mixtures of fibers in fabrics, and new finishes, there are new classes of dyes, new dyes within classes, new processes for dyeing, new equipment, and modifications of old processes and equipment. The thermoplastic fibers, in particular, have led to new dye procedures using high temperatures and pressures. Much dyeing is now carried on by continuous methods.

Dyestuffs may be added to the spinning solution of man-made fibers before they go through the spinnerets as solution or dope dyeing, or dyeing may be done in fiber (stock), yarn, or fabric stage.

Fiber or *stock* dyeing is more difficult to handle and more expensive than other methods, but results are likely to be quite uniform. *Yarn dyeing* in skeins or cakes presents more of a problem in uniform dyeing because the dye solution must penetrate through to the yarns in the inmost sections. Fiber or yarn dyeing must be done for fabrics that are to be woven in color, such as gingham or chambray, or as most brocades. *Fabric* or *piece* dyeing is easiest and most economical and offers a choice of dyeing in a liquid dyebath, or of applying pigment pastes as the fabric is passed between color-padding rollers. In *dope* dyeing the color is fixed throughout the fiber, in a liquid dyebath the color penetrates to some degree within the fiber, and in *pigment* dyeing the color is attached to the fabric surface.

Fabrics made up of different fibers may have two or more different dyes added to the same dyebath, with one fiber picking up one color and the other fiber another color. This is known as *cross-dyeing*. Colors are not all dyed for the same type of degree of fastness, and they vary in fastness among dyes in a class as well as among classes.

Color-destroying agencies include sunlight, either direct or indirect, weathering, laundering procedures and aids, gas and industrial fumes, abrasion wear, perspiration, drycleaning solvents, and sometimes ozone or oxygen from the air (see Figure 12-1). Colors tend to be less fast with fabrics having resin finishes than with similar fabrics without such finishes. Color change may be due to fading, darkening, change of hue, crocking,

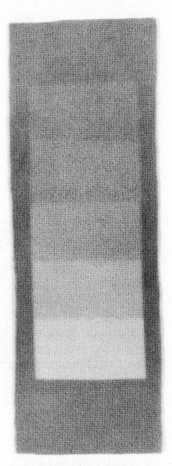

FIGURE 12-1. Fabric that exhibited unsatisfactory colorfastness when exposed to light in a Fade-Ometer. Progressive fading occurred with increasing hours exposure from 20 to 40, 80, 160, and 320 hours. Darker margin around the outside of the exposed area shows the original depth of color.

or bleeding. What do these terms mean? *Colorfastness* is usually defined to mean resistance to any type of color change.

Degradation or destruction of color is sometimes accompanied by degradation of fiber or fabric as well. Figure 12-2 includes photographs of three fabrics in which the fabric disappeared along with certain colors.

The *American Cotton Handbook* (second edition, p. 647) says, in relation to colorfastness, "The question of fastness is, to a large extent, a

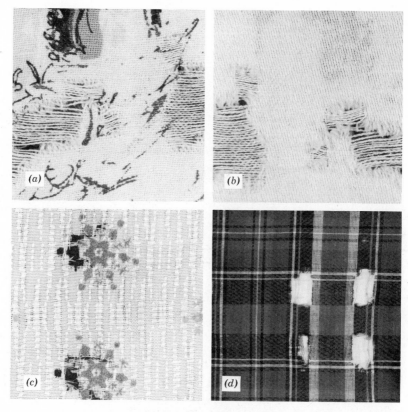

FIGURE 12-2. Fabric degradation: (*a*) right side, and (*b*) wrong side of drapery fabric in which warp yarns dyed in certain colors disappeared along with the color with light exposure at window; (*c*) window curtain in which a metallic print disappeared, taking the fabric with it; (*d*) deterioration of fabric with wear and washing in area dyed black—probably a sulfur dye.

relative matter. If the color on a textile material will resist the destructive agencies to which that material would normally be exposed during its useful life, it is for all practical purposes considered fast."

DESIGN

Design shares with color aesthetic appeal, variety, novelty, symbolism, and means to personal expression. As color often gives meaning to design, so design often gives meaning to color.

Design, as applied to textile fabrics, has a slightly different meaning

than that usually assigned to the term. In this field, design is pattern or figure that is repeated at regular intervals and is understood to refer to patterned fabric. Thus a rose stenciled on the left upper portion of a dress bodice, although it is a design on the fabric of that particular part of a garment, would not fit our definition of textile design.

Design is achieved on fabric in either or both of two ways: (1) by arranging or manipulating the yarns in fabric construction so that a design is formed; or (2) by applying a design to the fabric surface after the fabric has been constructed. The two types of design will be hereinafter designated as *structural* and *applied*.

An exception to the definition for applied design, but one that fits the description in all ways except the time of application, is that known as "warp print." In making warp prints, the design is printed on the warp before weaving, but until the yarns are woven, of course, there is no fabric. This type of design, however, fits into the second classification because it is applied to the surface and is not involved in the construction process and will not affect serviceability of the fabric any differently than other printed-on designs. You will often find warp print listed with the structural design processes in other books.

Often several methods of obtaining design are combined in a single fabric. You may be able to identify a number of design methods by looking around and seeing what other people are wearing. You probably have examples of a number of types of design in your own wardrobe. How can you distinguish between structural and applied design in fabrics?

Structural Design

Structural design, since it is produced by arranging or manipulating yarns for or during construction of the fabric, should be as durable as the fabric itself. Such design may, on occasion, itself limit the durability of the fabric. Structural design is more limited in its possibilities than applied design because of the limitations imposed by looms, knitting, and lace machines, and the methods by which the yarn may be handled by these machines or in conjunction with them. Removal of design yarns in a few instances might not destroy the fabric but would destroy the pattern and with it the original fabric designation. For example, it is conceivable that someone might, one by one, pull out all the extra design yarns in a clipped-knot dotted swiss. The resulting plain fabric would no longer be dotted swiss. Or one might pull all the pile yarns from corduroy, destroying its design and, with it, the fabric characteristics that make it corduroy. Durability of the remaining fabric would undoubtedly be affected by the removal of these yarns.

There are a few general types of structural design, under each of which

may be grouped several different ways of attaining that type of design. These are design produced by the use of different colored yarns, by different types of yarns, by yarns having different treatments, by grouping or spacing of yarns, or by the method of interlacing the yarns. Any one of these methods may be used alone, or they may be used together in any possible combination, or all may be used together in a single fabric.

DIFFERENT COLORED YARNS

Different colored yarns, usually in plain or twill weaves, may be arranged so that patterns such as checks, stripes, or plaids are formed. Examples are checked and plaid gingham, striped chambray, striped denim, color-striped seersucker, pin-striped flannel, etc.

DIFFERENT TYPES OF YARNS

Different types of yarns, usually in plain weave, may be used to form a pattern such as a check, stripe, plaid, or such design. The pattern may be developed by using heavier yarns than for the rest of the fabric, by complex textured yarns, chenille yarns, metallic yarns, yarns of different fiber and appearance, yarns of different degree of luster, with different amounts of twist or of differing structure, such as yarns that are a blend of different colors with simple yarns. Metallic striped or checked ginghams are examples of this type of design, and you can undoubtedly think of many more.

DIFFERENT TREATMENTS

Yarns with different treatments such as caustic-soda permanent shrinkage or treatment to affect dye affinity, or yarns with different shrinkage potential may be combined in pattern with regular yarns. Dyeing, washing, or steaming and relaxation of tension then develop the design. The alternating crinkled and smooth stripes of one type of seersucker are obtained by the first method, and the three-dimensional fabric Trilok by the last one mentioned.

SPACING OR GROUPING

Spacing or grouping of yarns may form a pattern. Examples of this are the grouping of yarns to form a stripe in dimity, grouping of yarns to form heavy ribs in bengaline, spacing of yarns to make the open cloth of Ephrata cloth and lace-stripe voile.

INTERLACING THE YARNS

The method of interlacing the yarns in weaving and knitting may produce design. Lacemaking always produces design; that is a primary

purpose of this method of construction. Figure weaves and figure knits also have production of a design as a primary purpose in their construction. Elaborate brocades and tapestries typify figure weave to many people, but there are many other possibilities not so readily apparent. For example, a one-toned satin-stripe fabric, such as is often used for men's dressing gowns, is made with a stripe of satin weave alternating with a stripe of plain weave—figure weave as truly as the more elaborate Jacquard designs. Corresponding knitted fabrics also fall in this class. Other weaves in themselves, except for satin, all-over pile, and perhaps double weave, may produce design if the yarns or groups of yarns are coarse or heavy enough to form a pattern on the surface of the cloth that is plainly visible to the unaided eye. Such plain weave forms a checkerboard pattern, and twill weave forms diagonal stripes on the face of the cloth. It becomes a problem when to consider that such interlacing is design and when to ignore it. Probably these weaves and leno should not in themselves be considered as forming a design, unless the interlacing pattern is so visible and prominent that it affects the style of garment or other item for which a fabric is suited, or if it affects the amount and type of decoration that would be added to the garment compared with a similar fabric with less prominent weave pattern.

Applied Design

Applied design, since it is a surface treatment, may or may not be as lasting as the fabric to which it is applied. Many factors enter into its durability, such as how it is applied and how well affixed, what medium is used for attaining the design, what type of wearing action it is exposed to, and durability to various cleaning methods. Printed design is by far the most important design method in this classification.

In all types of applied design, for satisfactory results it is essential to have the warp and filling held at the correct right angles to each other, and to have the designs applied in line with both warp and filling yarns.

PRINTING

Printing is well defined by H. A. Webb (*American Dyestuff Reporter*, November 29, 1948, p. 791), who said, "In printing, the dyestuff is applied in a definite pattern to the cloth by mechanical means and then by subsequent aftertreatment a fixing action of the dye takes place in the desired outline or pattern."

Printing is of several types—roller, screen, hand block, photographic, stencil, caustic soda, paste, flock, lacquer, batik—although all are not used in the same way or accomplished by the same processes. Since roller print-

ing is used more than all other processes together, we shall examine it rather closely.

ROLLER PRINTING. The first step after the design is chosen, and one that requires very careful precision work, is the preparation of the engraved copper cylinders, each somewhat longer than the width of the cloth to be printed and usually 15 inches in circumference. A separate roller must be prepared for each different color in the design except when one color can be printed over another to give the desired final color effect, as yellow over blue for green rather than a separate roller for green. How much overprinting can be done depends on the type of coloring matter used, its opacity, etc. The background color may be printed as well as the design itself.

The rollers must be tooled and polished to exactly the same dimensions to make the various parts of the design fit. A drawing of the design is used that has been made to the exact scale of the roller or a multiple of its circumference, and the entire circumference of the roller and its width must be engraved with repeats that are spaced exactly the same with no gaps and no overlaps in either direction. The copper rollers may be engraved by hand or they may be coated with an acid-resistant substance, have the design cut through this coat, then be etched to the desired depth in acid. There are several methods for transferring the design to the roller. Various shades of the same color can be printed by one roller, if it is correctly made. The *American Cotton Handbook* (second edition, p. 660) describes the preparation as follows:

In each case the engraving is cut into the copper shell. Lines are obtained by cutting a groove in the copper; solid objects are engraved by outlining the object and then filling in the space with a series of line grooves or a system of sunken dots, or *stipples*. The number of lines per inch varies with the depth of shade desired. A small number of coarse lines require deeper grooves and give a heavier print, whereas a shallower system of fine lines takes up less color paste and gives a light shade. The stippling is used generally for light shades also. Thus, it is possible to print different depths of shade from one roller by varying the depth of the engraving.

After engraving, the rollers are sometimes plated lightly with chromium, a much harder metal than copper, to protect the design from wear.

Once prepared, rollers can be used for many different color combinations and for printing hundreds of thousands of yards of fabric. The same set of rollers may even be used by different mills. This large-volume printing makes roller printing a cheaper method of producing design than other printing methods, although the initial cost of printing machines and of preparing the rollers is high.

When all the rollers for a particular pattern have been completed, they are assembled in place around a cylinder on a printing machine. The cylinder is covered with a soft roll of blanket, a back "gray cloth" against which the fabric being printed is carried, and perhaps another protective coating between it and the blanket. The engraved parts of the roller press the cloth firmly against the soft layers covering the cylinder and print the engraved part of the design rather than the flat high part from which the printing paste is scraped by a "doctor" blade before the roller touches the cloth. Figure 12-3 is a cross-sectional sketch of such a machine showing four rollers in place for printing. Printing machines are made to handle up to twenty rollers at one time, but four to six are commonly used. The rollers can be adjusted in any direction against the cylinder so that the

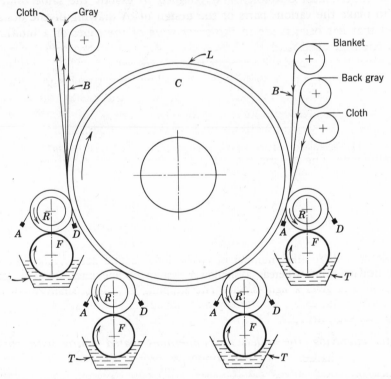

FIGURE 12-3. Cross section of roller printing machine: C, machine roller: R, engraved print roller; T, color box; F, color pad roll: D, doctor blade that scrapes excess color from raised parts of engraved roller before printing: A, doctor blade that scrapes adhering material from engraved roller after printing and before it is supplied with fresh color; B, printing blanket; and L, additional wool padding lap. (Permission *American Handbook of Synthetic Textiles*, Herbert R. Mauersberger and Interscience Publishers.)

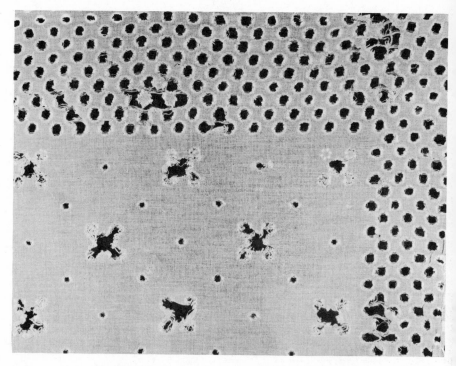

FIGURE 12-4. Handkerchief with discharge-type printed design, after use and laundering.

design of each roller will be printed to fit exactly into the right place in relation to that part printed by the other rollers. The printer must, of course, be an experienced, efficient, and careful worker.

The paste carrying the color must be thick enough, and the means of drying between print rollers efficient enough, that a color printed by one roller will not smear when the cloth is being printed by the subsequent rollers. After the design is printed in all its colors, it must be set by heat, usually steam, with possibly an acid or other chemical added; then the starch or gum that carried the pigment or other dyestuff is washed out.

RESIST PRINTING. Printing may be by direct methods, as just described, by resist, or by discharge methods. In resist printing the design is first printed with a type of dyestuff and paste with which the background color will not react; then when the solid-color "cover" is printed for background, the parts previously printed resist the new color and remain as first printed. This type of printing does not affect durability of the fabric.

DISCHARGE PRINTING. In discharge printing the fabric is first dyed or printed in a solid color; then the design is printed with a paste that contains a bleaching agent effective for the class of dyes used for the plain color, thus removing the color and producing a white design on the colored background. Sometimes a different color not affected by the bleach is printed with it. The bleaching weakens the fabric, and the design often wears through before the background fabric is worn out. Figure 12-4 is an example of this.

DUPLEX PRINTING. Duplex printing is done by identically engraved rollers set up so that one prints the front of the fabric and the other the back to make a print that has no right or wrong side. This method is adaptable to certain small designs, usually in one color, and is sometimes used for shirting fabrics.

BURN-OUT PRINTS. These are made like other discharge prints, except that the chemical used for discharging destroys the fabric, leaving holes for the design. Cheap fabrics that, at a distance, give somewhat the appearance of eyelet embroidery are made by this method. Blended fabrics may be printed with a chemical that will destroy only one fiber, leaving the other as the heavier design on a thinner or transparent background. What would you expect the durability of these fabrics to be? Such a print was photographed for Figure 12-5a. The solid black circles and petals are holes through which the black background is seen. Figure 12-5b is an eyelet embroidered batiste.

CAUSTIC-SODA PRINTS. Caustic-soda prints are made by having a part of or all the design printed with caustic soda, and allowing it to dry without tension, thus shrinking the fabric in those areas. The shrinkage produces pucker in the areas surrounding the caustic-soda-printed areas— a sort of pseudo-embossing. Caustic-soda printing may be done along with color printing of the embossed or other parts of the design.

PHOTOGRAPHIC PRINTS. Photographic prints are made in either of two ways that are quite different. In one method photographs supply the design. Negatives are arranged in the desired order and printed on a glass plate in a size to fit exactly the circumference and width of a regular printing roller. The design is transferred from the glass plate to a carbon tissue that is then pasted in place around the roller as a pattern for the engraver. A complete print and roller must be made for each color as for regular roller printing, and the roller engraved in the same way. Subsequent steps are the same as for regular roller printing.

(a)

Photographic printing is sometimes done by dyeing a cloth with a light-sensitive dye, then using regular negatives for printing the design directly on the fabric. Only one or two colors can be printed on a single fabric, and the process is adaptable to a very limited range of colors in the particular dyestuff used. Both range and depth of color are limited, and it is difficult to obtain matched-color lengths of fabric. Since this process is sometimes used for short lengths of drapery fabric and frequently for designs of large size, to be able to match sufficient yardage for the window treatment of a room may become quite a problem.

FIGURE 12-5. Photographs of (a) burn-out cotton percale print, and (b) eyelet embroidered cotton batiste.

PASTE PRINTS. Paste prints may be made by printing rather bare designs with a white paste or paint instead of color; the paste dries as a raised design and is often remarkably stable. Very short cut fibers, almost a dust, may be applied as *flocking* as the paste leaves the printing rollers,

before it has had a chance to d
stencil roller. Some so-called dott
tell by examining it closely.

STENCILING. Stencils are traditionally made on stencil paper, cardboard, or metal plates with the design cut out. A separate stencil must be prepared for each color, with only the parts to be made in the same color cut out; and if there are continuous lines within lines, or other areas that would fall out of the stencil if cut, a series of stencils to cover different parts of the same lines may be necessary. The flat stencils are applied to fabric fastened flat on padded tables; the same preparation of tables is made for stenciling, block printing, and screen printing. The color is brushed on and covers the cloth in the cutout areas of the stencil, or it may be sprayed on, giving a mottled effect, which can be shaded, if desired.

Engraved stencil rollers may be prepared as for regular printing, except that the acid is allowed to etch clear through the copper shell. Color is then applied from inside the roller, being forced out and onto the fabric through the design holes.

LACQUER PRINTS. Lacquer prints are made by forcing enamel or lacquer through stencil rollers onto the fabric. Since lacquers and enamels cover opaquely, lacquer printing can be done after other types of treatment and design have been applied. Metallic compounds can also be printed in this way.

SCREEN PRINTS. Screen printing makes use of silk fabric similar to flour-bolting cloth, vinyl fabric, or (more recently) fine-meshed metal screening to make a flat screen, which is fastened smoothly and securely to the bottom of a square or rectangular frame, forming a sort of shallow box. The design, in the exact desired size, is transferred to the screen, with a separate screen being prepared for each color. All parts of the design, except the part that is to be made the designated color for the specific screen, are blocked out by coating all the rest of the screen with lacquer or similar opaque material that will not let the color through. As an alternative method, the screen may first be coated all over with the opaque material; then the coating is removed in the desired area by means of a solvent for the particular substance used.

The fabric to be printed is fastened flat on a padded table. Then the first screen is placed on the fabric and moved from one position to the next down the entire length of the table; then the same procedure is followed with the second screen and the next color, etc. The color is squeezed through the screen onto the fabric underneath by means of a roller called

a "squeegee," which is operated by hand by one or two men, depending on screen size and width of the fabric. Evenness of pressure and dyestuff consistent thickness are essential for even-colored designs as the progress from one position to another. Actual printing may no by a machine which places the screens, one after the other, on the in a continuous operation, as the cloth is fed through the machine on a padded platform. Screens have a limited serviceability, depending on the screen material, but they are much cheaper than rollers for a limited yardage in a particular design. Screens are adaptable to larger designs and more brilliant colors than rollers and may be used for special orders of highly personalized designs. Photographic designs are adaptable to screen printing.

BLOCK PRINTS. Block printing, a hand-printing process, is believed to be the oldest method of printing. Designs are carved on the faces of wooden blocks of a size that can be handled readily—a separate block for each color. Fine parts of a design may be made· by inserting metal strips or wires in the face of the block. A number of blocks may be used to form a large design, with a part carved on each block, which then must exactly match. The uncarved raised areas print the colors and the carved-out parts remain uncolored. Great care is required to line up the blocks exactly and to overprint with different colors in exactly the right spots. Dots at the corners of each block facilitate alignment and are a means of identifying a true block print. The cloth is spread out and printed on a padded table.

Block prints are expensive and have limited use for fabrics, but the blocks themselves are practically indestructible. Wood blocks are frequently used for bookplates, illustrations, and note cards as "woodcuts."

BATIK. Batik, for which the Javanese people are particularly well known, is sometimes more a hand-painting than a printing operation. Batik is a resist-type of printing. In one type of batik printing the design is first outlined on the fabric, and then the parts to be left the original cloth color are wax coated. The material is dyed the next color, and wax is applied over the areas to remain that color. This process continues, alternately waxing and dyeing, until the last and darkest color has been dyed. After the final color has been applied, the fabric is put in hot water to remove the wax. Overprinting in this way mutes the colors and gives subdued and often subtle color effects.

In other methods wax is applied before each color, then removed after the color is applied, and reapplied before the next addition of color. In this way, printing of one color over another is avoided except for the lines and cracks that occur in the wax. This results in clearer, more vivid colors

in the design than is achieved by the first method described. Batik-like patterns are often printed today by regular roller printing methods.

OTHER METHODS

EMBOSSING. Embossing is done by means of a copper roller prepared about as the printing rollers except that the entire design is placed on one roller. The raised part of the design presses against the soft backing of the cloth and forms the raised design on the cloth. For thermoplastic-fiber fabrics, the embossing roller is heated to heat-setting range for that particular fabric; then immediate cooling after embossing sets the design and makes it permanent as long as the embossing temperature is not exceeded. Figure 12-6 is an embossed polyester print made in Japan. For nonthermoplastic fabrics, a thermosetting resin is applied and cured during embossing to retain the design. A color may be applied to the engraved portions of the design and thus print the background in color as the embossed design is being made; such designs are usually white on a colored background. Embossing may change the texture and opacity of a fabric.

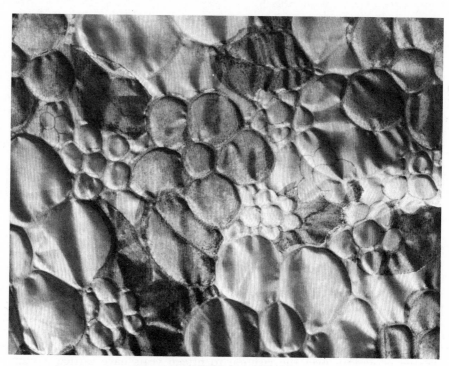

FIGURE 12-6. Embossed polyester print from Japan.

MOIRÉ. Moiré is a "watered" design that is usually made by an embossed roller that has been engraved in the traditional moiré silk patterns, or similar designs. Silk moiré is traditionally obtained by calendering two lengths of fabric of different thread count together. This results in flattening the yarns where they crossed each other, producing the watered effect.

EMBROIDERY. Embroidery design is made by applying floss or yarns, according to a pattern, to a fabric background; this is accomplished by means of needles. Embroidery, like lace, may be any width from narrow trimming to all-over embroidered full-width fabric for dresses, curtains, and other uses. Organdy, batiste, pique, and nylon sheer are popular background fabrics for embroidery. Eyelet embroidery has design holes which have been completely encircled with embroidery stitching that reinforces and covers the cut edges, thus forming open-work design as strong or stronger than the original background fabric. Most embroidery today is machine made; the machines were mentioned in the section on lace-making in Chapter 10.

APPLIQUÉ. In appliqué, designs cut from fabric or lace are applied, by means of hand- or machine-stitching around the design edge, to a background fabric. One type of lace is made by applying lace patterns to a net background; otherwise appliqué is not much used for fabric.

QUILTING. Quilting is hand- or machine-stitched design developed for holding together multiple layers of material. The layers consist of the face fabric, a backing fabric, and a padding layer, usually of cotton batting, between. The layered fabric forms puffy areas between the stitching rows of the design, emphasizing the pattern.

TIE AND DYE. Tie and dye is a design obtained by hand-tying areas of fabric, and perhaps winding them with string, so that the dye cannot fully penetrate them. The tied areas are released after dyeing is complete, forming the design. A variety of shapes and sizes is possible, all more or less circular in outline. The Japanese are adept at making very lovely and intricate tie-and-dye designs on their sashes (obis).

HAND PAINTING. Hand painting may be used for fabric design but is ordinarily used only to decorate small, individual items such as neckties.

This discussion has only introduced you to these fascinating procedures. Textile periodicals over the last ten to fifteen years have carried a number of interesting articles on some of these subjects which you may wish

to investigate. One series of such articles and some of the books are given in the following list.

FOR FURTHER READING

American Dyestuff Reporter.
Ciba Review.
Color Engineering.
Edelstein, S. M.: Historical Notes Series; *American Dyestuff Reporter,* Vols. 42–49.
Judd, D. B.: *Color in Business, Science, and Industry.*
Kaswell, E. R.: *Wellington Sears Handbook of Industrial Textiles.*
Linton, G. E.: *Applied Basic Textiles.*
Mauersberger, H. R.: *American Handbook of Synthetic Textiles.*
Merrill, G. R., A. R. Macormac, and H. R. Mauersberger: *American Cotton Handbook.*

DURABLE-PRESS, WASH-WEAR, AND MINIMUM-CARE FABRICS AND APPAREL

Fabrics and apparel that required, and probably received, a minimum amount of care originated in the animal pelts worn by the cave dwellers. Ever since, there have been fabrics that have received a minimum amount of care in terms of washing and dry cleaning by modern standards. Today we have, compared with former eras, much higher standards of cleanliness than many earlier ages could afford to have, and we are perhaps more careless in avoiding soil, stains, and wrinkles so that more care is needed. Certainly, wool and silk have always required a minimum of care.

Minimum-care washable fabrics and garments, as understood today, originated with knitted fabrics for undergarments. The celluloid collar invented soon after the turn of this century was surely a minimum-care item compared with the stiffly starched, detachable collars of the shirts of that time. Fabrics such as plissé and seersucker were designed specifically for easy care. Other fabrics such as corduroy, denim, and sateen have not required much care. With the introduction of nylon tricot in its many and varied uses, the modern minimum-care movement was really launched.

C'reas kisis. Durable Press
Drip Dry
Wash + Wear
Durable Press

Durable or permanent press is the logical outcome of developments that began with the application of resins to cellulosic fibers to produce the first crease resistant fabrics in 1929. Handwash–drip dry items were next; then this progressed to wash-wear fabrics and garments, and finally, in 1964, to the first durable press garments. The ultimate, insofar as the consumer is concerned, may well be a truly permanent-press–soil-release fabric. This should be a reality in the very near future. Each advance has been welcomed by consumers who have considered the advantages to far outweigh the disadvantages. We shall be interested in both the advantages and disadvantages and the kind of care that will insure making best use of the advantages.

Crease-resistant as well as durable-press fabrics are of value today as they serve different needs; varying needs are likely to continue. Fabrics intended for garments or interior furnishing end-uses that are expected to be dry-cleaned rather than washed often need no finish, and if finished, a crease resistant process is ordinarily all that is necessary. Such a finish may function in dimensional control as well. Crease resistance and wrinkle recovery are covered briefly in Chapter 11, p. 347.

Wash-wear, as the way station to attainment of durable press, perhaps will soon be a synonymous term for durable press. Today we still have a great many items and fabrics, much apparel, and many textile furnishing items on the market that qualify as wash-wear as defined in the DuPont *Technical Bulletin X-83*, "Test Methods to Determine Wash and Wear Properties," which says:

Wash and wear garments are those that will satisfactorily retain their original neat appearance after repeated wear and laundering with little if any touch-up ironing. This means that the garment will retain any pressed in creases or pleats and be essentially free from undesirable wrinkles both during wear and after laundering. In addition the garments will meet normal consumer demands for such properties as durability, color stability, and shrinkage.

Although this definition was written for apparel, it is equally applicable to other wash-wear items, whatever their end-uses.

The level of performance that will be accepted as satisfactory varies widely among individuals and for the end-use to which fabrics are applied. Outerwear that is seen by other people and that affects personal appearance usually demands a higher standard of performance than undergarments, lingerie, and sleepwear. An individual may demand much more rigid standards of performance in clothes for business or dress than for sports, travel, or other recreation. Some individuals demand the highest standards of appearance for all clothing and furnishings, and others are satisfied with a low standard for everything. Evaluation of a satisfactory

performance level must, in the end, meet the subjective standards of many consumers.

Much washable clothing, particularly that of women, girls, and children, many curtains, draperies, slipcover fabrics, bedspreads, and table napery are of this type. Many satisfactory wash-wear fabrics are 100 percent cotton although polyester/cotton blends account for the largest share of these fabrics.

C. M. Lee in the *American Dyestuff Reporter* for January 17, 1966 (p. 39) has given a good definition of durable press as

. . . the ability of a garment to keep its shape-retaining properties throughout its life. This means sharp creases, flat seams, and smooth appearance of the fabric after wearing, washing, and drying. In addition, the wear life of the durable press garment must be equal to or better than that of the garment it replaces. The wear life is necessary to have long-lasting acceptance and consumer satisfaction. . . .

The difference between wash-wear and durable press is explained by E. N. Alexander in *American Dyestuff Reporter* for August 1, 1966 (p. 28) as follows:

The appearance on the market of hundreds of millions of yards of polyester/cotton blended fabrics of outstanding durable press quality gave the impression of an entirely new type of resin technology. This is not the case because the entire difference between standard wash-and-wear and permanent press lies merely in the sequence of operations, a sequence that consists of deferring the cure until the fabrics have been sewed into garments and pressed. In this manner the crease is sealed into the position given by pressing, because the chemical fixation or polymerizing of the resin or cross linking agent occurs on the cellulosic portion of the blended fabric.

Since this explanation was made, variations of method have developed which we shall examine briefly. For those who may wish to study this subject further, the textile periodicals, beginning with 1965, cover the subject in considerable depth.

FIBERS USED

Although the first durable-press garments were made entirely of cotton, this fiber has not as yet been completely successful because of low resistance to abrasion and loss of tearing strength, breaking strength, and extensibility in the finishing process. All-polyester fabrics can be successfully heat-set for permanent-press apparel and fabrics and it is possible to use other thermoplastic fibers in this way. The thermoplastic fibers, however, are

not as absorbent and thus not as comfortable for the type of apparel for which durable-press fabrics are especially desirable; therefore, blends of cellulosic and thermoplastic fibers are most popular. Polyester/cotton blends are far more widely used than any other combination. Other fiber blends used for durable-press fabrics or apparel are: wool/nylon, wool/polyester, polyester/high-wet-modulus rayon, polyester/acrylic, acrylic/rayon, cotton/nylon, Arnel/cotton, and perhaps others. The polyester combinations tend to be the most satisfactory where creases or pleats are used, but other combinations may be as satisfactory where creases and pleats are not involved.

PROCESSES

The first durable-press garments, introduced in fall 1964, were women's slacks and skirts that were permanently creased or pleated by an apparel manufacturer, Koret of California. The finishing process developed by Koret was a delayed-cure process, now known nationally as the Koratron process, which covers fabrics sold under a number of trade names as licensed by the parent company. From this beginning, several durable-press processes have developed, including a precure-flat process, the Koratron delayed cure, a fiber modification process, a double-cure process, a high temperature-high pressure process that starts with a precured fabric, and a garment-treatment process. Trade names have been granted to different mills under each of these processes and some mills carry on more than one process. The differences with which we shall primarily be concerned are these: whether the fabric is precured, delayed-cured, or treatment is applied after the garment is constructed. Other differences are largely the different chemicals used and curing methods and temperatures.

The precure-flat process is used for fabrics that are treated and cured in the flat state, stay smooth in wear or use, and return to this smooth flat state after laundering. Fabrics for many garments, particularly for women's dresses and blouses, for the great numbers of permanent-pressed sheets on the market, for many curtain and drapery fabrics, as examples, are finished by this process. It is difficult if not impossible to put creases or pleats in such fabrics except as such creases or pleats are edge-stitched to hold the creases firmly in place, and it may be difficult to keep seams and hems flat. Most of these fabrics are polyester/cotton, usually in a 65/35 percentage blend. Some of the same problems may arise as with any wash-wear items, that is, puckered seams because of stitching tension, needle size, stitch length, or thread shrinkage; and the necessity to preshrink zipper tapes and other fabrics or materials to be used with the precured fabrics.

In the delayed-cure process, the fabric is resin treated at the finishing plant; the resin is not cured but stabilized enough in some manner to hold through shipping, storage, and garment making, and to avoid too high a concentration of formaldehyde or other irritating chemicals in the apparel manufacturing plants. The garments are then cut, assembled, sewn, and pressed very carefully to place creases and pleats in exactly the correct position, carefully clamped to a rack or hanger to hold the folds in correct positions, then given the final cure in a short trip through a high temperature oven especially constructed for the purpose. Some garment manufacturers carry on the final cure in a high temperature-high pressure pressing operation of short duration, or curing may be by intense irradiation. The cellulose component cross-links in this curing stage.

double-cured

The double-cure process differs from the delayed-cure in that the cellulosic fiber of the blend is at least partially cross-linked in the preliminary cure, and often is fully cross-linked at that time, so that the final cure at a higher temperature recures the cellulose and heat-sets the polyester component.

garment treatment

In the garment-treatment process, the fabric may have little or no finishing treatment before the garments are cut and sewn, that is, they go through apparel manufacturing processes as do any other untreated garments. Then the resin is applied in a bath and the garment is pressed and cured as in other permanent-press processes. The advantage of this process is that thread, tapes, pocket linings, and other findings all have the same treatment so there should be no problem of seam puckering, tape shrinkage, and such. This process is not as widely used as the others; it requires a different type of equipment and expertise that is usually not available at present apparel manufacturing plants. Thus, it is more difficult for the garment manufacturer to handle than the other processes.

Successful durable press results from a careful selection of fibers, fiber blends, fabric construction, choice of resins, and careful control of all finishing processes. Judicious choice of fabric for the specific end-use is also very important.

selection of fibers   choice
fiber blend
fabric construction

RESINS USED IN FINISHING

The resins used in several instances belong to the same general classes as for wash-wear fabrics but are not the same compounds; catalysts and some of the other chemicals are newly applied to this type of finishing. The resins used for wash-wear fabrics often are not stable enough for the longer time between application and curing of some of the durable press processes. Some catalysts cause changes in shade, lightfastness is reduced

for some colors, or objectionable odors may become a critical problem. E. N. Alexander, in the article cited early in this chapter, said:

The finisher must be more cautious and more careful in the application of the chemicals used because their final effect will occur later and beyond his control. He must avoid the many difficulties of odor development, premature catalysis, objectionable handle of cloth, excess resin concentration, loss of strength and tear beyond the normal tolerance.

Three types of resins are most widely used; dimethylol dihydroxy ethylene urea, dimethylol propylene urea, and, especially for cottons, a group of resins known as carbamates. Since all-cotton is not much used and there seems to be some question as to toxicity of carbamates, we shall not define them further.

The resin that seems to be generally favored is the dimethylol dihydroxy ethylene urea (DMHEU), a cyclic compound having this chemical structure

$$
\begin{array}{ccc}
 & \overset{\displaystyle O}{\underset{\displaystyle \parallel}{C}} & \\
\text{HOH}_2\text{CN} & & \text{NCH}_2\text{OH} \\
| & & | \\
\text{HC} & & \text{CH} \\
| & & | \\
\text{O} & & \text{O} \\
\text{H} & & \text{H}
\end{array}
$$

DMHEU is highly satisfactory for finishing colored fabrics but has poor resistance to chlorine bleach so it is not as satisfactory for white fabrics. Dimethylol propylene urea (DMPU), however, another cyclic compound with this chemical structure

$$
\begin{array}{ccc}
 & \overset{\displaystyle O}{\underset{\displaystyle \parallel}{C}} & \\
\text{HOH}_2\text{CN} & & \text{NCH}_2\text{OH} \\
\text{H}_2\text{C} & & \text{CH}_2 \\
 & \overset{\displaystyle C}{\underset{\displaystyle H_2}{}} &
\end{array}
$$

has high chlorine stability and is satisfactory for white fabrics.

In addition to the resins for durable-press properties, other resins or chemicals may be added in the same mixture to obtain other properties such as increased flame resistance, abrasion resistance, softer hand, bacteria and mildew resistance, and soil and stain repellence. Soil-release

finishes are getting most attention at present and several very promising durable press—soil-release finishes are on the market under a number of different trade names which either say "soil release" on the label or the names themselves reveal their purpose.

PROBLEMS ASSOCIATED WITH DURABLE-PRESS FINISHES

There are a number of problems associated with production of durable-press fabrics and also problems for the consumers who use them. The problems of producers include those arising in handling by all the people along the way from the person who makes the choice of fabric and finish to the final operation before the item is ready for the consumer. Those of choice of fiber, finish, and procedures are quite obvious. Other problems in addition to those already mentioned arise in handling uncured or partially cured fabrics. They must be rolled smoothly on rollers to avoid wrinkling and not folded or bolted as many fabrics are. They must be shipped and stored with rollers lying flat which may require special devices for holding or storage. They must be kept at a temperature that will not permit the resin to cure until the final curing treatment. The chemicals used must be fixed so that they will be stable through shipment, storage, and garment making, not deteriorating in storage or degrading the fabric, or posing a health or comfort hazard to employees who work with them, or in the mills where such fabrics are handled. Much more care than for other finishing is needed in aligning creases and pleats properly, seeing that seams lie flat and straight or at correct angles (not twisted), and that the curing process is carried on for a sufficient length of time and at sufficient temperature and/or pressure to cure the resins properly but not enough to overcure them, thus causing harshness or degradation of the fabric. Some dyes sublime in curing and disappear, or they may migrate and concentrate in spots. Optical whiteners are not as durable as could be wished. Patterns may have to be altered as compared to their use for other fabrics. Sewing machines must have careful adjustment of tension, needle size, length of stitch, and speed at which the fabric moves through stitching. Thread must be suitable for the fabric, as must linings and other findings. Zipper tapes must be preshrunk. No doubt you can add other problems.

Consumers, of course, are concerned with many of the same problems as producers but from a different viewpoint. Most of these are obvious. Few alterations can be made on permanently pressed garments; they can be taken up but cannot be let out without the marks of the former seams or hems being forever visible. Creases and pleats cannot be changed which

means that hems often cannot be changed. Incorrectly placed creases or pleats, poor seam alignment, or incorrect folding in pressing cannot be corrected. The consumer needs to look for these details before buying. Frosting sometimes occurs with wear; this is due to the cotton in a polyester/cotton blend wearing away with abrasion, thus exposing more of the polyester which, if not as deeply dyed, will look whitish. Other problems may be pilling, picking up of stains—particularly oily stains—which are difficult or impossible to remove. Light colors may pick up soil and it may not all be removed in washing, thus the item will gradually become gray-looking.

SELECTION AND CARE

Some of the problems are avoided, or at least are less apparent, if fabrics with printed or woven or knitted designs are chosen rather than plain colors; medium or dark plain colors may look better over a long period of time than white or light colors. Small or broken, closely spaced all-over designs in prints and plaids seem to be particularly satisfactory fabric patterns. The garment designs with few seams are most likely to retain a smooth appearance unless the finish is applied after the garment is completed.

Fiber content labels required by the Textile Fiber Products Identification Act are a great help in selection of fabrics and garments according to the end-use for which they are intended. This is also true of many of the tradenames and brands for the various finishes as one learns through experience which ones perform satisfactorily or are backed by quality control programs. It is the consensus of responsible groups working with these fabrics that terminology must have the same meaning at all times, that labeling must be honest in terms of performance and care, and that the seller must guarantee the accuracy of the labeling as long as instructions are followed. Such labels should be permanently affixed as a part of the garment or item for care is a continuing problem long after hang tags are lost or lose their identity among many others.

Insofar as polyester/cotton blends are concerned considerable experimentation with varying proportions of each fiber and consumer reaction to durable press garments made of them have pretty well established the most satisfactory levels for a number of end-uses. A 65 percent polyester/35 percent cotton thus far is the most preferred and widely used blend for trousers, shirts, blouses, dresses, and other such garments, although a number of 50 percent polyester/50 percent cottons have given satisfactory per-

formance in both appearance and durability. A blend of 50 percent polyester/50 percent cotton seems to be well on the way to acceptance as a standard percentage for sheets and pillowcases. Some dress and blouse fabrics on the market as yard goods are a smooth-textured 80 percent polyester/20 percent cotton.

Since much of the satisfaction in appearance and service of durable-press and other minimum-care items depends on care as well as wise selection it seems desirable to think through some suggestions for care and the reasons behind them. As in so many things, prevention is better than cure. Anything that avoids putting wrinkles into a fabric or setting them, or that avoids pulling pleats and creases out and distorting them, especially under conditions of high humidity and high temperature, also avoids the necessity for special care. It would seem a good idea to keep such garments on hangers, and flat goods folded even when soiled, rather than to throw them into the family clothes hamper, perhaps with heavy, damp, stained clothing thrown in on top, thus putting in creases that will have to be removed later. Reasonable care to avoid soiling and staining will also help keep garments and other items looking better for a longer period of time, especially if they are to be washed at the low washing temperature (100°F) sometimes advocated. Soils and stains can frequently be removed in laundering only at considerably higher temperatures than this. Some types of stains may require pretreatment before laundering. Pretreatment of heavily soiled or stained areas with detergent pastes, enzymatic products, full strength shampoo, liquid detergent, or with special solvents may eliminate the need for severe laundering.

Classroom experiments with stain and spot removal for a number of commonly occurring stains applied to normally finished, wash-wear, durable-press, and durable-press–soil-release finished fabrics led to some worthwhile observations. All stains were removed from 100 percent polyester fabrics in a single wash at 120°F. Several stains on the durable-press–soil-release fabrics also were removed in the first wash and by five washes nearly all stains were completely removed. However, there was variability among the different types of finishes and fabrics in this respect. Stains tended to be as effectively removed after being left a week as when washed as soon as the stains dried. Dark grease came out completely when pretreated with a colorless fat to remove the dark color, then with solvent to remove the remaining grease or fat.

Wash-wear and durable-press garments and other items today are designed to be washed in an automatic washer and tumble dried. It is frequently recommended that tumbling be continued for a few minutes with no heat at the end of the drying cycle; this would permit cooling of any

fibers softened by the heat. All items should be removed from the drier immediately when tumbling stops, the garments placed on hangers, and flat goods folded smoothly.

Durable-press garments and textile furnishings have certainly gained widespread acceptance by consumers who are willing to sacrifice some wear-life for the advantages gained in improved appearance and ease of care. Durable-press finishes are the final touch that probably will make knitted fabrics suitable for tailored garments such as men's and women's business suits, dress shirts, tailored dresses, and such items.

In summarizing research on all-cotton permanent press fabrics, B. M. Kopacz and R. M. Perkins, in *Textile Chemist and Colorist* for January 29, 1969 (p. 87/29) said:

At present, the innovation in textiles that appeals most to the American consumer is durable press. The product remains smooth and wrinkle free, creases stay in trousers, pleats return in skirts, seams lie flat—all without the chore of ironing or the expense of commercial laundering.

The production of durable press apparel began in 1964 but was limited to slacks, work pants and sport shirts. In 1967, more than a billion yards of polyester-cotton blended fabrics were processed into durable press items, not only apparel but also such household items as bed linens, bedspreads, table-cloths and draperies. It is forecast that the $2.5 billion a year durable press market will soar to $9 billion by 1970.

But all the problems are not yet solved, either for all-cotton products or for blends. In current commercial practice in the U.S., wrinkle resistance in all-cotton products is accompanied by losses in abrasion resistance, strength and extensibility.

It appears that there is no single solution to the production of a superior all-cotton durable press product. Obviously contributions from the various elements of a comprehensive research program are required including suitable modification of the cotton at appropriate stages in the conversion of the fiber to the finished product. These modications should involve mechanical as well as chemical and physical treatments. Although the various contributions may in some cases be minor, the composite should eventually lead to an all-cotton durable press product with qualities desired by consumers.

With the large numbers of people with their varied knowledge, experience, interests, and education working on the development of textile fibers, fabrics, finishes, apparel, and furnishings, and with the vast resources in materials and technology at their command, no doubt many of the remaining problems will soon be solved. But what makes the field so interesting is the fact that there is always something new and different ahead, presenting new problems that beckon for attention and new solutions!

FOR FURTHER READING

American Dyestuff Reporter.
Modern Textiles Magazine.
Textile Chemist and Colorist.

▪▪

MIXTURES AND BLENDED FABRICS

Combinations of fibers in fabrics have been used for many centuries; such fabrics usually had warp yarns made of one type of fiber and filling yarns of another. Reasons for such combinations were probably the ease with which fibers could be made into yarns sturdy enough for weaving (with the strongest yarns used for warp), the supply of fibers available, their refinement, and their capacity to be dyed with local dye materials.

With the wide variety of different type fibers that we have today, the trend toward combining two or more fibers in one fabric is growing rapidly and demands increasing attention from textile engineers, designers, and consumers. The problems of mixing and blending are being approached more and more scientifically.

Mixtures and blends are terms generally used to describe combinations of fibers in fabrics. Sometimes the terms are used interchangeably, but more often their meanings are different; we shall follow the latter practice. By our definition, *mixture* fabrics are those made up of two or more different kinds of yarns, each of which is composed of only one kind of fiber or of different fiber yarns plyed together; the yarns may be composed of filament or staple length fibers. *Blended* fabrics are made up of yarns in

which two or more different kinds of fibers are spun together; staple length fibers are used to make such yarns.

With these two types of yarns, one composed of only one type of fiber and the other spun of two or more, many possibilities of combining the yarns in different ways in fabric construction are possible. Blended yarns are most frequently used in both warp and filling directions in production of blended fabrics. One-fiber yarns are most often used, as for past centuries, with one type for warp and the other for filling, but the one-fiber yarns of different types are sometimes used alternately, or in other regular arrangement, in both warp and filling directions. It is possible to combine blended yarns and one-fiber yarns in the same fabric in a number of different ways. What possibilities for combining them can you envision?

REASONS FOR MIXING AND BLENDING

For many years the reasons for producing mixed or blended fabrics were to reduce cost, or to obtain a different appearance. Although they are still important, there are additional reasons for mixing and blending today, many of them related to the very different properties of the thermoplastic and nonthermoplastic man-made fibers which often complement each other, as do some of the natural and man-made fibers. There are also blends of thermoplastic with thermoplastic, cellulosic with cellulosic, and many other combinations and possibilities. Some of the properties obtained by blending are not obtainable in any other way.

Some of the reasons for mixing and blending today are: to obtain a greater number of the desirable characteristics than can be gained by using one fiber alone, such as increased washability, absorbency, comfort, and light fastness; improved resistance to hole melting and abrasion; quicker drying; improved wrinkle resistance, strength, elasticity, resiliency, dimensional stability, tear strength, fabric liveliness, transpiration of perspiration, eye appeal, texture, drape, and softness; reduced tendency to pilling, mildew, bacterial growth, and static electricity accumulation; for easier care such as durable-press, wash-wear garments with automatic washability, and dryer dryability; for better-appearing, tougher work clothing which is more durable, more acid-resistant, and can withstand the careless wear given to rental clothing and the rigors of commercial laundering; to permit application of special finishes; to create a mixture of colors or other design and color possibilities through cross-dyeing procedures; to enable permanent pleating, embossing, printing, or other special effects; to attain the body and hand desired; to permit utilization of different classes of fibers within a type, such as new, reused, and reprocessed wool; to com-

bine limited stock in order to avoid mill waste; and to improve functional properties within a price range that consumers can and are willing to pay.

The effects of blending and mixing fibers and yarns in fabrics are implied in the reasons for which such combinations are produced. The noticeable effects may be in appearance, utility, price, and fabric behavior, or primarily in the care required.

To attain these effects, the nonthermoplastic fibers, especially the cellulosic fibers, are often included in the mixtures or blends to give increased absorbency and comfort, decreased static electricity accumulation, hole melting and pilling, increased washability, and increased affinity for dyestuffs and chemicals used in finishing. Thermoplastic fibers are often used to improve crease resistance, dimensional stability, shape retention, abrasion resistance, strength, elongation, drying time, and to reduce the necessity or difficulty of ironing and permit permanent heat-setting, pleating, etc. Rayon and cotton in blends, for example, are often used to keep costs low and to increase absorbency and washability; the acrylics to improve softness and warmth with light weight; nylon to improve toughness and abrasion resistance; polyester fibers to improve wrinkle resistance and dimensional stability; and acetate to improve wrinkle resistance, drape, and texture.

PROBLEMS WITH MIXTURES AND BLENDS

There are many problems in producing a satisfactorily functional or appealing blend and, perhaps to a lesser extent, mixture. Which fibers to combine is a first problem, but then what proportion of each should be used is equally a problem, and optimum proportions for various end-uses vary widely with the fibers used. Some of the requirements and procedures for blending fibers are discussed in Chapter 9 on yarns and yarn processes. The effect is seldom an average of the properties of the two fibers—too many properties have a variable effect on each other, such as elasticity and strength. For example, it might be expected that a small amount of nylon added to cotton would increase its strength, but strength may be reduced because the greater elasticity of nylon will allow it to stretch when load is applied so that the load all falls on the less-elastic cotton, which is present in a smaller amount than it would be in a similar size all-cotton yarn. Conversely, sometimes certain properties are improved beyond the most optimistic expectations, or a different and unexpected effect may be obtained. Some pairs of fibers are much more compatible than others. This whole area needs much experimentation and research with all fibers in varying proportions and combinations in blends and mixtures in order to

build up a body of knowledge of how combinations perform and why. Such knowledge, however, can never be static because the fibers themselves, the processing, and the finishing are constantly changing.

It is difficult to obtain a uniform blend of fibers in a yarn because of differences in specific gravity, length, diameter, surface shape and texture, and hygroscopicity of fibers. There will always be some variation along the length of a blended yarn from one spot to another, and also in composition from inside to outside. It has been learned that longer fibers tend to travel toward the center and shorter fibers toward the outside of yarns. This fact may sometimes be used to advantage in attaining a desired result but more often it is not desirable. Some fibers may cut others, especially if one is tough and one soft, or if one is much heavier than the other. Blends and mixtures present special problems in dyeing and finishing and may require changes in conventional equipment and handling procedures. Too much special handling could well make the price prohibitive as far as competition with other fabrics for similar end-uses are concerned.

In mixing and blending, as in other types of yarns and fabrics, improvements in one set of properties must often be made at the cost of other desirable properties, so it becomes important both to produce and to select on the basis of the end-use for which the particular set of properties is best suited. Too often the right choice seems to be left entirely to the consumer, with very little information furnished her for guidance in selecting the combinations that suit her particular need.

Just as blends and mixtures have presented yarn and fabric producers, dyers, and converters with new problems, so has their optimum care often posed a problem to the consumer. With the Textile Fiber Products Identification Act in force, the consumer is able to know what is in a combination so that she can at least profit by her experience with known fiber combinations. Many labels carry specific instructions for care that have been found satisfactory for the type of fabric to which they are attached. But satisfactory care for one type of fabric is not necessarily equally satisfactory for other fabrics that are made in different proportions of the same fibers, or for other combinations of fibers. There can be no general procedure for care of all blended or mixture fabrics; care of each is dependent on the particular fibers included and on finishes that may have been applied. A safe procedure to start with is usually the kind of care required by the most sensitive fiber in the combination. A thorough knowledge of the properties of the major groups of fibers is invaluable in arriving at care procedures that will enhance and not harm or destroy the desirable properties of such fabrics.

Some of the oldest blends were cotton-wool, wool-linen, silk-cotton, and linen-cotton. Among blends available in fabrics, apparel, and furnishings

today are polyester-cotton, rayon-cotton, acrylic-cotton, cotton-nylon, triacetate-cotton, rayon-acetate, polyester-wool, acrylic-wool, wool-nylon, polyester-acrylic-modacrylic, polynosic-acrylic, wool-silk, wool-rayon, and many others. What would you expect each partner in these pairs to contribute to the finished product, and for what end-uses would it be desirable? With which combinations have you had experience? What was your reaction?

Three-fiber blends are on the increase too and may become more important than two-fiber blends eventually. Three-fiber blends may produce both a greater number of desired properties in a single fabric and more problems.

Combinations of fibers in a single fabric have made available fabrics different in appearance, texture, and drape from one-fiber fabrics and have thus given us wider aesthetic choice than we would otherwise have. Increased utility has often been combined with increased choice. By careful selection today's consumer can obtain any of a number of types of fibers in the apparel, fabrics, and furnishings to suit the particular requirements of her own situation. Price may be less than before if combinations have replaced a more expensive fiber, or price may be higher if desirable qualities have been attained with a more expensive fiber. Today, as it has ever been, the prestige value of a certain fiber or item will be more important than economic considerations to some consumers (all the time), and, upon occasion, to all consumers.

Blends and mixtures are found in all types of end-use—for undergarments, lingerie, sweaters, dresses, shirts, slacks, skirts, uniforms, suits for both men and women, coats, upholstery and drapery fabrics, rugs, blankets, work clothing, socks, simulated fur fabrics, nightwear, rainwear, sportswear, children's wear, and in many items of practically every kind. Such fabrics can be expected to continue to increase in both number and variety for all types of fabric end-uses.

FOR FURTHER READING

American Dyestuff Reporter.
Consumer Reports.
Modern Textiles Magazine.
Textile Chemist and Colorist.

STRETCH FABRICS AND APPAREL

Stretch in apparel is an old concept but today it is being achieved in new ways. A measure of stretch or "give" is essential in any body-conforming garment to permit ease for body movement and for comfort. Freedom of movement has been provided for traditionally through knitted fabrics—the loop structure being very flexible—or through woven fabrics, which are cut into shaped pieces and put together with seams at contour lines of the body, or have darts, pleats, folds, or gathers for motion and ease. *Stretch* now means a type of structure, whether garment, slipcover, or automobile headliner that conforms to the shape of the object to which it is closely fitted, and which, in the case of moving objects, assumes the different positions of that object in motion, whether the human body or the cover of a cushion as it is compressed and relaxed during use.

Stretch, as we are concerned with it, will be confined to two types of fabrics designed for different purposes, although there may be overlap at times. One type is elastomeric stretch, the other nonelastomeric stretch.

ELASTOMERIC STRETCH

Elastomeric stretch is elongation achieved by means of rubber and spandex fibers, yarns, and fabrics. They were probably a direct result of the develop-

ment of the automobile early in this century. The discovery that raw rubber could be made useful for tires by vulcanization was not only important in the development of the automobile but also for many other uses, including stretchable apparel and accessories. Rubber, spandex, and the newly-announced anidex fibers are discussed in Chapter 7.

Elastomeric stretch is characterized by potentially high elongation at break of 500 to 800 percent and high elasticity that results in an immediate and high degree of recovery when tension is released. Such fabrics are found primarily in foundation and other types of support garments including surgical garments, and narrow fabrics such as elastics of various types. Some swimwear utilizes elastomeric stretch fabrics.

Covered natural rubber yarns were the first elastomeric yarns to be successfully woven or knitted into garment form. Within a few years after their introduction, foundation garments of these fabrics had replaced a large proportion of the firm-fabric, boned, laced and/or hooked corsets, which were the foundation garments of the day. Natural rubber yarns were first made in a thin sheet form, then cut into narrow strips similar to thin rubber bands and covered by winding the rubber core with yarns of other "hard" fibers such as cotton, acetate, or rayon. Since 1925, rubber has been extruded as a round fiber or yarn core of varying fineness which, when cured, is ready for sheathing with any of a number of different types of fibers, including nylon. Rubber is heat sensitive, cannot be dried in a dryer, and its dark color sometimes shows through the covering sheath when stretched.

With the general availability of spandex fibers since 1961, the use of elastomeric fibers and fabrics has been greatly expanded, both in the foundation garment field and in many other uses. Because spandex is durable, dyeable in colors to match other lingerie, light in weight, and can be machine washed and dryer dried, it has taken over much of the elastomeric fabric field. Spandex yarns may be used covered or bare.

The degree of figure control or "power" and the degree of stretch of elastomeric fabrics depend on the type of fiber used for the covering sheath, how closely together the coils are wound, and whether single or double cover is used; double cover is usual for rubber yarns. The higher the percentage of cover and lower the percentage of elastomeric fiber the greater the control or power. Conversely, the higher the percentage of elastomeric fiber and the lower the percentage of cover fiber, the greater the degree of stretch. Bare spandex garments are most easily stretched (have lowest modulus), therefore, they stretch with little pressure to a great degree of stretch but do not give much figure control. Since percentages of each fiber must be shown on labels it is easily possible to have almost any degree of figure control or stretch desired—other than the extremes—

but not both great power and a great degree of stretch in a single garment. Covered elastomeric yarns may have stretch or extensibility as low as 30 to 40 percent or may go as high as several hundred percent.

Elastomeric fabrics may be woven or knitted. Many power nets and laces are knitted on raschel machines. Elastomeric fabrics are often dyed in delicate or brilliant colors as well as being available in white or black, or they may be printed in multi colors. Elastomeric fabrics usually have two-way or warp-direction stretch.

NONELASTOMERIC STRETCH

Nonelastomeric stretch fabrics first appeared as expensive, sleek, form-fitting ski pants at ski resorts in Europe in the late 1950's; they had He-lanca textured-stretch nylon warp and wool filling. All were heavy, warm fabrics suitable for ski wear in the mountains. Much of European-made ski wear is still this type of fabric though fiber content may vary. Pucci, in 1960, launched his famous series of high fashion pants for all types of oc-casions; these fabrics had Helanca stretch nylon warp and dupioni silk fill-ing yarns.

American producers attempted to copy the European stretch fabrics in a variety of cheaper, lighter weight fabrics for a much wider market than for ski clothing. Many mills jumped into production without sufficient knowledge, proper equipment, or quality control so that much of the potential interest in such fabrics was dissipated and the market fell far short of predictions. There are, however, many stretch garments of many types for many uses on the markets; the great upsurge in skiing alone would account for a fairly large market.

Although warp stretch is ordinarily used for ski pants, much more non-elastomeric stretch fabric is constructed with fillingwise stretch. The snug, sleek, tapered line of many of the ski pants, the effect of which is largely due to the fabric being held taut by a strap under the instep, is not the type found in most garments in which stretch is for comfort rather than fashion.

The Chemstrand Company's 1962 book *Stretch Woven Fabrics* (p. 1) gives a good description of what is probably agreed among the majority of fiber, fabric, and apparel producers who are involved in some stage of nonelastomeric garment production. It says:

Stretch woven fabrics—contrary to popular misconception—are not in-tended to create a bizarre silhouette or a skin-tight look. What they *are* in-tended to create, as in the case of cotton-stretch nylon denims for example, is action where one needs it—across the hips . . . in the seat . . . and at the knees. In addition, stretch woven apparel is more comfortable, can fit better

for a sleek look, retains its shape and has greater resistance to wear in strategic areas than non-stretch apparel. Shirts of stretch woven fabrics for example, will "give" across the shoulders without putting strain on the fabric; and this holds true in every area where the body bends, such as at the elbows and knees. Stretch woven fabrics also improve the sizing of garments. This is not to imply that one size will fit everyone, but that each particular size can adapt to individual variations of people within that size; thus, the garment can fit more customers. . . .

Nonelastomeric stretch is designed to give from a very low 5 to 10 percent stretch to a maximum of about 30 to 35 percent stretch. Recovery is not as rapid as for elastomeric fabrics and may not, in some types of fabrics, be complete until a garment is washed or dry-cleaned. There have been many complaints that all-cotton stretch garments lose their ability to completely recover after they are worn and laundered a few times.

Nonelastomeric stretch is attained in any of three ways; by use of stretch-textured thermoplastic yarns; by use of elastomeric core-spun yarns; or by mechanical and chemical treatment. Stretch-texturing processes for yarns are discussed in Chapter 9. Nylon is still the most-used fiber for this purpose but the polyesters, Arnel, and the acrylics are also used. Core-spun yarns are those in which spandex fiber is carried through yarn-spinning processes with other fibers and in the process become imbedded among the other fibers in the yarn, giving the yarn considerable elasticity. The success of both of these types of fabrics depends on proper weaving and finishing.

Slack mercerization of cotton is the usual mechanical-chemical method of obtaining stretch; it has been used for stretch denims but has thus far not been a completely successful method for stretch fabrics. In slack mercerization, always with filling stretch, the rather loosely woven cotton fabric must be put through the mercerizing bath with no tension in the filling direction though moderate tension is needed in the warp direction. The nontensioned caustic treatment causes changes in the cotton fiber; it becomes less crystalline, shrinks in length 15 to 20 percent, and swells in diameter, thus becoming more circular in cross section. These changes produce fabric filling shrinkage of 20 to 30 percent of which a part is crimping around the warp yarns. Such fabrics for apparel uses are usually given a resin treatment also to cause cross-linking of the cellulose in order to improve dimensional stability and crease recovery. For stretch bandages and such uses, resin treatment is unnecessary.

How fabrics are cut and stitched is very important in retaining their stretch properties, as are all finishing operations which, if improperly carried through, can nullify the stretch potential. Garment fabrics are designed to have from 5 to 10 percent more stretch than is actually needed for a specific

end-use in order to facilitate complete recovery. They must be cut to allow for maximum shrinkage in order to permit maximum stretch according to the potential of the specific fabric.

Nonelastomeric stretch is the type used for sportswear of all types, hosiery and socks, leotards, diapers, lingerie, lining materials for stretch fabrics, slipcover and upholstery fabrics, shirts, slacks, much swimwear, and some medical and industrial fabrics.

There are no commonly accepted standards for the amount of stretch for any specific type of fabric and no commonly accepted method for measuring stretch. Several methods have been developed, however, which are used by various producers and laboratories and which have considerable value in measuring the stretch properties of this group of fabrics.

FOR FURTHER READING

American Dyestuff Reporter since 1960.
Hathorne, B. F., Woven Stretch and Textured Fabrics.
Joseph, M. L., Introductory Textile Science.
Modern Textiles Magazine.
Textile Chemist and Colorist.

▄▄ 16

TEXTILE PERFORMANCE STANDARDS AND TEXTILE-ASSOCIATED ORGANIZATIONS

There have been, for many years, federal specifications by which the United States governmental agencies buy textile fabrics and apparel and furnishing items to supply the needs of the armed services, the government-operated hospitals, and the various other government services. The government standards are based on end-use performance as indicated by a series of specific standard test methods; the standards are often developed by the various agencies according to the particular needs of their service. The government standards are often not at all the type of standards in which the civilian consumer is interested.

A great many retail and mail-order stores, particularly the large chains, have also established performance standards for goods offered for sale to their own customers; the stores often maintain their own testing laboratories to determine and to insure maintenance of their standards. Manufacturers of fibers and yarns have also sometimes established end-use stand-

ards for fabrics that may have permission to carry the trade name of their products, as, for example, the requirements imposed by the producers of the high-wet-modulus rayons.

Although all these standards are of general interest and of some general value, there was, before the 1952 American Standards Association* L22 voluntary standards for rayon and acetate, no general group of standards specific to the end-use performances of apparel and textile furnishing fabrics of particular interest to consumers, to the manufacturers of fibers and fabrics, to finishers and converters, to garment cutters and manufacturers, and to producers of household furnishing items. The L22–1968 standards are the latest revision of the 1952 standards.

HISTORY   Nat. Retail Merchants Assoc.

The L22–1968 performance requirements are a direct outgrowth of the 1952-L22 voluntary standards and the 1960 revision of these standards. The National Retail Merchants Association has always been the sponsor of these standards, that is, furnishing the impetus and at least a part of the cost to get a movement toward standards established. The need for standards, although probably always present, became noticeable to many people with the appearance on the market of a seemingly bewildering array of unfamiliar rayon and acetate fabrics, and particularly with many fabrics of unpredictable serviceability at the close of World War II. A number of producers and retail stores had established, before World War II, performance standards for their own products. Notable among these was the "Crown Tested" program of the American Viscose Corporation.

On the recommendation of interested groups, the American Standards Association set up committees to evaluate end-use performance standards for apparel and home furnishing textiles, and to recommend for acceptance those that seemed suitable. In cooperation with the American Standards Association action most of the various agencies gave up their own performance standards, turned over whatever work they had done along this line to the Association, and cooperated in the work of the committees. The 1952 American Standard Association Standard Performance Requirements for Rayon and Acetate was the result.

By the time the 1952 standards were accepted, a great many new fibers were on the market, making a discriminating choice ever more complicated, and indicating a need for widening the scope of the standards. As a result, when the time came for a review of the 1952 Standards, they were revised

* Now the American National Standards Institute, Inc.

to include all fibers as well as to review the properties to be specified and to update the test methods. These revised standards were accepted in 1960; these have now been superseded by the USA Standard Performance Requirements for Textile Fabrics USAS L22–1968.

THE L22-1968 STANDARDS

The purpose and use of the standards are set forth on the flyleaf of the 1968 USA Standard in this paragraph:

A USA Standard implies a consensus of those substantially concerned with its scope and provisions. A USA Standard is intended as a guide to aid the manufacturer, the consumer, and the general public. The existence of a USA Standard does not in any respect preclude anyone, whether he has approved the standard or not, from manufacturing, marketing, purchasing, or using products, processes, or procedures not conforming to the standard. USA Standards are subject to periodic review and users are cautioned to obtain the latest editions. Producers of goods made in conformity with a USA Standard are encouraged to state on their own responsibility in advertising, promotion material, or on tags or labels, that the goods are produced in conformity with particular USA Standards.

Since the L22 standards are the result of a consensus among participants in the committee work and the hearings, they are necessarily a compromise among the interests of the various elements represented. Such standards are inevitably considered too high by some interests and too low by others. After a period of trial, a standard may be changed or dropped altogether, as was the standard for crease recovery in the 1960 revision.

The L22–1968 Standards cover three classes of textile fabrics; for women's and girls, apparel and accessories, for men's and boy's apparel and accessories, and for home furnishings.

The twenty-seven standards for women's and girls' textile fabrics cover the following end-uses: both woven and knitted fabrics for bathing suits (not elastomeric), blouses, dresses, brassieres, corsets, girdles, combinations, gloves, dressing gowns, negligees, nightgowns, pajamas, slips, and underwear; and woven fabrics only for coats, coveralls, dungarees, overalls, shop coats, handkerchiefs, linings, rainwear, scarves, sportswear, suits, uniforms, work pants, work shirts, and sheer dresses and blouses.

Twenty-one standards cover the following end-uses for men's and boys' apparel fabrics: woven and knitted fabrics for bathing suits (not elastomeric), bathrobes, dressing gowns, pajamas, underwear, sportswear, and dress shirts; and woven fabrics only for coveralls, dungarees, overalls, shop coats, handkerchiefs, linings, neckties, rainwear, beachwear, sports shirts,

suits, work pants, work shirts, and certain sheer and nonsheer pajamas, shirts, shorts, undershirts, and underwear.

Fifteen standards for home furnishings cover these end uses, all woven: awnings, canopies, bath mats, throw rugs, bedspreads, decorative pillows, blankets, comforters, drapery, sheets, pillowcases, shower curtains, slipcovers, napery, tablecloths, towels, umbrellas, upholstery, and window curtains. There is also a standard for knitted sheets.

Each standard consists of a list of minimum requirements for specific properties together with the designation of the standard test method by which the property is to be determined. Properties covered vary for the various end-uses but, in general, are the following: breaking strength, tearing strength, bursting strength, yarn shifting, dimensional change (always the maximum allowable although all others are minimum standards), degree of colorfastness to the various fading agencies (atmospheric conditions, laundering, light, crocking, perspiration, dry-cleaning), resistance to yarn slippage, and odor. Table 22 gives some of the more commonly-used requirements for selected items from all three classes of end-uses.

Although not appearing in any end-use requirements of the 1968 standards, other standards have been developed for claims for special characteristics, ready for use as they are needed and demanded. Some of these are for spot and stain resistance, wrinkle resistance, crease of pleat retention, resistance to insect damage, mildew, and rot, fire resistance, antistatic requirements, retention of appearance, and stretch properties.

Recommendations for labeling legends have also been developed. Letters have been assigned to designate care instructions and a colored strip the full width of the label and not less than $1/16$ inch wide is recommended to be used with each care designation as follows:

USAS L22–B washable at 160°F, with bleach—purple
USAS L22–W washable at 160°F, no bleach—green
USAS L22–C washable at 120°F, no bleach—blue
USAS L22–H washable at 105°F, no bleach—yellow
USAS L22–D dry-cleanable only—red

These should be permanently attached labels. Special care instructions may be included, such as "Washable—Do Not Dry-clean," "Hand Washable," "Dry-clean Only," "Do Not Bleach," "Iron on Wrong Side," and specifications for special ironing or drying temperature. Other types of information than care labels may be detachable tags.

All these recommendations, of course, are in addition to those required by the Textile Fiber Products Identification Act. Actually, both types of labeling can be combined in a neat and attractive label. It is desirable to have such types of permanent labels developed.

TABLE 22. United States Standard Performance Requirements for Selected End-Uses. USAS L22-1968

Specific End-Use	Break or Burst Strength		Tear Strength	Dimensional Change[a] (max)	Colorfastness Class[b]			Light Fading Hours
	Dry Pound	Wet Pound	Pound	Percent	Change in Washing or Dry cleaning			
					Shade	Stain	Shade	
Women's and Girls' Textile Fabrics								
Woven blouse or dress	20	12	1.0	2.5	4	3		L4–20
Knitted blouse or dress	32,50[c]	25,30[c]		3.5–5	4	3	4	L4–20
Woven coverall, dungaree, etc.	55	55	2.5	3.5	4	3		L5–40
Woven dressing gown, etc.	20	12	1.0	2.5	4	3	4	L3–10
Knitted dressing gown, etc.	32,50[c]	25,30[c]		3.5–5	4	3	4	L3–10
Woven rainwear	40	35	2.5	2.5	4	3	4	L5–40
Woven sportswear	30	25	1.5	2.5	4	3	4	L5–40
Knitted sportswear	32,50[c]	25,30[c]		3.5–5	4	3	4	L5–40
Woven uniform	50	25	2.5	2.5	4	3	4	L5–40 [d]
Men's and Boys' Textile Fabrics								
Woven coveralls, dungarees, etc.	55	55	2.5	3.5	4	3		L5–40
Woven dress shirt	25	25	1.5	2.0	4	3		L4–20
Knitted dress shirt	32,50[c]	25,30[c]		3.5–5	4	3	4	L5–40
Woven pajamas, shorts, etc.	25	25	1.5	2.5	4	3	4	L4–20
Woven rainwear	40	35	2.5	2.5	4	3	4	L5–40
Woven sportswear	30,40[e]	25	2.5	2.5	4	3	4	L5–40
Knitted sportswear	32,50[c]	25,30[c]		3.5–5	4	3	4	L5–40
Woven work pants	40	40	2.5	3.5	4	3		L5–40
Woven work shirts	30	30	1.5	3.5	4	3		L5–40
Textile Furnishing Fabrics								
Woven drapery	35	20	1.5	3.0	4	3		L6–80
Woven sheets and pillowcases	55	55		1½–6+[f]	4	3	4	L4–20
Knitted sheets (tricot)	100	75		3.5	4	3		L4–20
Woven slipcovers	75	40	2.5	3.0	4	3		L5–40
Woven towel	50	35		10W,5F	4	4	4	L5–40

Woven umbrella	35	20	1.0	5.0	4	4	L4–20
Woven upholstery	50	50	5.0	5.0	4	3	4 4 L5–40
Woven window curtains	12,20 g	8,15 g		4.0	4		L6–80

a Dimensional change standard varies according to type of knit; it frequently is lower for dry cleaning also.
b Explanation of classes of colorfastness and terms for describing degree of change:

Fastness to Light
Class 8—outstanding
Class 7—excellent
Class 6—very good
Class 5—good
Class 4—fairly good
Class 3—fair
Class 2—poor
Class 1—very poor

Alteration in Shade and Strength
Class 5—negligible or none
Class 4—slight
Class 3—noticeable
Class 2—considerable
Class 1—much

Staining
Class 5—negligible or none
Class 4—slight
Class 3—noticeable
Class 2—considerable
Class 1—heavy

c The lesser figure is for man-made cellulosic fibers and the greater for other fibers.
d This figure is for outdoor use; indoors is L4–20.
e Only jackets may be the lesser figure.
f Fitted sheets may change no more than 1½% either direction; flat sheets may change no more than 6% warpwise and 2.5% fillingwise.
g Sheer fabrics may be the lower numbers, all others must be the higher.

American Association Standards for Institutional Textiles L24 were sponsored by the American Hotel Association and were accepted (as revised) in 1957. They do for the institutional field what the L22 standards do for the home furnishings field. Many of these standards are the same for both groups.

Although use of the L22 standards is voluntary, and probably a majority of the groups who participated in their formulation and who recommended their acceptance do not use them in their entirety, the fact that the standards are available exerts a beneficial influence on all concerned. They furnish a readily available standard for comparison and are ready for use wherever and whenever they are needed or desired. They help bring order to a formerly chaotic condition. As long as things go along smoothly and consumers are reasonably well satisfied with the performance of the apparel and furnishings fabrics they use, the fact that the standards seem to be lying dormant is perhaps not very important; as the time comes when a number of fabrics fail to meet consumer expectations, we can expect that the L22 standards will be called forth in a hurry, and they will acquire great significance to all concerned. The danger is, of course, that if not used consciously, they may be allowed to become outdated and will lose their maximum usefulness through sheer neglect.

Consumers need to be aware of the L22 standards, to know their coverage, to look for evidence on labels that goods meet their requirements, and to ask for them when they are missing. That a fabric meets a USA Standard L22 performance requirement does not imply that it is the best fabric of its type that a consumer may buy, or the best one for his money, but it does imply a satisfactory minimum level of serviceability, all other things considered.

TEXTILE-ASSOCIATED ORGANIZATIONS AND AGENCIES

There are a number of organizations and agencies in the United States primarily concerned with the general textile field through establishment of performance standards, test methods for evaluating performance and their application, for interpretation and enforcement of textile laws and regulations, and liaison between national and international groups. Most important to our understanding of the field are: the American National Standards Institute Inc. (ANSI)*, the American Society for Testing and

* The American National Standards Institute, Inc. (ANSI) was the United States of America Standards Institute, Inc. (USASI) until October 6, 1969.

Materials (ASTM), the American Association of Textile Chemists and Colorists (AATCC), the National Bureau of Standards (NBS), the Textile Division of the Federal Trade Commission (FTC), and the American Association for Textile Technology (AATT). We shall refer to them by initials henceforth, and will consider each briefly.

In the front part of the book of L22–1968 standards the ANSI describes its function as:

The Standards Institute provides the machinery for creating voluntary standards. It serves to eliminate duplication of standards activities and to weld conflicting standards into single, nationally accepted standards under the designation "USA Standards."

Each standard represents general agreement among maker, seller, and user groups as to the best current practice with regard to some specific problem. Thus the completed standards cut across the whole fabric of production, distribution, and consumption of goods and services. USA Standards, by reason of Institute procedures, reflect a national consensus of manufacturers, consumers, and scientific, technical, and professional organizations, and governmental agencies. The complete standards are used widely by industry and commerce and often by municipal, state, and federal governments.

The USA Standards Institute, under whose auspices this work is being done, is the United States clearinghouse and coordinating body for standards activity on the national level. In 1966, the USA Standards Institute was constituted as successor to the American Standards Association, founded in 1918. It is a federation of trade associations, technical societies, professional groups, and consumer organizations. Some 2,000 companies are affiliated with the Institute as company members.

Headquarters of ANSI are in New York City.

ASTM is an organization that covers all types of materials. The part of the organization concerned with textiles is Committee D–13 on Textile Materials. On the flyleaf of the ASTM Standards, Part 24 for October 1969 the Society describes itself and how it functions as follows:

The American Society for Testing and Materials is an international, nonprofit, technical, scientific, and educational society devoted to . . . "the promotion of knowledge of the materials of engineering, and the standardization of specifications and methods of testing."

Since 1898, the Society, mainly through the activities of technical committees, has conducted a vast amount of investigation and research leading to a better knowledge of the properties of materials and the development of more than 4000 standard specifications for and methods of testing materials. These standards are used throughout the world by engineers, scientists, architects and builders, industries and governments in specifying and evaluating materials of all kinds. They are applied in design, manufacturing, construction, and maintenance.

More than 105 main technical committees (some 2500 committees including all subcommittees and sections) function in prescribed fields under regulations that ensure a balanced representation among the 18,000 producer, consumer, and general interest participants. Current committee activities cover materials in the fields of aerospace, atomic energy, surgical implants, housing and construction, highways, heavy industry, and durable consumer goods.

The standards developed by the committees and the hundreds of technical papers and reports presented at Society meetings are published and widely distributed.

The world-wide membership is drawn from a broad spectrum of individuals, agencies, and industries concerned with materials. More than 16,000 members include 12,000 individual engineers, scientists, researchers, educators, and testing experts; 1300 governmental agencies and departments (federal, state, and municipal), educational institutions, and libraries; and 2700 companies, trade associations, research institutes, and testing laboratories. In addition, about 8500 other individuals, though not personally members of the Society, serve as technical experts representing industrial members on committees.

And in relation to the standards (p. iii):

An ASTM standard represents a common viewpoint of those parties concerned with its provisions, namely, producers, consumers, and general interest groups. It is intended to aid industry, government agencies, and the general public. The use of an ASTM standard is purely voluntary. The existence of an ASTM standard does not preclude anyone from manufacturing, marketing, or purchasing products, or using products, processes, or procedures not conforming to the standard. Because ASTM standards are subject to periodic review and revision, those who use them are cautioned to obtain the latest revisions.

ASTM headquarters are located in Philadelphia.

AATCC was founded in 1921 at Lowell Textile Institute with a small group of members but long ago outgrew its quarters there and now has a national and international membership of almost 9000 members. In addition, there are approximately 300 corporate members and six college student chapters. To facilitate the functions of the organization in the United States seventeen sections have been established in different geographical regions. This enables members to meet for other purposes and other times than is possible at the annual meeting. Headquarters are at Research Triangle Park in North Carolina.

The objectives of the association, as set forth in the AATCC constitution are: "To promote increase of knowledge of the application of dyes and chemicals in the textile industry, to encourage in any practical way research work on chemical processes and materials of importance to the textile industry, and to establish for the members channels by which the interchange of professional knowledge among them may be increased."

AATCC

In the *Technical Manual* for 1968 (p. A–5) appear these descriptions of the functions and operation of the association:

Through the years, the Association has gained national and international recognition for its standard methods of testing dyed and chemically treated fibers and fabrics to measure such performance characteristics as colorfastness to light and washing, crease resistance, shrinkage, wash-and-wear, water resistance, flammability and the many other conditions to which textiles may be subjected.

Practically all of the dyes, finishes and many chemicals produced in the United States are controlled and checked by AATCC test methods. These test methods are a major factor in insuring the satisfactory consumer performance of the billions of yards of textiles that find their way across the retail counters and into the hands of Mr. and Mrs. U.S.A.

AATCC maintains co-operative relationships with many other societies of kindred interests and with departments and agencies of the Federal government. At the international level, the Association participates in the International Organization for Standardization (ISO) and the Pan American Standards Commission (COPANT) in an effort to bring about world-wide uniformity in testing procedures.

The work of AATCC has been further clarified by these statements by F. Fortess in the *American Dyestuff Reporter* for July 22, 1963 (p. 35).

What is most unique about our Association is the fact that hundreds of our members, in scores of laboratories and plants, voluntarily participate in cooperative programs leading to the development of new scientific data and in the gathering of information and technology for the benefit of the textile industry and in the public interest.

It must be clearly understood by all, that the primary purpose of these committees is the creation of new information and the establishment of tools and testing procedures which correlate with the behavior of textile products in service. It is definitely not the purpose of TCR (Technical Committee on Research) and its various functioning committees, to establish standards of performance of any textile product or to determine the quality of a textile material. It is a great enough achievement that many of our test methods have provided a common denominator in all parts of the world, but it is even more important that in the USA the same test procedure will be applied with substantially the same results in the laboratory of a textile school, a commercial dyehouse, a textile chemical manufacturer, a man-made fiber producer, a government agency, a retail distributor, or a converter. How this information, concerning the performance of the textile product, is used is entirely up to the various parties involved—the buyer and seller, dyer and converter, finishing plant and textile chemical supplier. AATCC is only involved in providing the tools and describing how the tests should be performed.

The NBS, as an agency of the Department of Commerce, has six functions assigned to it by Congress. These are: custody, maintenance, and development of the national standards of measurement; determination of the physical and chemical constants and properties of materials; development of testing methods; development of standard practices, codes, and specifications; scientific and advisory services; and special research and development projects for U.S. government agencies. The NBS does not set standards or have authority to impose them.

On May 14, 1969, Miss Josephine Blandford of the Product Evaluation Division of the National Bureau of Standards wrote especially for this book the following description of the NBS and its work:

The National Bureau of Standards was established in 1901 to serve as the Nation's central measurement laboratory. Today it serves also as a principal focal point in the Federal Government for assuring maximum application of the physical and engineering sciences to the advancement of technology throughout the Nation. Headquartered at Gaithersburg, Maryland, with additional laboratories in Washington, D.C. and Boulder, Colorado, the Bureau's staff of about 3400 is made up predominantly of chemists, physicists, engineers, mathematicians, and technologists, organized into three Institutes—the Institute for Basic Standards, the Institute for Materials Research, and the Institute for Applied Technology. In a 1962 reorganization, the Textiles Section, along with four other sections concerned with organic and fibrous materials, was abolished and the textiles staff absorbed by several divisions in the Institute for Materials Research and Institute for Applied Technology. The latter Institute, in 1967, formed a Plastics and Textiles Section which, however, has but a limited staff on textiles who, in addition to the section's projects on textiles, collaborates with others of the Bureau staff on work related in part to textiles, for example, chemical tests, flammability, fiber structure, static resistivity, and building materials.

With specific respect to textiles, the National Bureau of Standards investigates the physical, chemical, and performance properties of textiles, and contributes to the advancement of the technical and scientific knowledge of textiles. It cooperates with national and international standardizing bodies in the development of standards to evaluate the properties of textile fibers, yarns, and fabrics. It maintains close relations with textiles research and professional institutes and societies, universities and textile schools, government agencies, and the textile and apparel industries. It concentrates its activities in areas in which the expertise of its staff can make the most significant contributions to science and industry.

The FTC is also a part of the Department of Commerce. Its textile division is charged with administration of the federal textile laws and issuing trade practice rules. Some of these rules have concerned infants' and children's knitted outerwear, upholstery and drapery fabrics, hosiery, rayon

and silk dyeing, printing, and finishing, and shrinkage of woven cotton cloth, as examples. The new amendment to the Flammable Fabrics Act for the first time authorized the FTC to initiate action on its own.

Mr. H. Hannah, in *American Dyestuff Reporter* for November 7, 1955 (p. 797), said:

The purpose of the Federal Trade Commission is to protect both business and the public against unfair methods of competition in commerce and to stop those practices which would lessen competition or tend to create monopoly. It is also to guard both business and the consumer against unfair or deceptive trade practices.

The AATT was founded in 1933 as a local organization in New York under the name Association of Textile Laboratories and Technologists. Its purpose was social and exchange of information on textile testing and fabric developments. The name was changed in 1936 and again in 1954 to the present one. It became a national organization in 1960 and had 1200 members and several student chapters in 1965.

According to *Modern Textile Magazine* for February 1965 (p. 51) its objectives are

. . . to encourage mutual understanding in the fields of textile technology and marketing; the advancement of textile technology in all its branches; cooperation with established facilities for textile education; and the interchange and dissemination of professional knowledge among its members and with other industry groups.

The AATCC and ASTM cooperate in some of their work and each accepts the standard test methods developed by the other, thus avoiding repetition and duplication. ASTM and AATCC standard test methods are used for evaluating performance in relation to USA Standard L22–1968 textile performance requirements and for many of the international standards that have been adopted by ISO.

FOR FURTHER READING

American Dyestuff Reporter.

Modern Textiles Magazine.

United States of America Standards Institute: *USA Standard Performance Requirements for Textile Fabrics USASI L22–1968.*

INTERRELATIONS OF PROPERTIES
AND FABRIC PERFORMANCE

In our study of fibers, yarns, and fabrics we have used many terms relating to properties, such as length, diameter, specific gravity, hygroscopicity, breaking strength, tear strength, elasticity, resilience, elongation, dimensional stability, shrinkage, felting, crease recovery, abrasion resistance, pilling, thermoplasticity, static electricity accumulation, thermal insulation, effect of acid, alkali, weather, or sunlight, to name a few, in addition to terms ordinarily used to describe visual appearance. In fabrics, and indeed in yarns and fibers, none of these properties can be completely isolated and studied by itself—all influence some or many other properties to a greater or lesser degree.

Although the specific effect that one property has upon another property is known in relatively few instances for many fibers, it is important that we understand that there is an interrelation; and that such interrelatedness must make us cautious in attributing cause or effect to a certain property when we may be unable, even under the most carefully controlled experimental conditions, to completely isolate one factor from another, or to duplicate exactly the test conditions. Recognition of the limitation does not mean, of course, that we should not try to relate a specific cause

to a specific effect, but it does mean that we should weigh all factors that may influence this relation and acknowledge them.

Once we understand their interrelatedness, we should not be tempted to say, as has so often been said, "This fabric has higher thread count, therefore it is better," unless all possible factors have been weighed and this particular factor is the only one to which it seems logical to assign the difference. The only time the quoted statement would be true is when everything else about the fabrics is identical, and fabrics and conditions usually are not identical when such statements are made. "Thread count" seems to be a term understood by persons who otherwise have little knowledge of textiles, so that they have tended to attribute to it many effects not truly produced by this particular factor. *Identical* would mean the same kind of fiber from the same "batch" or, in the case of cotton, even from the same part of a field, with identical processing of fibers, the same yarn structure and processing, the same fabric construction and finishing processes on the same machines, handling of the same machines by the same operators, and testing by identical methods with the same operator handling any machines that are subject to operator differences in results. Then if higher strength, or any other factor being considered, accompanies the higher thread count, we may safely say that the difference is the direct result of the difference in thread count.

There are many difficulties, at best, in trying to produce identical fabrics. What can you see as some of these difficulties? In the first place, fibers are not identical. We saw that wool fibers from the same area and from different parts of an animal vary in a number of properties, and that there is variation of cotton fibers within a boll and in bolls from different plants and from different areas of the same field. You will recall that the first purpose of blending these fibers in the mills is to obtain a reasonably uniform quality of blend for a considerable yardage of fabric. But, of necessity, blends must vary as different lots come from a mill and from different mills. Careful grading and blending, however, insure a usable uniformity for all practical purposes. The man-made fibers too, although touted as being uniform, really are not so. They vary from batch to batch—you will remember that a number of batches are blended before the solutions are forced through the spinnerets—and fibers of the same kind vary with different temperatures, speeds, and other differences in details of processing. Variability in their product is recognized by some producers who recommend that different shipments be handled separately and not blended in yarn and fabric making with other shipments of the same type of fiber. There may be differences in reaction to dyestuffs, to finishing agents, or in other reactions. Raw materials vary for the man-made fibers as well as for the natural. As improvements or changes are made in proc-

essing anywhere along the line, these may be reflected in variations in the fibers produced.

The different fibers are affected differently by the various processes they undergo in being made into fabric and apparel or other items. As an example, we noted that increase in twist improves strength up to a point; then increase in twist leads to decrease in strength until the twist itself will cause the yarn to break. Spun yarns are more quickly and adversely affected by too much twist than filament yarns of the same fiber. Some fibers can withstand considerably more twist without damage than others. Twist is necessary, however, in making yarns and fabrics. Increased twist leads to firmer, harsher fabric, which may be undesirable from other standpoints. Conditions under which twisting is done and tests are made may also influence results.

As another example of interrelation, increased orientation of the molecules within the molecular chains of the fibers may lead to an increase in the percentage of crystalline area within the fiber and to a decrease in the percentage of amorphous area. This results in increased strength and rigidity but also in increased brittleness and decreased flexibility; the fiber also becomes less absorbent with all the other changes that accompany changes in absorbency.

We also saw that changes in physical, chemical, and biologic properties each have an influence on the others, that use of finishing agents affects fibers differently, and that some properties may be improved only at the expense of other and equally desirable properties.

Resin finishing of cottons for easy care improves wrinkle resistance, crease recovery, and probably dimensional stability, but it may decrease breaking and tear strengths, pliability, elongation, elasticity, and comfort. There must be a limit beyond which change cannot be carried if a satisfactorily serviceable product is to be offered the consumer. Use of carefully chosen fibers in mixtures and blends to attain easy care does not lead to some of the difficulties described for resin-treated fabrics, but the fabrics may be more expensive, less comfortable, require a different kind of care than what the consumer wants to give them, or perhaps not have the kind of appearance desired for a particular purpose.

In addition to differences in processing fabrics of different fibers and of different batches of the same fiber, there may be variations in processing the same fabric at different spots along its length as it goes through the mills, particularly in such processes as bleaching, singeing, heat-setting, shearing, napping, drying, tentering, resin application and curing, washing after resin treatment—or just the slight fluctuations produced by differences in voltage at different times through the machine controls, slight variations in the machines themselves and their operation, or even slight

differences among different batches of chemicals or the amounts used, even with fully automatic and continuous operation. When the human element enters into processing too, still other variations may arise among operators according to each one's skill at performing the same operation as well as their skills in performing one operation compared with another, their efficiency and carefulness as workers, the effects of fatigue, and innumerable other things.

The influence of different factors is recognized by the Union Carbide and Carbon Corporation in the pamphlet *The Story of Dynel* in these statements:

It needs to be emphasized, however, that neither fiber content nor any other single factor by itself determines the nature of a fabric. Fiber content, yarn construction, fabric construction, and the finish given the cloth all play a part in the drapability, porosity, warmth, strength, and texture of a cloth. In general, strong fibers can be depended upon to give strong fabrics and chemical-resistant fibers result in chemical-resistant fabrics. Other factors, such as warmth, are gained through the combination of the right fiber and the correct fabric construction. Softness, as another example, depends not only on the fiber but also on the size of the fiber, the amount of twist given the yarn, how the fabric is constructed, and how it is finished.

How then can identical fabrics be made for assessing the influence of different properties, and how can a relation be shown between one factor and another?

A common method of comparing fabrics is on the basis of weight and construction as nearly identical as can be obtained, sometimes even to the extent of supervising all steps in their production. For example, cotton may be supervised by choosing the seeds, choosing the fields in which they are to be planted, selecting cotton from only a particular area of a field, and supervising its processing all the way through the mills.

Comparison of similar fabrics on the basis of the same weight for a unit area, usually a square yard, favors the fibers with low specific gravity, such as nylon and the acrylics, over others with higher specific gravity, such as cotton and wool. Why is the fiber with lower specific gravity favored? Would this always be true? A fairer basis of comparison would be an identical cross-sectional area and unit length; the difficulty here is in achieving identical cross-sectional areas because of the differences in cross-sectional shape among fibers, and even to some extent among fibers of the same kind. Equal cross-sectional area, however, is not impossible to attain. There might still be slight differences caused by variations in the shapes, but such differences would probably be negligible.

Given fibers of equal cross-sectional areas and unit length, and the opportunity of making them into yarns and fabrics as close to identical

as possible with processing and handling all the way through as nearly identical as possible, and with testing done with standard methods by the same operator, we could begin to make valid comparisons. Then all factors could be held the same except the one that we purposely plan to vary, such as thread count, amount of twist in the yarn, the finish applied, or some one other factor; differences in results could then be assumed to be at least partially due to this change. Again, however, the effect the change would have had on related properties must be considered. For example, increased thread count may theoretically lead to increased strength but may cut down on flexibility, resilience, and elasticity, so that lack of give will actually make it no stronger than it was and may actually decrease the wear life.

Clusters of related properties need to be considered together in evaluating service satisfaction. Much work needs to be done to find out which properties may be most meaningfully grouped together for achieving and evaluating different end results.

Identical test methods carried through under the same conditions of testing are necessary in any type of comparison testing. Textile testing for all properties likely to be affected by differences in moisture or temperature are ordinarily carried out under specified conditions of relative humidity and temperature. Such standard conditions, adopted by ASTM and used in the United States and several other countries for fabric, yarn, and fiber testing, have been established as follows: relative humidity 65 percent, with a tolerance of 2 percent in either direction; and temperature 70°F, with a tolerance of 2 degrees in either direction. These conditions are not equally favorable to all fibers, and new conditions may eventually need to be established. Or it may be possible to show that these conditions, compared to the ideal, do not make enough difference to matter insofar as consumer products are concerned. They do make a difference, however, in strictly accurate comparisons. Temperatures within the specified range probably do not affect the different fibers to any extent, but relative humidity of 65 percent, at which the air contains considerable moisture, favors the strength data of fibers such as cotton and linen, in which strength increases with increased moisture; affects unfavorably such fibers as wool and rayon, in which strength decreases with increased moisture; and does not affect nonhygroscopic fibers at all. To be absolutely fair to all fibers, a relative humidity is desirable that balances increase in strength of one fiber against the decrease in another; this may, however, be an impossible assignment. Again, it may not matter in the long run, but we should be wary of drawing conclusions about the relation of cause and effect as long as we do not *know for certain* what the relation may be. As long as we use standard conditions or some other controlled con-

ditions, and state clearly what these conditions are, persons familiar with the properties of the fibers can arrive at a fair interpretation of the data. In every field the danger is always present that data will be incorrectly interpreted by persons unfamiliar with the basic facts of that field.

Few properties can be relegated to lists either of properties affecting appearance alone, or those affecting serviceability alone; nearly all properties in either group influence those in the other. Properties that have a definite relation to appearance include fineness, nature of the fiber surface, length, luster, opacity, affinity for dyestuffs and finishing materials, dimensional stability, crease resistance, resiliency, ability to be heat-set, abrasion resistance, resistance or tendency toward pilling, color, and colorfastness. Can you add to this list?

Those properties most important to serviceability include dimensional stability, shrinkage, breaking strength, tear strength, bursting strength, elasticity, elongation, resilience, crease resistance and recovery, absorption, hygroscopicity, abrasion resistance, colorfastness, light sensitivity, weather resistance, compatibility with or resistance to insects and other biological organisms, pliability, and flammability. Can you add to this list? How does each of these properties affect serviceability?

Fabrics must be planned for a specific end-use or group of related end-uses if they are to fulfill their purposes satisfactorily. And they must also be used for the kinds of end-uses for which they have been planned, to obtain maximum satisfaction. The producer must carefully weigh the relationships of properties to each other and must balance them against each other so that he may obtain as great a degree of as many desirable properties as possible while sacrificing as few other and equally desirable properties, and to the smallest degree, as possible. A description in terms of test results of the different properties is invaluable to mill men in producing an aimed-for quality of fabric, and such data should also be valuable to garment and furnishings manufacturers in enabling them to make the best possible utilization of a fabric. Test data for some of the properties most meaningful to consumers, together with standards established for such properties for specific end-uses, can be of great value to consumers who are interested in wise and economical choice of fabrics, apparel, and furnishings, and in acquiring knowledge through alert experience.

CONSUMER RESPONSIBILITY

The L22 standards are now available for all types of fabrics for apparel and furnishings. Consumers need to be acquainted with them, to demand

goods meeting such standards, and to make use of all information available to them. It is inconceivable that there could be any use for a textile fabric for which we would not be interested in at least a minimum standard of performance. The consumer also has a responsibility to make specific requests for the kinds of things she wants but cannot find on the market; otherwise consumers are dependent on what the producers consider to be the demands of the consumers, and this situation is often far from actual fact. We have seen altogether too much of it in recent years.

How can the consumer judge whether or not she is getting the properties she desires in a fabric, item of apparel, or furnishing? Experience is not an infallible guide in this day of many fibers, mixtures, blends, and special finishes, but it often helps. It is the responsibility of the consumer to know the legislative provisions that affect consumer goods and their labeling, and to study and evaluate all information given on the things she contemplates purchasing. Careful examination before purchase may reveal flaws in fabric and construction, poor-quality materials or workmanship, off-grain design or cut, poor colorfastness, uneven color, and other such visible characteristics. Potential disagreeable odor can sometimes be detected by sniffing alone, or it may be desirable to hold a corner of a suspected material closed tightly inside the bare fist for a short time—the warmth and moisture of the hand often reveal lurking odor danger.

Although high price is often not an indication of high quality, high-quality fabrics are not usually offered for sale on bargain counters. It may be possible to find high quality at a low price if the consumer has the knowledge to discriminate among properties; she also needs this knowledge to find high quality at high prices.

Not only does the consumer need to know about fabrics, legislation, and such things, but she also needs to have the specific end-use in mind for which she wishes to choose a fabric or an article, if she is to buy wisely. It may be as important to know what *not* to buy as what to buy. It would seem as unwise to buy an expensive, well-cured resin-finished wash-and-wear cotton fabric for a costume to be worn briefly for one time and discarded as to buy a cheap, shoddily finished fabric designed for a costume or other limited-life usage when a drapery, dress, or upholstery fabric is needed.

The consumer who has thought through her needs, what sort of fabrics or items will best serve these needs in relation to the care she wishes to give, and what she can afford to spend initially and in upkeep, and who has used the available information to help her arrive at a decision in making her choices among the various things offered on the market, has infinitely better chances of succeeding in buying wisely and satisfactorily than any amount of "lucky" haphazard buying can possibly give.

Consumer responsibility does not end with the purchase of an item. All hang tags should be kept in an accessible place, with an identifying description of the fabric, garment, or other item, place and date of purchase, and other pertinent information, so that the information is available whenever needed. If care instructions are given, they should be followed unless there is good reason to suspect that they are inaccurate. Fabrics, apparel, and furnishings that do not perform satisfactorily must be returned to the retailer with an honest explanation of wherein failure has occurred; taking the hang tags along may be very valuable to all concerned. The retailer has recourse to the manufacturer who must be informed what is wrong if he is to correct it or to prevent repetition of the same faults. Cooperation among all parties concerned can eventually lead to better satisfaction for everyone.

FOR FURTHER READING

Labarthe, Jules: *Textiles: Origins to Usage.*

Appendix A

REFERENCE BOOK LIST

Alderfer, E. B., and Michl, H. E., *Economics of American Industry* (1957), McGraw-Hill Book Company.

Baity, E. C., *Man Is a Weaver* (1942), Viking Press.

Bray, H. A., *Textile Fibers, Yarn, and Fabrics* (1929), The Century Company.

Carrol-Porczynski, C. A., *Asbestos* (1956), The Textile Institute, England.

Crawford, M. D. C., *The Heritage of Cotton* (1924), G. P. Putnam & Sons, The Knickerbocker Press.

Editors of American Fabrics Magazine, *Encyclopedia of Textiles* (1960), Doric Publishing Company.

Fieser, L. F., and Fieser, M., *Advanced Organic Chemistry* (1961), Reinhold Publishing Corporation.

Hadfield, J. W., *Linen Flax Fibre Production in New Zealand* (1953), Whitcomb and Tombs, Ltd.

Hamby, D. S. (Ed.), *The American Cotton Handbook*, Vol. I (1965), Vol. II (1966), Interscience Publishers, a Division of John Wiley & Sons, Inc.

Harris, M., *Handbook of Textile Fibers* (1954), Harris Research Laboratories, Inc.

Hathorne, B. L., *Woven Stretch and Textured Fabrics* (1964), Interscience Publishers, a Division of John Wiley & Sons, Inc.

Hollen, N. R., and Saddler, J., *Textiles* (1968), The Macmillan Company.

Joseph, M. L., *Introductory Textile Science* (1966), Holt, Rinehart & Winston, Inc.

Judd, D. B., *Color in Business, Science, and Industry* (1952), John Wiley & Sons, Inc.

Kaswell, E. R., *Wellington Sears Handbook of Industrial Textiles* (1963), Wellington Sears Company, Inc., a sales subsidiary of West Point Manufacturing Co., Inc.

Labarthe, J., *Textiles: Origins to Usage* (1964), The Macmillan Company.

Leggett, W. F., *The Story of Linen* (1945), Chemical Publishing Company.

Linton, G. E., *Applied Basic Textiles* (1966), Duell, Sloan & Pearce.

Linton, G. E., *Natural and Manmade Textile Fibers* (1966), Duell, Sloan & Pearce.

Lyle, D. S., *Focus on Fabrics* (1964), National Institute of Drycleaning.

Mark, H. F., Atlas, S. M., and Cernia, E. (Eds.), *Man-Made Fibers: Science and Technology*, Vol. I (1967), Vol II (1968), Vol. III (1968), Interscience Publishers, a Division of John Wiley & Sons, Inc.

Marsh, J. J., *An Introduction to Textile Finishing* (1966), London, Chapman & Hill.

Mauersberger, H. R. (Ed.), *Matthews' Textile Fibers* (1947, 1954), John Wiley & Sons, Inc.

Mauersberger, H. R., *The American Handbook of Synthetic Textiles* (1952), Interscience Publishers.

Moncrieff, R. W., *The Man-Made Fibres* (1957, 1963), John Wiley & Sons, Inc.

Peters, R. H., *Textile Chemistry*, Vol. I (1963), Elsevier Publishing Company.

Potter, M. B., and Corman, B. P., *Fiber to Fabric* (1967), Gregg Division of McGraw-Hill Book Company.

Press, J. J. (Ed.), *Man-Made Textile Encyclopedia* (1959), Textile Book Publishing, Inc.

Sherman, J. V., and Sherman, S. L., *The New Fibers* (1946), D. Van Nostrand Company.

Strong, J. H., *Foundations of Fabric Structure* (1953), London National Trade Press, Ltd.

Von Bergen, W. (Ed.), *Wool Handbook*, Vol. I (1963), Interscience Publishers, a Division of John Wiley & Sons, Inc.

Von Bergen, W., and Mauersberger, H. R., *American Wool Handbook* (1948), Textile Book Publishers, Inc.

Walton, P., *The Story of Textiles* (1936), Tudor Publishing Company.

Ward, K., *Chemistry and Chemical Technology of Cotton* (1955), Interscience Publishers.

Weibel, A. C., *Two Thousand Years of Textiles* (1952), Pantheon Books for the Detroit Institute of Arts.

Appendix B

TRADE-NAMED FIBERS OF THE UNITED STATES AND PRODUCERS TO WHOM THE NAMES ARE GRANTED

A.C.E. nylon[1]
Acele acetate[2]
Acrilan acrylic[3]
AeroROVE glass[4]
Amco olefin[5]
Amcostrap olefin[5]
American olefin[5]
Anovor saran[6]
Anso nylon[1]
Antron nylon[2]
Anywear acrylic[3]
Aralac azlon[7]
Avicolor acetate[8]
Avicolor rayon[8]
Aviloc rayon[8]
Avisco vinyon[8]
Avlin polyester[8]
Avril high-wet modulus rayon[8]
Avron rayon[8]
Ayrlyn nylon[9]

Barbara nylon[9]
Beamette olefin[10]
Bembella rayon[11]
Beta glass[12]
Blue C nylon[3]
Blue C polyester[3]
Briglo rayon[13]
Cadon nylon[3]
Cantrece nylon[2]
Caprolan nylon[1]
Caslen azlon[*]
Celacrimp acetate[14]
Celacloud acetate[14]
Celafil acetate[14]
Celaloft acetate[14]
Celanese nylon[14]
Celaperm acetate[14]
Celara acetate[14]
Celarandom acetate[14]
Celatow acetate[14]

Celatress acetate[14]
Celaweb acetate[14]
Chadalon nylon[15]
Chemfit nylon[3]
Chemlux nylon[3]
Chemstrand acrylic[3]
Chemstrand nylon[3]
Chemstrand polyester[3]
Chevron olefin[16]
Chromspun acetate[17]
Colacril acrylic[3]
Coloray rayon[18]
Comiso rayon[11]
Cordura nylon[2]
Courtaulds nylon[18]
Crepeset nylon[13]
Creslan acrylic[19]
Crowelon olefin[20]
Cumuloft nylon[3]
Cupioni rayon[11]
Cupracolor rayon[11]
Cuprel rayon[11]
Cuprussah rayon[11]
Dacron polyester[2]
Dawbac olefin[10]
Darvan nytril [14]
Diane nylon[9]
DLP olefin[10]
Drapespun rayon[21]
Dream Slub rayon[11]
Dul-Tone rayon[21]
Dy-Lok rayon[21]
Dymetrol nylon[2]
Dynel modacrylic[22]
Elura spandex[3]
Encron polyester[13]
Englo rayon[13]
Enka nylon[13]
Enka polyester[13]
Enka rayon[13]
Enkalene nylon[13]
Enkaloft nylon[13]

Enkalure nylon[13]
Enkasheer nylon[13]
Enkatron nylon[13]
Enkrome rayon[13]
Estron acetate[17]
Estron SLR acetate[17]
Fair Haven rayon[23]
Fiber 24 rayon[21]
Fiber HM high-wet-modulus rayon[13]
Fiber 700 high-wet-modulus rayon[13]
Fiberfrax ceramic[24]
Fiberglas glass[12]
Fibro rayon[18]
Fibro DDC rayon[18]
Firestone nylon[25]
Firestone Nytelle nylon[25]
Flaikona rayon[11]
Floterope olefin[5]
Fortisan rayon[14]
Fortrel polyester[14]
Fortrel 7 polyester[14]
Fulflex spandex[26]
Garan glass[27]
Garanmat glass[27]
GC glass[28]
Glospan spandex[29]
Grip polyester[3]
Hazel nylon[9]
Herculon olefin[30]
Hi-Narco rayon[11]
Hyten nylon[2]
IT rayon[8]
Jetspun rayon[8]
Kodel polyester[17]
Kolorbon rayon[8]
Krispglo rayon[13]
Lambeth olefin[31]
Lactron rubber[32]
Lastex rubber[32]
Lirelle high-wet-modulus rayon[18]
Loftura acetate[17]
Loktuft olefin[33]

Lowland nylon[13]
Lowland polyester[13]
Lowland rayon[13]
Lycra spandex[2]
Marvess olefin[33]
Modiglas glass[34]
Monosheer nylon[13]
Multi-Cupioni rayon[11]
Multi-Strata rayon[11]
Narco rayon[11]
Narcon rayon[11]
Newbray rayon[35]
New-Color rayon[35]
New-Dull rayon[35]
Nomelle acrylic[2]
Nomex nylon[2]
Nub-Lite rayon[11]
NUF glass[36]
Numa spandex[19]
Nupron high-wet-modulus rayon[21]
Nylon by Enjay[37]
Nypel nylon[1]
Nypel olefin[1]
Ondelette rayon[11]
Orlon acrylic[2]
Orlon Sayelle acrylic[2]
Parfé rayon[11]
Patlon olefin[38]
Phillips 66 nylon[33]
Pittsburgh glass[39]
Poliafil nylon[9]
Poly Bac olefin[38]
Polycrest olefin[40]
Polyex olefin[41]
Polyloom olefin[16]
Poly Needl Bac olefin[38]
Polynosic high-wet-modulus rayon[13]
Polytwine olefin[41]
Poly-Weve olefin[42]
PPG glass[39]
ProPex olefin[38]
Purilon rayon[8]

Qiana nylon[2]
Quintess polyester[33]
Qulon nylon[11]
Radiant Twine olefin[41]
Rayflex rayon[8]
Rovana saran[6]
Rovcloth glass[43]
Rovmat glass[43]
Ruvea nylon[2]
S-3 nylon[45]
Saran by Enjay[37]
Sarelon azlon[*]
Shakespeare Wonder Thread polyester[44]
Skybloom rayon[13]
Skyloft rayon[13]
Softglo rayon[13]
Sooflex nylon[45]
Source polyamide/polyester[1]
Speckelon nylon[3]
Spectrodye nylon[13]
Spectran acrylic[3]
Strata rayon[11]
Stratella rayon[11]
Strawn rayon[21]
Superflex nylon[45]
Super L rayon[8]
Super Narco rayon[11]
Super Rayflex rayon[8]
Suprenka rayon[13]
Teflon tetrafluoroethylene[2]
Textilmat glass[43]
Touch nylon[1]
Trevira polyester[44]
Tri-Dye nylon[1]
Tusson rayon[11]
Twisloc nylon[3]
Type F acetate[14]
Type K acetate[14]
Tyron rayon[21]
Tyweld rayon[21]
Ultrastrand glass[46]

Unel spandex[22]
Unicure glass[36]
Unifab glass[36]
Uniformat glass[36]
Uniglass[47]
Unirove glass[36]
Unistrand glass[36]
Unitape glass[36]
Vectra olefin[37]
Verel modacrylic[17]
Vicara azlon*
Villwyte rayon[21]
Vitro-flex glass[27]
Vitron glass[27]
Vitro-Strand glass[27]
Voplex olefin[48]
Voplex vinyon[48]
Vycron polyester[11]
Vylor nylon[2]
Vyrene spandex[40]
Weatherbright acrylic[6]
Wellene polyester[49]
Xena rayon[11]
Xtra-Tuf polyester[11]
Zantrel high-wet-modulus rayon[13]
Zantrel 700 high-wet-modulus rayon[13]
Zefran acrylic[6]

* Not clear who holds producer's rights at present.
[1] Allied Chemical Corporation, Fibers Division.
[2] E. I. duPont de Nemours & Co., Inc.
[3] Monsanto Company, Textiles Division.
[4] Glass Fiber Products, Inc.
[5] American Manufacturing Company, Inc.
[6] Dow Badische Company.
[7] Virginia-Carolina Company.
[8] FMC Corporation, American Viscose Division.
[9] Rohm and Haas Company.
[10] Dawbarn Division, W. R. Grace & Co.
[11] Beaunit Corporation, Beaunit Fibers Division.
[12] Owens-Corning Fiberglas Corporation.
[13] American Enka Corporation.
[14] Celanese Corporation.
[15] Chadbourn Gotham, Inc.
[16] Chevron Chemical Company.
[17] Eastman Kodak Co., Tennessee Eastman Company Division.
[18] Courtaulds North America, Inc.
[19] American Cyanamid Company.
[20] Crowe Rope Company.
[21] Midland-Ross Corporation, IRC Fibers Division.
[22] Union Carbide Corporation.
[23] Fair Haven Mills, Inc.
[24] The Carborundum Company.
[25] Firestone Synthetic Fibers & Textiles.
[26] Carr-Fulflex, Inc.
[27] Johns-Manville Fiber Glass Inc.
[28] Golden Crescent Manufacturing Co., Inc.
[29] Globe Manufacturing Company.
[30] Hercules, Inc., Fibers & Film Department.
[31] Lambeth Rope Company.
[32] U.S. Rubber Company.

[33] Phillips Fiber Corporation, Subsidiary of Phillips Petroleum Co.
[34] Modiglass Fibers.
[35] Mohasco Industries, Inc., New Bedford Rayon Division.
[36] Ferro Corporation.
[37] Enjay Fibers & Laminates Company.
[38] Patchogue-Plymouth Division.
[39] PPG Industries, Inc.
[40] Uniroyal Fibers & Textiles.
[41] Columbian Rope Company.
[42] Langston Bag Company.
[43] Fiber Glass Industries.
[44] Hystron Fibers, Inc.
[45] Soo Valley Company.
[46] Gustin-Bacon Manufacturing Company.
[47] Uniglass Industries.
[48] Vogt Plastics.
[49] Nichols & Company, Inc.

INDEX